THE CAGE OF DAYS

The Cage of Days

TIME AND TEMPORAL EXPERIENCE IN PRISON

K. C. Carceral and
Michael G. Flaherty

Columbia University Press
New York

Columbia University Press
Publishers Since 1893
New York   Chichester, West Sussex
cup.columbia.edu

Library of Congress Cataloging-in-Publication Data
Names: Carceral, K. C., author. | Flaherty, Michael G., author.
Title: The cage of days: time and temporal experience in prison / K.C. Carceral and
Michael G. Flaherty.
Description: New York: Columbia University Press, [2021] | Includes bibliographical
references and index.
Identifiers: LCCN 2021022072 (print) | LCCN 2021022073 (ebook) | ISBN 9780231203449
(hardback) | ISBN 9780231203456 (trade paperback) | ISBN 9780231555050 (ebook)
Subjects: LCSH: Prisoners—Time management. | Time perception. | Prisoners—Psychology. |
Imprisonment—Psychological aspects.
Classification: LCC HV8706 .C368 2021 (print) | LCC HV8706 (ebook) | DDC 365/.6019—dc23
LC record available at https://lccn.loc.gov/2021022072
LC ebook record available at https://lccn.loc.gov/2021022073

Columbia University Press books are printed on permanent and durable acid-free paper.
Printed in the United States of America

Cover design: Milenda Nan Ok Lee
Cover image: Nastco © iStock

For our mentors, Thomas J. Bernard and Norman K. Denzin

CONTENTS

ACKNOWLEDGMENTS

There are a number of people I have learned to appreciate over my life. I want to thank them for giving me the tools that helped through this project. My life is different from most. I was raised in the working class, then I ended up in the school of hard knocks. While there I sought education, which changed my life for something better.

To start, I must reflect on those individuals I have harmed. The past and guilt can be overwhelming, yet one has to strive to be a better person and to pay amends. I admit my past transgression. In the end, a person was gone at my hands. To my family and those I hurt, I am truly sorry for the pain and suffering I caused. Some have received me and blessed me with kindness and love. A sincere gratefulness goes to all of them for my mistakes.

In my journey of life, I would like to thank all those who helped me grow—most importantly, my coauthor who decided to take a chance to create knowledge through the written word. He is an individual who has never worked with a person like me and my background. I also want to again thank Thomas J. Bernard, who is no longer here. Sadly, my mentor died while I was still locked up. I am hoping to meet him on the other side. Both have made me a better man to walk this journey.

Next, I must thank the people who took time from their lives to share it with me: Stephen C. Richards, Jeffrey Ian Ross, and Rebecca L. Bordt. Stephen was the one who visited me while in "the cage of days." He is a person who has a felony behind his name, like I do. He took time out of his life for me, he earned his PhD, only to be hit by a drunk driver who destroyed his life. Karma is crazy. Jeff has always helped me and is direct. Much love goes to Jeffrey Ross. Rebecca brought me into her classrooms and taught me much. You have all helped and taught me.

Finally, I have to thank those I walked with on the inside. They blessed me with their friendship and love. Maxwell is my brother from another mother of a different color and the man who saved my life plenty of times. He walked the journey with me, and is still walking it with me. I am waiting to meet his offspring. Aarif is a devoted brother and now a family man. *As-Salaam-Alaikum,* peace be with you. Thank you for your love and friendship. I am grateful to have the opportunity to show those who helped me that I have become a better person.

I hope all readers enjoy the material. I could never write with proper, clear wording. I just tell a story. Thank you.

K. C. Carceral

Our book is centrally concerned with time and temporal experience, so it seems sensible to begin with some words of heartfelt gratitude in roughly chronological order.

This book would not have been written if my coauthor had not reached out to me with an invitation to pursue the study as colleagues. I thank K. C. Carceral for taking that initiative, and I am grateful for his willingness to share this project with me. I also appreciate his commitment to ethnographic research under the most difficult conditions one can imagine. He became a scholar in prison, of all places, and it has been a pleasure working with him.

Soon after hearing from Carceral, I shared the invitation with my administrative assistant, Linda F. O'Bryant. From these earliest days onward, she expressed continued interest in our study. Her enthusiasm bolstered my own sense of the potential in this line of inquiry, and she typed the first two chapters of our book. Even after retiring, she regularly checked on our progress and helped to sustain our work with benevolent goading.

In the summer of 2010, I was attending a meeting of the International Society for the Study of Time in Santa Elena, Costa Rica. Out of the blue, I received an email from Anne Line Dalsgård, an anthropologist at Aarhus

University in Denmark. Having found my work helpful in their own research, she was writing on behalf of her colleagues to suggest future collaboration. This was the same summer that I first heard from Carceral, and these seemingly unrelated invitations would become entangled with one another.

By 2016, only four chapters of this book had been written, and progress had been slowed by competing demands on my time. However, a forthcoming sabbatical offered a release with which to focus on the study of temporal experience in prison. With the support of Dalsgård and two of her colleagues, Lotte Meinert and Dorthe Refslund Christensen, I was awarded a year-long Marie Curie Fellowship at Aarhus Institute of Advanced Studies (AIAS). This fellowship provided a rare and valuable chance to concentrate exclusively on this project.

AIAS is heaven on earth for the fortunate scholars who assemble there each year. Morten Kyndrup, the executive director during my tenure, has created a perfect place for every kind of academic work. The handsome Institute is full of intriguing art, and fellows at AIAS receive generous financial support, of course, but of far greater importance is the unique opportunity to devote oneself to research. Kyndrup has put together a tremendously talented and dedicated staff, and I am deeply grateful for the assistance of Maya Jepsen, Helle Villekold, Lena Bering, Vibeke Moll Sorensen, Tanya McGregor, Pia Leth Andersen, and Dorte Mariager. Moreover, it was inspirational to work among an international and interdisciplinary group of distinguished scholars.

In 2016, when this project was still in its formative stages, I mentioned it briefly in the sociology of culture newsletter. Almost immediately, I was contacted by Eric Schwartz, editorial director at Columbia University Press, who suggested that this book would be a great fit at Columbia. After that initial conversation, the two of us would discuss the study once a year or so, and Eric's interest was tremendously heartening at a point when there was still a great deal of this book left to write. I thank Eric for his encouragement and support as well as his enduring confidence in our project.

I am grateful to Cosima Rughiniş, a sociologist at the University of Bucharest, for sharpening our analysis with her insightful comments and astute critiques. In addition, as always, I am indebted to Gretchen Flaherty for improving our writing with her insistence on clarity and precision.

Michael G. Flaherty

THE CAGE OF DAYS

Arrested in 1973 for possession and trafficking of hashish, Andreas Schroeder served eight months in the British Columbia correctional system. It was his first offense, but his experience with incarceration would be more extensive than this short sentence might suggest. Eventually, he was an inmate at Oakalla Maximum Security, Haney Correctional Centre, Pine Ridge Camp, and Stave Lake Camp. An accomplished Canadian writer, he is a discerning observer in his prison memoir.[1]

Following his arrest, Schroeder was taken to the district lockup where he was "held incommunicado for forty-eight hours."[2] Never having been in jail before, and lacking the usual cues, he was irritated by his trouble with time reckoning:

> I'm starting to lose my sense of time completely. There's virtually no out-side light in here; the only window is a panel of thick glass brick which barely registers any light at all. What little light filters through seems entirely ambiguous; I can't tell whether it's morning or evening or lamplight. The disorientation is made complete by a small light bulb here inside that burns constantly. Strange, how damned annoying it is not to know the time of day.[3]

Eventually, with numbing repetition in prison, the days of the week would become just as indistinguishable. Schroeder found this temporal disorientation "damned annoying," and his aggravation is justified. Asking someone to identify the time of day and day of the week are common ways to check for concussion or dementia. One's inability to answer questions of this sort is a clear sign of disconnection from the rest of us. For the same reason, this condition is profoundly unsettling.

Weeks later, violence erupted in the truck transferring Schroeder and other inmates to Stave Lake Camp. "Somebody said we had us a skinner in the back of the truck."[4] The skinner, prison slang for anyone convicted of sexual assault, was "a thin, frightened-looking eighteen-year-old kid."[5] Schroeder watched as fellow prisoners taunted and punched him, kicking him when he fell to the floor: "The beating continued for what was probably only minutes but seemed like half an hour, and the guard's eyes never left the peephole."[6] Whatever else this incident achieved, the motivation included seizing an opportunity to break the monotony with a bit of excitement that was rarely punished. Indeed, the correctional officers may have instigated the whole thing in order to enliven their own temporal experience. For Schroeder, this situation brought about another form of distortion in the perceived passage of time. In this instance, distortion is marked by translating objective "minutes" into a subjective "half an hour." His sense of prolonged duration was a product of intense concentration on shocking circumstances. It would not be the last such occasion.

Six months into his sentence, however, Schroeder realized that drama is not the primary driver of time in the penitentiary. Regimentation and boredom have a more pervasive impact on temporal experience:

> When I looked at my calendar this morning I discovered I have now been in prison half a year. It feels like an awfully long time. Somehow, Prison Time is Outside Time quadrupled or even more; in here you live by ontological rather than chronological time, the kind of time lived by drunks, by stoned or panicked people. Time Inside stretches irrationally in all directions, and most of all in length.[7]

Unlike Schroeder, a long-term prisoner would learn to rid himself of the calendar and disregard dates in an effort to compress the sentence by losing track of time: "At half a year in prison, the repetitions begin to occur so regularly that that's normally the point at which a long-timer draws in his horns, lets himself go numb and settles in for the ride, developing a steady, almost drugged rhythm that most effectively kills the time."[8] Periodically indulging in retrospection, this inmate may be shocked at how much time has passed. Convicts try to hurry time along, but what they lose in the bargain cannot be recovered.

ORIGINS OF THE PROJECT

K. C. Carceral (his pen name) was convicted of murder in 1982, when he was nineteen years old. He was in one prison or another for the next thirty-one years, until his parole in 2013. He knows what it means to endure a long stretch of time behind bars.

On July 18, 2010, he wrote a letter to Michael Flaherty, a professor of sociology with research interests in time and temporal experience. Finding it in his mailbox a few days later, Flaherty was surprised to see that the sender's name was followed by a six-digit number. A curious message was stamped in red on the back of the envelope: "THIS LETTER HAS BEEN MAILED FROM THE WISCONSIN PRISON SYSTEM."

In his letter, Carceral stressed that he was "serving *time*." Moreover, having become "enthralled by the subject," he had written a doctoral dissertation on how prison inmates struggle with temporal experience. He had come across Flaherty's research on the perception of time while working on his dissertation. Now, he invited Flaherty to read it and collaborate with him as he pursued its publication. His invitation was open-ended and irresistible: "The role you take in this would be up to you."

As of 2020, we have been working on this project for ten years. We have spoken on the telephone and exchanged emails since Carceral's parole in 2013, but dozens of letters and edited copies of the manuscript have been our primary means of communication. First and foremost, this study is based upon Carceral's observations and experiences during more than thirty years in prison. With the persistent questions of an outsider, however, Flaherty helped Carceral to broaden and deepen his analysis. During a decade of collaboration, Carceral's dissertation served as the starting point for a far more extensive study, with the collection of considerable data as well as new lines of inquiry. This book is, therefore, a product of our correspondence.

Conducting this project via letters was necessitated by the geographic distance between us as well as prison regulations, and it made our collaboration challenging in uniquely temporal ways. We had to make time for writing long letters, a laborious effort to keep each other informed of our progress (or lack of it). These letters became more elaborate and digressive as our relationship developed, and it was quite time-consuming to write and read them. In addition, there was the prolonged and unaccustomed delay of waiting days or even weeks for a reply—a "reply" that may have been mailed before the arrival of one's last letter, which meant that none of one's most recent and relevant questions had been answered. Our letters often reflected the writer's current mood or perspective, rather than the issues raised by one's correspondent at an earlier date. All of these temporal discontinuities established the framework for a long-distance and time-fraught relationship akin to something from the eighteenth century.

Our letters may be anachronistic, but our topic is both timely and timeless. It is timely because, of course, Carceral had plenty of company behind bars. During the last four decades, America embarked upon an unprecedented policy of "mass imprisonment."[9] By any measure, the scope of this policy is astonishing. In 2008, the Pew Research Center found that, "for the first time, more than one in every 100 adults is now confined in an American jail or prison."[10] After reaching that mark, the number of prisoners under the jurisdiction of state or federal correctional authorities declined by 9.4 percent between 2009 and 2018. Nonetheless, there were 1,464,385 prisoners nationwide during 2018, yielding an incarceration rate of 556 per 100,000 U.S. adults.[11] In Russia, the 2018 incarceration rate was 413. In England, it was 141. In France, it was 102. In Germany, it was 78. Today, both the absolute number of people in prison and the rate of incarceration in the United States are higher than the comparable figures for any other nation.[12]

"I live in an environment that is all about time," writes Carceral in his first letter to Flaherty. Indeed, from a certain point of view, the American penal system is something akin to a massive experiment concerning the relationship between involuntary confinement and temporal experience. Millions of people here and abroad are behind bars. Carceral calls them "time junkies." They are obsessed with the passage of time, and all facets of their existence are ultimately temporal in nature. According to Stephen Stanko, an ex-con and subsequently a sociologist, "The first realization that a prisoner has, once incarcerated, is that he is 'doing time.' "[13] In this regard, at least, prison inmates do not misperceive their circumstances. The clockwork logic of our criminal justice system dictates that those who must be punished are "sentenced to 'time.' "[14] It is the aim of our project to understand how prison inmates experience and modify time. We want to know what time does to them and what they do to time.

Yet, in asserting that prison inmates are possessed by temporal experience, our argument threatens to fold back on itself, for an obsession with time per se does not distinguish them from the rest of us. Arguably, a self-conscious awareness of time is one of the defining attributes of human nature. Still, one could declare that the circumstances of imprisonment are extremely divergent from and, as such, unrepresentative of temporal experience for most of us in everyday life. A similar case might be made that the behavior of inmates at mental asylums is unique to their special circumstances, but, in his justifiably famous study of one such institution, Erving Goffman discovered that extreme circumstances can reveal important things about life outside of the mental asylum—things that are not as easy to see in the commotion of everyday life: "Extreme situations do, however, provide instruction for us, not so much in regard to the grander forms of loyalty and treachery as in regard to the small acts of living."[15]

We make a parallel argument on behalf of our own inquiry. Prison and other types of involuntary confinement predate the current policy of mass incarceration, and prison is not the only place where people are held against their will. Moreover, the various ways that people suffer time within the context of involuntary confinement have significant implications for our understanding of how human beings, always and everywhere, perceive the passage of time and strive to manage their temporal experience. Ironically, then, there is a timeless quality to our investigation of temporal experience among prison inmates. In fact, far from being unrepresentative and irrelevant, their extreme circumstances provide an instructive *distillation* of diverse dimensions of lived time, thereby making more apparent essential, but often obscured, features of human temporal experience.

CONVICT CRIMINOLOGY

This book is a product of dialogue between coauthors who approach the same subject from two very different perspectives. Carceral comes to our line of inquiry from the standpoint of convict criminology—the study of crime and corrections by convicts and ex-convicts. A noteworthy precursor to this perspective can be found in writings by Hans Toch, who began to employ convicts and ex-convicts in his research during the 1960s. They interviewed fellow convicts using the language of the cellblock and, with the knowledge of insiders, helped Toch to interpret the resulting data. With this modest initiative, Toch and his colleagues challenged a customary distinction: "We have tried to blur the line between the observer and the observed."[16]

Convict criminology erases that line. Those who advocate this perspective start from the assumption that "it takes one to know one." However, unlike the convicts who worked for Toch, they not only do the labor of research but frequently do so from the position of scholars with doctoral degrees and, crucially, they author or coauthor the resulting publications. Jeffrey Ian Ross and his colleagues identify different versions of convict criminology.[17] In one version, an inside guy collaborates with an outside guy. One of the earliest instances is *The Time Game: Two Views of a Prison* by Anthony Manocchio, a former counselor in the California penal system, and Jimmy Dunn, a prison inmate.[18] Despite its title, the authors have very little to say about time and temporal experience behind bars. As is typically the case with books of this sort, the insider has been quite busy *disregarding* the passage of time and other temporal matters in order to ease his way through a sentence. At the end of the book, and the end of his three-and-a-half year stretch in a correctional institution, Dunn's aspirations cannot be described as scholastic: "I'm going to shoot junk, pimp whores, and tear holes in business roofs."[19]

In another version of convict criminology, an inside guy becomes an outside guy, thereby combining within a single person the direct experience of a convict and the academic agenda of a scholar. This convict scholar is epitomized by John Irwin. He served five years in prison for armed robbery before earning his PhD in sociology at the University of California, Berkeley, where he studied with Erving Goffman and David Matza.[20] One of his first books, *The Felon*, was published in 1970, but, unlike current practitioners, Irwin was not yet explicit with readers concerning his status as an ex-con.[21] On the back cover, the synopsis euphemistically states that his research was based on "in-depth interviews and two years of participant observation." By 1985 and publication of *The Jail*, however, he was out of the correctional closet: "Having been a prisoner in eight different city and county jails for periods up to 120 days, I have firsthand experience with jails."[22] Irwin practiced convict criminology without ever calling it that, but his trailblazing career set the stage for further developments.

The two-person model of convict criminology did not disappear, but, in contrast to Dunn's obdurate commitment to criminal ambitions, the inside guy and the outside guy began to have equally academic motivations. When, for example, Richard Jones and Thomas Schmid examine identity transformation in a maximum-security prison, the reader is presented with a professional analysis but also learns that "one of the authors was an inmate serving a felony sentence."[23] That convict scholar is not identified, but these individuals increasingly encountered colleagues with comparable backgrounds: "By the 1990s, there were a significant number of ex-convict graduate students and professors using their prior experience in the criminal justice system to study jails and prisons."[24] Toward the end of that decade, they coalesced at annual meetings of the American Society of Criminology and, emboldened by their numbers, began to offer sessions devoted by name to convict criminology. This new line of inquiry integrates the conceptual framework of critical criminology with ethnographic research methods. Practitioners hope to reform the penal system, and their studies are based upon the unmediated experience of participant observation.

Inspired by convict criminology, and wanting to make his own contribution, Carceral wrote the manuscript that would eventually become his first book. Members of the faculty at a nearby university were not interested in working with him, but, as consolation, they sent him a copy of *Life Without Parole* by Victor Hassine.[25] Carceral noticed that the book had two editors and sent his material to them. Both were enthusiastic about his manuscript, but one bowed out upon learning the identity of his rival, telling Carceral that he would be in much better hands with Thomas J. Bernard. In Bernard, Carceral found a benevolent mentor who also happened to be one of the most renowned scholars in the field of criminal justice.[26] It was Bernard who gave Carceral his pen name, borrowing Michel Foucault's famous term for the system of incarceration.[27] Carceral learned a great deal from Bernard, who served as his editor for his first two books, but he lost his outside guy when Bernard died in 2009. Fascinated by time and temporal experience in prison, a neglected topic in his previous research, Carceral began to look for a new collaborator.

In his first book, *Behind a Convict's Eyes*, Carceral examines day-to-day life inside maximum- and medium-security prisons.[28] One enters prison with Carceral via his initial experiences at the Receiving Center. He must take off all his clothes in front of strangers. He folds his clothing neatly before handing it to a correctional officer and then watches him shake each item carelessly before throwing it into a box. He is asked a seemingly endless number of questions during his intake interview as he stands naked in front of the officers. The reader accompanies Carceral to the Assessment and Evaluation Center where he is given various tests before being assigned to a prison job. We see how an inmate earns a reputation behind bars and makes money in the yard as part of the underground economy. The staff attempt to control and abase even the most minute aspects of his temporal experience. One of the first lessons he learns is that correctional officers "hurry only when a prisoner is in leg irons. Any other time, they're casual and slow moving."[29]

In 1997, Carceral was among the 1,500 convicts transferred from prisons in the North to a new for-profit prison in the South. Woefully unprepared for their arrival, this correctional facility quickly degenerated into near-anarchy. Carceral's second book—*Prison, Inc.*—is a case study of dysfunctional conditions and resulting turmoil.[30] An inexperienced and poorly trained staff permit inmates to roam freely through the cellblocks. Some inmates take advantage of the opportunity to steal from others. These thefts and unrelated grievances lead to rampant and unrestrained fighting. Gangs can be found in every prison, but Carceral witnesses something he has never seen anywhere else: the formation of "beat down crews" who wander through the prison "purposely scouting for other inmates to assault."[31] Belatedly, the staff tries to regain control, which brings about a full-blown riot. In the aftermath, there is lockdown and extensive use of segregation (or "seg"). The outsourcing of corrections to privately owned prisons is frequently defended as a cost-saving measure, but Carceral's thoroughly detailed description suggests that these correctional facilities cut dangerous corners in order to realize their highly touted economies.

TIME AND TEMPORAL EXPERIENCE

Time is a socially constructed dimension of human experience. We perceive the passage of time by virtue of self-consciousness—the uniquely human awareness of our own existence and continuity. We see ourselves enduring against the backdrop of an ever-changing environment. I was; I am; I will be. Language provides a vehicle for self-consciousness as well as the tenses of time. In other words, self-consciousness requires a synthesis of memory, immediate experience, and anticipation. Norbert Elias asserts that "the potential for this kind of synthesis is a property peculiar to human beings."[32] An awareness of time is our quintessential quality, and temporal autonomy is precisely what prison takes from us. What happens to people when they lose control of time?

A capacity to integrate our experience of the past, present, and future is not bestowed on us by nature but by society. New parents can vouch for the fact that their infants cannot tell time. Self-consciousness is a by-product of socialization, and the latter is a culturally relative phenomenon. We are not aware of time as atomized individuals—only as members of social organizations and societies with distinct temporal cultures; we are born into an ongoing and collective system of time reckoning. Mastery of this system is one of the prerequisites for full-fledged participation in that society. For example, children in Madagascar must learn that " 'rice cook-ing' often means half an hour, 'the frying of a locust,' a moment."[33] In that society, and everywhere else, "systems of time reckoning reflect the social activities of the group."[34] So how does incarceration shape the time reckon-ing of inmates?

Systems of time reckoning and temporal norms vary across national bor-ders and historical periods. The people of Pakistan and Switzerland have very different understandings of punctuality. We have a seven-day week because ancient astrologers could see seven "planets" (including the sun and the moon) and concluded that these "signs" determine our destinies. Yet Eviatar Zerubavel has shown us that some societies have no weekly rhythm (especially those who rely on hunting and gathering), while other societies have had weeks that consist of three, four, five, six, eight, nine, ten, twelve, or even nineteen days.[35] Our international system of time zones is no less a product of social conventions. The date line and prime meridian could have been drawn anywhere. Their respective locations on the globe reflect political considerations at an international conference.[36] In a related vein, Robert Levine's research reveals that societies differ markedly in their pace of life.[37] This factor has profound implications for health, wealth, hap-piness, and altruism. Such variation is not what we would expect to see if time reckoning and temporal norms were hard-wired into the human organism. Is there one all-encompassing pace of life in prison, or does the perceived passage of time vary across the diverse situations comprising incarceration?

By dint of socialization, a system of time reckoning is typically taken for granted and, consequently, unquestioned. Thus, systems of time reckoning are highly resistant to reform, although they can be changed in radical fashion by ruthless regimes.[38] In 1793, victorious revolutionaries imposed a decimal system of time reckoning on the people of France. This system featured a ten-day week, with each hour divided into one hundred minutes and each minute divided into one hundred seconds. In 1929, the Soviet government initiated a five-day week. With only one-fifth of the population allowed to rest on any given day, the regime hoped to make continuous use of its industrial machinery. There are, as well, the kindred experiences of countless aboriginal people who have had a new system of time reckoning imposed on them by colonial powers. Individuals may be born into a taken-for-granted system of time reckoning or an unfamiliar system may be imposed upon them by the state. Either way, the system in question confronts the individual as "the temporal structure of everyday life," and it is inherently "coercive."[39] Convicts inhabit a mercilessly coercive system of time reckoning. Their modes of adaptation may clarify our own unresolved issues with the temporal structure of relationships, organizations, and society.

Systems of time reckoning facilitate social interaction by standardizing temporal experience. Nevertheless, there is variation in the perceived passage of time. Eugène Minkowski refers to this dimension of temporal experience as "lived time."[40] For Alfred Schutz and Thomas Luckmann, it is "subjective time" or "inner duration."[41] This terminology reminds us that our subjective experience of duration often diverges from the shared or collective time of clocks and calendars. We can conceptualize this variation as three segments of a continuum. At one end, the perception is that time is passing slowly. At the other end, the perception is that time has passed quickly. In between, one's lived duration can be roughly synchronized with standardized measures of time reckoning. This variation is not random, and it cannot be reduced to personality differences. All kinds of people will tell you that "time flies when you're having fun." And, vice versa, individuals with quite different personalities report that time passes slowly when they suffer physical or emotional discomfort. Our perception of the passage of time is conditioned by the relationship between self and situation.

This relationship alters with transitions from one realm of experience to another, such as drugs, dreams, travel to an exotic locale, and, of course, when we are taken from everyday life by involuntary confinement.[42]

Flaherty has studied temporal experience for as long as Carceral has been in prison. In his book, *A Watched Pot*, he formulates a theory that accounts for variation in our perceived passage of time.[43] We have the impression that time is passing slowly in distinct circumstances: physical or mental anguish, intense emotions (pleasurable or disagreeable), violence and danger, waiting and boredom, altered states of consciousness (drugs, dreams, etc.), extreme forms of concentration and meditation, or shock and novelty. These situations are quite diverse, but they share an underlying commonality: they provoke intensification of subjective information processing within the mind of anyone ensnared in such circumstances. With this intensification, standard temporal units (e.g., seconds, minutes, or hours) become saturated with far more information than they carry under normal circumstances. It follows that time is perceived to have passed quickly in circumstances where subjective information processing is abnormally low. This type of temporal experience can be brought about by routine complexity (such as a busy day at work) for which one has sufficient training or expertise, thereby demanding only a low level of attention or subjective information processing. In addition, the impression that time has passed quickly is produced by the erosion of episodic memory (i.e., our recollection of ordinary activity), which, as time passes, reduces the level of remembered information processing per standard temporal unit. Under normal circumstances, finally, the recurrent social structuring of our schedules roughly synchronizes the perceived passage of time and the standardized time of clocks and calendars. By virtue of our learned familiarity with the normal volume of information processing, we are capable of translating experience into standard temporal units, and vice versa.

The foregoing analysis presumes that, in regard to temporal experience, the individual is akin to a victim of circumstances. From this standpoint, time is something that happens to us. However, we do not always accede to the temporal dictates of our circumstances. We may ask ourselves, in effect, "What kind of temporal experience would I rather have?" The answer to this question guides our ensuing attempts to create circumstances that are thought to bring about a desired form of temporal experience. In his book *The Textures of Time*, Flaherty examines temporal agency or "time work"—the strategies we use to control, manipulate, or customize our own temporal experience or that of others.[44] Time is multidimensional, and so are our efforts to modify it. On behalf of our temporal desires, we regulate duration, frequency, sequence, timing, and the allocation of time. We steal time from others, notably our employers and employees. From this perspective, then, time is not something that simply happens to us. On the contrary, we routinely exert our will in the construction of temporal experience.

These theories have very different implications for our understanding of lived time. Are we victims of our temporal circumstances or architects of our temporal experience? This project offers an unprecedented opportunity to assess these theories within the context of incarceration—an organizational setting that reduces one's circumstances to the essentials of time and temporal experience.

METHODS

This book is a product of "dialogue" between two people who come from dissimilar circumstances. One has spent most of his life behind bars; the other has never seen the inside of a prison cell. Working together, we unite observational intimacy with analytical distance. Therefore, a description of our research methods should not be consigned to an appendix.

Convict criminology and the sociology of temporal experience differ in terms of substantive content, but they overlap with regard to theory and method. According to Richard Jones and his colleagues, the theoretical framework of convict criminology is "rooted in Goffman's study of total institutions and stigma" as well as his commitment to qualitative methods.[45] Stephen Richards adds that the "use of ethnography and autoethnography to study prisons has a long history."[46] Likewise, Goffman's theory and methods have been crucial in the sociology of temporal experience. Equally influential, however, has been that parallel version of social science inquiry formulated by Herbert Blumer.

It was Blumer who called for "direct examination of the empirical social world," which consists of what people "experience and do, individually and collectively, as they engage in their respective forms of living."[47] Carceral has lived behind bars for more than three decades, giving him firsthand acquaintance with the social organization, time reckoning, and temporal experience of penitentiaries. For an extended period of time, he has conducted participant observation in multiple prisons, which makes him the consummate insider. Carceral has devoted his life, albeit involuntarily, to the twin goals of ethnographic research: "intimate familiarity" with one's subject by means of "becoming the phenomenon."[48]

Time became the focus of Carceral's research when he began to work on his doctoral dissertation in 2008. For the purposes of this study, then, he is at once coauthor and key informant, subject and object, knower and known. He has recorded his meticulous observations concerning temporal experience in hundreds of journal entries spanning the years of his incarceration. This rich trove of data describes his perception of the passage of time in various circumstances as well as his efforts to modify or customize temporal experience. These chronicles encompass the ordinary and the extraordinary: meals and cell counts but also violence and solitary confinement. He has been an inmate at twelve correctional facilities in three states (Wisconsin, Minnesota, and Tennessee). Most of these penal institutions were run by the states, but he also spent years in a for-profit prison. He has served more than eighteen years in maximum-security prisons (each referred to as "Gladiator School"), almost two years in medium-security prisons (each referred to as "Ridgewood"), and more than ten years in minimum-security prisons (each referred to as "Cherry Flats"). We use pseudonyms for these correctional facilities in order to protect his identity.

In our letters, we might consider a particular passage in Foucault's writings or discuss racial and class biases in the criminal justice system. Frequently, however, Flaherty posed questions that were meant to amplify Carceral's observations or bring them into sharper focus. With these questions, Flaherty asked him to address specific aspects of time and temporal experience in prison and to describe how he perceived the passage of time throughout the segments of a typical day. In addition, he asked Carceral to characterize his efforts to control, manipulate, or customize temporal experience. When the possibility of parole arose, Flaherty asked Carceral if this idea altered his temporal experience or blunted his ability to "do" time. Gustav Ichheiser's statement concerning social reality is also an important methodological principle: "Nothing evades our attention so persistently as that which is taken for granted."[49] Questions from an outsider prodded Carceral to elaborate on his observations.

In addition to recording field notes in his journal, Carceral questioned others concerning the perceived passage of time and their efforts to modify temporal experience. On occasion, his questions were embedded within ordinary conversations, but he also conducted interviews over meals in the cafeteria, while at work, during walks in the recreation yard, and in the cells at night. The interviews were flexible and semistructured, but he found that other prisoners were also preoccupied with these issues and eager to answer his questions. Throughout our analysis, we use pseudonyms when referring to people observed or interviewed in the course of this study. Carceral interviewed thirty-nine inmates or former inmates. All were male and most were middle-aged because they were serving long sentences. Thirteen of them were white, twenty-two were Black, two were Hispanic, and race was not ascertained in one instance. He also conducted interviews with nine guards. Two were officers (one male, one female, both white) and seven were sergeants (six white males, one Black male, one white female). As well, he interviewed one white male medical officer, one white female nurse, one white male staff coordinator, and one white female reentry counselor.

Ironically, prison can bestow the gift of time on those who are prepared to take advantage of their temporal circumstances, but this is not quite the "opportunity" outsiders may imagine it to be. In one of his letters, Flaherty appears envious of Carceral's temporal autonomy: "I have the impression that a lot of your time is free . . . to use as you wish." Carceral refutes this impression: "Is it my time? My time is state time." Yet he admits that "this is an interesting point," one that is laden with "paradox." Inmates at most medium- and maximum-security prisons traverse vast expanses of empty time. True, they do not suffer the swarming distractions of life on the outside, but it is also true that correctional institutions offer only meager provisions for these temporal journeys. Most inmates lack the skills and other attributes with which to use the time at their disposal. Eighty percent of them are high-school dropouts. What is more, they have far less temporal autonomy than we might think. Much of their time is scheduled by prison authorities or squandered by security procedures (e.g., cell counts and waiting for doors to be unlocked). However, subsequent to being paroled in 2013, Carceral acknowledged that he found writing "extremely" difficult now that he had so many different things to do and, for the first time in more than thirty years, no external temporal structure organizing his activities.

It would appear that incarceration grants one who is inclined to write at least some time to do so, constricted and put upon though these intervals may be. Like all forms of social organization, prisons give us time with one hand and take it away with the other. Diandra, an inmate at Fluvanna Correctional Center for Women, comments on this temporal enigma: "If it seems that the prisons are full of a lot of gifted artists and craft persons, it's because being incarcerated gives you the time to hone the talents you already possess."[50] It is no accident, then, that there are so many authors behind bars, and one person's book is another person's data. Thus, autobiographical accounts of incarceration represent a third source of information concerning time and temporal experience in prison. We have examined fifty-one of these texts, and they are listed in the Selected Bibliography.

These autobiographical texts extend the reach of our analysis because their publication dates span more than one hundred years of incarceration and feature great diversity in authors and their circumstances. Forty-one of these texts were written by inmates at American prisons. Twenty-nine were published since 2000, the most recent one in 2019. Three were published in the 1990s, two in the 1980s, five in the 1970s, one in 1930, and one in 1912. It is noteworthy that these sources tilt toward white authors and include a number of women, whereas the inmates interviewed by Carceral are all male and disproportionately Black. Two of these authors (one white male and one Black male) are avowedly homosexual. Different crimes bring these authors to prison: murder, manslaughter, robbery, burglary, aggravated assault, pimping, drugs, writing fraudulent checks, statutory rape, corporate income tax evasion, paying kickbacks to government subcontractors, contempt of court, political protest, and civil disobedience. As with any ethnographic informant, something of each author's personality emerges in our analysis.

There are, as well, kindred forms of imprisonment or involuntary confinement once removed. Here, we find a smaller, mixed bag of autobiographies. Some of them were written by common criminals who were held in a foreign prison or juvenile detention center. Yet others were written by hostages, POWs, and political prisoners or people considered enemies of the state.[51] The latter have not been convicted of any "crimes" in the ordinary sense of that word but are held against their will in conditions that are often more unpleasant than those typically found at correctional institutions. In an ancillary way, their abject stories illuminate variation in the perceived passage of time and offer instructive comparisons with prison memoirs. These sources represent ten of the fifty-one autobiographies.

To be sure, these autobiographical sources represent different forms of captivity. Hostages view themselves as victims, not perpetrators, of crime; POWs and political prisoners are frequently tortured. Should we compare people who confront such different circumstances? Pushed to its logical conclusion, a negative response to this question would lead us to presume that men and women or Blacks and whites cannot be compared in our analysis, leading to a balkanization of the data that prevents discovery of underlying similarities. To see only the differences between people produces analytical paralysis. While we acknowledge relevant differences among people who inhabit various social categories, we also find fundamental similarities in their temporal experience that reflect the common existential conditions of captivity. In its particulars, of course, each prison is unique, but in the essential ways that they condition time and temporal experience, all prisons are alike. Our agenda is in accord with principles of research in the social sciences. We seek an empirically grounded understanding of time and temporal experience under various forms of involuntary confinement.

Social scientists have produced a rather large literature on prisons, although remarkably little of it concerns time and temporal experience. Typically, these writings allot no more than a few pages to what is, in fact, the central issue of incarceration.[52] More germane for our purposes are studies by two sociologists. Thomas Meisenhelder collected life histories from twenty-five inmates at two medium-security prisons. He was a visiting scholar, not an inmate, at these correctional facilities. Rik Scarce combined the roles of insider and outsider by spending 159 days in jail for contempt of court, where he engaged in participant observation. Despite differences in their methodological particulars, their conclusions are disconcertingly divergent. Meisenhelder depicts inmates as victims of their temporal circumstances or, as he puts it, "effects rather than causes."[53] In contrast, Scarce finds that "inmates negotiated with time quite directly, attempting to make it do [their] will and refusing to bend to its heavy omnipresent hand."[54] These paradoxical statements call for further investigation.

Each of these observations, interviews, and texts provides only fragments of information, but from these bits and pieces, we hope to assemble a detailed mosaic of how one struggles with time in prison. Regrettably, this book will not change penitentiaries for the better. Issues pertaining to the criminal justice system or the legal efficacy of incarceration are not our concern. Rather, we want to learn what life behind bars can teach us about that peculiar form of temporal experience. Along the way, moreover, we will have occasion to consider some common features of time reckoning among convicts and people who are not so confined.

Chapter One

A TEMPORAL REGIME

Prior to the eighteenth century, European criminals were routinely tortured and executed in public spectacles. After efforts at reform, however, these gruesome events were replaced by imprisonment for a period of time commensurate with the perceived seriousness of the crime. Michel Foucault observes that punishment of the body was gradually supplanted by a cloistered "time-table."[1] Rather than inflicting physical pain in public ceremonies, authorities chastised the psyche of offenders through the regimentation of time in private confinement. A temporal regime took control of criminal law.

Foucault does not ask how life behind bars conditions the temporal experience of prisoners, nor does he ask how inmates use time work to achieve a measure of temporal autonomy. To address these issues, we must accompany Carceral as he encounters the rhythms and routines of correctional facilities. In one of his letters, he describes how fellow convicts talk about the struggle to endure their lengthy sentences. Many of them will say, "I'm still in this cage," but what is the nature of their confinement? We misunderstand their predicament if we focus on architecture and surveillance. Incarceration is about time, and prison is a cage of days.

RHYTHM AND ROUTINE

The earliest prisons in America were founded by religious sects—the Puritans and Quakers—each of which put a particular spin on this experiment.[2]

What they had in common, however, was the belief that one's time is a gift from God. As such, it must be used wisely. From this spiritual standpoint, the regularity in one's rhythm and routine signified mental hygiene and social order. Temporal regimentation became analogous to individual and collective well-being. It follows that criminals (and the insane) were threatening precisely because they represented temporal disorder. The unwavering enforcement of a temporal regime in prisons (and asylums) was meant to "reform" or "correct" the way inmates use time. From their origins, reformatories or correctional facilities were centrally concerned with temporal regimentation.

Yet rhythm and routine are no less important in our lives outside of prison. One's routine consists of the regular tasks that, together, compose one's schedule. Rhythm is the rate at which these tasks are completed, as measured by the standard temporal units of clocks and calendars. In other words, rhythm is the pace of our activities. One person may prefer to write in the morning and run in the evening. She adjusts her schedule accordingly. Another person likes to feel busy, so he fills his nights and weekends with chores, socializing, and volunteer work. Nevertheless, the rhythm and routine in our lives are seldom determined by individual fiat. Obligations entailed by relationships and organizations dictate much of what we do and when we do it. Our circumstances typically force us to work, worship, shop, sunbathe, eat, and sleep at particular times. It is tempting to celebrate our temporal autonomy vis-à-vis prisoners, but careful consideration of the facts suggests that we exercise much less control over time than we might think. We have a say, though rarely a decisive one. In regard to temporal experience, at least, the difference between them and us is one of degree, not kind. There is a temporal regime in everyday life, and the individual does not wear the crown.

The individual always inhabits a chronological commons. Our shared temporal circumstances bring about a joint perception of time. We often think of time as an individualistic experience, but, in concert with one another, human beings create systems of time reckoning. "The people in one society may agree to meet at a certain hour, but in a society without clocks, people may agree to meet when the sun is at a certain point in the sky."[3] These systems of time reckoning are the basis for our coordinated actions, but they also act back upon us with externality and constraint.[4] By way of contrast, then, it will be useful to understand how a person perceives time before entering prison. Inside or outside of prison, one's perception of

time is conditioned by the temporal regime that governs one's social location. Thus, the essential contrast is not between captivity and "freedom" but
between two different shades of captivity.

The religions at the roots of Western civilization posit a "Genesis" and
"Judgment Day." They comprehend the entire universe in terms of a beginning and an end—the alpha and omega of all that exists. In between, there
are "historically specific events," such as "Exodus" and "GoodFriday."[5]
These religions established the foundation for a linear time perspective
in the West. Aided and abetted by the invention of calendars and clocks,
this theological tradition created a distinct temporal orientation that
depicts time as an artificial linear sequence of unique dates. Your days are
numbered. You have been granted only a limited amount of time, and you
are running out of it. To waste any of it is sinful.[6] The secularization of our
society has transformed "sinful" into "slothful," but there is continuity in
the underlying admonition: stay busy.

This perspective on time is also an artifact of linear progression through
the stages of one's life. The child becomes a teenager; the teenager becomes
a parent; the parent becomes a grandparent. Elementary school is followed
by middle school, which is followed by high school and possibly college.
A clerk is promoted to assistant manager and in due course is promoted
to manager. These sequences are typically institutionalized by one's society
into an expected series of steps or stages that Anselm Strauss refers to as a
"regularized status passage."[7] Moreover, there are standardized transformations of identity associated with the social organization of the life course.
Especially in regard to school and work, success is often defined as moving
through these stages as quickly as possible. Those of us who strive for self-
esteem are usually in a hurry.

Contemporary America, consequently, is characterized by a pervasive
sense of time famine. Most of us are paid for our time, and we view it as a
scarce and valuable resource. We develop time-saving devices and strategies (e.g., email and speed reading), but there never seems to be enough
time for the things we want to do, and we frequently feel rushed. The resulting hustle and bustle of daily life threatens to overwhelm us. Rampant
individualism exacerbates our sense of temporal urgency; people in collec-
tivistic societies are patient with one another as a mutual sign of respect.[8]
A chronic and widespread sense of temporal scarcity pushes people toward
"time deepening behavior"—that is, our efforts to do more with the time

available to us.[9] We attempt to speed up our activities and substitute shorter activities for those that take longer. We try to do more than one thing at the same time (i.e., multitasking) and strive to maintain a schedule for our activities. These forms of adaptation often backfire, however, leaving us feeling frustrated and inadequate, and with the faulty perception that we have less time than we actually do. Time junkies live outside prison as well.

The rhythm and routine of life in prison are quite different. So much so, in fact, that one's introduction to this new temporal regime is experienced as a cataclysmic shock. Alfred Schutz conceptualized "finite provinces of meaning upon which I may bestow the accent of reality."[10] He observes, furthermore, that we experience a kind of "shock" when we make the transition from one realm of social reality to another. Nowhere is that more apparent than in the transition one makes from the outside world to life behind bars. Victor Serge depicts an abrupt and comprehensive change of pace when he is imprisoned: "A runner, suddenly immobilized, experiences a shock. So does a captive."[11] In one of her conversations with Carceral, his mother asked plaintively, "Where does all the time go?" He did not see it that way, of course, but she was not trying to be cruel. Among those of us on the outside, the prevailing perception is that "time flies." The new inmate leaves that realm of time scarcity and enters a realm of time glut. "I've got nothing but time," writes Erin George.[12] For the murder of her husband, a crime she denies committing, she is serving a 603-year sentence at Fluvanna Correctional Center for Women in Virginia. The irony is that so many of us long for more of what she has in abundance, but prison inmates are as desperate to kill time as we are to save it.

The temporal regime in prison is totalitarian. It aspires to control all aspects of time. In this way, incarceration is the epitome of bureaucratic standardization. Convicts are treated as numbers, and units of time exhibit a comparable uniformity. The goal is a temporal symmetry wherein the same intervals are repeated endlessly. A young inmate laments, "All's I do here is eat, sleep, and sit on the yard." Crucially, the rhythm and routine are *preestablished*. Outside of prison, we often take the initiative to "make time" for one activity or another. This is a necessary feature of social interaction, for it is frequently the case that the activity in question will not occur absent our intervention. Inside of prison, there is an enforced passivity. Time happens to inmates, and they wait for everything. In her study of culture and personality under the new Soviet regime, the anthropologist Margaret

Mead noted the ruthlessness with which authorities imposed a system of time reckoning on Russian citizens: "Punctuality has been exceedingly difficult to instill into a population unused to regular hours, and heavy fines and jail sentences have been introduced on a drastic scale—for example, lateness of twenty-one minutes might mean a loss of a third of the salary or a three-month jail sentence."[13] Likewise, convicts are punished for failure to conform with the temporal regime behind bars, but the more they become accustomed to the dictates of this system, the less prepared they are for life outside prison.

Those of us on the outside can vouch for the fact that there is plenty of repetition in our lives, but prison ratchets it to nightmarish levels. The routine is ironclad; the rhythm is snail-paced. Jeffrey Ian Ross and Stephen Richards attest that "everyone goes through the same routine upon arrival."[14] Moreover, this unchanging routine has a harrowing effect on the emotional state of new prisoners. "After a week in intake," writes Erin George, "I found myself so depressed I could barely function."[15] The distress among long-term inmates is not lessened by their familiarity with this routine. "After the 6 A.M. standing count," observes James Paluch, "I usually go back to bed or meditate on what I am going to do today, which is usually the same thing every day."[16] Ceaseless repetition makes for days that are difficult to distinguish or remember. "The days never hurried or slowed," for Jimmy Baca; "they settled like heat waves at dawn that evaporated like mist at dusk."[17] As Jimmy Lerner points out, the disorienting impact on temporal experience is worsened under certain conditions: "In a prison lockdown, time is distorted. It bends and swirls and circles until nights dissolve into days that are perhaps Monday or Friday, but no one knows for sure and no one cares 'cause we're not going anywhere."[18]

To some extent, these effects are imposed on prisoners by a temporal regime bent on machinelike uniformity, but not knowing the date or even the day of the week is also grudgingly embraced by some inmates as a way to make time pass more quickly. Days perceived as distinct entities seem to pass slowly. In truth, therefore, many convicts are at least complicit in disregarding the days of the week. They make it a point to not know what day it is, contradicting the stereotype of prisoners tracking time with crosshatched tallies on their walls. As a fully intended consequence, it becomes that much easier for their days to slide by seamlessly in a blur of undifferentiated time. When, finally, the date or day cannot be avoided, one is surprised by how much time has passed. Of course, it is best not to dwell on the fact that, in so doing, one hurries through a sizable segment of one's life.

Recent sociological research draws our attention to the problematic aspects of "social acceleration," and rightly so.[19] Increasingly, we inhabit a world where things happen too quickly. An individual may feel overwhelmed by conflicting demands on his or her time. The opposite problem afflicts those who enter prison. Incarceration brings about a dramatic *deceleration* in the pace of temporal experience with attendant, if quite different, challenges. Instead of too much happening, there is far too little. This stimulus deprivation is exasperating, and it creates the kind of boredom that makes for desperate measures. "Cackling laughter. . . . Wild screams. Pleasured rage"—that is what Timothy Leary hears when fellow inmates start a fire on the floor of their own cellblock: " 'Yay man, burn mudderfucking joint down! . . . Burn to ground. Pour it on.' "[20]

DAYS OF THE WEEK

The date is typically of little relevance in prison, and there are good reasons to ignore it. Except for convicts in solitary confinement (or "segregation"), however, it is difficult to disregard the days of the week even though some inmates strive to do so. Like it or not, the days of the week impinge upon one's awareness of time. The seven-day cycle may be socially constructed, somewhat arbitrary, and ultimately despotic, but inside and outside of prison, it is the primary basis for sociotemporal rhythms in our routine activity. Indeed, for inmates, the week is much more important than the month or the year, since the weekly cycle provides a temporal framework for meals, mail, hygiene, laundry, cleaning, recreation, education, and work. All prisons organize these and other activities into a recurrent seven-day pattern. It has no beginning, and it has no end. Outside of prison, we have a complicated intermeshing of annual, semiannual, monthly, bimonthly, and weekly cycles. The new inmate, consequently, must make a wrenching adjustment to temporal reductionism. Behind bars, our annual and monthly calendars are reduced to the days of the week—a much shorter and endlessly repetitive cycle.

In the prison and nonprison worlds alike, Saturday and Sunday are viewed as qualitatively different from other days of the week. The weekend is associated with leisure, recreation, and sacred assemblies on the outside.

Conversely, it represents closed areas and fewer activities behind bars. At a minimum-security facility, for example, Carceral was bemused to discover that the chapel was one of the many buildings closed on Sunday. Among inmates, the weekend signifies less of everything except, notably, large tracts of empty time. Big Byrne expresses a common complaint: "Man, the weekends drag for me. Monday through Friday is okay. My part-time job is okay; work in the mornings, read the paper in the afternoon, and get some recreation. But there is nothing to do on Saturday and Sunday. By Sunday night, I'm waiting to go to work. I mean, I'm dying to go!"[21]

The adjacency of days of the week colors our perception of time. Outside of prison, many of us suffer the "Sunday blues" due to the unwelcome resumption of our work on Monday.[22] In contrast, prisoners dread the inactivity imposed upon them by the weekend.

Members of the prison staff want the same days off that others have in order to synchronize their leisure activities with those of friends and loved ones. To have them working on Saturdays or Sundays requires extra pay or more employees, and neither option is terribly attractive at a time of cost cutting and privatization of prisons. Consequently, the weekend has a new temporal significance for inmates who are not scheduled to work and therefore have decidedly less to do. "I tend to dread weekends," writes Erin George, "mostly because there is no mail call."[23] The routine is nearly vacant, and the rhythm slows to a crawl. In turn, the lack of daily events on the weekend alters how prisoners perceive the passage of time. They are ensnared by the perception that time is passing slowly, or what Flaherty calls "protracted duration."[24] Some prisoners attempt to avoid this frustrating experience by manipulating their schedules. When Carceral was approved for work release, he purposely let his employer know that he wanted to work on weekends. That way, he would have weekdays off when all members of the prison staff were at work, especially his assigned social worker. In addition, this schedule reduced the otherwise excruciating temporal drag of the weekend.

Of course, this strategy is only ever partially successful. Some of the convicts who have janitorial or kitchen assignments are required to work on Saturdays and Sundays and have two days off on other days of the week. Still, they perceive their days off as passing slowly. Lacking work, they are forced to fill these days with fewer activities. The following comments, for example, are from Carceral's interview with a unit janitor:

GRAYSON: "On my two days off, I go to the library for fifty minutes to get a break from the unit, sleep when I get back if possible, and sit around watching TV."
CARCERAL: "Wouldn't you rather have Saturday and Sunday off for TV?"
GRAYSON: "Yes, for TV, but everything else is closed except for the gym and yard."

In short, days off from one's job assignment always pose a serious challenge to a convict's efforts to manage temporal experience, but the problem is far worse if one has Saturdays and Sundays off. Work is important for prisoners but not because of its intrinsic satisfactions. Instead, the job assignment is a temporal milestone; it gives inmates something to do, something to which they can pay attention other than time itself.

Among prisoners, work is typically ineffective as a way to manage the perceived passage of time. The work is usually mind-numbingly tedious, unrewarding, and worst of all (ironically), there is not enough of it. Not everyone is eligible, of course, yet the supply of jobs does not meet the demand. Note, for instance, that Big Byrne only works part-time. As with Robert Berger's job in the kitchen, many assignments demand very little time or effort: "Our work day begins at 11:45 A.M. We clean up the dining room after lunch, take a three-hour break until dinner, then clean up again and we're out by 5:30 P.M."[25] Likewise, Michael Santos reports that he and fellow inmates could do their janitorial cleaning in ninety minutes on most days.[26] The upshot is that inmates learn to ration or conserve their work by means of a slower pace. For a time, Carceral worked in the kitchen at a minimum-security facility while also working on the outside at a nearby diner. The work was similar, but the pace of work at these respective locations was quite different. At the diner, he was in constant motion; at the prison, no one noticed if he took an hour-long break. Job assignments do not solve a prisoner's problem with the perceived passage of time; they are instead part of the problem.

Just as days off and the weekend have new meanings behind bars, so do the holidays. In prison, holidays mean activities are further limited or temporally suspended. Erin George's experience is representative: "Weekends and holidays are slightly different because there are few classes to allow us the chance [to] get out of the wing and we are only fed two meals a day instead of three."[27] The details vary from one prison to another, but there is always less scheduled activity. At most prisons, only chow and confined recreation are offered. Some only feed inmates and hold no off-unit activities. Other prisons serve breakfast and a hot lunch but only distribute a meal in a bag for dinner. Lerner helps us debunk a myth propagated by the entertainment industry: "In the movies, convicts in prison always get a special meal for Christmas. In here it's the same ol' same ol'—we were served soybean patties with mashed potatoes on top, green Jell-O on top of the mashed potatoes, purple Kool-Aid."[28] While the nonprison world is celebrating, inmates are sitting around, waiting for regular activities to resume, and more restricted than is usually the case. During twelve years at Gladiator School, Carceral spent many Christmas days in his assigned cell, leaving only for one recreation period and three ordinary meals. He and fellow prisoners did not celebrate anything, which is a total reversal of the temporal expectations one has for the holidays prior to incarceration. The lack of celebration magnifies the sensation of an overabundance of time, and it contributes to the difficulty many have with their adjustment to life behind bars.

It is always challenging to visit convicts, so visits are rare events, but they are more likely during the holidays. The importance of these visits is enhanced by the fact that they occur during a period when almost all routine activity has been stopped. It follows that family and friends can become associated with certain holidays. One year, Carceral's family visited him on December 24. "What does the prison have planned for you?" his mother asked. "Nothing," he replied. "I'm having my Christmas right now, in these short hours, visiting you." If they had not arrived, he would have spent that day in the usual way: reading, sleeping, and watching TV. Such "holidays" bring about widespread depression, but visits are burdened with their own temporal quandaries. Megan Comfort discloses that those who wish to visit loved ones in prison must endure "enforced time wasting" as they run what amounts to a temporal gauntlet: "The three types of waits imposed on visitors of San Quentin—the morning waiting line, the count period, and the redial purgatory of appointment scheduling—converge to signify the devaluation of prisoners' intimates and kin in the eyes of the authorities."[29]

For friends and loved ones, visits represent a way to maintain their relationships with those who have been imprisoned. Some convicts appreciate these visits, but many others dread or even avoid them because they disrupt one's ability to manage temporal experience. Rose Giallombardo addresses this issue in her study of a women's prison:

In order to survive in the prison world, then, time, according to the Alderson inmates, must be psychologically collapsed to the immediate present, a present that places severe limits on the extent to which the inmate is psychologically bound up with events and individuals associated with the past and present in outside society.[30]

Visits from family and friends undermine one's efforts to ignore everything beyond the rhythm and routine of incarceration. Conversely, the absence of such visits facilitates a convict's "successful" management of temporal experience. A male inmate quoted by Stanley Cohen and Laurie Taylor provides the following testimony:

> One of the reasons I always did easy time was I had nobody who would write or visit me. Also, I had no life outside. My mind was usually always in the here and now. I lived a day at a time and had no thoughts of the streets or getting out.[31]

Cohen and Taylor suggest that this insight often evolves into a strategy: "There was some evidence here that men had deliberately severed all contacts early in their sentence."[32] The temporal regime in prison sets the stage for this peculiar form of time work.

Modern societies are characterized by a linear perspective on time that emphasizes a sequence of unique dates (March 15th, March 16th, etc.). In contrast, premodern societies typically exhibit a cyclical time perspective because activities are organized on the basis of the rising and setting sun, recurrent phases of the moon, and seasonal oscillations.[33] Like premodern societies, the temporal regime in prison has days but disregards dates. It is an endlessly repeating seven-day cycle of rhythm and routine. Moreover, the days of the week do not add up to a month or a year. In other words, the day is not part of some larger unit of time. If one identifies (and therefore cares about) months or years, it creates a mental friction that slows the perceived passage of time. Experienced convicts learn to refrain from such calculations. Temporal norms are typically taken for granted and, consequently, difficult to discern. The crucial role they play in the organization of social interaction only becomes evident when violations and reprimands make them visible. In the following instance, Big Byrne chastises Carceral for losing track of the seven-day cycle:

BIG BYRNE: "Are you going out tonight for recreation?"

CARCERAL: "I might; I didn't know we had it tonight."

BIG BYRNE: "We only have it Monday and Thursday nights; how can you forget this? Sunday and Wednesday are Gym nights! We only have seven days to remember!"

Dates lose their symbolic significance because almost all prison activities recur on particular days of the week.

Our calendars put Sunday in the privileged position as the first day of the week. In prison, however, it is Monday. The central issue is access. Monday is the first day of the convict's week because that is when most of the staff return to work, thereby giving inmates access to various services that were closed over the weekend. On Saturdays and Sundays, correctional officers respond to almost all requests with a familiar litany: "You'll have to wait until Monday when they return." *They* are social workers, unit managers, counselors, librarians, record clerks, or other people who manage practically everything behind bars except security. Normal operations resume once the staff returns to the institution. The library is open; the social worker meets with prisoners; the unit manager hears complaints; the boss is back to supervise work in the shop.

Try as they might to disattend the passage of time, nature intrudes on the lives of convicts in ways that cannot be ignored. The rhythm and routine behind bars are affected by a variety of natural periodicities, such as sunset, seasonal changes, and the weather. These factors impose limits on the timing of prison activities and modify an inmate's temporal experience.

More than a century has passed since sunset marked the cessation of most outdoor activities. Subsequent to the invention of electric lights, Americans began to colonize the night as a temporal frontier—a trend that has steadily accelerated.[34] At most correctional facilities, however, inmates must adjust to the fact that their access to any outside areas is severely restricted after sunset. For example, all outside recreation will be terminated as sunset nears. Generally speaking, only someone on the way to work or the visiting room is allowed outside after sunset. One of the great changes confronting those who enter prison, especially maximum security, is not spending a customary amount of time outside. Once incarcerated, the individual will spend most of each day indoors. "During the thirty-day intake processing phase," writes Lerner, "new fish are locked down twenty-four hours a day, seven days a week."[35] At Gladiator School, Carceral's cell had no windows, but his wing of the prison had frosted panels of glass that grew lighter or darker with the hours of the day (unless it was cloudy). These panels were less than six inches tall and positioned near the ceiling of the central hall, making it impossible to look out a window. At 6:00 A.M., seven days a week, a loud electronic hum could be heard for about fifteen seconds. Then, large hanging lights began to glow. It would take five minutes for them to fully illuminate. At 9:00 P.M., these lights dimmed to the glow of a lightning bug. That process was Carceral's sunrise and sunset for twelve years.

Seasonal changes often mark the passage of time for those of us outside prison, but we also resist the temporal dictates of the seasons in disparate ways. We go north or south to a second home, put on warmer or cooler clothing, make a fire, or go to the beach. It is typically difficult or impossible for prison inmates to modify their temporal experience of the seasons. Instead, they suffer these changes. The cinder-block walls of Berger's cell are cold in the winter; the walls of Jorge Renaud's cell are sweaty in the summer.[36] Convicts at northern prisons miss going outside when winter weather cancels recreation periods for weeks at a time. Yet even prisoners who rarely, if ever, go outside come to recognize seasonal changes in their environment. For Carceral, one of these rhythms was a disgusting "funk" during the winter months. Most prisons (north and south) lack air conditioning. In the north, windows and vents are closed during the fall, winter, and spring but opened in the summer to bring in fresh air. When everything is closed, however, a musty smell of dirty laundry pervades the cellblock.

Prisoners who spend almost all of their time inside begin to know only the rhythms of artificial light or darkness. Their temporal experience is altered, and they learn to recognize the passage of time without recourse to the sun or seasons. Their units of time become meals, showers, announcements, and guard changes. Amanda Lindhout was kidnapped and held hostage in Somalia for 460 days. For months, she was locked in a room with no light whatsoever. "When you are in darkness," she recalls, "time folds in on itself, surreal and elastic. It bellows like an accordion, stretching and then collapsing. An hour becomes indistinguishable from a night or a day."[37] Nonetheless, she was able to measure the passage of time in a devoutly Muslim country: "I marked the days by following the summonses to prayer."[38] Lerner provides a related, if secular, variation: "There are no windows in my cell, and of course they took my watch, but I can estimate the time by the food trays. Three times a day an unseen hand shoves a plastic tray through a slot in the bottom of the solid steel door."[39]

Weather has related effects on the rhythm and routine of life behind bars. It can, for example, bring about an abrupt change in scheduled events. Due to snow, Berger and fellow convicts are locked in their cells for the day, cancelling both outdoor *and* indoor activities.[40] Thunderstorms can unexpectedly halt the one hour for outdoor recreation that inmates have per day, leaving them with nothing to do. Carceral was housed at a prison where tornado warnings over the summer repeatedly forced all prisoners to stand in a wet, cramped basement for hours, where they could smell each other's breath and sweat. Similarly, vicious sandstorms in Nevada keep Lerner and fellow convicts inside where the temperature in his cell is over one hundred degrees.[41] Lerner's cellmate "likes to say the weather is part of the punishment."[42] But weather can also impart opportunities that are otherwise unavailable: "If Nevada had a robust summer fire season, these inmates would be paid minimum wage to help fight fires. Convicts pray for devastating fires harder than farmers pray for rain."[43] Fires spring inmates from prison and alleviate the boredom that makes time pass so slowly. With its impact on temporal experience, the weather is a two-edged sword.

SCHEDULE

In her short story "Autres Temps" (Other Times), Edith Wharton's protagonist is struck by "the irony of perceiving that the success or failure of the deepest human experiences may hang on a matter of chronology."[44] With this word, she draws our attention to the temporal arrangement of events—that is, the order in which they occur. Her protagonist is distressed to learn that timing and sequence determine so much of our destiny.

The rhythm and routine in prison are not subject to inmate caprice; they are structured by a rigid schedule. This schedule was formulated by the staff, not prisoners, and it dominates the sociotemporal experience of incarceration. A daily schedule consists of specific time slots for every conceivable activity. As such, it is the shadow of a temporal regime. With this schedule, the staff decides what will occur, when it will occur, in what sequence it will occur, and the rate at which it will occur. A schedule distributes temporal resources. In everyday life, people use schedules to organize their own time and that of others. Thus, one's schedule represents a mix of temporal autonomy and temporal negotiation. In prison, the schedule exists prior to one's incarceration. It has been preestablished by the staff, and convicts have no say in its design.

The staff breaks each day into the same temporal increments. Time slots are unerringly symmetrical. Every Monday is the same; every Tuesday is the same; every day is identical. Eviatar Zerubavel points out that, in accord with temporal norms, the staff of hospitals and other organizations typically make appointments at fifteen-minute intervals, beginning at the top of the hour.[45] In prison, where every minute is counted by the staff, the schedule is comprised of five-minute increments. This excruciating concern with punctuality may signify the temporal regulation of convicts (for "correctional" purposes), but Carceral and fellow inmates viewed it as an authoritarian form of temporal taunting. In any case, the recognition that time is now absolutely inflexible is an important psychological adjustment for prisoners. Any deviation from the schedule will require permission, which is unlikely since it would invite similar requests from others. Those of us in the outside world enjoy an exaggerated sense of temporal autonomy regarding our schedules, but convicts can harbor no such illusions.

At Gladiator School, a maximum-security prison, Carceral's day began at 6:00 A.M. with a buzzer blasting and the lights brightening. Convicts were allowed to leave their cells for breakfast at the 6:25 ring-out, but they were herded back into their cells at 6:55 for the 7:05 morning count. Monday through Friday (except holidays), school ring-out in the cellblock was at 7:45 A.M. Classes did not stop during the summer. Convicts with jobs left ten minutes earlier, from another cellblock, at 7:35. There were four periods of school in the mornings (7:50–8:25, 8:35–9:10, 9:20–9:55, and 10:05–10:40). Prisoners returned to their cells after classes. They were released at 11:30 for lunch, but there was another in-cell count at 12:15 P.M. There were four more periods of school during the afternoon. Dinner started at 4:35, and there was a nightly count at 5:20. In combination, counts appropriate more than two hours of a prisoner's day, most of which is spent waiting.

Standing counts also structure the schedule at medium- and minimum-security prisons. Carceral was at the Ridgewood medium-security facility in 1995. The standing counts were at 7:30 and 11:30 A.M. and 4:30, 7:30, and 9:30 P.M., seven days a week. Prisoners were fed after the second two counts. Almost twenty years later, he still remembers the times for counts and how they cut up the day. At the minimum-security facility, Cherry Flats, the daily schedule was equally symmetrical. The first prisoner count was at 5:15 A.M. Once that count was cleared by announcement, inmates were allowed out of their cells for breakfast. Other counts were called throughout the day with five to ten minutes' notice. Stephen Stanko describes a comparable system:

> At 7:30 A.M., the institutional intercom announces "ten minutes to count," giving notice of count procedure to all parties. At 7:40 A.M., "count time" is called. Count procedures vary slightly from one institution to the next. Some require inmates to stand in their respective cells, while others demand each inmate to stand outside the door. . . . In the event that a count does not tabulate exactly, an immediate "recount" is called.[46]

"Standing count is held at least four times a day" at the maximum-security prison where Erin George resides with other female convicts.[47] "Until count has cleared, inmates remain locked in their cells."[48] Each count interrupts the temporal flow of all other activity. Moreover, as noted by Sunny Jacobs, convicts spend considerable time waiting for the count to be verified: "We have been sitting on our beds for forty-five minutes waiting for them to clear the count and I am getting itchy to go. There is no talking during count and you can't leave your bed, even to go to the bathroom."[49]

Further corroboration can be found in Theodore Davidson's careful fieldwork among Chicano convicts at San Quentin in the 1960s:

> Prisoners are awakened by a bell at 6:30 A.M. Cell doors are opened at 7:00 and the men file to the mess halls to eat, finishing by 7:30. After a half hour to mingle on the upper yard, "work call" is sounded at 8:00. Assigned men go to their job or to school (including vocational training). Unassigned men and those with evening or night jobs either stay in the yard (to pass the time there, in the gymnasium, on the lower yard, in the library, or in some out-of-the-way place) until lunch lineup, or voluntarily lock up their cells for the morning. At 11:30, prisoners line up in the upper yard for lunch. The mess halls are cleared by 12:30, giving the men another half hour on the upper yard until work call is sounded at 1:00 P.M. Again, the men either go to their assignments or pass the time until the work day is over. Beginning at about 3:30, men gradually gather in the upper yard prior to filing into the

cellblocks for the regular count. Between 4:00 and 4:30, the guards carefully count every prisoner in the prison—most prisoners are required to stand at the bars of their cell while count is being taken. Dinner is served at 5:00, after which the prisoners return directly to their cells. At 6:20 the prisoners who are scheduled for early evening activities are let out of their cells. Some who are scheduled only for later evening activities are let out at 8:20. Other activities such as scheduled showers [once a week] and clothes changes take place within each block during the evening. All evening activities are concluded by 10:00, with all prisoners being locked in their cells by "lights out time" at 10:30. Prisoners control the lights in their individual cells, so they may do things such as read or listen to the radio (if they have earphones) as late as they wish.[50]

And tomorrow will be exactly the same. Hence, Stanko brings us back to the heart of the matter: "Schedules in prison do not change from day to day."[51]

At Cherry Flats, Carceral worked in the upholstery shop Monday through Friday. He ate breakfast at 5:40 A.M. because he was required to be at work by 5:55. He had to keep travel time in mind. It took four minutes to walk to the dining room and another six minutes to walk to work. Lack of punctuality could have cost him a job that was not as valuable monetarily as it was temporally. There was an outdoor recreation period after the morning count from 5:35 A.M. until 6:50. Given that it was simultaneous with breakfast, convicts had to choose between eating and recreation. It may come as a surprise to learn that cells in medium- and minimum-security prisons do not have toilets. What is more, some officers would not allow prisoners to use the toilets prior to 5:15 A.M., forcing inmates to be late for work or to lose precious time outside while using the bathroom. Here, as with countless other instances, convicts were at the mercy of the temporal regime.

Correctional officers changed shift at 7:00 A.M. For the prisoners at Cherry Flats, it was noteworthy due to the informal count the officers operated between 6:50 and 7:10. During that period, no one could be outside the unit except convicts with jobs. In addition, the shift change was an important temporal marker for inmates because officers brought unique characteristics to each shift. These shifts are, consequently, part of the unwritten schedule for convicts. They get to know each officer's temperament: disciplinarian, laid back, hack, whiner, and so forth. More to the point, they learn what particular officers do or do not permit when they are on duty. A common refrain heard on the cellblock was, "Damn, we have to put up with this crank until 3:00," the time when that shift would end. As a variation on this theme, there was a systematic difference between the "relief" and "regular" sergeants, both of whom were assigned to a specific shift. The relief sergeant fills in for the regular sergeant on weekends, holidays, or whenever the latter has a day off. One becomes used to relief sergeants answering all questions in the same way: "This isn't my shift; I just relieve the regular sergeant. You'll have to get with him [or her] for a decision." In short, relief sergeants deflect any requests onto regular sergeants, which postpones all initiatives during that shift. And, of course, regular sergeants complain that relief sergeants do nothing.

Even at a minimum-security facility like Cherry Flats, access to recreation time is governed by the temporal regime. Inmates were supposed to have at least one hour and fifteen minutes of outdoor recreation per day (minus travel time). The 5:35 A.M. recreation period was available seven days a week for all units of the prison, but only because hardly any of the men took advantage of this "opportunity." Other recreation periods started at 8:10 and 9:40 A.M. and 1:00, 3:10, and 6:15 P.M. Each unit was assigned to a particular recreation period on a rotating basis. If, for example, you're in Unit 1, your recreation period will be 8:10 on Monday, 9:40 on Tuesday, 1:00 on Wednesday, 3:10 on Thursday, 6:15 on Friday, 8:10 on Saturday, and so forth in an endless cycle. It is noteworthy that the recreation periods begin at very different times, indicative of the fact that they were not selected for the ease with which inmates might remember them. Another interesting aspect of such schedules is that they become more temporally complex as the level of security decreases. In other words, more time outside of the cell is associated with more rules regarding how one uses it. John Irwin argues that the situation is usually worse in jails where "few activities punctuate the long periods of idleness."[52] The prisoners in jail with Rik Scarce confirm that assessment: "It surprised me that jail time, not prison time, was considered hard time."[53]

There were, then, specific segments of time for being out of the cell or off the unit, and this schedule controlled the temporal framework for social interaction among inmates. Given that housing units had different scheduled times for outdoor recreation, the convicts who lived in each unit would socialize almost exclusively with men who lived in the same unit. As a result, this temporal structure made it difficult to establish relationships with prisoners in other housing units. Inmates who resided in different housing units might never see one another. Authorized segments of time determined the movement of convicts to and from meals, hygiene, work, school, and recreation. In effect, this schedule created temporal relationships. Furthermore, identities were shaped by physical and temporal location. It follows that prisoners were known by their scheduled period for recreation. Carceral would hear someone say, "I'll see Fred at 9:40 rec."

Correctional officers knew that the schedule restricted social interaction among inmates and used this knowledge to orchestrate prisoners' relationships. If they wished to separate two convicts, they simply moved one of them to a different living unit. The prisoners could then no longer spend time with each other because they had different schedules. Curiously, this system resembles the aforementioned Soviet five-day week in that it proved to be problematic for Russians to maintain relationships of any kind with people who had a different day off.[54] The Russians found this system quite frustrating and ultimately rejected it.

Travel time is another important aspect of the schedule. This is ironic because, strictly speaking, it is not part of the official schedule. Like a bridge, travel time connects two temporal slots. It is the time it takes a convict to travel from one interval (and activity) to another. Put differently, it is the prison world's version of commuting. Convicts pay close attention to these transitional intervals, but they are typically ignored or at least unacknowledged by the correctional staff. Prisoners realize that these transitional intervals are subtracted from the time available for other activities. Travel time can reduce the official size of an interval, eliminate certain opportunities altogether, and create temporal competition among inmates. Jimmy Lerner depicts a standard dilemma: "We are let out of our cells for ten minutes every *other* evening after chow. During this so-called 'tier time,' we can take a shower or line up to use one of the three phones on the lower tier."[55] Not wanting a riot on their hands, the correctional officers "open only three cell doors at a time."[56] Nonetheless, a violent race against the clock (and five fellow inmates) ensues:

The ten-minute limit imposed a tough choice. With Fish Tank [i.e., the intake unit] temperatures rarely dropping below 100 degrees, we all wanted to take a cool shower. Of course, every fish [i.e., new prison inmate] also desperately longed to use the phone. No way to do both in ten minutes. Eight minutes actually—subtract two minutes for travel time to and from the showers and phones.[57]

Travel time is a harsh facet of temporal reality in prison. Inmates quickly learn that they will actually have only a fraction of the official time allocated for any activity.

Carceral's worst experience with travel time was in a private prison. The staff established a forty-minute period for recreation, but it took fifteen minutes to get one unit in and another out. Obviously, this transitional period reduced the actual time available for recreation, but the correctional officers would say, "You got forty minutes for rec." Travel time is also affected by the location of one's cell. At Cherry Flats, use of the basketball court or access to special programs (such as a movie) was on the basis of first come, first served. To one degree or another, the same is true of all prisons. In a maximum-security facility, the prisoners were rung-out (or released) by tiers. If your tier was rung-out first, then you would have greater temporal access. A typical cellblock would have four tiers, each housing forty men. Those in the first tier would arrive before the others and thereby have better access to activities during the ensuing period. Men who lived on the last tier would have at least 120 inmates ahead of them. Similarly, at a minimum-security facility, inmates have differential temporal access, as evidenced by the following excerpt from an interview:

DOUGLAS: "Our cottage is down by the Administration Building; the Activities Building is up near Units 5 and 7."
CARCERAL: "Right."
DOUGLAS: "We go to rec with Unit 5. It takes them three minutes to get to the building to sign up for special programs, and it takes me ten minutes to hustle there."

Travel time diminished his temporal access. Tacitly, he recognized that leaving earlier was not an option. Because he lived further away, he had to compete and struggle for that which came more easily to fellow convicts. Sometimes, as a work-around, men would ask prisoners in closer units to sign their names on the lists for special projects. This was one way to alter travel time and improve one's access to various programs, but you did not want the correctional officers to catch you.

In prison, as in society, there is not enough work for everyone who wants it. Likewise, not all inmates go to school. Convicts without jobs or classes are part of the unassigned population, which represents at least 30 percent of the inmates. The rhythm and routine of their lives differ from those of other prisoners, as does their temporal experience. They are the prison world's unemployed. Inside and outside of prison, unemployed people have more time on their hands and intensified self-consciousness concerning the passage of time. There are no reasons for them to leave their units or cells, save for recreation periods or meals. In maximum, they only had recreation on Tuesday and Thursday for an hour. Their schedule was characterized by fewer activities and a slower pace. Sleeping during the day is one form of adaptation, but this "solution" does not come without cost. Baca discloses that he would have trouble sleeping at night, so he would sit in the darkness talking for a few hours with Macaron in the next cell, their "backs against the bars."[58] Prisoners with jobs have tasks, no matter how trivial. Unassigned convicts have hardly any responsibilities. Most of their activities are voluntary, and they find precious little to occupy their attentional resources. Moreover, their relationships with fellow inmates (and staff) are diminished. Given less time out of the cell or away from the unit, they have fewer opportunities to meet and socialize with other convicts. Not surprisingly, most of the men they get to know share their unassigned status.

When we consider the scheduling of everyday life versus that of prison, it becomes apparent that hostages confront the worst of both worlds. They suffer the grinding repetition of involuntary confinement interspersed with the frightening capriciousness of their captors. A religious schedule was imposed on Amanda Lindhout by her Somali kidnappers: "Five times a day, we all folded ourselves over the floor to pray."[59] Despite this temporal structure, however, her "days felt increasingly like a long wait for nothing."[60] She never knew how long she would be kept at a particular location: "When the gunfire and grenade blasts between warring militias around us grew too thunderous, too close by, the boys loaded us back into the station wagon, made a few phone calls, and found another house."[61] Her comments are echoed by Ingrid Betancourt, who was held for six years by the FARC in Colombia: "There was nothing to do but wait, without knowing what we were waiting for. The minutes stretched into an oppressive eternity, and to fill them required a determination I didn't have."[62] Any revision of her schedule was welcome relief: "The idea of a change in routine made us lighthearted."[63] Otherwise, there was only "eternal boredom."[64] When two of the guerrillas taught her how to weave, they unintendedly showed her how to manage temporal experience: "With my work in front of me, I no longer felt the burden of time. The hours passed quickly."[65] With that breakthrough came an instructive contrast between her plight and that of unassigned convicts.

DESTINATION LOG

At many prisons, rhythm and routine are recorded in the destination log. This document tracks the pulse-like temporal flow of inmates to and from their cells. Whenever a prisoner leaves or returns to the unit, he must provide certain information by completing a written form. A log of this type is generally maintained at medium- and minimum-security facilities. It is kept next to the officer's station for easy access and nearly constant supervision.

Symbolically, the destination log is a temporal indicator of the convict's travels and activities in prison. Where is he, and what is he doing? To answer these questions in absentia, every inmate who leaves the unit must print his name, number, destination, and the time on this log. Upon returning, he again notes the time. His penmanship must be legible. Typically, the log is not dated because a new one is presented each day. Officially at least, it documents his location at any particular moment. It is, in essence, an archive of the prisoner's temporal discipline.

The destination log is used by correctional officers to monitor inmates' behavior. Its functions include surveillance and control from a distance. An officer can check a convict's whereabouts at any time throughout the day. As previously noted, the officers at a minimum-security facility change their shift between 6:50 and 7:10 A.M. Consequently, Carceral was already at work prior to the arrival of the first-shift officer. From his desk in Carceral's assigned unit, the officer would check the log to see that he had signed out for work. In order to verify his presence at work, the officer would call Carceral's supervisor. If other inmates were signed out, he would call their destinations, as well.

The system, however, is not foolproof. Mistakes happen, and some of the more adventurous convicts seek to exploit it. Honest mistakes are usually recognized and corrected, although the response varies with the offender. One day, Carceral's supervisor called him into his office at about 7:05 in the morning (i.e., near the start of the officers' first shift): "Hey, your sergeant wants you back on the unit. You forgot to sign out." When he returned to his unit, Carceral noticed that the first-shift sergeant was the regular, laid-back officer. "Just sign the log for me," said the sergeant. His security routine had revealed that Carceral's whereabouts were missing from the destination log. When had he left the unit? Where had he gone? Carceral observes that this officer had been calling his supervisor to check his location for at least a year, so he expected Carceral to be at work if not on the unit. That the officer viewed this as a minor infraction can be inferred from the way he joked with Carceral about it: "If I'd thought you escaped, you would have made sure you signed the log!" Yet the second-shift officer reacted in a very different manner to a similar incident. Carceral was returning with other prisoners to sign in from being outside. Apparently, one prisoner had forgotten to sign the destination log before going outside. It is probably not irrelevant that he was a newcomer or "fish."

OFFICER: "Walsh, you didn't sign out when you left the unit."
WALSH: "I didn't? I must've forgot, I. . . ."
OFFICER: "You can't do that. I need to know where you're at, at *all* times. You have to sign out. What if you had a visit or something came up where the administration wanted you. I have to be able to locate you any time you leave this building. I could put you in seg for escape and write a disciplinary!"
WALSH: "I must have forgotten. . . ."
OFFICER: "Don't let it happen again."

The prisoner's temporal experience is an artifact of the rules and efforts to control his behavior.

An officer in Carceral's living unit once lost his destination log. He was a relief sergeant, and seldom worked there, but, when present, he was consistently rude and demanding. Apparently, a convict took the log and destroyed it, thereby usurping time and control from the officer, if only temporarily. When Carceral came back from work, he could not sign in. A prisoner is not allowed to be on the unit if he has not signed in, so Carceral asked the officer for his log sheet. Realizing that it was missing, the relief sergeant ranted for more than ten minutes. "I should call an emergency count," he snarled at Carceral. "How would you like that? Everyone to his cell for an hour, hmm?" Carceral was not impressed by this bluster. It would have brought the temporal routine of the entire prison to an immediate halt for an in-cell count of all prisoners. Almost certainly, those in authority would have viewed it as an overreaction to an irksome but trivial incident. In any case, Carceral had nothing to do with taking the log and was not interested in hearing the relief sergeant's invective. It is noteworthy, however, that this officer felt Carceral was there to listen as he complained about the actions of another prisoner. Temporal access is connected to status and power. As Barry Schwartz puts it, "the lowly are summoned."[66] We can approach a sales clerk whenever we like, but we usually need an appointment to see our physician, and we may be summoned by the boss at any moment. Carceral only wanted the officer to tell him what to do (i.e., how to sign in). Yet, like most officers, the relief sergeant saw Carceral as directly available for whatever he might want.

On another occasion, Carceral overheard two inmates talking. One of them had been cussed by the correctional officer for not recording the time he returned to the unit. For his more experienced colleague, it was a teachable moment:

"Fuck that crank. . . ."
"The reason he's digging into your ass is because he does his count by that sheet. If his count is wrong and they catch him, he'll be taking some days off without pay."
"So, what're you saying?"
"Hey, I'm on your side. He won't say nothing to you if you be sure to sign in. Otherwise, he is going to dog you."

In short, the destination log also helps an officer count the number of prisoners in his charge.

At maximum-security prisons, where there is a need for greater control over inmates, officers do not rely on a destination log. Instead, each prisoner who leaves his cellblock receives a pass. These passes are color-coded for various destinations. There are a limited number of them, and any officer along the way can check one's pass.

UNSCHEDULED TIME

In prison, unscheduled time is the dark matter of temporal reality. There is a great deal of it, with significant implications, but it is difficult to see. It consists of the time that inmates spend at their living unit or in their cells and the intervals between scheduled activities. Despite being by far the largest portion of time during a prisoner's day, it is easily overlooked because it is essentially interstitial and not part of the printed schedule. During the weekend at Gladiator School, for example, the men were allowed only one recreation period (for a little more than an hour) and three meal times per day. Unless one had a job or a class, all of the remaining time was spent in one's cell. The staff did not include this time as a component of their schedule, but it represents much of the inmate's temporal experience.

Outside of prison, there is a widespread assumption that unscheduled time offers welcome relief from school, work, and other responsibilities. Many of us have the temporal autonomy and, crucially, the resources with which to fill otherwise empty intervals "with varied and interesting experiences," as William James put it.[67] Time seems to pass quickly, and we enjoy our amusements. This stereotype is, however, only valid for an increasingly narrow segment of the population. Tea Bengtsson has shown that delinquent teenagers in Denmark face frustrating boredom in the streets as well as juvenile detention centers.[68] More broadly, Anne Line Dalsgård and her colleagues have found that the youth of diverse cultures experience time objectified as an external and troubling factor in their lives.[69] There can be no doubt that the youth in these studies are harbingers of a dystopian future. Whose work cannot be automated or outsourced? What are underemployed and unemployed people supposed to do with their unscheduled time? These questions will become increasingly relevant if capitalism continues to reduce the need for labor.

In kindred fashion, prison inmates quickly learn that no one needs most of their time. Convicts inhabit what Erving Goffman calls a total institution: "A basic social arrangement in modern society is that the individual tends to sleep, play, and work in different places, with different co-participants, under different authorities, and without an overall rational plan. The central feature of total institutions can be described as a breakdown of the barriers ordinarily separating these three spheres of life."[70] Prisoners are subject to "an overall rational plan" that dictates enormous periods of passive inactivity. Put differently, unscheduled time is an intended part of the temporal regime. At a minimum-security prison, off-unit activities account for five hours per day, leaving inmates with eleven hours of unscheduled time on the living unit or in a small concrete cell. On the weekend at a maximum-security prison, convicts have fourteen hours per day of unscheduled time locked in their cells. They do not desire this extensive dormancy, but, lacking scheduled activity, they must figure out what to do with this time. Their past exploits do not suggest that they are well prepared for this challenge.

At Gladiator School, Carceral and fellow inmates were locked in their cells all evening on Thursday, Saturday, and Sunday. There was a brief recreation period every Tuesday night. On Monday, Wednesday, and Friday evenings, they were released from their cells in a staggered sequence for a twenty-minute shower interval. Men waited expectantly for their tier to be released while others showered. Twenty minutes may not seem like much, but a period of anticipation, the moment one actually leaves the cell, the short walk across the tier and down the stairs, the abbreviated time for the shower itself, and the walk back to one's cell divided the evening in a welcome way. Carceral's unscheduled time, in contrast, seemed endless.

It is tempting to imagine that convicts take advantage of unscheduled time with amusements that POWs lack, but prison inmates who are restricted to their living units or cells have a short list of activities from which to choose. Some convicts write letters, read, or work on a hobby, but most of them watch television, play games, or socialize. In practice, however, all of these activities are controlled by the staff and problematic in one way or another. "I'm not permitted any books or newspapers," writes Lerner, "and up until about an hour ago my requests for paper and a pen have been laughed at."[71] Reading and writing are not feasible options for the many prisoners who are functionally illiterate. Very few of the convicts pursue hobbies due to the expense and hassle associated with procuring equipment and supplies. Television was the main activity during unscheduled time at Gladiator School, providing that one owned a television, which had to be purchased with one's own money.

Prisoners at medium- and minimum-security facilities were less isolated during unscheduled time than their colleagues in maximum. In addition to their cells, they typically had access to a common area (or room) where they watched television and played board games or cards. The television had only four to six channels, and the common area was often so noisy that no one could hear it. Temporal access to the television was controlled by the staff. A correctional officer would change the station on the television at the top of the hour (or whenever he got around to it). Prisoners were not allowed to stand while watching the television, so access was also regulated by the number of chairs the officers permitted. The living unit at a mini-mum-security prison would hold forty-eight men, but, during Carceral's stretch, the number of chairs went from twenty to ten. In addition, the officers replaced comfortable upholstered chairs with hard plastic chairs in an effort to reduce the time prisoners spent watching television. At every level of security, formal rules and informal practices ensured that unscheduled time would be a punishing temporal experience.

STRUCTURE AND ANTISTRUCTURE

For a small minority, time in prison is burdensome but functional, in that they are able and willing to take advantage of what incarceration affords them. This is not to say that they enjoy being behind bars, and they suffer the same distortions in temporal experience as other prisoners, but they understand and even appreciate the benefits that can accrue from captivity. Baca admits that prison can be an improvement over conditions faced by some inmates prior to incarceration, a point anticipated by the narrator of Clifford Shaw's book *The Jack-Roller*.[72]

These convicts see prison as a chance to pursue remedial education, dry out from drug habits, or separate themselves from dangerous confederates. More often than not, their aspirations are thwarted by the circumstances of incarceration, but a few of them view their time in prison as beneficial. For Peter Pringle, IRA soldier and POW at Portlaoise Prison, "not having a drink would do me good."[73] At a Florida correctional facility, Jacobs is vexed by a fellow convict who has "been in and out of prison all her life. They say she comes back for some R&R, rest and relaxation, to fatten up, get healthy and get her teeth fixed."[74] It is noteworthy that Jacobs longs for release and resents her colleague's willing recidivism.

The anthropologist Victor Turner distinguished between structure and antistructure.[75] Structure consists of recurrent (and therefore predictable) patterns of social interaction, and antistructure is that which disrupts the establishment and maintenance of such patterns. The regimentation of time facilitates social coordination, but the externality and constraint of structure are chronically opposed to the immediate self-interests of the individual, which provokes antistructural forms of resistance. Our study of time and temporal experience in prison makes the dynamics of structure and antistructure visible.

What we find noteworthy is the ambivalence of prisoners toward the temporal regime. Their attitude is not one of unadulterated resistance. In his autobiographical account of incarceration, Albert Woodfox acknowledges that the monotony of life in prison takes a terrible toll on the convict's psyche: "The repetitiveness of every day could feel very painful."[76] Moreover, he describes his own efforts to compensate for the boredom by purposefully creating novelty in his daily routine:

> I tried to make the routine different. I might sit on my bunk to eat breakfast for months or maybe a year. Then I'd stand to eat breakfast for months. Then I'd sit at the table to eat breakfast. Deep down I always knew it was the same routine. I couldn't really trick myself into believing otherwise.[77]

In this passage, we witness Woodfox engaging in temporal agency and resistance, but with little or no success. His efforts are in the expected direction because he attempts to increase novelty, rather than decrease it. More surprising is the fact that he and fellow prisoners often embrace the temporal structure of prison, instead of resisting it:

> As much as we hated the routine, though, we needed it for mental stability. It gave us familiarity, a sense of confidence and the illusion of control over our surroundings . . . when people know their surroundings, they know how to survive in that environment. To have the lights go on at the same time, to eat at the same time. It brought order to our lives. Once we were used to the structure of the day it was something we could count on. The smallest change could feel devastating.[78]

Clearly, it would be a mistake to view the individual as always and utterly opposed to the external constraints of temporal structure, even in the penitentiary. People create or accede to temporal structure for their own sake, and with good reason. Temporal structure is the basis for social organization; it is the foundation for our ability to do things with others.

Goffman helps us theorize our ambivalence toward temporal structure:

> [We should define] the individual, for sociological purposes, as a stance-taking entity, a something that takes up a position somewhere between identification with an organization and opposition to it, and is ready at the slightest pressure to regain its balance by shifting its involvement in either direction. It is thus against something that the self can emerge.[79]

Human beings choose to conform with temporal norms or choose to resist them. If, as Goffman suggests, we are self-guided and stance-taking entities, these attributes have troubling implications for the predictability of our behavior. We want our cake, and we want to eat it, too. Here and there, now and then, we want temporal structure or temporal antistructure as it suits our personal interests. This ambivalence is true for us as well as prisoners, but incarceration magnifies these dynamics.

Chapter Two

TIME AND SPACE

Alcatraz, Angola, Attica, Florence, Folsom, Leavenworth, Marion, Rahway, Rikers Island, San Quentin, Sing Sing, and Soledad; these are notorious locations for cruelty, suffering, and degradation. They are physical settings for the punishment of body and soul. Every prison, be it infamous or less familiar, is a brutal sensory experience. There are, then, intriguing parallels between prison and poverty. The people who inhabit a ghetto or similarly impoverished place suffer many indignities, not the least of which is the fact that they have nothing to do. The upshot is widespread boredom that can only be alleviated by means of illicit activities. Robert Levine provides a cogent description of life in these settings: "Many of these people are unemployed, have little prospect of employment, and . . . almost no future time perspective."[1] Moreover, the inhabitants (especially young men) "congregate loosely each day and wait for something to capture their interest. Their problem is not so much finding time for their activities as it is to find activities to fill their time."

Temporal experience is conditioned by the relationship between time and space. Our perception of time reflects the situated stream of experience across our senses. It follows that the physical environment can impose constraints on the perceived passage of time. Daphne Demetry asserts that "one feels time pass far differently when in a restaurant than in a jail because of the different spatial circumstances."[2] Indeed, all physical settings affect temporal experience in ways that are, as yet, poorly understood. How do the sensory dimensions of place influence the perceived passage of time? We can begin to address this question by conceptualizing any given location as a specific *sensorium*—a unique experiential world. Physical settings comfort or assault the senses, and they facilitate or impede intended action. In so doing, they condition our temporal experience. Can we design spaces that affect our experience of time in desirable ways?[3] These questions implicate an architecture of time. We can learn something about the possibilities of a temporally informed architecture by examining the relationship between time and space in prison, where the intended and unintended consequences of the physical setting for temporal experience are more evident than they are in everyday life.

THE PRISON SENSORIUM

As one might expect, convicts rarely have an opportunity to contemplate the exterior of their prisons. When they do glimpse their prospective residence from the outside (for only a few moments through a window on the van that delivers them), they often see a forbidding structure in a desolate landscape. A "stifling-hot van" brings Jimmy Lerner and his fellow fish to a repellent place: "Like a nightmarish desert mirage, the state prison compound looms ahead. Barbed wire, gun towers, more barbed wire, and concentric circles of fences, all topped with swirls of razor wire."[4] We find a similar description of Florence State Prison in the writings of Jimmy Baca: "Menacing granite and razor-wire coils unspooled the length of the looming wall enclosing the prison. Manned gun towers jutted up with guards in sunglasses cradling rifles and pacing catwalks, clocking the cons, monitoring their every step."[5] Upon arrival, prisoners proceed "through a series of checkpoints . . . [to] a massive iron gate."[6] This is the architecture of intimidation; among convicts, it instills anxiety, despair, and, not incidentally, the perception that time has slowed to a crawl.

There are many different areas in a prison. New inmates are typically herded through a reception area (or "Intake") to the "Fish Tank" where they are held until reassigned to cells in the "general population." In addition to cellblocks, there may be a chapel, library, property room, canteen, chow hall, recreation yard, infirmary, workshops, classrooms, and administrative offices. What is more, the cellblocks are not identical, which makes for a strange approximation to neighborhoods. There are racial and ethnic enclaves, different levels of security (e.g., protective custody), punishment or segregation cells, as well as solitary confinement for inmates with severe forms of mental illness (e.g., "Nut Run").[7] Nonetheless, the prison's immutable layout recapitulates the irrevocable rhythm and routine of the schedule. Thus, the physical setting is monotonous when it is not ominous: "While doing time, inmates see the same buildings day in and day out without change. They have walked the same cement path to the cafeteria, to work, to the laundry, to the canteen, to medical, and back. It never changes."[8] These conditions, too, occasion a sense of protracted duration.

A prison may encompass a variety of places, but a convict will spend most of his or her time in a cell. Remarkably, human beings can adapt to and even cherish the most meager and frustrating circumstances, which makes for a two-edged relationship with one's cell that is imbued with irony and ambiguity. This ill-furnished and frequently dangerous setting is, simultaneously, the place where one lives. The cell is a "dehumanizing environment" for Baca.[9] "To most of us," avows James Paluch, "these cells are nothing more than cold coffins, leaving a chilling effect on anyone forced to live inside them."[10] Victor Serge concurs with his assessment, and he adds an instructive comment concerning the impact of this environment on temporal experience: "I am already in a sort of tomb. I can do nothing. I am nothing. I see, hear, and feel nothing. I only know that the next hour will be exactly like this one."[11]

Yet prisoners gradually assume a defensive and even possessive attitude toward their cells. Notice, for example, how Lerner's cellmate refers to one's cell as "the house" and invokes a possessive pronoun in reference to "their front porches" (i.e., the area directly in front of one's cell): "They can't count for shit here, O. G. In Kansas they line ya up *outside* the cell door, stand the cons up on their front porches, outside the house, three, four, *five* fucking times a day."[12] Later, Lerner himself embraces these terms when he lays claim to "my front porch" and offers the following observation: "In prison you *never* enter a man's house without permission. Unless you intend him some harm."[13] Luckily, he has a trustworthy cellmate, which means they can stay inside "the relatively safe cocoon of our locked cell."[14] The territorial etiquette he espouses is ironic given that convicts do not have any enduring claim to a particular cell. Timothy Leary is "led handcuffed into seven jails in six weeks. Fourteen different cells."[15] With another cellmate, moreover, one's cell may become a contested or even predatory environment, not a sanctuary. Lerner reports the suicide of a sixteen-year-old who had been repeatedly raped by his cellmate, and someone attempts to kill Paluch by throwing a firebomb into his cell.[16]

Prisons differ in the size of their cells, and estimates vary because convicts rarely have a tape measure. Unquestionably, however, the sheer amount of space is shockingly small, and, except for prisoners held in isolation, it will be shared with one or more cellmates. Baca decries "living in a six-by-nine cage," the same size as Stephen Stanko's cell.[17] Lerner must "share an eight-by-six cage" with a gigantic cellmate (or "cellie").[18] Paluch's cell is ten feet by seven feet; for Erin George, it is seven by twelve.[19] In our eighteen estimates, the average size of a cell is sixty square feet, and the average height is nine feet. Outside of prison, the average size of a bathroom ranges from forty to fifty square feet, and the average size of a bedroom is approximately 144 square feet (with a primary bedroom at 250 square feet or more). Yet it is not arithmetic but how space in the cell is experienced that really matters. Standing in the middle of his cell, Baca "could touch both walls."[20] Jacobo Timerman, a political prisoner in Argentina, cannot extend his arms, but he can stretch out his entire body when he lies down, which he could not do in his previous cell.[21] Serge paces "around the cell in twelve steps."[22] Carceral finds two feet of space between the floor beds at a minimum-security prison. Two men cannot pass by one another in Jorge Renaud's cell because the distance from the wall to the bunk beds is so small.[23] Lerner suffers claustrophobia in a cell where "only one man at a time could comfortably stand up."[24] Like Stanko, convicts encounter "a constant sense of enclosure and confinement," with attendant effects on temporal experience.[25]

As with space, there is some variation in the furnishings of prison cells, but the range extends from very little to nothing at all. For Gresham Sykes, the official contents are "harshly Spartan."[26] Sleeping accommodations are invariably uncomfortable and contribute to overcrowded conditions: "A set of steel bunk beds and an additional mattress either on the floor or an antiquated 'army-cot' style foldout bed generally make up the sleeping arrangements."[27] Atop these beds, Lerner notes, are "three-inch-thick vinyl pallets that the prison generously referred to as mattresses."[28] Yet convicts in suicide watch or segregation cells may well discover that there is no mattress whatsoever, no sheets, and no blanket.[29] Aside from beds, "one stainless steel toilet/sink combination" is the only other item in most maximum-security cells.[30] Typically, the sink and toilet are operated by push buttons, but both may be inoperative.[31] It is not difficult to imagine what one sees, hears, and smells in a small cell where two or three men share a single toilet. The perceived passage of time is altered by these circumstances. A more primitive system was used in the not-so-distant past. The anonymous narrator of *The Jack-Roller* tells us that, during the 1920s, his "cell was barren except for the dirty bunk and the open toilet bucket in the corner."[32] Decades later, according to Theodore Davidson, comparable conditions could be found in segregation cells at San Quentin: "In the mid-1960s, there was only a hole in the floor where the toilet had been and no wash basin; the prisoner was given a bucket of clean water for drinking and washing, and an empty bucket in which to perform bodily functions. The buckets were changed daily."[33]

There is more to a prison than walls and razor wire. Sometimes, for example, there are tiny desks in each cell. "At the end of my bed," writes Paluch, "is a small steel desk with a swivel chair, also bolted into the floor. This doubles as a dining table and a writing desk."[34] The desk's size, however, and the fact that it must be shared, affect the rhythm of activity as well as temporal experience. In the following excerpt from an interview, Carceral asks Evan and Felix to comment on the desks in (refurbished) cells at a minimum-security prison:

FELIX: "Desk? What desk? It's a small shelf! You're lucky if you can write a letter on it. You can't set a typewriter on it and have room for the material you want to type."
CARCERAL: "That sounds small."
FELIX: "It is! Then, in a two- or three-man room, there is only one desk and one chair! For you [i.e., Carceral], you couldn't do any school work at it. It's ridiculous, the size."
EVAN: "Then they expect men to eat meals in their cells. The dining room is too small for the whole unit, so the guys from upstairs eat in the dining room, but the downstairs guys have to eat in their rooms."
FELIX: "Imagine two men eating, and one small desk and one chair. One guy is going to be eating on his bed!"

Echoing their comments, Carceral recalls trying to study at Gladiator School with "a typewriter on the desk, a book in my lap, and another on the floor. Maybe a notebook on the bed." Taking turns (at a desk, a sink, or a toilet) slows the pace of life and builds unavoidable delays into the most mundane facets of one's daily round. What if one cellmate decides that the desk is a shelf for his hygiene items? The quantity and quality of time for study would be reduced, and progress toward a desired future would be impeded or blocked.

Sykes summarizes the entry procedures that all convicts undergo immediately upon their arrival at a prison: "Before he leaves the outer hall he is taken to a room where he is stripped and searched. His age, name, crime, sentence, and other information are duly recorded; his civilian possessions are taken away and he puts on the prison uniform."[35] His use of masculine pronouns notwithstanding, George confirms an identical process in operation at a women's prison more than fifty years later: "I kept nothing: no panties, no T-shirt. . . . I couldn't even keep my bra."[36] One enters prison only after having all of one's personal property taken away, including clothing. Multiple convicts recount their humiliation during these procedures. The reader meets Lerner when he is "naked in Suicide Watch Cell No. 3," and Leary invokes the Biblical "shame" of Adam at his own nakedness.[37] Relinquishing all of one's personal property is one of the most searing aspects of intake. It is the epitome of what Harold Garfinkel calls a "degradation ceremony."[38] Subsequent to imprisonment, however, convicts begin to acquire property of one kind or another, especially when they have disposable income. "If the inmate can afford it," says Carceral, "he will have a television or radio, writing supplies, and hobby items." At Angola, Billy Sinclair's possessions include an old Underwood typewriter and a dictionary.[39] Like convicts, POWs are allowed very little property, but, as Christopher Burney points out, what they have is highly valued: "Those who live only with the barest elements of life are keen judges of their meager assets and set great store by them."[40] Lerner adds that strong feelings are linked to these modest possessions: "When all you have in this world is a half roll of toilet paper and a little piece of gray soap the size of a chiclet, any property loss is an occasion for mourning."[41]

Inside every prison, ironically, there is a wealth of one particular kind of property: contraband. "I never took a shower without my shank in reach," states Baca.[42] For the most part, weapons are constructed on the premises, but drugs are brought inside by those who come and go. Corrupt members of the staff deliver drugs to inmates, but so do friends and loved ones, as noted by Baca: "After visits he [Macaron] came back and drank salt water and threw up a balloon of hash his wife had tongued him in a kiss."[43] There are countless ways to distribute contraband once it has entered the prison. Some convicts sign up to attend religious services, for instance, so that they can conduct business on the way to and from these meetings.[44] Theodore Davidson adds that "in the blocks with limited evening movement, the prisoner 'tier tenders' legally carry hot water to the prisoners and pour it through their bars to them; and illegally, the tier tenders pick up and deliver all sorts of things for those who are locked in their cells."[45] There is, then, property in the cells, both legal and illegal, but all of it can be taken away at a moment's notice.

Subsequent to imprisonment, declares Aleksandr Solzhenitsyn, "nothing that belongs to you is yours any longer."[46] The convict's sentiments to the contrary, a cell and its contents are not his or her property. Rather, a prisoner "owns" these things only temporarily and by the grace of those in authority. Prisoners who are put in punishment cells relinquish all of their possessions. Davidson reports that a prisoner in segregation "is allowed no personal property other than the clothes on his back."[47] Sinclair itemizes what he is permitted to bring: "I was given an orange jumpsuit, a toothbrush, a tube of toothpaste, a sheet, and a worn yellow blanket—nothing else."[48] Nor is it the case that convicts outside of segregation are safe from search and seizure. Knowing that contraband is prevalent, correctional officers send shakedown crews through the cellblocks with no prior warning. In a Russian gulag, "violent searches and unscheduled visits were frequent, requiring the complete turning out of one's belongings and undressing down to one's skin."[49] Back in the United States, Baca and fellow convicts know "the shakedown crews usually inspected one or two cells while cons were out on the field or working."[50] At a women's prison, however, the officers engage in temporal gamesmanship: "Shakedowns like this almost never happen during the day. Instead, the ominous sound of officers moving plastic chairs in an otherwise empty dayroom awakens you at midnight."[51] The correctional officers do not restrict themselves to search and seizure. "Destruction of an inmate's belongings was a favorite tactic of the shakedown crew," avows Sinclair, an observation corroborated by Lerner: "A photograph of my girls, Alana and Rachel, taken at Disneyland when they were eleven and ten, is ripped off the wall. The sergeant examines it briefly before tearing it in half and tossing the pieces in the air."[52]

Prison cells are terribly small and lacking in all amenities; moreover, their physical condition is frequently abominable. Carceral says, "It was hard at first to get used to the dirt and grime." Likewise, Robert Berger comments on the ubiquitous filth.[53] At Angola, Sinclair is put into a cell where the "roof leaked directly above the bed, flooding the cell when it rained," and Timerman endures similar conditions in Argentina:

> The floor of the cell is permanently wet. Somewhere there's a leak. The mattress is also wet. I have a blanket, and to prevent that from getting wet I keep it on my shoulders constantly. If I lie down with the blanket on top of me, the part of my body touching the mattress gets soaked.[54]

Lerner encounters equally disgusting circumstances at intake in Nevada: "We're all trying, without much success, to avoid stepping into the puddles of brown water that are fed from the overflowing toilets behind the cell doors."[55] And one finds comparable conditions in the Yuma County Jail: "Every time someone in another cell flushed their toilet," Baca tells us, "particles of sewage bubbled up from my commode and puddled on the floor."[56]

A great many autobiographies bear witness to the fact that prisons are infested with all manner of disgusting pests. The anonymous narrator of Clifford Shaw's book *The Jack-Roller* provides this commentary in the vernacular of the 1920s: "I fell into a slumber, only to be awakened by vermin crawling all over my face and body."[57] Seven decades later, Baca describes "slapping lice from rancid mattresses."[58] Paluch discovers that his "cell is infested with all kinds of roaches."[59] "I am taking a shower," he adds, "when I turn to see a big, fat rat facing me. Instead of running away, he seems to be staring me down."[60] The inmates at Angola are beset by voracious mosquitoes, but they have worse problems to contend with:

> Death row cells were infested with rats and roaches. After heavy rains, rats often crawled into the pipes and came up through the commodes. They emerged into toilets while condemned inmates were using them. Some were so afraid of the rats they refused to sit down on the toilets, opting instead to squat over the edges when nature called.[61]

For convicts, the temperature is either "unbearably hot" or "terribly cold."[62] As is so often the case, these aggravating circumstances are brought about by the absence of temporal autonomy. Paluch must put up with "bitter cold" in his cell because "they officially start the heat each year on November 15, another three weeks away."[63] The central issue, then, is nearly complete lack of control over how one experiences the temperature. "Florence is in the desert," states Baca, "so like almost everyone else I wore boxer shorts, dressing in prison blues and brogans only for family visits, counselor interviews, chow time, or infirmary."[64] During the winter, however, we find him "under my blanket, wearing my pants and T-shirt and beanie cap because of the night cold."[65] In certain climates, prisoners can suffer both extremes every twenty-four hours: "It stays desert hot in the days, cold now at nights."[66] Carceral helps us understand how this problem is exacerbated by a specific form of architecture: "From my past experience at Gladiator School with living on tiers, I remember that during the winter, men on the top tier wore only lightweight boxers while in their cells, but men on the lower tier wore long underwear, pants, and a sweatshirt or jacket." Paluch serves time at SCI-Rockview, where the main housing units are five tiers high: "The problem is that heat rises. On the highest tiers when the heat is on, it is too hot to even breathe, resulting in irritable and frustrated inmates. But those on the lower tiers experience refrigerator-like temperatures that are also very uncomfortable."[67] Such powerlessness makes for suffering, frustration, antagonism, and protracted duration.

Incarceration reeks of "the vile odor of men living in cages."[68] Most convicts share a toilet with at least one other inmate in a very small space. "An oven-hot eight-by-six concrete cell in a post-dookie environment stinks," asserts Lerner.[69] Thus, he celebrates solitary confinement, which frees him, temporarily, from his cellmate's "interminable rants and dookie sessions."[70] Yet even prisoners in solitary confinement cannot escape the smell of previous occupants. "Inside the cell," states Paluch, "the stench of feces and urine stings my senses."[71] Similarly, when Baca is thrown into the drunk tank, it "smelled like urine and whiskey vomit."[72] Lerner describes the Fish Tank as "broiling hot and filled with the stench of sweat, urine, and something worse—the thick oppressive odor of fear and despair."[73] Once again, architecture plays a role. Davidson cites "poorly ventilated cellblocks" as a contributing factor, and Carceral recalls a tiny, windowless game room that had a strong odor during the summer.[74]

Prisons also differ concerning the availability and control of light. Some inmates, under certain conditions, exercise a modicum of control over the lights in their cells, but this appears to be atypical.[75] At most penitentiaries, correctional officers resist any attempt by prisoners to change the scheduled timing for lights:

> I was writing a letter later that month when it started to rain. The skies darkened outside and it got hard to read. I called down to the tier officer, "Yo, man, turn the light on in cell 14." He ignored me. I called out again, thinking he hadn't heard me. No light. I asked him at least five different times to turn my cell light on. He didn't. I called down to him to get the supervisor. He said, "You ain't running nothing, I'll turn the light on when I want."[76]

Light is the epitome of the temporal regime. In this regard, as with all others, convicts must cede control over the timing of personal conduct.

For those in jail, according to Irwin, "life begins early in the morning, about 6 A.M. when deputies turn on the lights."[77] Controlling the rhythm of light is a fundamental way in which the staff structures the temporal experience of prisoners. Yet, as Jimmy Dunn argues, such efforts may seem pointless or even sadistic because they usually result in nothing more than enormous swaths of empty time:

> The first thing is the light. Consciousness comes fast in the penitentiary. The bull throws the master switch in the cellblock and each cell is flooded with light. I know the bull is a sadist. He enjoys his work. He wakes us up every morning at six o'clock with the jar of a hundred watts, while it's still dark outside, knowing we have no place to go.[78]

Just as arbitrarily, the absence of light brings the prisoner's day to a close: "'LIGHTS OUT!' screamed Strunk, and Kansas [his cellmate] flicked off the switch."[79] Darkness denotes the loss of temporal autonomy for Baca: "After a while the lights flickered, signaling bedtime, and went off a few minutes later."[80] Even after "lights out," correctional officers impose temporal discipline on their prisoners by means of light. Dunn remembers that officers on the third shift would take "two or three counts, flashing lights through the bars on the sleeping faces to make sure they haven't lost anyone."[81]

In correctional facilities, there is either not enough or too much light. Both conditions bring about temporal disorientation as well as various forms of psychopathy. Solzhenitsyn suffers both ends of the continuum and notes the destructive side effects that accompany such treatment:

> The *light* in cells was always "rationed," so to speak, in both the thirties and the forties: the "muzzles" on the windows and the frosted reinforced glass created a permanent twilight in the cells (darkness is an important factor in causing depression). They often stretched netting above the window "muzzle," and in the winter it was covered with snow, which cut off this last access to the light. Reading became no more than a way of ruining one's eyes. In the Vladimir TON, they made up for this lack of light at night: bright electric lights burned all night long, preventing sleep.[82]

Sleep deprivation is, of course, part of the standard repertoire of torture in contemporary interrogation.

It is certainly not the case that such circumstances afflict only political prisoners in foreign lands, for it is easy to find comparable passages concerning punishment cells in American prisons. "Days and nights blurred" when Baca's "cell was pitch black."[83] But at the other end of this continuum, the circumstances are no less wretched. "Above my bed is a wall light of two bulbs," writes Paluch, "one of which stays on twenty-four hours a day."[84] Sinclair endures kindred conditions in Louisiana: "The jailers had installed a large light bulb in the ceiling light fixture. It was controlled by a light switch outside the cell. The jailers kept it on twenty-four hours a day. There was no escaping its blinding glare."[85] Moreover, Davidson makes it clear that manipulation of light is an intended part of the punishment at San Quentin:

> The lights are controlled from the outside (as they are in all isolation and grade 1 and 2 segregation cells); and, if the guards are really down on the prisoner, they will shut the door and keep the lights off—except during meals. If their feelings are extreme, they may not even turn the lights on at meal time, when the food is pushed in to the prisoner through the slot in the bars.[86]

And what is there to see? What does the light in prison reveal? "I look around my cell," writes Paluch. "Its walls and floor are constructed of dense pockmarked concrete, except for the thick iron bars that enclose the cell front and its door."[87] The physical condition of one's surroundings articulates a dismal fate. For Lerner, there are "cinder block walls yellow-brown from decades of cigarette smoke."[88] In Baca's cell, there is "caked grime on the walls and floor."[89] What you see makes it clear that no one cares. "The rusting bunk was anchored to a shit-smeared wall," notes Baca, "and the putrid commode was barely attached to the wall with rotten bolts."[90] The agony of previous inhabitants is inscribed on the walls, where Baca observes the "graffiti of despair and vengeance."[91] Lerner describes the graffiti in his cell as "a mural of misery and enigmatic engravings."[92]

The regions outside of one's cell offer little if any respite. What there is to see signals that prison is a dangerous, desolate, and demeaning place. "Chain link fencing is welded outside the rails of the walkways that run along the second through fifth tiers," states Theodore Davidson, "making an additional cage that is used to control prisoners and prevent them from throwing guards or other prisoners over the railing when they are moving to or from their cells."[93] At Lerner's prison, "the main yard is about the size of two football fields, a huge rectangle of dirt with a crumbling asphalt walkway."[94] In the name of outdoor recreation, Paluch and other prisoners in the Restrictive Housing Unit "are strip-searched in their cells, handcuffed, then transferred to fenced cages similar to dog kennels, averaging seven by twenty feet in size."[95] Everywhere one looks, there is racial segregation with its menacing implications. In the chow hall, recalls Baca, "whites sat with whites, Blacks with Blacks, and Chicanos with Chicanos."[96] And on the yard, adds Sinclair, "all ethnic groups had their own turf. Whites had the weight pile; Blacks, the basketball court; Mexicans, the handball court; and Indians, the baseball diamonds."[97]

Staring is a form of social control. We garner the stares of passersby whenever we violate mores or folkways in public places. By the same token, we earn what Erving Goffman called "the civil inattention that passersby owe each other" if we behave ourselves.[98] In these latter circumstances, others do not have a right to stare at us, and it would be considered rude or intrusive for them to do so. To be stared at is stressful because, as Goffman taught us, our performances in social interaction are fragile productions and vulnerable to sustained scrutiny. So, it comes as no surprise to learn that public speaking (during which strangers stare at us) is perennially listed as one of the most stressful experiences in everyday life.

In prison, the people who stare at you are armed and dangerous. "Above us a guard patrolled," says Baca, "walking around the catwalk, cradling a rifle and peering down into the cells."[99] The stress associated with being stared at is a ubiquitous feature of life behind bars. Writing in 1958, Gresham Sykes observed that "prisoners live in an enforced intimacy where each man's behavior is subject both to the constant scrutiny of his fellow captives and the surveillance of the custodians."[100] Recent developments in penology have only worsened this experience. Lerner describes the architecture of surveillance: "Forty cells on each floor, or 'tier,' are arrayed in a compressed horseshoe pattern around a lower-tier staff office and the upper-tier Plexiglas-enclosed gun bubble."[101] This arrangement is a manifestation of what Michel Foucault refers to as Bentham's *panopticon*, but with the contemporary addition of closed-circuit cameras almost everywhere.[102] In a small-town jail, Sinclair is an object of fascination: "For the first few days, the jailers brought people to the cell at all hours to peer at me."[103] Yet Sykes is correct in asserting that much of this "constant scrutiny" comes from one's fellow prisoners, and it begins immediately upon arrival:

> A reception committee greeted the fresh fish as we moved down the Walk. They lined the rails, eyeing us, forming a gauntlet of leers, wisecracks, and lewd laughter.[104]
>
> All around us and above us, convicts are standing and shouting from behind their cell doors, faces pressed up against the square glass windows. The spectacle of sixteen naked, sweating bodies has apparently inflamed the current guests, inspiring them to scream out their respective welcomes.[105]

Subsequently, the scrutiny of fellow inmates is inescapable: "The cons across the landing . . . looked at us and we looked back."[106]

Tomorrow, they will still be there. Convicts see the same things day after day. Scholars who conduct research inside correctional facilities (even if only briefly) are invariably troubled by their "sensory deprivations."[107] "When we examine the physical structure of the prison," reports Sykes, "the most striking feature is, perhaps, its drabness."[108] Thomas Meisenhelder links "the gray sameness of prison space" to distortion in temporal experience: "Like the experimental subject in a sensory deprivation tank, the prison inmate often creates out of the lack of change in his environment the feeling that time is creeping along."[109] This lack of visual stimulation is a pervasive source of stress in correctional facilities. Moreover, the findings of these academic studies run parallel to observations in convict autobiographies. "One of the greatest hardships for me in the first few months I was at Angola was getting used to the sameness of every day," recalls Albert Woodfox.[110] From this standpoint, it is what the convict does not see that shapes the perceived passage of time:

> At most prisons, there are no VCRs, no microwaves, no movies, no weights, and few, if any, recreational activities. The daily actions of life include eating, going to a job assignment, and outdoor recreation for no more than a few hours daily. The cells contain no rugs, no comforters, or any such luxury. The floors are concrete, no pictures of any kind can be displayed on walls or lockers, and any form of decorating is strictly forbidden. There are no choices of any kind for meals.[111]

In solitary confinement, Christopher Burney discovers that "variety is not the spice, but the very stuff of life."[112] Baca ruminates on "this place with no color, no stimulation, nothing to feed my senses."[113] Erin George echoes his frustration: "We are so starved for color here—almost everything is white or gray."[114] She adds, "Of course, we weren't allowed to put anything on the walls or metal desks."[115]

If prison is akin to a sensory deprivation experiment, then it is one regularly punctuated by scenes of degradation and violence. Lerner witnesses a fellow convict picking at the scabs on his skull until blood and pus trickle down his face.[116] From his cell "on the disciplinary tier," Sinclair watches fellow convicts resist authority with the scant resources at hand: "Feces and urine were slung at guards on occasion."[117] Baca looks at other residents of the drunk tank: "Men sat and stared at the wall in front of them. Some were crumpled on the floor where they had passed out."[118] Inmates glimpse the suicides of friends as well as strangers.[119] Woodfox is witness to a predatory environment: "I was constantly seeing acts of violence, constantly seeing guys being raped."[120] Convicts see inmates assault each other, and they notice that the correctional officers do not intervene:

> There is a fight today on the block. Through my cell door, I observe two prisoners severely beating down a third, while two more inmates watch. The guards wait until the fight is over.[121]
>
> I witness a prisoner getting stabbed today near the end of the block. The guards lock themselves in on the other side of the gate.[122]

From observations like these, convicts learn that no one will protect them from the predation of others.

And what, finally, do they hear? The sounds of prison can only be truly understood as variations on sonic torture. Anyone who has ever been inside a correctional facility comments on the extraordinary noise. To a great extent, this noise is produced and amplified by the structure of prison as well as its operational procedures. John Irwin directs our attention to the material environment of the jail: "Its cement and metal refract sound, and the clanging, talking, and shouting bounce around and mix together into a steady, dull roar—a frightening sound to those unaccustomed to it."[123] Most cells, furthermore, only have bars on one side, leaving inmates chronically exposed to this noise. The rhythm and routine in prison are marked by an irritating assortment of sounds:

> In all 26 State Correctional Institutions across Pennsylvania, bells, sirens, and buzzers sound throughout the day. They start at 6 A.M. for standing counts, then at 7:30 A.M. for breakfast lines. Then comes . . . lunch . . . and supper, then more standing counts. Prisoners hear these bells, sirens, and buzzers a minimum of 10 times a day, 70 times a week, 3,640 times a year.[124]

Convicts' eardrums also are pummeled by a never-ending stream of curt announcements: "Tier 3, out for showers!"[125]

"If you have never been inside a prison, it is hard to imagine the *noise*," states Paluch.[126] Yet the lion's share of the noise is generated by the inmates themselves. Carceral helps us understand how their circumstances create a sonic competition, which, in turn, brings about this nightmarish babel. The men on his cellblock would yell across the landing at each other in an effort to be heard above the din. Convicts with radios or televisions would turn the volume up in order to hear them. Other inmates would set up chess boards and shout numbers to each other for hours. Most of them, however, simply screamed back and forth—talking, laughing, arguing, threatening. "The earsplitting roar sounded all day," writes Baca in corroboration.[127] This sonic competition results in a "maddening opera of noise" that makes it difficult or impossible to read or sleep.[128] "The years I studied on the cellblock were frustrating to say the least," recalls Carceral. "Most men would give up." In segregation, a convict confronts the opposite extreme of solitary confinement. "When you neither move nor think in your cell," avows

Jack Abbott, "you are awash in pure nothingness."[129] It is a different kind of sonic suffering, but one with comparable effects on temporal experience: "Time descends in your cell like the lid of a coffin in which you lie and watch it as it slowly closes over you."[130] Lerner finds the quiet soothing at first, but not for long: "After three days of isolation, I am climbing the walls, desperate for some conversation."[131]

Unavoidably, one hears the grief and distress of other inmates. "Intermittent shrieks crackled throughout the night," according to Baca.[132] "At night I can hear screams and wild sobbing," echoes Lerner, including "one of the teenagers' cells" where the younger prisoner is repeatedly raped by his much older cellmate.[133] The teenager's "cellie . . . calls him 'punk' or 'little bitch' to his face" until, unable to stand the physical and verbal abuse any longer, he kills himself.[134] Prisoners also listen to intended aggression directed at themselves or other inmates. "I overheard two cons talking on the first tier below about the contract on my head," recalls Baca.[135] At Chino, Timothy Leary records this exchange between fellow prisoners:

"You miserable Motherfucker, I'm going to get you. You's dead you Motherfucking fool. I get out of this cell tomorrow, I'se going to whip you ass so hard you die. Die, Motherfucker! You hear me?"

"Yay bo." Mocking. "You scare me."

"Done you 'yay bo' me you Motherfucker. I'se going to get you dead, Motherfucker. What you name?"

"My name is Shackleforth, baby."

"Well you po fool, Shackleforth, you dead. Dead, Motherfucker."[136]

There is a constant flow of scorn and the promise of harm from correctional officers as well as other prisoners. Indeed, Lerner reflects "on just how much the C.O.'s sound like the convicts."[137] Upon their arrival at a prison in Nevada, Lerner and other fish are greeted by the following speech from the officers:

"LISTEN UP, DICKWADS!" . . .

"I want all you cum-sucking maggot convicts down on your fucking knees, *right now!*" . . .

"All right jerkoffs! After I uncuff you, you still don't move, you keep your hands on top of your heads *until* your name is called. . . . There will be a cavity check in the holding cell for the benefit of any ignorant motherfucker that thinks he can ass-keister a hypo or crack pipe or even a naked photo of his sister Kate doing the shimmy." . . .

"I SAID HANDS ON YOUR HEAD! ARE YOU FUCKING DEAF OR STUPID?" . . .

"MOVE AGAIN AND I'LL BLOW YOUR FUCKING HEAD OFF!"[138]

Drenched in a cascade of insults and threats, convicts are relentlessly coarsened or demoralized by their environment. Either way, the pace of temporal experience slows to a disabled crawl.

The convict's perception of time is not only conditioned by a cell's physical environment, but also by its occupancy. Given that politicians are reluctant to raise taxes for the sake of new correctional facilities, a policy of mass incarceration has the direct consequence of overcrowding. Carceral observes that convicts' preferences with respect to occupancy can be arrayed along a continuum. Of course, the most desirable situation is a single-occupancy cell. Like early feminists, the convict longs for a room of one's own.[139] "I have the cell to myself and it feels wonderful," exults Lerner.[140] Except for protective custody and other types of segregation, however, this living arrangement is nearly nonexistent. Baca celebrates the tradeoff: "Yes, I missed being in general population and the freedom that went with it. But in the dungeon I had my own cell and I enjoyed my privacy and the time I had to write and read."[141]

Most prisons have double-occupancy cells now (with bunk beds), but, confronting chronic overcrowding, officials often resort to makeshift measures that shoehorn a third or fourth inmate into each cell. Thus, a prisoner is likely to spend a great deal of time in a very small space with one or more strangers. Such conditions set the stage for conflict and violence: "The anger, frustration, and tension in the air could be cut with a knife. Three men per six-foot-by-nine-foot cell with one stainless steel toilet/sink combination."[142] It is worth noting, moreover, that these cells were designed for a single occupant: "Even though each of these 2500 cells in San Quentin was planned to house a single prisoner, a second steel bunk bed has been added to most cells."[143] Jails for women have recourse to related forms of expediency:

RRJ had gotten so overcrowded that in cells designed for one inmate, they would house three: two in bunks and a third on the floor. The woman assigned to the floor slept in a "boat"—a heavy plastic frame that took up every inch of the available floor space. I couldn't even use the toilet in the cell without having to put my feet on someone's mattress.[144]

The resulting interpersonal relations are predictable: "There were more than one hundred women crammed in a unit designed for fifty. Tension ran high and fights broke out several times a day."[145]

Everyone seems to agree that the worst accommodations are found in dormitory—or barracks-style—forms of incarceration. Lerner explains why he quickly rues his assignment to the "twelve-man barracks": "Inside my new dorm, I am immediately assaulted by a bedlam of competing sounds—boom boxes blasting, TV talk show hosts inciting guests to riot, radios blaring, and convicts yelling and jumping around."[146] In this setting, each prisoner is always accessible to all of the other residents: "They are staring at me. I already long for the relative privacy and peace of my two-man Fish Tank home."[147] At Angola, Sinclair was housed in a "dorm" with "four rows of army-style bunks. Each row consisted of fifteen bunks."[148] Soon, however, there were "as many as eighty" prisoners in that unit.[149] Yet even these circumstances pale beside reports from other countries. Aleksander Solzhenitsyn provides this vignette: "Vlasov was put into Cell 61. This was a cell intended for solitary confinement, sixteen feet long and a little more than three feet wide. Two iron cots were anchored to the floor by thick iron bolts, and on each cot two condemned men were lying, their heads at opposite ends. Fourteen other prisoners were lying crosswise on the cement floor."[150] Much more recently, Martin Frederiksen documents comparable conditions in the Republic of Georgia, where one of his informants is put into "a sixteen-bed cell crammed with fifty-four inmates; they had to sleep in turns."[151]

Overcrowding is not the only issue. The comportment and demeanor of cellmates are equally consequential. Day in, day out, convicts are at close quarters with people who are acknowledged criminals. They are assumed to have sinister motives; by definition, they are untrustworthy. Moreover, many of them are diseased or disfigured. At intake, Lerner is welcomed with disturbing information: " 'This prison has a combined HIV and hepatitis C infection rate of 60 percent' "[152] In short, a prisoner's experiential surround encompasses what cellmates say and do as well as their identities or public personae. Yet convicts rarely have any say concerning who their cellmates will be. Lerner is Jewish but is assigned to share a cell with Kansas, a huge con with a large swastika tattooed on his neck and confederates in the Aryan Nation.[153] Lerner is assigned to the lower bunk, but Kansas takes it.[154] "Between exercise sets," Kansas "would fart out the aroma of rotten eggs."[155] And he likes to talk: "For thirty days in the Fish Tank, Kansas never shut up."[156] A cellmate's behavior is frequently brazen, unsettling, or worse. "My first cellmate . . . offers to perform oral sex on me," recalls Paluch.[157] A subsequent cellmate "seems to have mental problems."[158] When authorities add a man to Baca's cell, Baca beats him senseless.[159]

"A bad cellmate in prison (as in jail) can be one of the most stressful aspects of inmate life," asserts George.[160] This statement implies a "bad cellmate" is an occasional problem, but her foregoing observations reveal that such cellmates are typical, not exceptional: "Most are sick, drunk, detoxing, mentally ill, or some combination thereof."[161] With vivid thumbnail sketches, she catalogs "the unpleasant roommates that appear with distressing regularity."[162] There is "a ragged blond . . . smelling unspeakably of vomit, sweat, and some other odor that I couldn't identify."[163] There is Kelli, "in on her fourth or fifth prostitution charge. . . . She was detoxing from her heroin habit and she had AIDS."[164] In jail, her worst roommate was Gloria: "It was her habit to masturbate vigorously [and loudly] several times a day."[165] Other prisoners fare no better with their cellmates. "Felicia walked up to her roommate, who was watching *Oprah* on the dayroom television, and slugged her. . . . 'She snores too loud,' she was explaining to the officer as they passed me."[166] One pregnant inmate knocks another pregnant inmate unconscious with her dinner tray because " 'that bitch stole my extra milk.' "[167] George recalls that "tiny Rachel . . . was so severely beaten once during count time by her 240-pound roommate that she had to spend two weeks in the infirmary."[168]

Cellmates come and go, but their behavior is consistently aberrant and objectionable: "Fingernail clippings would appear in my water cup. My radio was accidentally brushed off my desk. Appointment slips or mail that was slipped under the door by an officer while I was asleep would disappear before they reached me."[169] A "sissy" who is punked by other convicts on the tier is assigned to share a cell with Leary's young companion: " 'Jeez, he's crazy. You know what he did? He used my toothbrush. Can you dig that? After I told him not to and marked mine with a red pencil. Now I can't use it after all the stuff that's been in his mouth.' "[170] The outrage and suffering occasioned by cellmates cannot be attributed to a few bad apples. Victor Serge makes it clear that cellmates themselves are the problem, not just "bad" cellmates:

> Three men are brought together in a cell by chance. Whatever their differences, they must tolerate each other; relentless intimacy twenty-four hours a day. . . . Rare is the day when at least one of them is not depressed. Irritable or gloomy, at odds with himself, he exudes a sort of invisible poison. You pity him. You suffer with him. You hate him. You catch his disease.[171]

In an era of mass incarceration and deinstitutionalization of the mentally ill, cellmates are increasingly part of the punishment.

From Jack Abbott, whose expertise cannot be impugned, we learn that convicts inhabit a predatory landscape: "Many times you have to 'prey' on someone, or you will be 'preyed' on yourself."[172] In this dog-eat-dog setting, deterrence cannot be achieved by means of posing or bluffing. As Sykes puts it, "the inmate is acutely aware that sooner or later he will be 'tested'— that someone will 'push' him to see how far they can go and that he must be prepared to fight for the safety of his person or possessions."[173] Not surprisingly, this perilous environment provokes intense anxiety. "*Everyone* is afraid," admits Abbott, and Sykes confirms a "tense and fearful existence."[174] "No one can be trusted," states Paluch, and Sinclair reports that inmates "slept with Sears Roebuck catalogs tied to their chests."[175]

Precautions of this sort are prudent but ineffectual against other dangers, such as rampant extortion (i.e., the "protection" racket) and kindred forms of exploitation. Lerner's cellmate is illustrative:

> Kansas always allocates a portion of his one-hour tier time to terrorize fish into donating a percentage of their store to him. He tells them it is the standard "cell rental" charge and he is the collection agent for the landlord. Or he allows them to purchase a "life insurance" policy from him.[176]

There is, Lerner adds, "predatory extortion for all manner of things," including "using the phone," a "seat in chow hall . . . or just the 'toll' for walking in the yard."[177] Moreover, George assures us that women's prisons have the same dynamics. She characterizes Fluvanna Correctional Center as a "volatile mix of predator and prey."[178] There are "sexual manipulators," of course, but "another tack is strong-arming a newbie into coughing up some commissary."[179]

Uppermost in the convict's mind are questions that seldom trouble those of us in everyday life: "Would I be attacked today for bumping into someone at 'chow,' or would I be robbed of all my belongings while eating?"[180] In prison, cell robberies and rape are commonplace. Amy Fisher recounts that she "was raped numerous times in prison."[181] Violence flares up quickly and with little or no provocation. While held in a minimum-security prison, Carceral witnesses a fight between two inmates. Afterward, one of them needed 150 staples and stitches. "Fights occurred on a daily basis for any and every reason," affirms Stephen Stanko. "It might be over a prior argument in society, a good seat in front of the television, or a piece of corn bread."[182] It may be tempting to attribute this chronic belligerence to the inclinations of those involved, but it is the predatory setting that brings even avowed pacifists like Leary to the brink of violence: "It is completely impossible to do a long prison term and not have moments of fierce, blind, murderous . . . rage."[183] Rage is not an absurd response to repeated victimization. Witness, for example, the experiences reported by Paluch: "I go to court today for some type of hearing. On the bus trip back, another prisoner attacks me. . . . As I return from the library, a prisoner spits in my face. I have no idea who he is."[184] Sinclair's observations are equally instructive. One of his colleagues "killed an older inmate who made aggressive homosexual advances toward him," and, in a later instance, "another inmate was stabbed to death because he wouldn't give up his Timex watch."[185]

A predatory environment sets the parameters for merciless and ubiquitous violence. With uncommon insight, Macaron clarifies the situation for his younger protégé, Baca:

> On the streets, you lose a fight you go home; that's it. Here, you get fucked, you get sold, punked out; cons don't respect you. Cons who went to Nam say it's worse than jungle warfare. You live with your enemies here. There ain't no going home. You live hour to hour with your enemy standing next to you, eating next to you, walking next to you.[186]

His sage lecture is one instance of widespread efforts to resist victimization—that is, "the constant need for inmates to establish the fact that they cannot be, in any way, mocked, stolen from, and/or disrespected."[187] The corollary is, simultaneously, a central irony of incarceration: all of this predatory behavior (and resulting violence) transpires within *maximum-security* institutions. "In 1972," recalls Sinclair, "Angola was known as 'the bloodiest prison in the nation.' "[188] Paluch is held at Holmesburg in 1991, "a maximum-security prison that the prisoners call 'The Terrordome.' "[189] Carceral and fellow convicts refer to their prison as Gladiator School.

TEMPORAL EXPERIENCE

The Lady and the Unicorn tapestries date from the sixteenth century and hang at the Cluny Museum in Paris (Musée national du Moyen Âge). No one is quite sure, but it is widely believed that five of them represent a meditation on the senses. In one tapestry, the Lady is surrounded by things she can see; in the other four, by things she can hear, taste, touch, or smell.

Here, we have been engaged in a far less elegant meditation on the senses. Step by step, we have toured the prison sensorium—that is, a convict's experiential world. Despite the social sciences' avowed devotion to empirically grounded procedures, they have largely overlooked what the senses can tell us about human experience. Jack Katz has accused criminology of being negligent in this regard: "The social science literature contains only scattered evidence of what it means, feels, sounds, tastes, or looks like to commit a particular crime."[190] Yet neglect of the senses is especially inexcusable for penology. In part, the persistence of prisons can be attributed to their cloistered practices and a corresponding reluctance by the public to consider what it is really like to live behind bars. An unflinching study of the prison sensorium serves to correct the prevalent (and ideological) misconception that correctional facilities are akin to pampered country clubs, albeit with less freedom of movement. More to the point, however, systematic attention to the sensations of incarceration enables us to discern what happens to time and temporal experience in that setting.

The physical setting is, by turns, monotonous or menacing. Living space is inadequate to the point of claustrophobia. Furnishings are meager and decrepit. One's own property has been taken away, and, by official fiat, cells lack almost all amenities. The constant requirement of turn-taking makes for the frustrations associated with waiting and delay. A prisoner suffers dirty and deplorable conditions. Cells are infested with frightening, annoying, or loathsome pests. Prisons stink, and much of what an inmate smells is disgusting. It is usually too hot or too cold, and the convict has no control over the temperature. Likewise, there is too much or not enough light. The former disrupts sleep; the latter brings about temporal disorientation and depression. A convict sees dismal circumstances and ubiquitous signs of abandonment. These sights lead to feelings of despair and self-loathing. Prisoners are under constant surveillance from correctional officers and other inmates. This lack of privacy is enormously stressful and renders ordinary modesty irrelevant. Convicts see an unchanging environment that is characterized by sensory deprivation. Together, the architecture and operational procedures produce a noxious level of noise as everyone tries to be heard over the competing roar. One hears the distress of fellow inmates as well as demeaning and threatening speech from prisoners and officers alike. Convicts share small overcrowded spaces with cellmates who are often diseased, disturbed, or predatory. For Albert Woodfox and other inmates, constant vigilance is crucial to survival: "There was the potential for danger every day, twenty-four hours a day."[191]

How do these conditions distort the perceived passage of time? Analytically, we can identify six factors that, in combination, bring about the perception that time is passing slowly (i.e., protracted duration). First, the prison sensorium features multiple dimensions of physical discomfort and mental anguish. Second, there is omnipresent waiting and boredom due to the systemic thwarting of initiative. Third, violence and dread are prevalent, which calls for chronic watchfulness. Fourth, even experienced convicts repeatedly confront shock and novelty. Fifth, the widespread availability of drugs (especially narcotics and hallucinogens) results in altered states of consciousness. Sixth, all of the preceding factors provoke an abnormal concentration on one's present circumstances. The individual's mental focus is narrowed to the here and now. Subjectively, the prisoner is obsessed by self and situation as well as time itself.[192] This increased attention to one's immediate circumstances creates a heightened level of situated stimulus complexity even where there is little or nothing happening from an overt standpoint (e.g., solitary confinement). In effect, these seemingly "empty" intervals are filled by a massive volume of self-consciousness. As a result, there is an extraordinary density of experience per standard temporal unit (minute, hour, day, etc.). These are precisely the ingredients for protracted duration.[193]

Ordinarily, such circumstances are few and far between in the world outside of prison. By definition, they are relatively rare situations at the extremes of our experiential range. They are, however, the modal settings for protracted duration. It follows that the relationship between situated stimulus complexity and the perception that time is passing slowly can be modeled with a U-shaped curve.[194] Put differently, we experience protracted duration when situated stimulus complexity is either abnormally low or abnormally high (i.e., the left and right "tails" of this distribution). In prison, time is perceived to pass slowly during episodes of solitary confinement (or, more generally, waiting and boredom) but also during instances of violence, as when Jack Abbott murders a fellow inmate: "Things register in slow motion because all of your senses are drawn to a new height."[195] Outside of prison, the bulk of our experiences fall in the moderate middle of this continuum, where we do not perceive time passing slowly. Prisoners, in contrast, nearly always find themselves confronting abnormally low or abnormally high stimulus complexity. As we have seen, the prison sensorium stacks these circumstances into towers of causal impact with stark implications for temporal experience. Through the looking glass and into prison, we enter a distorted world where that which is unusual becomes that which is typical. Thus, for prison inmates, protracted duration becomes the norm.

Unexpectedly, variation in temporal experience has important implications for perceived justice. The convict is sentenced to a specific period of time—one, moreover, that is viewed by those in authority as a just interval, given the crime he or she has committed. Yet the cons are conned; a trick is being played on them, and it is temporal in nature. Invariably, the circumstances of incarceration will make the time they serve *feel* much longer than its objective length. It is, of course, impossible to measure this distortion with any certainty, but there can be no doubt that it severely lengthens the sentence as it is experienced by the inmate. By and large, the public is blissfully unaware of this elasticity in prison sentences, but it is something with which convicts are keenly and bitterly familiar.

Pious believers in the cult of incarceration may applaud these circumstances as well as the temporal distortion they occasion. Yet those who approve of such conditions would do well to consider the biographical particulars of Jimmy Dunn—the epitome of what this system produces. Like so many of his confederates, he is "a career offender" who was "raised by the state," and, rather than being deterred by the prospect of prison, "views incarceration as an occupational hazard."[196] People who are exposed to the prison sensorium for extended periods of time are steadily changed by the experience in ways that make them unfit for the civil society into which, sooner or later, most of them will be released.

Chapter Three

TEMPORAL ALLOWANCES

Time is the indispensable resource for all of our activities. Do I have time for that? Tacitly or explicitly, this question is preliminary to every human endeavor. With the answer, we strive for a semiautonomous balance between our wishes and obligations.

The allocation of time in everyday life is a facet of our efforts to control, manipulate, or customize our temporal experience. "Outside," writes Timothy Leary, "we richochet [*sic*] each day through [a] billion-faceted traffic-jam of choice points."[1] We allot a certain amount of time to various activities with the understanding that, unless we set a few minutes, an hour, or a day aside for whatever we want to do, there may be no time left for purely personal experiences after our disparate duties have been discharged. Our distribution of temporal resources, then, is akin to a zero-sum game: time allocated for this will be unavailable for that. The idiomatic (if not quite literal) phrase for this effort at self-determination is evocative of something quite dear to us: our ability to *make time* for what we want to do. Likewise, we must determine the optimal timing for the things we want to do, which involves choosing when something should happen. What hour of the day or day of the week is best for certain activities and experiences? For us, the answer to this question is often discretionary. Time is never limitless in the world outside of prison, but, relative to life behind bars, there is a real (if approximate) sense in which many of us have the wherewithal to do whatever we want, whenever we want, for as long as we want.

Much of the punishment in prison is realized by limiting the time available for the fulfillment of any and all human desires. We punish convicts by "giving" them time, yet incarceration restricts what they can do with it. Behind bars, those in authority allocate temporal resources and determine the timing of one's activities or experiences. There is, consequently, an abundance of time until you try to do something with it. Then you discover that there is never enough time to eat a meal, take a shower, wash your clothes, talk to loved ones on the telephone, play a game, watch television, further your education, or enjoy a moment of privacy. The predefined and always insufficient interval allotted for each of these activities will have nothing whatsoever to do with desired duration, frequency, or timing. In prison, time is both limited and limitless. This paradox is rooted in ubiquitous restrictions on the allocation of temporal resources. For convicts, these restrictions are readily visible along two dimensions: access and immediacy. *Temporal access* concerns how much time one has for a particular activity or with a particular resource, either physical or social. *Temporal immediacy* concerns when or how soon one can engage in a specific activity or make use of a specific resource. When, how often, and for how long may the prisoner pursue a personal agenda?

ACCESS AND IMMEDIACY

Every prison is a cramped world with programmatically scarce resources. Structural and procedural aspects of incarceration govern access and immediacy, thereby regulating social interaction and temporal experience. The systemic lack of availability has baleful implications for the human spirit. Prisons are designed to impede intended action. A convict evinces the resulting frustration in the following dialogue with Carceral:

BIG BYRNE: "I can barely stretch out. If I use the chair to watch TV, then I have to sit in the area between the beds, since the headphone cord is too short. How is my cellie gonna move around? He can't get to his bed!"

CARCERAL: "He can't? [smiling] Little Tanner can get around your big ass!"

BIG BYRNE: "No! So, I will sit or half lay on the bed. Then, my back will begin to hurt. A mattress two inches thick does nothing for a 250-pound, six-feet-five-inch tall man!"

CARCERAL: "Can't win."

BIG BYRNE: "No, I can't. You know how it is; TV on a stand at the end of the bed, sitting on the floor, antenna taped to the wall. Taped until the sergeant rips it down! Our hygiene supplies on the desk, no room for storage. This place sucks!"

Any inmate who tries to pursue a personal agenda feels as if he or she is swimming against a strong current. It is exhausting until you surrender to the system and become the passive creature the authorities want you to be. Lacking initiative, the convict's time will have a molasses-like quality.

Carceral observes that the game room at a minimum-security facility had eight chairs for forty-eight inmates. At any given time, only one-sixth of the men had temporal access to those activities. It was a small space with nothing but hard surfaces, so all of the noise echoed clamorously. Whenever the gaming became "too loud," the sergeant would imperiously close it down, effectively eliminating temporal access altogether. Further fueling frustration was the fact that a day room adjoining the game room was not used for any purpose whatsoever. Prisoners viewed this area as a wasted resource:

DIESEL: "If the idiots would bring two picnic tables inside, we'd have plenty of space to sit. They don't want it any better here."

CASINO: "All the sergeant has to do is call my boss; we have extra picnic tables stored in the back of Maintenance."

One's inability to make use of certain spaces and objects precludes spending time in desirable ways. Note, however, that the prisoners expressed bitter fatalism instead of suggesting these changes to correctional officers. They have learned that such initiative is routinely rebuffed. Jimmy Baca reveals kindred resignation when he admits having to "sharpen my pencil with my teeth."[2]

Incarceration is about *time served*, not *time for* whatever one might like to do. The temporal regime dictates how much time a prisoner can allocate to any particular activity. "For instance," reports Rik Scarce, "inmates might be in the midst of a pinochle game when the time for a lockdown came. Because they lived in different cells, they would have to suspend the game."[3] As with the aforementioned game room, temporal access to television is always at the correctional officers' discretion. Scarce states that some of them let us "stay out of our cells past lockdown to watch the end of a football game on television."[4] Stephen Stanko refers to television as "the proverbial prison babysitter," but only four channels (ABC, CBS, NBC, and FOX) are available: "Contrary to the media's portrayal of 'cablevision prisons,' inmates are not given a cornucopia of satellite-dish choices for viewing."[5] He adds that the channel "was decided by the officer in the control room."[6] John Irwin notes that "reading is also popular, although the supply of reading material is quite limited."[7] Thematically, then, the inmate lacks access to resources for killing time, either because they are not available within that prison or because access is at the discretion of others. Both issues have severe implications for the convict's ability to manage his or her own temporal experience.

Contrastingly, authorities make a great deal of *time for* security procedures. In prison, ubiquitous gates are emblematic of the relationship between architecture and temporal experience. The very design of these gates is temporal. Imagine trying to walk down a hallway where you are forced to pass through multiple gates. At each of them, you must pause, open it, pass through, and close it behind yourself before proceeding to the next gate. Commas in the preceding sentence symbolize moments of time that will be magnified by this process. The construction of this hallway impedes your intended action. This physical setting slows the pace of movement and alters your sense of time. Now imagine that these gates are controlled by someone else. You cannot open or close them yourself. In prison, inmates must stop and wait for a correctional officer to open each gate using a key or control panel. The officer may see a prisoner coming and open the gate upon arrival, but some obstruction is much more likely. An officer may be busy talking to someone or completing paperwork, or may choose to simply ignore the prisoner. Whatever the inmate is trying to do will be delayed, which affects access and immediacy as well as the perceived passage of time.

Like other convicts, Jorge Renaud is outraged by the temporal mathematics associated with such obstructionism: "Inmates waste hours every day, weeks every year, just waiting for the officers to roll the doors and let them into their cells."[8] Carceral recalls walking the hallways of a private prison where the staff operated its gates by means of cameras and remote control. It could take thirty minutes to walk fifty yards. One day, he only went halfway before giving up. In order to walk through a particular hallway, prisoners would have to wait for four successive gates to be opened. On average, an inmate would spend three to ten minutes at each gate, but a single gate could take twenty minutes. During these intervals, convicts feel thwarted and angry because the delay can determine whether they gain access to a desired activity. Jaylen, one of Carceral's fellow inmates, finally blew his top one day: "Fucking gates! We'll be last in line for the library and not get in!" Much of the seemingly interminable delay is clearly unnecessary, especially in the eyes of well-traveled prisoners. During one of Carceral's torturous trips down that hallway, Maxwell, another fellow inmate, commented on security procedures at different prisons: "Man, these gates are slow here. I liked the state system where lots of them are left open." Nevertheless, the convict must wait submissively because, as Carceral puts it, "there is nothing that can be done."

The strip search, another part of routine security procedures, causes further delays and humiliation. James Paluch describes the male version:

"Open your mouth," directs the guard. "Let me see your tongue. Pull out your bottom lip. Top lip. Okay, stretch your arms towards me and let me see the tops of your hands. Turn them over. Good. Raise your arms over your head. Now run your fingers through your hair. Let me see behind your ears. Uh-huh. Okay, lift up your penis. Your balls. Now turn around and lift up your left foot. Wiggle your toes. Your right foot. Wiggle your toes. Now bend over. Spread your cheeks. Okay, get dressed."[9]

Piper Kerman describes the female version:

"Strip." I kicked off my sneakers, took off my socks, my jeans, my T-shirt, my bra, and my underpants, all of which she took from me. It was cold. "Hold your arms up." I did, displaying my armpits. "Open your mouth and stick out your tongue. Turn around, squat, spread your cheeks and cough." I would never get used to the cough part of this drill, which was supposed to reveal contraband hidden in one's privates—it was just so unnatural. I turned back around, naked. "Get dressed."[10]

Each episode begins with an officer's intrusive command. The imperative violates our common concern for modesty and provokes intense feelings of vulnerability and embarrassment. Not only is time perceived to pass slowly, but the encounter is also quite literally time consuming. Kerman repeats this ritual "hundreds of times in the next year."[11] Her experience is not uncommon. "There were days when I was strip-searched as many [as] six times," remembers Albert Woodfox. "Some days I didn't leave my cell at all to avoid being strip-searched."[12] This tactic gave him some control over the frequency of a repugnant performance, but restricted mobility was the price he paid.

Access and immediacy are affected by the number of people who want to use time in specific ways. As prison populations have exploded during recent decades, there has not been a corresponding increase in temporal resources. Consequently, the intervals allocated for various activities are sliced thinner and thinner, a fact that is not lost on the inmates at a medium-security facility:

DESMOND: "You know, Ridgewood only has one gym and one library."
CARCERAL: "Yeah, I was there."
DESMOND: "Well, they built unit after unit, growing from about 700 men to 2,100, all still using the same little gym and library."
CARCERAL: "Makes you wonder how much they care."
DESMOND: "They don't!"

The time a convict can spend in the gym or library shrinks as the population confined within that prison grows, which makes for harder time. Moreover, the severity of their punishment is incrementally worsened due to overcrowding, not bad behavior.

Because of disinterest or antipathy on the part of our citizenry, most prisons are small places holding a lot of people, with little or nothing for them to do. As Richard Jones and Thomas Schmid put it, "prison walls . . . become the outer boundaries of the inmate's day-to-day world."[13] Ken Lamberton remembers that a cherished daily ritual was walking across the grounds of Santa Rita Prison in Tucson, Arizona. He especially enjoyed a tiny visitation park, where inmates could picnic with loved ones, but, by official fiat, they "no longer have access" to it because "picnicking inmates quickly fell into disfavor with the public."[14] The prison got a little smaller; the list of ways to kill time got a little shorter. "Over the past three years," writes Robert Berger, "I was never more than a few minutes' walk from my room."[15] For Berger and other convicts, the diminutive environment in prison creates a "concentrated world of sameness."[16] While we all mark time by observing change, below a certain threshold, the perceived absence of change brings about boredom and the feeling that time is passing slowly. Most of us do whatever we can to avoid this experience, but in prison these circumstances are inescapable.

Temporal resources are characterized by quantity and variety. By restricting the quantity of temporal resources, prison authorities limit the time inmates have for various pursuits. Likewise, if temporal resources lack variety, then one's behavioral choices are reduced. Certain options cannot be selected; they are simply not available. With hardly any say in the allocation of time, a prisoner's sense of self-efficacy erodes toward the vanishing point.

WHEN, AND FOR HOW LONG?

Impatience is a product of social expectations. Relative to most nations in the southern hemisphere, the United States has an impatient culture.[17] A market economy ensures that everything is available whenever we want it. Access and immediacy have become cultural values in the United States. Instant gratification is for sale in our consumer society (epitomized by credit card purchases). We expect quick access to whatever we desire.

In prison, access is constricted and available resources are unused or forbidden. Immediacy is chronically delayed by overcrowding and security procedures. Prison is the opposite of a market economy. The distribution of time for disparate activities does not respond to demand. The quality of time for study is impaired; the quantity of time in the library is reduced. Temporal allowances for meals, laundry, recreation, personal property, mail, and programs are minimized. Even access to conversation is restricted. All of this is by design. Accustomed to their world prior to incarceration, first-time inmates feel out of sync with the pace of life behind bars.

"Wait" is something parents say to children, but, as the sociologist Javier Auyero explains, it is also something an authoritarian regime says to its subjugated citizens.[18] The same is true of the command to "stop" what you are doing. Prisoners wait for recreation periods to begin, and they are told when to stop. There are variations, of course, but, as with other temporal resources, recreation is always dispensed grudgingly. "At most I would have four hours a day out of the cell," states Erin George, "but usually it was two."[19] These figures may seem pitiable, but they put her at the more generous end of the continuum. Jacobo Timerman, a political prisoner in Argentina, is "given one hour of recreation a day."[20] At an American penitentiary, Paluch reports that convicts in the Restrictive Housing Unit have outdoor recreation only "five days per week for one hour in length."[21] Yet our prisons resemble Russian nested dolls in that "outside" is frequently just another version of confinement. Baca's description is apt: "We were let out for an hour, twice a week . . . in the enclosed exercise cage out back."[22] Paluch provides further testimony:

> Prisoners are strip-searched in their cells, handcuffed, then transferred to fenced cages similar to dog kennels, averaging seven by twenty feet in size. Once a prisoner is locked inside the cage, a guard removes his handcuffs. Some institutions only permit one prisoner per cage, while others allow two men to share a cage.[23]

At the least generous end of the continuum, convicts hardly ever leave their cells. Schooling Jimmy Lerner on life behind bars, Kansas tells him that convicts in protective custody " 'sit in their fucking houses [i.e., cells] twenty-four-seven. Fuckers never see the light of day.' "[24] Billy Sinclair and other condemned prisoners at Angola were not "let out of [their] cells for more than fifteen minutes, three times a week."[25] And when Kerman is transferred to Chicago, she and fellow inmates are "granted 'privileges' [including recreation time] only once a week."[26] In the language of incarceration, prisoners are "given," "let out for," or "granted" recreation.

When we turn our attention to time with friends and loved ones, there is continuity in the theme of temporal resources as "privileges." Like recreation, temporal opportunities for contact with outsiders are dispensed with an eyedropper. Once again, the world outside of prison provides revealing contrast. Cell phones have altered our social expectations concerning access and immediacy. Prior to their invention, any person away from a landline was practically incommunicado. Those wishing to speak with that person lacked access; they were forced to wait (often for an uncertain period of time) until communication could resume. With the advent of cell phones, this waiting period has nearly disappeared. It is almost expected that everyone is available all of the time. We can talk with anyone in our social circle, whenever we want, for as long as we want. By the same token, however, an individual who lacks cell-phone service for one reason or another is out of sync with everyone else. Access and immediacy are impeded and the pace of social interaction slows to a crawl. This person, mired in something resembling enforced solitude, is apt to be quite frustrated even though the problem is easily remedied and short lived.

Behind bars, this out-of-sync feeling taints an inmate's entire sentence. There are, of course, other prisoners with whom to socialize, but most of them are strangers, and the inmate is frequently contemptuous or fearful of them. The people a convict cares for are typically out of touch. Cell phones are not permitted (which makes them a risky but valuable form of contraband). Without their own phones, Carceral observes, inmates depend on the correctional facility for access to this temporal resource, which was always inadequate: "I remember being in Gladiator School where the phones that prisoners could use were at recreation. If I wanted to call my family or a friend, I had to delay doing so until I got to recreation." Carceral adds that he and fellow prisoners could only place collect calls, and the length of these calls was strictly limited, rarely leaving enough time for what they wanted to say. George confirms that the financial burden reduces the frequency of these calls:

> For most lifers, visits are a rare or nonexistent joy, so we rely on our phone calls home to stay connected with our loved ones. The problem is that these phone calls are so expensive that in many cases families have to regretfully limit these vital contacts because they simply cannot afford to pay the phone bills. It is not unheard of for one fifteen-minute call to cost as much as twenty dollars, quite a luxury for families who have to struggle to put food on the table each day.[27]

The frequency of various activities is a key aspect of our temporal experience. Reducing the frequency of these calls retards the perceived movement of time.

Prior to incarceration, George would call her mother "almost every day." She argues that the loss of such contact is among "the hardest deprivations inside."[28] In her study of men wanted by the police in Philadelphia, the sociologist Alice Goffman depicts a poignant scene when one of them calls his younger brother from jail: "Chuck kept talking until his minutes ran out."[29] It is impossible to say how much time he will serve, but his time on the telephone is precisely apportioned. Kerman finds this temporal restriction maddening: "In no time at all, the infuriating click on the line was telling me my fifteen minutes were up and the prison system was going to end the call."[30] Over and over again, programmatically limited resources turn rights into temporally restricted privileges. "Four phones for making collect calls were available only in nonlockdown time periods," notes Stanko.[31] Having only a small number of telephones for a large and growing number of prisoners makes for a lot of wasted time. "I stood on line for twenty-five minutes to call Larry," Kerman remembers, "just to hear his voice."[32] Yet special circumstances can always make things worse, as when George is held in protective custody:

> If I were lucky, I had fifteen minutes out of my cell during the day to make phone calls. Because the rest of the pod had to be locked down when I was out of my cell, every phone call was accompanied by clamorous jeers, threats, and the vilest profanity imaginable.[33]

Prisoners have no access to telephones during lockdowns, which occur several times each day and all night long, or when they are assigned to the Special Housing Unit (SHU).[34]

Typically, access to telephones is denied or restricted as an intended matter of policy or punishment. All too often, however, access is blocked by the programmatic inefficiency that is endemic at correctional facilities. When Berger, formerly a wealthy corporate executive, is transferred to the prison at Fort Dix, he cannot call anyone due to bureaucratic ineptitude and indifference:

> My phone account has still not been validated so I submitted a written request, and met with the unit manager. . . . I haven't been able to speak to my family since January 6 and I'm upset and frustrated about this issue. As a prisoner I am entitled by law to certain privileges and it irks me when a prison administrator takes it upon himself to try to fuck with me when it comes to my rights.[35]

When he could make a call, it would be limited to ten minutes. Berger expends a great deal of time gaining access to the prison's telephone system. He also conflates "rights" and "privileges," but they are distinct. From his standpoint, telephone access is a right, but the prison administration views it as a privilege. Unlike rights, privileges can be revoked at the whim of those in authority. For prison administrators, *all* of the ways to allocate one's time are privileges.[36]

The rationing of time behind bars is exemplified by aptly named "visiting hours." Inmates are not allowed to see friends and family whenever they wish. On the contrary, time is prescribed for this purpose in rather more meticulous fashion than it was at their sentencing. Physical setting and temporal allocation vary, but George avows that the worst conditions are found in jails:

> Visitation at the jail was awful, a dim and clamorous room oppressive with the smell of Wal-Mart cologne and mildew. All conversations had to be shouted through a few tiny holes punched into the metal and plastic barrier that divided us from our visitors. At RRJ, the visitation room didn't look like it does on TV or in the movies. There wasn't even a telephone to let me speak more clearly to my parents or the friends who would wait an hour or more just to have a scant twenty minutes with me surrounded by the weeping children, pissed off relatives, and loudly (and often obscenely) affectionate boyfriends of my fellow inmates.[37]

Once convicted, she is transferred to a prison where visiting hours are more humane, but "almost a year" passes before she can hug her mother, and it is "even longer" before she can hold her children.[38] Prisons may permit greater physical contact and longer hours, but they are typically further away from friends and family, so available time with visitors is limited in any case: "Now my parents live in another state and I am fortunate if I have a two-hour visit from them every few months."[39]

Visiting hours are more generous at a minimum-security facility, such as Danbury, Connecticut: "three to eight P.M. on Fridays."[40] Obviously, however, one's time with visitors is limited, and the temporal boundaries are strictly enforced: "The guard came by to remind us that it was time to say goodbye."[41] When Kerman's fiancé leaves at the end of his first visit, she suffers temporally induced sorrow: "I wouldn't see him for another week."[42] It is also noteworthy that physical affection serves as temporal brackets for these encounters: "Hugging and kissing your visitors (no tongue!) was permitted at the beginning and end of the visit."[43] The same temporal brackets can be found at Lerner's prison in Nevada: "Inmates are permitted one brief kiss and hug . . . upon both the arrival and the departure of their visitors."[44] Moreover, prison administrators do not want inmates devoting too much time to physical affection with their visitors: "Signs are posted everywhere warning that PROLONGED KISSING will result in IMMEDIATE TER- MINATION OF THE VISIT!"[45] Despite various restrictions and frustra- tions, these visits represent an important exception to the general impact of the temporal regime on the perceived passage of time: "The hours I would spend in the prison visiting room . . . sped by, the only occasion at the Camp in which time seemed to move quickly."[46]

On the one hand, visits are subject to temporal prohibitions. Correctional officers curtail or cancel visiting hours as a form of punishment, and visi- tors are not permitted during lockdowns. On the other hand, considerable time that could have been allocated to visiting hours is, instead, devoted to ineffectual efforts at intercepting contraband. The standard procedure includes frisking inmates before each visit and strip-searching them after- ward.[47] Visitors also contend with these temporal restrictions. Kerman's fiancé and his parents drove a long distance to see her, but they got "stuck behind a highway accident for hours" and arrived "fifteen minutes before visiting hours were over."[48] The waiting that visitors do is prolonged, mul- tifarious, and programmatic. Megan Comfort concludes that such treat- ment is indicative of a certain attitude toward their temporal resources: "The lengthy and inefficient waits required for visiting a prisoner do not just belittle the worth of his family's and friends' time—they deprecate the importance of the visit itself, the preciousness of moments spent with those who are otherwise physically barred from one's presence."[49]

TEMPORAL SCARCITY

Outside of prison, many of us have immediate access to whatever we need for the sake of personal hygiene. We take such access for granted because time does not stand in our way. In prison, temporal scarcity is manufactured by a combination of mass incarceration, inadequate funding, and a policy of retribution. Thus, time allowed for personal hygiene becomes another rationed privilege. In a place where time is plentiful, temporal allowances for personal hygiene are meager. Administrative regulations (and discretion) throttle the immediacy inmates were accustomed to prior to incarceration. The prisoners' temporal reality is altered by the timing of personal hygiene.

When can I take a shower? How long can it last? In everyday life, these simple questions are addressed (if at all) with the offhand self-determination exercised by anyone at liberty. Behind bars, however, the timing, duration, and frequency of one's showers are matters of policy decided by those in authority. Individual desires are not taken into account. "The guards let us out one at a time for showers," recalls Baca.[50] Time for personal hygiene is dispensed by correctional officers. One inmate takes a shower while the rest wait. At SCI-Frackville, reports Paluch, prisoners "in the general population are able to shower once a day for a period of ten minutes. Guards stand watch and usually give a two- or three-minute warning before one's time in the shower stall expires."[51] Yet in the Restrictive Housing Unit (RHU), prisoners are only allowed to shower "three times per week . . . for a period of no more than five minutes. This enforced five-minute rule begins once an inmate leaves the cell."[52] Conditions are worse for those who displease the correctional officers and wind up in solitary confinement. Billy Sinclair "was kept in the cell for sixty-three days without being allowed to shower, shave, or brush [his] teeth."[53]

When, moreover, temporal dimensions of personal hygiene change (usually in response to increased pressure from overpopulation), a systematic contraction of services invariably occurs. Reluctantly, Carceral got used to taking a shower only three days a week when he first went to prison. Later, however, that level of access was further reduced when the time allotted for showers was restricted to ten minutes. Inmates wait and are then forced to hurry, with detrimental implications for their temporal experience. As Ingrid Betancourt points out, this waiting period feels both prolonged and shameful: "The wait for the appointed bathing time seemed to take forever, far too long for someone who had nothing better to do than ruminate on her own repugnant state."[54] In Florida, Sunny Jacobs fumes over infrequent showers at the Broward Correctional Institute: "And why only two showers a week? That was ridiculous, especially since it was so hot in here and the shower was right down the hall."[55] Like hostages, convicts must adjust to feeling out of sync with their normal pace of personal hygiene. Others decide how often they clean themselves.

In sum, the temporal allowance for an inmate's shower is brief, strictly enforced, and further abridged by travel time. What is worse, the remaining interval is little more than an official conceit because dilapidated facilities at most prisons impair the quality and quantity of the experience. How much

water will flow from the shower head? For how long and at what temperature? Those of us in the nonprison world assume that hot water will always
be readily available; we are deprived of it only under extraordinary circumstances. In prison, however, hot water is merely a memory from one's
life prior to incarceration. "'Rule number one,'" an officer drawls to Lerner
and the other new prisoners, "'y'all got *nothin'* coming!'" He is right: "The
shower produces only cold water."[56] Consider, as well, the length of time
that water flows for George:

> The shower was nothing like mine at home. Instead of having controls for
> adjusting the temperature and turning the water on and off, there was only a
> small metal button embedded into a mildew-blackened wall. When I pressed
> it, the stream dribbled on for about forty seconds, then petered out. The
> temperature just skirted the edge of unbearable—so cold that when I fin-
> ished, I stood shivering, unable to dress myself for several minutes after I had
> attempted to dry off with the sodden, dishcloth-sized towel.[57]

A convict's shower is scheduled and of short duration; the water is cold, the
flow intermittent.

Prisoners experience their environment from a scarcity perspective.
Programmatic scarcity strangles access and immediacy. Inmates must
always wait to fulfill their needs and desires. This perspective is propagated
by the prison administration. Correctional officers and other members of
the staff routinely suggest that scarcity is the result of too many prisoners
in the facility. They can be heard to say, "If y'all stop committing crimes,
there won't be so many people here," or "The weight machine wouldn't be
broken if there weren't so many people using it." With statements of this
sort, members of the staff loop responsibility for scarcity back onto prisoners themselves. Inmates are blamed for scarcity, but they have no control
over sentencing policies, the building of prisons, or the allocation of funds
within the criminal justice system. This perspective breeds fatalism on the
part of staff and frustration on the part of prisoners. Nothing ever seems to
get done. With culpability folded back onto inmates, there is no need to fix
anything. When told that a toilet is flooding onto the floor, a correctional
officer shrugs and says, "Why call maintenance? Someone plugged it up,
and they'll just do it again."

On one occasion, Carceral listened as fellow convicts discussed this very issue. For Sully, it was about laundry detergent:

I asked the man for more laundry soap. He says, "It's all gone." I ask, "When will more be coming?" He says, "Next week, Monday." I ask, "Am I supposed to wait three days to do clothes?" He gets upset and tells me, "Well, if there weren't so many guys locked up, we'd have more soap!" Like I'm responsible for all the guys locked up!

Josh commented on his inability to have his cell assignment changed:

It's fucked up how they do us. I've heard, "If you'd stop coming to prison . . ." so much, it's making me mental. I asked to be moved to another cell, where there's an empty bed. The sergeant that's supposed to do it says he doesn't do it. I ask why and he starts in about all of us coming to prison. If one is moved, then everyone after me will expect to be moved. I'm not the one controlling everyone else!

Given that our perception of time is based upon the sensation of change, one's inability to alter one's own circumstances makes for a seemingly endless stasis.

Temporal experience in prison is conditioned by ubiquitous scarcity. The time one has for any particular activity is limited by the distribution of that resource across a large and ceaselessly growing population. For Carceral, that could mean temporally relevant ratios of twelve guys per shower and toilet, twenty-four guys per telephone, and almost five guys per chair in the television area (where sitting in a chair is mandatory). By and large, prisoners are not permitted to offset the resulting frustrations with their own possessions. Convicts are allowed very few amenities. Jorge Renaud observes that the correctional officers in Texas "write disciplinary cases on any inmates who in any way try to personalize their cells."[58] Prisoners in the federal system are required to fit their personal belongings into a locker. "These lockers very [sic] in size," but Renaud reports that they "average twenty-four inches wide, twelve inches tall, and eighteen inches deep."[59] In Carceral's experience, the few items one is allowed to keep are often lost or broken during transportation from one prison to another. The limited amenities inmates are permitted magnify their grating sense of scarcity.

Prisoners and staff adapt to scarcity in different ways. Convicts learn to relinquish their desires and put up with disagreeable conditions. Members of the staff learn to define everything a prisoner has access to as a privilege, not a right. Doing so absolves them of the responsibility for providing almost anything to a population bereft of nearly everything. Even eating is considered a privilege. The staff may not be able to totally suspend this privilege under normal circumstances, but they impose harsh temporal restrictions on access and immediacy. Food is doled out during fleeting intervals, and always at the staff's discretion. Unlike people in everyday life, prisoners are not allowed to eat whenever they want. "Department of Corrections rules prohibit taking food out of the dining hall," notes Paluch.[60] And prisoners are not allowed to eat whatever they want. Trays carry a standard (and typically inadequate) number of calories: "There are no choices of any kind for meals," writes Stanko.[61] Paluch describes the usual process: "Prisoners . . . stand in line and move toward a small window, through which food trays are handed to them. Each food tray is basically prepared the same way."[62]

In his film *Annie Hall*, Woody Allen tells an old joke. Two women are having lunch in a restaurant. One says, "The food here is terrible." The other says, "Yes, and such small portions." This joke is an apt way to summarize the food served behind bars, but prisoners would not find it terribly amusing. What they eat is poor in quality and quantity. "The food in the place was not fit for human consumption," recalls the anonymous narrator of *The Jack-Roller*.[63] Decades later, George decries sitting down to "another scanty, poorly prepared meal."[64] Fruits and vegetables are rare "and frequently range from merely aged to the obviously moldy."[65] For Lerner, a meal consists of "a peanut butter and jelly sandwich and half an apple, the flesh the color of mud."[66] Again, at breakfast, he is fed in his cell: "Another plastic airline tray hurtles across the concrete [floor and] collides with the far wall, releasing a spray of Rice Krispies. The fuzzy white orange rolls like a tennis ball under the toilet."[67] Nonetheless, Lerner cannot afford to let any of it go to waste: "I'm so hungry I collect every bit of cereal from the floor and wolf it down with the help of a handful of suspiciously cloudy cold water from the rusted sink."[68] Not surprisingly, Sinclair complains about losing weight, as does Paluch: "When I first arrive at the Detention Center, I am over 200 pounds. Nine months later, the nurse tells me I weigh

130 pounds."[69] Hunger slows the perceived passage of time with the painful awareness of each lingering moment.

The situation is dire for convicts held in segregation. George tells us that the women in punishment cells are "perpetually underfed" and "emerge from seg time significantly thinner than when they went in."[70] Their circumstances mirror those of POWs and political prisoners. "Hunger was always in the background," recalls Christopher Burney.[71] In *The Gulag Archipelago*, Aleksandr Solzhenitsyn takes us into a penal system (like our own) where prisoners do not eat when they are hungry, but at the temporal convenience of the staff:

> Whatever cooked food we got would be served at 1 P.M. and 4 P.M., one meal almost on the heels of the other. You could then spend the next twenty-one hours remembering it. (And that wasn't prison brutality either: it was simply a matter of the kitchen staff having to do its work as quickly as possible and leave.)[72]

We can conceive of *temporal stress* as something human beings suffer whenever they must endure an undesirable schedule. Paradigmatically, members of the staff address their own temporal exigencies by producing temporal stress among the prisoners.

In prison, eating is hemmed in by temporal restrictions concerning sequence and duration. Prisoners eat when they are told to eat (i.e., when it is their turn). Likewise, the ration of time they have for eating is brief and strictly enforced. For Lerner, one meal begins with a contemptuous command that specifies the time allocated for eating his food: "Ten minutes for chow, convict, then roll it the fuck up" (i.e., pack your belongings because you are being transferred).[73] In Baca's writings, however, we find a description of the typical regimentation:

> [The chow hall] held about a hundred cons at a time; as one group finished eating, deposited their trays at the wash window next to the slop cans, and went out at the south end, a new set of cons came in through the north. We were allowed fifteen minutes to eat, and if we took longer we got a write-up.[74]

The privilege of eating is regulated by the quantity and quality of available food as well as the temporal order in which housing units enter the chow hall and how much time convicts have for their meals.

Water represents another set of privileges. *When* will I have water to drink? *When* will I be able to visit or flush the toilet? Questions of this sort (so rare in everyday life) are commonly occasioned by the temporal stress of imprisonment. Consider the following excerpt from Carceral's interview with Jaylen:

> Man, we were all locked down because the water main broke. At least that's the story we heard. A day later, they finally brought in drinking water! A whole day we had to wait. They told us it would be fixed the next day. Two days after that, when the guard came around with water, I got a bucket filled with it to dump into the toilet. Man did the cell smell! These private people can't run a prison! It took a week to get it going.

As Berger points out, help is not available when the inmate needs it: "Yesterday our toilet clogged up and because we couldn't get a guard I had to clear it with my hand before the cell flooded."[75]

Readers may find it surprising to learn that, generally speaking, there are no toilets inside the cells at minimum- or medium-security prisons. Inmates with jobs are allowed to use the toilets on their way to or from work, but, Carceral recalls, "a time was set for nonworkers to use the bathroom." Their access to a toilet was regulated by the temporal regime. This does not mean that conditions at maximum-security prisons are less oppressively organized. At San Quentin, notes Theodore Davidson, "the guards flush the toilets from the outside only once a day."[76] Baca and fellow convicts would hear the same warning every night from the officer on their tier: "Piss and shit before water's off."[77] With sardonic undertone, Solzhenitsyn reminds us that scheduled access is established for the temporal convenience of the staff:

> The shifts change at 8 A.M. and 8 P.M., and it was more convenient for everyone to take the prisoners to the toilet at the end of a shift. (Letting them out singly in the middle of the day was extra trouble and meant extra precautions, and no one got paid for that.)[78]

Prisoners, hostages, and POWs do not find scheduled access "convenient," of course, but they do learn that the timing of events is controlled by others.

If anything, however, unscheduled access is still more frustrating. In seg, Paluch finds that he must secure an officer's uncertain cooperation: "If I want to use the toilet, I have to ask the guard to turn it on."[79] Timerman suffers comparable circumstances: "I must call the guard to take me to the bathroom. It's a complicated procedure, and they're not always in the mood."[80] (Similar restrictions apply to vision services and dental or medical care.) In Nevada, Lerner shows us that prisoners are punished for misdeeds brought about by indifference and delay on the part of correctional officers. A "confused Black teenager" is put into a cell without a toilet. He asks "to use the bathroom," but the officer tells him to "hold it" because he is "too busy to come to the holding cell right then." When the inmate urinates on himself, the officer charges him with "failure to keep one's person or assigned area neat and clean."[81]

In everyday life, we readily point to people who have been "silenced" in one way or another as an instance of injustice or oppression. To be silenced, however, is the common lot of prisoners. Timerman's account is indicative: "I'm in an isolation cell, given one hour of recreation a day, at which point I'm allowed to walk around the yard but not talk to other prisoners."[82] *At certain times*, it is against the rules to talk. Most prisons outlaw talking during count, and many restrict talking in the hallways. Clare Hanrahan, an inmate at a federal prison, offers the following observation: "Women must each stand in the threshold of her cubicle in absolute silence while the officers walk up and down the corridor counting."[83] She argues that "enforced silence is a throwback to the complete silence required in early penal experiments," but that "practice was abandoned due to the large number of prisoners who developed serious mental health problems."[84] Yet talking was forbidden in the hallways when Carceral was transferred to a for-profit prison, and, at Gladiator School, talking was banned in segregation except to the staff when they came around with meal trays. Only during this brief interval was a prisoner permitted to request toiletries or report an emergency. At Sumter Correctional Institution in Florida, six teenaged inmates were denied food for talking to each other during lunch in the mess hall.[85]

TIME FOR EDUCATION

Throughout his sentence, Carceral felt like the underdog as he pursued his education. Trying to study in the midst of clamor and despair was enormously difficult. Like many prison authors, Berger notes that "educational facilities are inefficient and substandard."[86] When he arrives at Marion, Stephen Richards finds that "there are no college courses taught at the prison."[87] Nothing is less important in the eyes of the administration. Members of the staff ensure that educational opportunities are poor in quantity and quality. At correctional facilities, anything out of the ordinary must be preapproved by the staff, and trying to advance one's education is not part of normal operating procedures.

Carceral managed to take college correspondence courses while at a minimum-security prison, but invariably there was an interminable delay while he waited for approval to do so. The citizens of autocratic regimes confront kindred delaying tactics.[88] There was an Education Director named Henderson at the minimum-security facility, but he never acted on any of Carceral's petitions. Eventually, the Assistant Warden had these courses approved, but only after Carceral's brother wrote to her. When Carceral shared this story with a fellow inmate, he reported a similar experience but with the typical outcome:

BRANDON: "That's Henderson. He drags his feet on everything. I was at Ridgewood when he was the Education Director over there. I wanted to take courses, but he kept dragging it out. I gave up."
CARCERAL: "It's like they don't want a guy in college."
BRANDON: "Nope, unless it's their school, their GED school, that's it."

Delaying tactics are intrinsic to a prison's temporal regime. They circumscribe one's perception of time but also shape behavioral choices and their consequences.

Carceral worked as the librarian while he was at the minimum-security facility. In that capacity, he asked the Captain if men doing GED or college correspondence studies could have periods of time allocated for their work in the library. Her response exemplifies how time is and is not allocated in prison:

No! We are a work release facility. Anything that I grant will make those men special. Other prisoners will come running to me asking why they cannot have that same privilege. If I do grant it, those men who are doing school will begin to believe it is a right to have that particular time. The computers in the library are a privilege. I will not make any special considerations.

Inmates do not have a right to spend their time in any particular way—no matter how uplifting it may be. The time a prisoner devotes to any activity is either required by the state or is a privilege granted by the state. As a representative of the temporal regime, and a person with power, she defined access to the library and its computers as a privilege. Like most administrators, she preferred to avoid problems with the management of activity by suspending the "privilege" for everyone. She often threatened to remove the computers so no one could use them.

During the previous two years, and unbeknownst to Carceral, he had been granted access to the computer lab for his correspondence course assignments. Never having been notified, he only discovered this after the fact, and accidently, when a tutor told him that he was on a list of approved inmates. Carceral checked this information with the Education Director, from whom he received confirmation as well as another dose of the reigning doctrine: "You guys are lucky to have computers at all." In any case, Carceral's time in the computer lab was governed by further issues related to access and immediacy. The lab was open from 2:00 to 4:00 P.M. and, conveniently, Carceral was finished with his job at 2:00. However, he was not a GED student assigned to the class that occupied most of the seats during that period. His temporal status was college student with a job, so he was not allowed to sit in one of the empty seats. As the teacher put it, "I'm sorry, but you can't be here from 2:30 to 3:30. You are not a student on the roster. There is shift change and count."

Carceral's understanding of temporal reality was subjective and simultaneous. He saw two or three empty seats and unused computers. The teacher's understanding of temporal reality was linear and sequential. The lab should be occupied for one purpose at a time. "In the bureaucratic method of management," writes Michael Santos, "the printed policy most frequently prevails; the objective trumps the subjective."[89] By official fiat, then, Carceral's access was limited to half an hour before class (2:00–2:30) and half an hour after class (3:30–4:00). Subtract travel time for walking there, and his effective access was further reduced to two ten-minute intervals, essentially eliminating this opportunity. The lab was open one night per week from 6:15 to 8:00 P.M. on a first come, first served basis. Carceral worked the morning shift, so he was quite tired by 6:15, and the gap of a week between sessions in the lab demanded a great deal of review. Without warning or explanation, the lab was closed for six months despite the fact that Carceral was in the midst of schoolwork.

Put differently, the computer lab was closed holidays, weekends, and four of the five remaining nights. During weekdays, it was occupied for GED preparation. It is revealing to contrast this opportunity schedule with that of recreation—specifically, basketball. Paradoxically, Carceral could attend recreation on weekends, holidays, and any night of the week in the very same building. In addition, he could play basketball on the court next to his unit if the court at the recreation area was occupied. The unit court was open sunrise to sunset except during counts. If the basketball facilities were damaged, they were quickly repaired or replaced. Eventually, the administration established a limit on the number of prisoners who could be on the unit court at the same time, but many guards overlooked this rule. In short, more temporal resources were allocated for basketball than for schooling.

LAUNDRY CYCLES

Even when a society, such as our own, is dominated by a linear perspective on time, it will still exhibit subordinate and cyclical patterns. The latter are brought about by recurrent activities and experiences, exemplified by that most prosaic of tasks—laundry. All prisons arrange for the cleaning of inmate clothing, yet each locally organized "solution" for this universal problem entails limiting access and immediacy in accord with the strictures of a particular temporal regime.

When Carceral arrived at one minimum-security prison, he was assigned to a unit that housed forty-eight men. There was no institutional laundry at this facility, but the state provided free laundry detergent. Each inmate was required to wash all of his own clothes—personal and state-issued. The laundry room was about twice the size of a cell with two washers, two dryers, and a large slop sink that backed up every three months. Correctional officers could not see into the room without standing at the doorway, and it was off-limits during count.

At first, there was temporal certainty. Correctional officers left the laundry room unlocked from 7:00 A.M. to 10:30 P.M. every day. They disliked this arrangement, however, which the second-shift sergeant, "Walls," revealed during a brief conversation with Carceral while he washed his clothes. "I need to lock the door, since too many men are hanging out in here," Walls said. "These guys do such small loads." He pointed toward a pile of laundry on the floor. "I hate that," he continued, "they want to only wash a little load to tie up the machines. Then, when they are doing loads, they want to hang out in the room."

His criticism presaged a sudden change in policy. A few days later, Carceral was standing by the officer's station for another purpose when a new prisoner asked a sergeant, nicknamed "Linebacker," about laundry detergent:

"Linebacker, can I get some soap and get into the laundry room?"
"No, we don't have soap."
"Oh . . . I thought they had it earlier? Delivered it earlier?"
"No. Too many men are just washing too few things. Laundry is closed."

The laundry room door was then locked at all times, forcing prisoners to ask for the key and permission to wash their clothes. With no prior consultation, temporal access and immediacy were drastically reduced. Clothes were washed when correctional officers allowed it. Obtaining their consent made for unpredictable delays and, in dictatorial fashion, slowed the pace of life.

For inmates and officers, the ideal pace of laundry was quite dissimilar. Correctional officers wanted inmates to wash larger loads *less frequently*. Like other activities, the officers defined laundry as a privilege and, from their standpoint, prisoners were abusing it. Prisoners had a different perspective—one that was temporally inflected. The state provided them with only three days' worth of clothing, which is why they tended to wash small loads frequently. They could only postpone doing laundry by wearing dirty clothes. This is another instance of a general phenomenon: prisoners and correctional officers operate within the same organizational context, but their temporal experience is quite divergent.

Later, the first-shift sergeant instituted a sign-up sheet, but this only made matters worse. Getting your name on the list became a race with winners and losers. Some inmates erased other men's names or signed acquaintances' names. A scarce resource became even more so. What had been characterized by temporal certainty became an arbitrary and very uncertain process. Previously, Carceral knew he could do laundry as soon as he finished his early morning shift. The timing of laundry had been a temporal benchmark. Now, immediacy had been supplanted by incalculable delay and waiting. Inmates learned that their lives are controlled capriciously by others—an essential ingredient in the recipe for paranoia.[90] Carceral found himself devoting attention to time itself. He stared at his watch to make sure that he did not miss the moment when the door to the laundry room was supposed to be opened. The more he stared, however, the thinner and thinner these temporal increments became, producing the sensation that time was passing slowly.

Inundated by requests for access, correctional officers discovered that they could not enforce the new system, so some of them went back to opening the door whenever they felt like it. Still, prisoners had to ask for permission to use the machines, a degrading requirement that made them feel like children. The short cycle on the washing machines took forty minutes, and the dryers were usually finished in thirty minutes, for a minimum time of one hour and ten minutes per load of laundry. No one could sign up before 7:00 A.M., yet this was also the first time slot. The first-shift guard never opened the door right away because coffee and count were his priorities. If, however, the officer brought a second prisoner to the laundry room at 8:00 A.M. or earlier, the machines would still be cleaning the first inmate's laundry. "Come on," the sergeant would growl, "I'm not gonna stand here waiting for it to stop." Any delay at the opening time slot would reverberate through the rest of the day.

So many policy revisions in such a short period of time exacerbated prisoners' confusion and frustration. There were bitter complaints within earshot of Carceral. "Why did they change it in the first place?" asked Tanner. "That first-shift fucker in the office is just inventing shit," declared Zeke. "Shit don't make no sense," groused Maxwell. The men also expressed their displeasure to the correctional officers, but more tactfully; of course, nothing ever came of it. It is worth noting that all of this transpired at a minimum-security facility, a fact not lost on Tanner:

> We can't even use this laundry room without an escort. The guards got it locked down like we're kids. Other units aren't like this. Other prisons aren't like this. At Ridgewood, it was better. And Ridgewood was a medium [i.e., a medium-security prison]. I thought when we moved down in security level, we were given more trust.

He expected more access with less security, but members of the staff did not share Tanner's assessment. They associated lower security with greater temporal regulation—further evidence that they inhabit a distinctive "timescape," as Barbara Adam would put it.[91]

There was a centralized laundry at Ridgewood, the medium-security facility where Tanner and Carceral were previously held, but it would clean only state-issued clothing. Most of the inmates owned some personal items (sweats, shorts, T-shirts, etc.), and the institutional laundry would not clean them. Ostensibly, the temporal availability of washing machines and dryers was regulated by means of a schedule. Times when prisoners had access to the machines were posted. There was no sign-up list, and Carceral never remembers waiting. Nonetheless, the temporal allowance for this resource was restricted through the use of a pay-to-play plan. Washing machines and dryers were coin operated. A load of laundry cost fifty cents to wash and usually a dollar to dry.

Poverty has temporal implications. These charges may seem trivial, but they greatly reduced the amount of time prisoners could devote to laundry. Due to the expense, Carceral and many of his fellow inmates rarely used the machines. To put these laundry charges in perspective, the average prisoner earned about twenty dollars a month. Much of this money was taken from them through various fines and fees (or child support, in some cases). For example, the state in question collected a sample of every prisoner's DNA and charged him three hundred dollars for it. Most of the inmates paid this fee on the installment plan. A prisoner runs out of clean clothes quickly because he has so little to wear. If he washed all of his personal clothing twice a week, it would cost three dollars (i.e., twelve dollars per month). A large majority of the inmates were in no position to give up this much of their income for laundry.

At Gladiator School, the maximum-security prison, there were two methods for handling personal laundry. Given available resources (or lack thereof), both of them were quite time consuming. Prisoners had no access to washing machines or dryers, so all personal clothing had to be cleaned inside one's own cell. A typical load included socks, T-shirts, underwear, sweat suit, and bath towel. Men complained to the correctional officers about not having access to laundry machines, but they were simply told, "This is maximum lock-up!"

The sink in one's cell held less than a gallon of water, yet it was one of only two options for personal laundry. A single bath towel or a pair of sweatpants barely fit into it, so washing clothing was a laboriously sequential task. Clotheslines were considered contraband. Some guards would overlook them, but others would not. Typically, then, wet laundry would be draped over the chair, bunks, toilet, and any other furnishings. Moreover, the temporal burden of personal laundry was multiplied by the two or three inmates sharing each cell.

With the second method for washing personal laundry, prisoners took advantage of the only other source of water in their cells: the toilet. Carceral learned this technique while sharing a cell in segregation. One day, while reading a book, he noticed that his cellie was scrubbing the toilet with unusual diligence. His cellie could not afford the extra expense of laundry detergent, so he was cleaning the toilet with shampoo. Then he put his sweatshirt and sweatpants in the toilet and scrubbed them together with his hands. When finished, he flushed away the soap, rinsed both items in the toilet, and hung them on a clothesline. Noticing Carceral watching him over his book, he exclaimed, "I gotta do it somehow!" At first, Carceral thought his cellie had lost his mind, but reservations concerning unsanitary conditions were gradually displaced by the alluring temporal autonomy in this new way of dealing with laundry.

This practice is not unique to Gladiator School. "Some inmates in the RHU will first clean out their toilet," reports Paluch, "then proceed to wash their clothes in it."[92] Like Carceral, he is initially appalled by the practice: "I thought that prisoners who did their laundry in the toilet were crazy. I could never imagine myself performing such a humiliating act." However, "soon tiring of the manual labor of sink laundry," Paluch takes it up himself:

> Once, while in the RHU, I was washing my clothes in the toilet, when a nurse came to my cell to give me medication for a stomachache. She saw me sitting on the cold concrete floor with my soapy hands in the toilet and reacted with horror: "Don't you know that toilets have bacteria, germs, and viruses?!"
>
> Somewhat embarrassed, I told the nurse, who was young and newly hired, that it takes too much time to wash my clothes in the sink.

Like countless others, Carceral and Paluch discover what they are willing to do for the sake of a little time. In order to wash your clothes, you must find your way through something that resembles an obstacle course. Prisoners are awash in time, yet they go to extraordinary lengths for small measures of temporal autonomy. Doing so does not free them any sooner, but it makes the time they serve a bit more bearable.

MICROMANAGEMENT

Convicts struggle with temporal access and immediacy during every moment behind bars. When, how often, and for how long will they be allowed to engage in any particular activity? Time served does not mean there will be time for eating, drinking, sleeping, getting from one place to another, hygiene, grooming, laundry, medical or psychiatric care, dental or vision care, education, recreation, shopping, conversation, communication with outsiders, or solitude.

Here, we have been concerned with resources because one's inability to make use of certain things precludes spending time in desirable ways. "Prison is designed to take everything from an inmate," avows Sylvester Long, "and hopefully force an inmate to depend on this form of lifestyle."[93] More to the point, prison takes all of an inmate's time and then doles it out in predetermined increments, but only when it is convenient for the authorities to do so. Prisoners have plenty of time unless they try to do something with it.

Budgetary restrictions and the physical design of prisons occasion the chronic scarcity of temporal resources. In turn, scarcity creates the need for temporal rationing, and rationing makes for the micromanagement of inmates' time. The micromanagement of time in prison is realized by means of needlessly punitive policies that limit temporal access and immediacy. In the manner of a self-fulfilling prophecy, micromanagement becomes a requisite, albeit frustrating, feature of the convicts' world because the staff has eliminated so much of their temporal autonomy.

The micromanagement of time in prison complicates the flow of action and, consequently, slows the perceived pace of temporal experience to a crawl. Much of what occurs in the name of security is actually gratuitous, erratic, and only for show. Nonetheless, it is a major source of wasted time in prison because convicts must devote countless hours to figuring out when something will be permissible—something that is handled in nearly thoughtless fashion on the outside.

Such conditions bring about the temporal experience of want, which explains why life in prison can seem so petty. Everything (including time) is rationed, which supports the privilege system as well as various forms of corruption. Members of the staff become tyrants who control tiny fiefdoms. When Lerner asks a correctional officer for toilet paper to replace what was taken during a recent shakedown, the officer rebuffs his request by citing Administrative Regulation number 22: "You know the rules, O. G. You get two rolls of toilet paper per cell per week."[94]

In Carceral's unit at a minimum-security facility, prisoners were not allowed to have toilet paper in their cells. It was considered contraband and, as such, a punishable offense. Yet toilet paper was the only available item with which to blow one's nose. Prisoners were not allowed to have facial tissues or handkerchiefs. Imagine being sick with a cold, and confined to your bed, without any toilet paper with which to blow your nose. You cannot run to the bathroom with diarrhea without first requesting toilet paper from a correctional officer.

From the outside, these issues of access and immediacy may appear trivial, but within a context of pervasive shortages, rationing, and micromanagement of the convict's time, these resources can play a decisive role in the temporal quality of one's life. It follows that, with so little available, there is always much at stake. In this setting, people serve countless years of incarceration, yet time is a scarce resource. A prisoner learns that it is often worth fighting and dying for a few minutes more or less.

Chapter Four

SERVING TIME

Deciding what to do with one's time is intrinsic to human conduct, yet prisons deprive convicts of precisely this capacity. Prisoners are victimized by time; it is something that happens to them. Lacking temporal autonomy, it is difficult for them to modify or customize their perception of time. They are serving time, not ruling it. Outside of prison, most of our time work is directed toward avoiding or alleviating temporally induced frustrations of one kind or another, whereas convicts must simply endure them. Consequently, the sensations of waiting and an overabundance of time are inescapable. In one of his poems, Albert Woodfox writes, "Seconds turn to years, years turn to centuries, and I wait!"[1]

CUT OFF AND ALWAYS AVAILABLE

Prisoners give up the temporal autonomy they used to take for granted. Having been consigned to a custodial facility (and thereby separated from society), they relinquish the governing of their own time. Ordinarily, we decide *when* we will be available, but, as the sociologist Eviatar Zerubavel observes, prisoners surrender this temporal sovereignty: "The individual's basic right to be inaccessible at certain times is also evident from the way society punishes offenders by taking control over their social accessibility out of their hands."[2] They are not permitted to close themselves off from fellow convicts or the demands of the temporal regime. In his semiauto-biographical novel, *The House of the Dead,* Fyodor Dostoevsky's narrator learns that this is a distinct and severe form of punishment: "Later on I realized that besides the loss of freedom, besides the forced labor, there is another torture in prison life, almost more terrible than any other—that is, *compulsory life in common.*"[3]

It is easy to say that "prisoners lose their freedom," but such statements are too simplistic. A prisoner is free to imagine anything that comes to mind, although this may entail majestic feats of disregard for one's immedi-ate circumstances. Likewise, the prisoner is ever capable of resistance, but rebellion brings punishing consequences. There is, however, a definite loss of freedom. What you do, when you do it, and who you do it with are not of your choosing. Instead of making autonomous decisions concerning their availability, prisoners cede control of their lives to the state. The prisoner no longer enjoys *time with* friends and family, and this is a calamitous transi-tion. In prison, Robert Berger finds that which is absent more punishing than that which is present: "The trauma of being separated from my fam-ily was . . . horribly gut-wrenching."[4] Cut off from everything beyond the walls and razor wire, Sylvester Long avers that incarceration is "like going to another country."[5]

A counterculture emerged among American youth during the 1960s. Fred Davis, an astute observer, noted their preference for a "structureless round-of-day" as well as their "disdain for appointments, schedules, and straight society's compulsive parceling out of minutes and hours."[6] In a related vein, Karen Stein reports that the temporal norms of conventional society are often overturned in less radical (but more prevalent) ways by holidays and vacations: "During their time off people may ignore, invert or alter the hours and days that make up their experience, or enter into an area with a different temporal organization from that of their everyday life."[7] Among hippies and those of us on holiday, time is a resource for playful experimentation.

For prisoners, however, time is a burden, not a resource. The loss of temporal autonomy begins when they are sentenced to time in prison and the state assumes control of their temporal experience. The convicted felon serves an uncertain number of days. We are apt to say that "they have . . . been given time as a punishment," but, notwithstanding the language we use, Stanley Cohen and Laurie Taylor help us see that this perspective is quite misleading: "Their own time has been abstracted by the courts . . . and in its place they have been given prison time. This is no longer a resource but a controller. It has to be served rather than used."[8] The loss of temporal autonomy has repercussions beyond the study of time. As noted by Sunny Jacobs, long-term prisoners lose their capacity for personal agency: "One of the results of institutionalization was that I was not able to make decisions for myself about such things as entering and leaving an area without official direction."[9] By eroding their capacity for self-determination, incarceration makes prisoners unfit for social interaction.

With incarceration, a prisoner no longer controls his or her own temporal reality, leading to alternating phases of despair, acceptance, and frustration. The fact that one's freedom of movement is restricted to the penal facility may seem obvious, but it demands a huge psychological adjustment on the part of prisoners. Within this institution, choice and initiative are all but nonexistent. A prisoner's contact with the outside world is limited to mail, visits, and telephone calls—all of which are heavily regulated. "The only real bright spot of the day is at mail call," writes Erin George, "when you keep your fingers crossed and hope to get a real letter."[10] Long echoes her sentiment: "Mail . . . usually brightens an inmate's day and in my situation, it really did."[11] The prisoner is segregated from the environment he or she once knew. Jimmy Baca notes that "writing for me was my connection to the streets."[12] Telephone calls can only be made from a community phone, collect to the receiver, at designated times. Visits are always difficult, often expensive, and typically demeaning.

Suddenly, prisoners are severed from the people, settings, and pursuits of the outside world. Forced confinement turns their availability upside down, with two distinctive but complementary effects. On the one hand, overcrowding, limited resources, and the perceived need for constant surveillance combine to eliminate almost all opportunities for privacy, solitude, or modesty. On the other hand, prisoners who are now inaccessible to practically everything in the outside world are expected to be always available to members of the staff as well as fellow convicts.

In *The House of the Dead*, Dostoevsky's narrator is astonished by the suffering this produces at a Siberian prison: "I could never have imagined, for instance, how terrible and agonizing it would be never once for a single minute to be alone for the ten years of my imprisonment."[13] Behind bars, time for privacy, modesty, and solitude is in short supply, yet these temporal enclaves are critical for the establishment and maintenance of one's identity. They provide the scaffolding for one's self-esteem, self-efficacy, and sense of personal authenticity. The systematic deprivation of these temporal resources corrodes a convict's capacity for a dignified presentation of self.[14]

Inside or outside of prison, time for privacy is highly esteemed, and with good reason. The psychologist Robert Gifford observes that it facilitates social interaction: "Privacy allows us the time and space to reflect on the meaning of events, to fit them into our understanding of the world, and to formulate a response to them that is consistent with our self-images."[15] Privacy can be instrumental to the realization of our goals. Flaherty writes in the privacy of his study at home. He may choose to ignore the telephone and email. In so doing, he makes time for writing by making himself unavailable to others. The resulting interval of time is his own to do with as he pleases. Prisoners have no comparable control over their temporal availability.

Cohen and Taylor argue that privacy is fundamental to a sense of personal autonomy: "Solitude is typically required in everyday life [so] that we can go out of play for a while."[16] Yet prisons are characterized by a lack of privacy that is all but inconceivable for those of us on the outside: "There are 'Judas holes' in every cell door and in one wing electronic devices under the floor enable prison officers to monitor the actual movements of the prisoners in their cells."[17] Mere surveillance, however, is only one aspect of the absence of privacy in prison:

> Every prison officer knows in detail the lives of the men he observes. Their mail is read, their visitors' conversations overheard, their life histories are available on record for general inspection. Their health problems are matters for public discussion. They are watched during the performance of intimate toilet functions. Their domestic problems become public troubles.[18]

A convict has almost no time alone, and every facet of his or her life is scrutinized by others. The resulting hunger for privacy motivates much of the clandestine and illicit activity behind bars.

Women who write prison autobiographies devote considerable attention to these issues. At Alderson, where Clare Hanrahan is held, female inmates learn to expect a strip search after they have been with a visitor, but there are altogether unexpected intrusions, as well: "On one occasion I witnessed an incident where two female officers flanked a male officer in the prison yard and stood looking on as he stopped and did pat-searches on dozens of women returning to the barracks after a meal."[19] When unexpected intrusions are added to routine security procedures, all of one's time is at the mercy of the temporal regime. In telling fashion, she corroborates the constancy and ubiquity of surveillance:

> I felt always and everywhere observed during my time in prison. Guards walk in and out of cubicles at any time. I was startled out of sleep on several occasions by a male guard pulling down the sheet that covered me as he made the rounds on a pre-dawn "count."[20]

If guards can intrude on inmates "at any time," then inmates have no privacy. One's cell is not a private space. As George points out, some convicts only learn this the hard way: "I remember when a cellmate of mine was put into seg merely because she had been bitching to me about a particular officer while we were locked in our cell. Kitty didn't realize it, but the officer had been dipping, in inmate slang, through the intercom."[21] This nearly limitless temporal dominion drives Piper Kerman to make unintended use of the facilities: "I would just flee to the bathroom for a few blessed minutes of privacy and quiet."[22] As with other facets of life in prison, however, there is great variation in the degree to which toilets offer refuge. "In Albion," recalls Amy Fisher, "guards were 80 percent male. They looked through the big glass part of the door and watched female prisoners when they used the bathroom."[23]

It is tempting to attribute these concerns to an essentialist version of gender roles, but Carceral and many of the men who pen prison autobiographies are equally disturbed by a lack of time alone. They object to public nakedness and an audience of strangers for their bodily functions. "I want to not be standing naked in a puddle of convict piss," writes Jimmy Lerner, "waiting to take a group shower with a bunch of criminals."[24] It is difficult to maintain a sense of dignity in the absence of privacy. "Most cells house three new arrivals," notes Stephen Stanko, "and all business, private and personal, is conducted with everyone in the cell at all times."[25] Carceral is chagrined to learn that one cannot even find time alone in segregation:

Seg does not necessarily mean being by oneself. I personally find it worse to live in a cell under twenty-four-hour lockdown with another man. Imagine being in a little cell, and having to shit in front of another dude. Toilets always face the bed. Seg changed as prisons became more crowded. The state began to place two men in one cell under lockdown. Some men are alone, but now most are doubled in a very small space.

One's most basic sense of modesty is constantly violated, but Victor Serge helps us understand that there is much more at issue in the loss of solitude: "Each does his business in front of the other two. But perhaps the worst intimacy is not that of bodies. It is not being able to be alone with yourself. Not being able to remove your face from the prying glance of others."[26] "There is no place to be by oneself," laments Jorge Renaud.[27] This is the plight of those who are sentenced to relentless scrutiny.

Long avows that the state will "put anybody with anybody and expect us to get along or kill each other."[28] The prisons where Carceral served time operated in the same fashion. At a minimum-security facility, he recalls, "I had four cellies I never met before I was placed in the cell with them." It follows that cellmates must exercise *temporal discretion* with one another if they are to maintain good relations. In his response to a question posed by Flaherty, Carceral reveals the intricate mindfulness that makes this possible:

Malik was a respectful person, one of the better cellies at Gladiator School. This is day and night when it comes to your cellie. He liked to stand at the end of the bunk and write, read, or watch TV. Sometimes he would sit in the chair, but seldom. I painted with all my free time, so I sat. Yet if I was painting and Malik hinted that he needed to sit at the desk, I would relinquish the area. Even if I would rather use my time painting, I shared the area and moved to my bunk to watch TV or find something else to do. I had to relinquish that time to let him use it. Then, if he laid down, the cell light was about three feet above his bunk, so I would stop anything I was doing if it required light. I would also remain quiet. For example, I would not rip open chips or spend time flushing the toilet. If he was standing and reading at the foot of the bunks and I had to use the toilet, I gave him a few moments to gather his material and move to the other end of the cell. We could not walk past each other in the cell since the area was too small. I would wait at one side; he would come to that side; then I would slip past him and the desk.

Time in a shared cell is communal. Prisoners must learn how to apportion their time together. In face-to-face situations, or what Alfred Schutz calls the "we-relationship," two or more people share "a community of space and a community of time."[29] Within the confines of that space, it is not my time or your time; it is our time, and we have "grown older together" in that "our experiences have been simultaneous."[30]

Temporal discretion requires sensitivity and a willingness to make allowances for the sake of others—uncommon attributes behind bars. What does the opposite of temporal discretion look like? At Florence State Prison, Baca has the rare privilege of a cell to himself until another inmate, Boxer, joins him at the insistence of one of the Chicano gangs: "As soon as he came in, he said the typing bothered him and told me to stop. Then he changed the channel on my little radio to his station, and that evening he said he couldn't sleep and wanted me to turn off my reading lamp."[31] The very next day, Baca attacks and nearly kills him before being pulled away by guards. Routinely, the absence of temporal discretion has violent consequences.

Different but equally vexing dynamics operate in prison dorms, where dozens of inmates are housed within a single large room. Given such numbers, noise is an incredible problem, and group conflict is the norm. As Berger shows us, enforced mutual presence can be not only annoying but also dangerous:

> It's 9:30 on Monday night in the Dorm. As I am writing this there is trouble brewing between the Black and Spanish inmates. They have been arguing about a bunk being too close to the walk-through aisle by about six inches. Every time the Blacks move it the Spanish move it back. Finally one of the Blacks threw a punch sending a Spanish inmate flying into a table full of food. Everyone jumped in to break it up. However, this is just the beginning, retribution comes at night in prison, and the Spanish have been disrespected. I know there are weapons here.[32]

Sooner or later, each prisoner is admonished to "do your own time," but this advice can be misleading. Berger is neither Black nor Spanish, but, in the dorm, their time is also his time. No time for solitude means no time for peace and quiet, no time for safety and security.

Subsequent to incarceration, temporal availability is extremely one-sided. Prisoners are always available to officers who patrol that tier. For prisoners, however, initiating contact with members of the staff is difficult, punishable, or simply impossible. "They locked me in The Cage [i.e., isolation] for three months," writes Fisher, because she wrote a letter to a correctional officer.[33] Rules aside, prisoners have no means of communicating with staff most of the time. By the same token, however, temporal asymmetry dictates that prisoners should always be available. Carceral is awakened in the middle of the night by a third-shift guard screaming at him: "Don't pull your blanket over your head while sleeping!" Only semiconscious, Carceral responds slowly as the officer continues to yell at him. It is noteworthy that the officer feels entitled to this behavior. He does not consider it *temporal trespassing*, as it would be in everyday life. The correctional officers expect Carceral to be available even while sleeping. Like Hanrahan, prisoners gradually grow accustomed to having flashlights shining in their faces at various times of the night.[34] Or, like Woodfox, they must assent to having their sleep interrupted for routine medical services: "When medical personnel needed to do lab work or other tests, they came to get us in the middle of the night—anytime from one to three in the morning."[35]

Even when correctional officers are not enforcing the temporal regime, the unrelenting presence of other prisoners can be oppressive. Most inmates share a small cell with one or more strangers nearly twenty-four hours a day, which wears on a person's patience. Carceral records the following exchange with Roscoe in his field notes:

ROSCOE: "My cellie left to the other building."
CARCERAL: "I suppose you're looking for a couple of days of peace?"
ROSCOE: "Yes, I had hoped, but they moved another dude in there right away. I didn't get any peace. After ten years, I'm so tired of being around other men. We don't never get no peace. Then, I may get one of those dudes who don't ever leave the room."

In a subsequent entry, Carceral acknowledges that moments of privacy are rare and fleeting:

Next, he may develop a hunger for solitude. No one likes to be hungry, but in a social setting like this seldom does one find any solitude. Even when I have it, I really know I don't. It's paradoxical. Let me explain. As I'm writing this, I'm in my cell. My cellie is at work. Yet the reality of the setting dictates that, at any moment, he or a guard could open the door. Further, the door has a glass window in it. Anyone passing by can look into the cell. And, sure enough, in between these sentences, I get called to the office where I work. By the time I get back, my cellie has arrived. He talks while making his bed.

Who is here? And when? One wishes for the presence of particular others and the absence of strangers but cannot bring about either of these conditions. Prisoners exercise almost no control over temporal aspects of social interaction.

That which you desire is unavailable; that which you find undesirable is plentiful. This paradigm is epitomized by sexuality. There are no opportunities for licit heterosexuality, so Berger is "sex starved."[36] Long's cellmate masturbates throughout the day, however, and other prisoners must ward off unwanted (yet ceaseless) homosexual advances.[37] Under the watchful eyes of staff and fellow prisoners, time for sexual privacy is practically nonexistent.

Privacy norms are characteristic of our cultural emphasis on individuality. Consider, for example, our compartmentalized homes. The anthropologist Edward Hall observes that, in contrast to Japan, the design of our homes displays a greater concern for privacy.[38] In accord with this emphasis, Zerubavel examines the always shifting and contested line between private time and public time.[39] For inmates, however, there is no time they can call their own. Like Roscoe, they share their time with others; like Carceral, they are at the beck and call of the staff. There is naught but *communal time*. Given their cultural background, this requires a wrenching adjustment. In short, conditions at most prisons make for nearly constant temporal trespassing. With ubiquitous overcrowding, others encroach on a prisoner's time more often. Such conditions are aggravating to say the least. Research demonstrates that unlimited proximity stokes interpersonal tensions, which, in turn, bring about much of the violence behind bars.[40] The state creates the temporal circumstances for this violence.

Prisoners must be available at all times, but the same is not true for members of the staff. This temporal asymmetry is especially problematic when (as is frequently the case) prisoners need something from the correctional officers. The system is purposely designed so that prisoners must talk to an officer to request even the most basic things: toilet paper, soap, toothpaste, permission to speak to another prisoner, daily job assignment, sign-out log, mail, passes for movement from one place to another, protection, and so forth. In the outside world, none of that would need permission. Prior to imprisonment, Carceral could make telephone calls whenever he chose to do so. Where he is first incarcerated, however, officers must be asked to dial telephone numbers for the prisoners, calls cannot last longer than six minutes, and officers listen to the call while it takes place. Indeed, much of one's time in prison is spent seeking permission.

And, if permission is necessary, then it can be (and often will be) denied or granted only grudgingly. Carceral notes that members of the staff typically impose punishing conditions on prisoners who deign to make such requests, including belittlement, demeaning lectures, and pointed delays. One morning, Carceral finds himself waiting for access to the laundry room at 9:14. One of the two officers on duty was supposed to unlock the door at 9:00, but, in full view of the convicts, they sit and chat at the officers' station. Carceral records the following incident in his field notes:

"Man, what is he doing in there?" asks a new guy.
"Wished I knew," Maxwell replied.
The new guy walks to the officers' station despite a sign on the door that reads, "Do not bother staff while they are talking, on the phone, or busy!" He is quickly sent back to us. "Man, this shit is a trip," says the new guy. "What do they think we are on? I point out that it's past nine. One says, 'Give me a minute, it's not that late,' and the other points to the sign on the door!"

As usual, such treatment is considered part of what prisoners deserve. With this tedious process, the tempo of prison life slows to a snail's pace.

Waiting signifies subordination. If a staff member summons a prisoner for an appointment, the latter is expected to arrive early and wait to be acknowledged. This punctuality is the temporal norm whenever prisoners attend official hearings such as parole and program review, appointments with social workers and the medical staff, other services having to do with property and mail, or simply to speak with an officer. Thematically, prisoners refer to this expectation with the well-worn phrase "hurry up and wait." Carceral heard this statement on countless occasions when inmates discussed their appointments. One prisoner would complain that the unit guard told him to hurry up, but, upon arrival, he was made to wait for the staff, whereupon those listening would nod their heads in unanimity while one of them would reply, "hurry up and wait."[41] This temporal norm leads to chronic waiting and the perception of protracted duration. It disrupts synchronicity in social interaction and ritualizes disrespect.

In jail, declares Rik Scarce, "nearly all appointments will be controlled by someone else."[42] Carceral confirms that this testimony is equally true of prison. Where norms are asymmetrical, so is deviance. As Carceral puts it, "If, God forbid, the prisoner is late, an apology is expected!" Members of the staff have no reservations about chastising a late prisoner as if they are speaking to a recalcitrant child. At a minimum-security facility, Carceral once arrived at the Medical Center about an hour late for his appointment. He immediately heard from the medical officer: "Well, it's about time!" Carceral did not respond, and the medical officer marked the absence of any apology: "Nothing to say, I see." Carceral heard it again as soon as he entered the nurse practitioner's office: "Now you know your appointments, and you may not want to come, but I need to see you when you are called." Come when you are called. Punctuality is imperative in spite of the fact that prisoners have no control over notification, release from prior location, or impediments to movement due to security arrangements.

The asymmetry of temporal norms in prison can have life-or-death implications. During a conversation with Carceral, Grayson describes an incident at Walls, his previous prison. While he is outside at recreation, another man with him develops severe chest pain. Yet he cannot go straight to the Medical Center. Instead, he waits while correctional officers call to see if a nurse will treat him. In addition, he must wait for an officer to roll the gates so he can leave the yard. Grayson notes that he is able to walk a few laps around the perimeter track while this takes place. By the time he finishes a third lap, the prisoner in pain has arrived at the Medical Center, but it is Saturday and the door at the main entrance is locked. He sits down, slowly falls over, and dies there.[43]

Expectations concerning punctuality reflect one's status in the social organization. In turn, these expectations shape the temporal dynamics of interpersonal relations. New prisoners find these practices strange and stressful. Among experienced prisoners, they are an irksome and chronic source of alienation. Members of the staff think it is proper that those serving time are made to wait. Unlike those of us in everyday life, prisoners cannot wait for and choose the proper moment for social interaction. Staff members determine when (and with what conditions) they will be available. Having no say in the matter, prisoners must resign themselves to a great deal of waiting. And, while they wait for one person, they will be under surveillance by another. In short, members of the staff routinely make themselves unavailable but demand that prisoners be always and immediately available.

Anyone suffering from an illness perceives time to pass slowly, and the impact on temporal experience is compounded by having to wait for medical care.[44] With migraine headaches and two impacted wisdom teeth (misdiagnosed for a year), Carceral was summoned to the Medical Center at Gladiator School on numerous occasions. He remembers these visits as brutal, invariant, and "hard to cope with." Nauseous and in pain, he must wait to be recognized as he is buzzed through a series of doors. He joins the end of a long line that snakes away from an officer's desk. Once that officer sees his pass (a bright orange slip of paper about the size of an index card), he activates an electronic switch that unlocks the door to the Medical Center. Then he waits in another line that leads to another officer's desk. That officer takes his pass and gives him the customary command: "Sit on the bench over there and wait to be called." Carceral joins the other prisoners on one of two wooden benches that face the officer's desk. He has been seen by several correctional officers, but he is yet to see any medical personnel.

Gladiator School is a maximum-security facility, so it stands to reason that procedures at the Medical Center are in keeping with this designation. Inexperienced convicts are told that procedures will be far less restrictive at prisons with lower levels of security. On many occasions, Carceral overheard fellow convicts being regaled with such fables: "Once you're at medium- or minimum-security, you can be out of your cell all day. At minimum, you go shopping." When they arrive at such prisons, however, they quickly realize that these stories are illusory. Indeed, procedures at medium- and minimum-security facilities can be more intrusive and allow even less temporal leeway. Carceral encounters such procedures when he is transferred to a minimum-security prison. A convict is buzzed through an electric door; he checks in with the correctional officer, is told to wait, and then falls under the scrutiny of that officer while doing so. Instead of being issued a pass, however, a prisoner would be summoned to the Medical Center by means of a telephone call to his housing unit or work site.

Within the context of a minimum-security prison, the effects of such procedures on temporal experience are still more frustrating. The staff supervisor at Carceral's job site summons a prisoner: "You need to report to Medical; they just called for you." The prisoner in question is not pleased: "I hate going up there! We work 6:00 A.M. to 2:00 P.M. They can't call us *after* work?" Another prisoner chimes in with "hurry up and wait." Carceral is summoned to the same Medical Center an hour later but finds that the prisoner who had been called earlier is still there in an increasingly agitated state. A third prisoner, acquainted with both of them, exclaims, "Man, I've been here an hour and a half!" "What are they doing?" asks Carceral. The third prisoner replies, "I don't know, but I guarantee I will *never* be on time again!" The prisoner summoned from Carceral's work site provides this coda: "We sit here waiting on them, but constantly hear it when we're late if they call for us." Members of the staff regularly summon prisoners without taking their schedules into consideration.

It is easy for outsiders (and members of the staff) to dismiss the difference between a pass or telephone system. From their standpoint, it is a trivial issue. Among prisoners, however, there is widespread recognition that these systems have very different implications for one's temporal availability. In a maximum-security facility, the pass sometimes arrives ten to thirty minutes before the appointment, and the prisoner does not always leave immediately. He or she has some time to prepare for the transition. In contrast, a telephone call allows no such adjustment. The same is true of a public address system. A prisoner must report immediately once the summons is broadcast. Carceral especially resented this system when he was using the toilet. Upon arrival, he would be asked about the delay, and the toilet was viewed as a questionable excuse.

Prisoners also confront the problem of availability for each other due to temporal segmentation. As we have seen, each housing unit is assigned to various activities during specific time slots. This rigid schedule creates temporal segmentation as the population is compartmentalized into groups of prisoners who do things at the same time. Under these conditions it is difficult for prisoners to form or maintain relationships with those on a different schedule, but they have devised illicit (and often ingenious) methods for circumventing temporal segmentation.

In a general sense, of course, other prisoners are almost always available, but one may not know or care for those who inhabit one's own temporal segment of the schedule. Frequently, a prisoner wants to communicate with someone—perhaps a friend or business associate—who occupies a different temporal niche. Doing so will require working around institutional restrictions on interpersonal availability. The simplest solution involves the use of third parties. During outdoor recreation, for example, prisoners from one housing unit may be on the track at the same time that prisoners from another housing unit are outside the entrance to their own building. One of those on the track may call to one of those standing near the entrance to that housing unit, asking him to bring a particular person outside. Once he emerges from that building, they have a brief, loud, and necessarily public conversation:

INMATE 1: "Tell Carter to bring my cigarettes up to the Activity Building tonight."
INMATE 2: "You're going to be there?"
INMATE 1: "Yeah, I'm on the list for special projects."
INMATE 2: "I'll go get him."

Job sites assemble prisoners from various housing units, thereby serving as another unintended opportunity to communicate with colleagues who inhabit other temporal segments of the schedule. "Hey," says Carceral to another prisoner, "will you give this message to Nelson?" He hands him a note. "Two dollars, pony express service," he replies, jokingly. Carceral and Nelson lived in two different housing units and, consequently, their respective segments of the schedule did not overlap. One's use of a third party transcends temporal segmentation, but at the cost of personal privacy. The man who conveys the message to Nelson could read it on the way and add that information to the pool of prison gossip.

Communication between prisoners in different cells is conditioned by the physical setting and the security level of that facility. On the tiers at Gladiator School, prisoners used four methods to extend their temporal availability. The cell halls were comprised of four tiers stacked on top of each other, with forty cells per tier. During in-cell periods when doors were locked, prisoners would circumvent their mutual inaccessibility by means of yelling, passing, sliding, or stringing. To illustrate these methods, let us consider the case of a prisoner who is hungry after the evening lockdown. How can his acquaintance, four cells down, know about this, and what can he do about it? Prisoners do not have refrigerators, and no further meals will be served before breakfast. Bear in mind that any communication on this matter is risky business. Correctional officers will confiscate notes because they represent unauthorized communication. Likewise, any food will be forfeited. The prisoners in question will be subject to disciplinary reports. Hand mirrors were not permitted because prisoners could use them to watch for the officers.

Yelling was the most common, but least effective, way to communicate with someone in another cell. A prisoner wishing to speak with an acquaintance who was four cells down would simply yell. In theory, doing so makes that other prisoner available now, not later when the doors have been unlocked. In practice, however, it also contributes to the cacophony that is characteristic of life behind bars. Under these conditions, the noise level may be such that only the loudest prisoners can be heard. Moreover, the prisoner who is seeking a snack may not want to disclose his source or the fact that he cannot afford items from the canteen. In that case, the convict can write a note, fold it up (Carceral would glue it), and write the intended recipient's cell number on it. This note can then be passed from one adjoining cell to another, assuming that all prisoners in between the sender and receiver are willing to cooperate.

Sliding offers another way to evade the temporal regime and its restrictions on mutual availability. Passing a note may not be a viable option. A prisoner may not want others to read that note, or he may not be able to count on their cooperation. As an alternative, sliding the note is particularly well suited to sending a private message across a longer distance. This procedure entails putting the note into something that slides—typically, a paperback book. Carceral's neighbor was one of many who favored this method in Gladiator School. The sender yells until he has the attention of the intended recipient and then tells him to prepare for the incoming message:

SLY: "Leon! Leon!"
LEON: "Yeah?"
SLY: "Put out a towel in front of your cell."

The intended recipient folds (or rolls) a towel and then pushes it onto the floor outside the bars of his cell. To ensure that he can catch the book, he extends the towel as far as possible. Having stopped the book, the recipient simply picks it up or uses the towel to drag it within reach.

For the sake of greater privacy, some prisoners would toss a book with an attached string. If the string is too short, the sender knots a second segment of string to the first. Through trial and error, one learns the length required to reach particular colleagues. Dental floss works very well for this purpose. The receiver could use the string to pull the book into his cell or, if the sender missed the intended recipient, he could use the string to pull the book back to his own cell and try again. This procedure also helps to prevent others from hijacking the note (or small package). As a variation on this technique, Carceral observed a pillowcase loaded with canteen items being pulled past his cell.

Some prisoners turn mutual scrutiny into still another form of illicit communication. Baca tells us that "Chicanos hand-signed to homeboys across the landing, a coded language that went on for hours."[45] While Billy Sinclair is imprisoned at Angola, his fellow convicts dig holes in the walls between cells, despite the certainty of severe punishment if they are discovered.[46] They are not escaping from prison; they are simply trying to be present for one another, not at scheduled intervals, but whenever they wish to be. They seek respite from the temporal regime.

By means of these improvised and invariably clumsy efforts, prisoners endeavor to achieve mutual presence. They attempt to transcend temporal segmentation and restrictions on interpersonal communication. Prisoners are almost never alone but frequently find that those they wish to be with are inaccessible. The state places physical and temporal barriers between prisoners, impeding their interaction. Hence, prisoners are deprived of control over their own availability—something those of us on the outside take for granted.

These circumstances alter temporal experience. Transactions with anyone in particular will be slow, uncertain, and often dangerous. A prisoner must wait for an opportune moment; there is, consequently, always needless delay. Carter was told to bring cigarettes to the Activity Building, but the intended recipient must now wait until their schedules coincide. He cannot go to Carter's cell. Our perception of time is conditioned by the pace of activity, and, in prison, all of one's activity is encumbered by the temporal regime.

RULING TIME

With imprisonment, temporal availability is determined by an elaborate set of rules. All social interaction is rule-bound, but the rules that govern life in prison are written, exhaustive, and rigidly enforced. By virtue of these regulations, those in authority decide when people, activities, places, and equipment will be available. For prisoners, lack of control over availability produces vast quantities of empty time during which they must wait for designated intervals.

A prison is more than buildings and grounds. Quintessentially, it is a set of rules for what one can do with time. No social organization is more highly regimented. The rules are constantly invoked by correctional officers and other members of the staff in order to justify their treatment of prisoners. Thus, due to their substance as well as their multiplicity, rules empower officers and disenfranchise prisoners. By ruling time, those in authority decide how prisoners will serve time.

Adherence to the rules brings into being recurrent temporal patterns— the rhythms of life behind bars. The rules are both prescriptive and proscriptive; they dictate everything a prisoner can or cannot do. For the most part, however, they are subtractive; they prohibit enjoyment in that a prisoner is not allowed to savor time spent eating, sleeping, bathing, or socializing. You can lengthen your sentence by taking stale bread from the dining hall to feed the birds in the yard.[47] Enforcement of the rules makes for temporal regimentation, which is ceaselessly monitored by the staff.

Substantial research demonstrates that temporal norms vary across history and geography.[48] Yet the people in each locale tend to take these temporal norms for granted. How a particular society defines punctuality or waiting one's turn is a by-product of the social construction of reality.[49] As such, the origins of temporal norms (e.g., the seven-day week) tend to be shrouded in antiquity. In contrast, however, the temporal norms that govern life in prison are known to be authored by members of the administration. Lacking the legitimacy conferred by what Max Weber called traditional authority, they are understood to represent the arbitrary and coercive exercise of administrative power.[50].

Although strictly enforced, the rules are never static. Moreover, the arbitrariness of these rules is evident in the frequency with which they change. When George first arrived at Fluvanna Correctional Center, she recalls, "We were still allowed to have a small crocheted afghan on our beds."[51] The cells were "bitterly cold" during the winter, but this quaint mercy was not permitted to continue: "We all had to send our afghans home when the rules changed."[52] According to Jeffery Ross and Stephen Richards, even correctional officers complain about swiftly changing rules.[53] Like prisoners, they are often on the receiving end of policy revisions. On occasion, however, both prisoners and correctional officers have a hand in the creation of new rules. Some rules begin when members of the staff order prisoners to follow particular procedures for the sake of their own convenience. Improvisational at first, these procedures are eventually formalized as printed policy. Less commonly, if prisoners are vociferous and cohesive in protesting a specific problem, members of the staff may be motivated to manage the controversy by formulating a new rule. Inconsistently, then, the rules are strictly enforced and frequently changed. This combination is highly unstable because it makes the rules seem purely imperious.

By shaping the schedule, rules establish the parameters for temporal experience. The weekly routine is an artifact of power residing in a temporal regime. Similarly, institutional procedures bring about temporal segmentation by allocating different access times across the prison population. Each facility will have its own rule-bound rhythms that govern when prisoners should eat, sleep, use the toilet, take a shower, stand for count, have recreation, do their laundry, shop at the canteen, make a telephone call, receive a visitor, report for work, or go to class. They are told what to do and when to do it twenty-four hours a day.

With these rules, the administration imposes a temporal framework on one's life behind bars. More often than not, this framework is responsible for monotonous certainty and protracted duration—the hallmarks of time in prison. It is a starkly simple and regimented world. Other subordinate populations (e.g., slaves and children) enjoy far more temporal leeway.

Certain Uncertainty

Yet now our analysis begins to fold back on itself because, in prison, one can be certain that time will be ruled unpredictably. On this point, Carceral's observations echo Megan Comfort's concept of "certain uncertainty."[54] Even prisons at the same level of security have different rules. The staff at one facility may define recreation and library as options within the same temporal slot, thereby forcing prisoners to choose between them. At another facility, library and recreation may occupy separate temporal slots, which enables prisoners to partake of both. As Carceral observes, a prisoner must adjust to these variations in policy whenever he or she is transferred to a different institution:

After serving time for almost thirty years, I was removed from a minimum-security facility, picked up from my job site outside of the prison, and immediately taken to Gladiator School's segregation unit. I went from writing, exercising, and free movement to and from working at a specific outside location to a cell with a toilet, sink, bunk beds, and a new cellie under twenty-four-hour lockdown. I did nothing wrong to induce this except be a member of a group called lifers. This time I serve is not my time; I have no control over it. It belongs to the state.

At any moment, and without explanation, the staff can restructure a prisoner's temporal reality. Lacking control over their own time, prisoners inhabit an environment that is temporally capricious.

With only rare exceptions, prisoners can be certain that they will have no say in the timing of events. It follows that temporal expectations arise from this rigidly enforced schedule. For example, dispossessed of temporal autonomy, a prisoner counts on going to recreation at a certain time. Yet prisoners are even deprived of the humble benefits that accrue from predictability. The churning effects of shift work and frequent turnover in staffing introduce new people with the power to impose new rules (plus discretion concerning rules that, theoretically, are still in effect). In short, prisoners suffer as a result of certainty as well as uncertainty. When rules change, moreover, so does temporal experience. Almost invariably, these unexpected changes make matters worse by reducing the time prisoners can devote to a particular activity. Lack of control is an aggravating factor. The interval of time previously allotted to the activity in question is now reduced or eliminated. Typically, prisoners learn of the changes just before or even after the expected activity was scheduled to begin. And, crucially, the prisoner cannot simply elect to do something else instead. If, for instance, the library is closed, prisoners cannot fill this unexpected gap with outdoor recreation. They are not scheduled for that activity and, in any case, limited resources prevent the addition of unscheduled prisoners.

In prison, it is a certainty that all activities will be viewed as privileges. The uncertainty is manifest in how members of the staff at a particular prison choose to allocate these privileges. Officially, the allocation is guided by a set of rules, but it is apparent to prisoners that members of the staff make and remake these rules whenever they feel the need to do so. Depending on immediate interests of the staff, therefore, a temporal regime can be flexible or inflexible. Either way, the temporal experience of prisoners is conditioned by this variation. "Inmates . . . were not restricted in the extent of free time that they could spend in hobby-shop or recreational programs" when Iqbal Karimi arrived at Fort Dix, New Jersey.[55] Subsequent to staff turnover, however, this schedule was drastically altered:

> A few years later, a new supervisor began to restrict hobby-shop participation to two hours per day. Such is a perfect example of how the Bureau of Prisons bureaucracy functions. Prisoners develop routines, then new employees take over a department and introduce new rules that disrupt those routines. In many instances, no reasons are provided, nor are appeals from disgruntled prisoners considered. The hobby-shop participants were dismayed over the change, but the only explanation provided was that the new supervisor of recreation had determined that two hours was enough time for hobby-craft activities in any given day. End of story.[56]

Correctional officers and other members of the staff decide how much time is enough. Within the context of enforced dependency, small adjustments to routine practices can have large effects on temporal experience, as witnessed by Carceral in the following excerpt:

> At Gladiator School, the guard would walk down the tier telling prisoners in each cell that it was time for them to head for the canteen. One Saturday morning, the guard decided to yell from the front gate. With all the noise, half the men on the tier never heard him. I was one of them. As the day passed, no one could figure out why we weren't going to the canteen. At lunch, men learned that they had missed out. Men relied on getting to the canteen each week. The reaction was fierce, to say the least.

Each day, a different tier is scheduled to visit the canteen. Through no fault of their own, the men on Carceral's tier would have to wait until their turn came around again. Prison riots have erupted for less.

Prisoners hate uncertainty, associating it with the restriction of activities and suspension of privileges. During more than three decades behind bars, Carceral has seen the transition from single- to double- and triple-occupancy cells, repeated reductions in permitted property, and cutbacks in educational opportunities from college-level to GED. "Up until 1996," recalls Fermin Martin, "inmates were allowed to use their funds to purchase electronic keyboards, guitars, and other musical instruments. . . . One of the casualties of the new rules was limiting inmate access to personal property; among other things, federal prisoners no longer were allowed to purchase musical instruments."[57] Other long-term prisoners echo Desmond's assessment: "Take, take, take; alls these people do is take." Uncertainty recapitulates their original loss of temporal autonomy. In the beginning, when a temporal regime is imposed on each new prisoner, it is characterized by certainty, exteriority, and constraint. In consequence, it provokes anxiety, despair, and resentment. After a while, however, prisoners become accustomed to the routine. They learn to expect and even relish its comforting predictability. Uncertainty brings the loss of temporal autonomy back to the fore and, in so doing, reignites resentment as well as the latter's effect on the perceived passage of time.

Uncertainty can be used to signal institutional control or serve as a weapon of authoritarian vengeance, but, just as often, it is simply a by-product of temporal dependency rather than malicious intent. When staff members do not come to work, regularly scheduled activities are canceled. They could be librarians, teachers, social workers, or records office personnel. The administration does not fill these posts with other members of the staff. Prisoners expecting to conduct certain business suddenly discover that they are not allowed to do so, and their plans have to be put on hold. They must wait (no one knows for how long) until the staff member in question returns or is replaced. Temporal dependency is the central issue when Carceral overhears two prisoners discussing a Hobby Director who is frequently absent:

INMATE 1: "It don't seem like he is ever here. Then, when he is here, he isn't in the shop."
INMATE 2: "If they would have two hobby employees, then we could get our time in."

The prison never lacks for correctional officers, of course, but different personnel introduce distinct types of discretion. At Gladiator School, the schedule for outdoor recreation rotated each weekend. If your section of the cellblock went at 8:00 A.M. last Saturday, then you would go at 1:00 P.M. this Sunday, and vice versa. Aside from meals, this was the only time

Carceral and fellow prisoners were out of their cells. Then the regular sergeant took a vacation. Carceral's section went at 8:00 A.M. for three weekends in a row. Men who had stayed up late on Friday nights (anticipating recreation at 1:00 P.M.) were furious because they were too tired. "What's up with these fools," Darnell groused. "I can't get my weight lifting schedule right. And you know the only good TV is late-night." Another prisoner argued with one of the correctional officers:

Inmate: "Hey, we're supposed to go to recreation at 1:00 P.M.!
Officer: "The sergeant says no."
Inmate: "Tell the fucking sergeant we've had early rec three weekends straight!"

The certainty of their previous schedule returned with the regular sergeant.

From George Herbert Mead's research, we learn that the "inhibition of action" occasions intensified thought and self-consciousness concerning one's predicament.[58] In the absence of any solution, however, one is left with a heightened sense of waiting and boredom.[59] This is the disappointment of thwarted desires. It is worse than the boredom that results from not trying to do anything in the first place because it is colored by what did *not* happen, what the prisoner could *not* accomplish. To avoid this frustration, some inmates renounce involvement of any kind. They sit in their cells and let life pass them by. One prisoner put it this way: "If you don't get involved in all those activities or programs, you won't be disappointed when they don't come to work or cancel them." By means of uncertainty, the state teaches these prisoners futility.[60] Yet serving a sentence devoid of distractions is just a different form of suffering. Inmates eschew recurrent disappointments, but the "solution" entails consigning themselves to empty days, weeks, months, and years. These prisoners succumb to resignation instead of thwarted desires—admittedly, an alternative temporal lifestyle, but one that leads to the same agonizing perception that time is passing slowly.

The Disciplinary Cycle

"Prison is a place," reports George, "where almost anything can be a violation of the rules if the officer writing the charge couches it in the correct terms."[61] Lacking rhyme or reason, it is difficult to evade discipline.

Correctional officers and other members of the staff differ greatly in their use of disciplinary charges. By the same token, enforcement becomes another aspect of uncertainty. Berger offers further confirmation and explains, correspondingly, why it is so hard to mind your own business:

> It's very easy to get into trouble in prison. One only has to be in the wrong place at the wrong time. That's the reason I'm in the Hole now. If two guys start to fight in the gym and you happen to be there innocently working out they'll lock you up as well. If they decide you covered up information when they interviewed you as to what happened, you suddenly have a serious problem. Now you have implicated yourself.[62]

Yet, frequently, there is no need to implicate yourself. Snitching is cultivated by those in authority, which exacerbates uncertainty. Clearly, "doing your own time" is a precarious undertaking. Time is communal even when it concerns getting into trouble.

The people who run prisons find discretion functional. It follows that rules are written to foster ambiguity. Renaud's comments are incisive as well as generally applicable to other penal systems:

> The Texas Department of Corrections once had a rule called Disrespectful Attitude. It was left to the guards to determine which attitudes were sufficiently respectful or not. As you can imagine, any inmate who walked, talked, or even looked at a guard in a remotely challenging way was given a case. This rule was struck down by the courts in *Ruiz v. Estelle* as being too ambiguous."[63]

Nonetheless, the Texas Department of Corrections was not deterred by this legal setback:

> There are two rules that were created to take the place of the late Disrespectful Attitude. One is Creating Unnecessary Noise, which is whatever an officer says it is, at any level, including a whisper and in one case I personally know of, a burp during count. The other is Failure to [C]omplete a Reasonable Amount of Work. Reasonable is left to the officer to define, and if he says it is reasonable and you don't do it, you've got a case.[64]

If ambiguity is functional and institutionalized, so is uncertainty. What is more, the resulting uncertainty has significant implications for time served as well as the quality of one's temporal experience.

The disciplinary cycle operates as a temporal loop with recurrently tragic outcomes. Prisoners are sentenced to serve time as punishment for their original crimes. In prison, however, they discover that it is all but impossible to avoid violating the myriad ambiguous rules that govern their behavior. "There were so many compulsories that very few of us could manage to stay out of trouble even with our best efforts," writes George Jackson.[65] "Women in the jail were constantly getting into trouble for both minor and major offenses," recalls George.[66] Then, in order to punish them for these subsequent violations, they are sentenced to more time and harder time— in effect, pushing back their release dates indefinitely. Berger illustrates this pattern when he ruefully considers the fallout from being swept up in the aforementioned fight: "So, now my release date will probably change, and there's a chance I will miss Travis's graduation. Something I have been looking forward to."[67] If a prisoner objects to the disciplinary report, adds Renaud, this only serves to escalate the situation and amplify the resulting temporal penalty: "When an inmate protests over the petty nature of a case, the guards will upgrade what was a minor rule infraction into a major confrontation."[68] Prisoners struggle to extricate themselves from this vortex of retribution. Objectively, their sentences grow longer. Subjectively, their perceived passage of time drags.

Many of the rules that govern a prisoner's behavior establish boundaries for various dimensions of time, including duration, frequency, sequence, timing, and allocation. To begin with, there is a rule that prohibits "group resistance." In the eyes of those charged with maintaining discipline, a group is defined as two or more convicts. As a case in point, a violation occurs if the group does not move from its present location when told to do so. The guards do not want them to occupy that area, and loitering is viewed as resistance. This situation can easily segue into "starting a riot" when prisoners fail to comply with an officer's order: "Move along," "Let's go," or "Get moving" (now). The correctional officers are hypersensitive to delay, as is apparent in these instructions for new arrivals: "Any motherfucker tries to slow-play me or the property sergeant, I'll lock your ass down all day."[69] How quickly should a group of prisoners disperse? In every order, "immediately" is the explicit or implicit adverb.

With an escape, a prisoner shortens his or her sentence unilaterally. Instead of being released by the staff, an agentive individual reappropriates time. Needless to say, the state frowns on any effort to circumvent the penal system by leaving early. Escape is exceedingly uncommon, of course, but it exhibits noteworthy temporal features. Subsequent to being apprehended (and most of them are), prisoners who leave the premises without permission are sentenced to a lot more time in prison—the very place they were trying to flee. Almost certainly, then, they lengthen their captivity. Sunny Jacobs cites the case of a fellow convict, Louise, who "had been part of an escape attempt with three other women. They each got another fifteen years."[70] An escape is an escape from a physical standpoint, regardless of whether the prisoner simply walks away from a minimum-security facility or scales a twenty-foot wall at a maximum-security facility. Symbolically, however, these transgressions are quite dissimilar, and this is signified by the much more severe temporal punishment meted out in the latter case where one embarrasses the elaborate procedures designed to prevent such excursions.

A rule demanding "punctuality and attendance" is plainly temporal. With it, those in authority strive to ensure that prisoners are where they are supposed to be when they are supposed to be. It represents an effort to impose the moral strictures of a temporal regime. Each inmate has a schedule to uphold and, in cyclical fashion, will be given more time in prison for being late to or absent from classes, programs, or jobs. A prisoner in an "unassigned area" is courting trouble. Rules proscribe doing things at the wrong time or not doing things at the right time. A related rule targets "refusal to work or attend school." Prisoners are not permitted to take a day off or quit. To do so is tantamount to escape because prisons are centrally concerned with dictating how time is served. Having refused to work or attend school, the prisoner now occupies an "unassigned area" (i.e., one's own cell, for example) and is "disobeying orders." The interrelatedness of these rules typically makes for a cascade of violations and severe temporal punishment.

Rules that forbid "loitering" and "leaving an assigned area" link time and place. Loitering subsumes failure to leave a certain place quickly enough or traveling too slowly through a restricted area. The pace of one's movement is deemed delinquent. One prisoner may walk slowly, for example, so that another can catch up with her. A prisoner may linger at recreation in order to finish a conversation with someone from another cellblock. The prisoner may be sitting at a picnic table designated for a different unit. The opposite case occurs when a convict is in his or her assigned location but leaves it without authorization to do so. Prisoners must not only be in the correct place but also remain there for the regularly scheduled interval. Potentially, this rule is violated whenever you leave your cell to use the bathroom. And, in turn, "leaving an assigned area" is necessarily paired with another violation: "being in an unassigned area." Given the redundancy across these rules, convicts usually come before the hearing officer with three or more charges and are found guilty on all counts.

Research by the sociologists William Reese and Michael Katovich shows us that, in everyday life, much of deviance entails the violation of temporal norms.[71] This principle is nowhere more applicable than in prison. A rule that prohibits "violation of institution policies and procedures" invokes the complex timetables that govern one's life behind bars. At a private prison in the South, Carceral recalls that inmates without jobs were not allowed to shower before 5:35 A.M. No one could use the bathroom during count. Two days a week, unassigned inmates were allowed passes to the library in the morning. The telephone was available at 6:00 P.M. Prisoners were forbidden to sign out any earlier than ten minutes before they were supposed to arrive at their destinations. All inmates were required to be in their cells for each of five counts: 8:00 and 10:00 A.M. and 2:00, 7:30., and 9:30 P.M. On odd days, the ring-out in the cellblock for meals was top down; on even days, it was bottom up. At every moment of the day, a prisoner is subject to an elaborate set of temporal controls.

Erving Goffman's conceptualization of "total institutions" is primarily spatial. As previously noted, he begins his analysis by distinguishing total institutions (such as prisons and mental asylums) from everyday life, where "the individual tends to sleep, play, and work *in different places.*"[72] Contrastingly, our findings suggest that the totalitarian character of life in prison is essentially temporal.

Segregation

"I spent about three of my seven years in prison in The Cage, in solitary," affirms Fisher.[73] She was put there "for hemming my prison-issue pants," for "having my fingernails too long," for trying "to dye my hair with their lye soap."[74] With the proliferation of rules, this secondary form of punishment is not uncommon.

The same system that punishes people with time in prison disciplines misbehaving convicts with confinement that is more severe and, from a perceptual standpoint, further protracted. Thus, segregation is a key phase in the disciplinary cycle. Once the hearing officer writes a disciplinary report, the inmate is transferred to segregation, which operates as a distinct realm within the prison.

Segregation has spatial connotations, and, in truth, these inmates are separated from (most of) the other prisoners. At base, however, segregation is a temporal process with three stages. The first stage is Temporary Lock Up (or TLU) during which a prisoner is placed in a segregation cell under twenty-four-hour lockdown. This prisoner will probably be "in solitary" or isolation, but, despite Fisher's testimony, prison overcrowding dictates that inmates in the TLU stage of segregation sometimes share a cell.

Either way, a prisoner is supposed to have his or her property transferred to the new cell, but correctional officers are not much interested in moving that stuff, so they interpret this rule as they see fit. Technically, this is not considered a punishment status because the allegations against that prisoner are still being investigated. Under these circumstances, however, prisoners view this stage as punishment that precedes conviction. There are regulations that limit the amount of time a prisoner can be kept on TLU status, but, in practice, officers exercise a great deal of discretion, and a prisoner can spend six months in this "temporary" stage.

Sooner or later (no one is in a hurry), the charges are brought before a hearing officer and, almost always, the prisoner is found guilty. The hearing officer writes a disciplinary report that goes into the prisoner's file, where it reduces his or her chances for early release. Now a prisoner enters the second stage of the segregation process: Adjustment Segregation. From the administrative perspective, it is the first of two punishment stages. With this status, the prisoner is moved to an empty cell with no property whatsoever. Alone and bereft of any distractions, the prisoner cannot communicate with anyone except the correctional officers, and most of them have no interest in talking to inmates. The temporal rhythms of Adjustment Segregation are more punitive than those of ordinary incarceration. No time is allocated for recreation. Typically, there is no window from which the prisoner can see outside, inmates are not allowed to have clocks or watches, and correctional officers control light in the cell. The prisoner is permitted to shower once every four days.

The deleterious effects of isolation are well known, so—officially, at least—there are legal limits on the length of time a prisoner can be held under such conditions. Still, most inmates are unfamiliar with the relevant penal codes, there is no one around to verify compliance, and correctional officers routinely work around these restrictions. At one prison, recalls Carceral, the official maximum period for Adjustment Segregation status was eight days. Yet members of the staff could shuffle paper, assign the prisoner in question a different status, and leave him in the same cell under the same conditions. A prisoner who has been held in Adjustment Segregation status for eight days can be charged with a new offense, reassigned to TLU for a day or so (but not given any of his property), found guilty, and then reassigned to Adjustment Segregation for eight more days—all without ever leaving a particular cell.

The German word for boredom, *langeweile* is translated as a "long while." One suffers time during Adjustment Segregation, but this is not the boredom experienced by people in everyday life who find themselves, only temporarily, in tedious or unchallenging circumstances. It is, in fact, no easy matter to survive Adjustment Segregation with one's mental faculties intact. Baca remembers his efforts to endure the resulting madness:

> My eyes weren't alone in playing tricks on me: I scratched and slapped at insects crawling over my flesh, which turned out to be tiny bits of iron shavings that had been embedded in my flesh when I was smashed to the welding-floor ground by the guards. . . .
>
> But these physical delusions were trivial compared to the insanity I got lost in. Ominous howling noises came through the walls. I was certain that Black gang members were coming to kill me through the crawl spaces behind the cells where the wiring and plumbing was. Lying perfectly still in the dark for hours, I could hear them gathering outside the door. . . .
>
> To keep from going insane, I started to do sit-ups, push-ups, and jumping jacks. I'd splash cold water over my naked body and sleep on the cool concrete floor, with no blanket, mattress, or sheet. I was constantly clawing at itches in my growing beard. Here in my own dark world, I had control only over the cold button on the sink, and I pushed it a hundred times a day, gulping until I was bloated, bathing until I was drenched. To squeeze every

last drop of restless energy from me I masturbated, sometimes six times a day. I tried anything to pass the time, but the moment finally came when I was tired of waiting. I was so depressed I couldn't stand it anymore. I wanted to get out. I curled up naked on the cot and quit eating. I forgot about life, forgot about myself, and just let time pass.[75]

"I was so bored," remembers Fisher, "that I actually felt like I was losing my mind."[76] Renaud describes Adjustment Segregation as "twenty-four hours of enforced loneliness."[77] At high-security facilities, he continues, the "level of isolation is such that most of the inmates I've spoken to all agree that merely holding on to one's sanity required a level of strength and inner resources they did not know they had."[78] Segregation "is the slowest time I ever experienced," says Carceral. "Slower than when I was sent to my room and had to wait for my father to get home. One's mind never stops processing the environment, and the solitude will have a man talking out loud to himself. I had nothing but my own mind to drive myself nuts."

The third stage of the segregation process is Program Segregation. In this status, the prisoner is given certain property rights (usually less than with TLU but more than with Adjustment Segregation). "From personal experience," states Carceral, "I can assure you that after doing ten days straight in a cell, by myself, with nothing, I was happy to have a TV or radio to break up the time." At this stage, many prisons place two inmates in the same cell, which did not make serving this time any easier for Carceral:

I have always told others that seg was boring, but it is much more. One may ask, "How do you survive?" It is all about survival. The state unknowingly teaches survival skills merely by placing a man in a cell, cut off from everything. I prefer to be in seg alone, versus with another man. I can pace the cell when I choose; I can talk out loud; I don't have to use the toilet in front of another prisoner. Each man will dig into himself to find something to occupy his mind. Segregation is state-sponsored terrorism. To overcome the terrorists, a man does not look toward the outside, but looks inside himself to survive. He must fill his unstopping mind with activity to pass the time.

During Program Segregation, prisoners are supposed to receive recreation for one hour every other day. However, Carceral offers the usual caveat concerning this temporal amenity: "Don't believe everything you hear.

Prisoners are out of sight and out of mind. If no one's present to enforce the rule, then the rule can be ignored." Similarly, the maximum stay in Program Segregation is officially 365 days per disciplinary report, but prisoners who pick up another disciplinary report while under this status can be kept in these conditions for a much longer period. Carceral attests to the fact that the latter contingency "is common with this type of deprivation." Once the prisoner's stay in Program Segregation is completed, he or she returns to the general population.

Like the original prison sentence (of which it is merely an installment), the segregation process is a timetable for retribution. Segregation consists of temporal progression through three stages, which are measured in twenty-four-hour increments from one's disciplinary hearing. If a prisoner is found guilty at 1:15 P.M., then he or she will be scheduled for release at 1:15 P.M. and not a minute sooner. In kindred fashion, one's property and activity allowances (such as recreation) vary across stages of the segregation process. The prisoner is deprived of intervals of time—at certain activities and with one's property. These changes to the regular schedule alter the pace of life and the prisoner's temporal experience.

The segregation process is only part of the disciplinary system. Like segregation, however, these other penalties are time-related forms of reprisal. As Carceral puts it, "At this point, I'm sure you've picked up on the fact that all punishments are temporal." Unsubmissive prisoners may be deprived of recreation for weeks at a time. They may be confined to a "feed cell" for thirty days (i.e., they must eat all of their meals in that cell). They may be restricted to their housing unit for a specified period of time or suffer a month without access to the canteen. They may be kept from attending agreeable programs or they may be assigned hours of extra duty at onerous tasks. Prisoners view these punishments as secondary sentences. Carceral hears them complain, "I have to clean the shitter for the man for two weeks" or "When I'm paroled from my cell, I'll get recreation back."

TIME AS PUNISHMENT

On the first page of Michel Foucault's book, *Discipline and Punish*, he quotes from documents that describe the public torture and execution of "Damiens the regicide" in 1757. Given the nature of his crime, Damiens was condemned to extraordinary suffering:

The flesh will be torn from his breasts, arms, thighs and calves with red-hot pincers, his right hand, holding the knife with which he committed the said parricide, burnt with sulfur, and, on those places where the flesh will be torn away, poured molten lead, boiling oil, burning resin, wax and sulfur melted together and then his body drawn and quartered by four horses and his limbs and body consumed by fire, reduced to ashes and his ashes thrown to the winds.[79]

Despite the barbarity of this itemization (from our contemporary perspective), a version of quantitative rationality is both tacit and intended. With these seemingly redundant penalties, those in authority meant to convey the magnitude of his crime via the enumerated dimensions of his punishment. Still, what was done to Damiens cannot be understood as the consequences of a rational calculus. As the sociologist Emile Durkheim taught us, it represents instead the discharge of moral emotions (especially collective outrage) and the furious retribution that is its correlate.[80]

The people who invented prisons prided themselves on having abandoned such gruesome spectacles. In place of vengeful violence, they substituted the cold and calculable punishment of time served in prison. Ostensibly, the measurement of time in standard (i.e., quantitative) units provides a basis for the rational calculus of justice that is missing in physical torment. What they have achieved, however, is not as rational as it may appear to those of us who take this system for granted. A sheriff's deputy faced forty-five years in prison for three counts of sex with a sixteen-year-old girl. A girl in Indiana received a sentence of sixty years in prison for a crime committed when she was fifteen years old. A paroled inmate was sentenced to one hundred years in prison for shooting a store clerk during a robbery. Another young man was sentenced to life in prison for a number of unarmed robberies and aggravated assaults. In Florida, the law calls for a prison sentence of at least twenty years whenever a gun is fired during the commission of a crime. Thus, Randal Ratledge, 58, faced a 120-year sentence for firing two shots in the air and shouting profanities at six neighbors (none of whom were injured). Ariel Castro was sentenced to life plus one thousand years. James Holmes was sentenced to twelve consecutive life terms plus 3,318 years in prison. Sentences of this sort are quite common, and they represent the temporal equivalent of redundant torture inflicted on someone who killed a monarch centuries ago. Time in prison has supplanted punishment of the body, but, beneath surface differences, our criminal justice system continues to be centrally concerned with angry and gratuitous retribution.

How much time should one serve for a particular crime? Is it even possible to specify that figure by means of a rational calculus? Should one serve more time for burglary or battery? Legislative and judicial bodies constantly tinker with our laws without ever arriving at definitive answers to these questions. When we ask ourselves questions of this kind, it quickly becomes apparent that, with our sentencing guidelines and procedures, we are not doing something akin to measuring the flour we need to bake a cake. In the mistreatment of Mark DeFriest, the judicial allocation of time as punishment is revealed to be the mere semblance of a rational calculus. "He was originally sentenced to four years on a burglary conviction for taking his father's tools before his will could be executed."[81] Yet suffering from autism and unable to "handle the prison system because of his mental health issues," the original penalty "turned into a virtual life sentence" due to several escapes, attempted escapes, and "nearly four hundred disciplinary reports."[82] As Florida Commission on Offender Review chairwoman Melinda Coonrod put it, "He's not a murderer, he's not a rapist, he doesn't have a history of violence." What was the outcome of this review? "In 2014, the commission knocked seventy years off his parole date after he went more than two years without any disciplinary issues."[83] Two years later, he was paroled, his release coming "thirty-six years after being convicted of stealing mechanic tools his father bequeathed to him."[84]

Punishment should fit the crime. Officially, at least, this is one of the guiding principles of our legal proceedings. The chief derivative is a top-down perspective on the social construction of time in prison. Our criminal justice system is based on the conceit that all crimes have precise temporal equivalencies, and those in authority claim to manipulate the time convicts serve through early release for good behavior. In actuality, the sentence is an artifact of public indignation, state-sponsored vengeance, prejudice and discrimination, personal competence, legal representation, plea bargaining, and other extraneous matters. The time one serves is not a rational metric for the severity of one's crime. Likewise, instead of operating as a numerical quid pro quo for the extraction of good behavior, early release reflects the vagaries of rules and their enforcement, demographic pressures due to overcrowding, and widespread efforts to game the system. At all prisons, moreover, but especially those that are run for profit, early release is antithetical to the commodification of convict time.[85] From this commercial standpoint, time in prison *is* a resource, but, of course, not for the convicts themselves.

Prison administrators use an inmate's disciplinary record to assess his or her institutional adjustment. In so doing, they invoke a distinctive temporal orientation. Disciplinary reports concern past misconduct. The state seldom records anything positive about a prisoner's behavior. Confronting a complex and fluctuating set of rules, prisoners find it hard to stay out of trouble. In everyday life, observed Goffman, one can engage in stigma management by withholding discrediting information from others.[86] In prison, however, an inmate's disciplinary record is public and permanent information concerning his or her previous transgressions. It follows that disciplinary reports lengthen sentences in largely indeterminate fashion because most prisoners find it difficult to elude trouble of some kind with the correctional officers.

Caught in a vortex of capriciousness, uncertainty, commodification, and temporal retribution, prisoners serve time that cannot be understood as a rational calculus of the debt they owe society. For prisoners, the time they serve is neither a resource nor a precise number of days between now and their release. It is, rather, an indefinite and punitive period of temporal discipline.

Chapter Five

NO FUTURE ON THE HORIZON

We have examined the structural and procedural factors that shape temporal experience in prison: unchanging schedules, the sensorium of incarceration, limited resources, lack of autonomy, and baffling enforcement of ubiquitous but ambiguous rules. Together, these factors constitute a temporal regime with problematic implications for one's perception of time. Here, we shift the focus of our analysis to the ways in which this regime diminishes a prisoner's attention to the future.

Today is the tenth of August. In less than two weeks, Flaherty will be attending the 2016 meeting of the American Sociological Association in Seattle. In less than two months, he will begin a one-year fellowship as Visiting Professor of Sociology with the Aarhus Institute of Advanced Studies in Denmark. Barring unforeseen circumstances, he can look forward to these events. Thomas Meisenhelder states, "It is one's personal projects *in the future* that give structure and meaning to the life-world."[1] Why does the future play this crucial role in our lives?

Our view of the future is determined by our cultural context. Historically, human beings have rendered time meaningful by virtue of two distinct cosmologies. Ancient systems of time reckoning were predominantly cyclical, but a linear system of time reckoning emerged in Western civilization. As Peter Berger notes, the origins of this linear system can be traced to the "messianic-millenarian" Christianity that arose in the Middle East some two thousand years ago.[2] This cosmology assumed that "the suffering or injustice of the present" would be "overcome in a glorious future."

A secular (or scientific) version of linear cosmology developed during the sixteenth century. Like its religious predecessor, however, it presumed that the future would be different and better than the past (due to invention and discovery, of course, rather than a messiah). This perspective values change and progress instead of tradition and the status quo. Whether religious or scientific in content, this linear cosmology serves as a symbolic universe. "With regard to the future," moreover, "it establishes a common frame of reference for the projection of individual actions."[3]

Socialization is the causal linkage between culture and consciousness. It follows that the meaning of time is conditioned by social institutions. "Temporality is an intrinsic property of consciousness," argue Peter Berger and Thomas Luckmann, because human beings are self-consciously aware of their own endurance: "Every individual is conscious of an inner flow of time."[4] The subjective meaning of time will vary with one's circumstances, but in Western civilization, at least, this stream of consciousness has been conceptualized as the tripartite conjugation of human experience: past, present, and future.[5]

Our emotions are derived from the socially constructed meanings in this symbolic universe. We can reflect on the past, but we cannot undo it. In contrast, the future seems open and flexible. As a people, we are imbued with positive feelings for the future. It is the temporal locus for optimism. With proper anticipation and planning, it is where our dreams will be realized. While planning confidently for the future, our lives seem stable and marked by self-control. Hope is a facet of the future. The attainment of goals leaves us with a deeply satisfying sense of progress toward desired outcomes.

Inmates must relinquish this cultural orientation once they enter prison. Suddenly, they find themselves in the grip of a temporal regime with no future on the horizon. Behind bars, inmates learn that the future is irrelevant or aversive. This transition is another wrenching aspect of their temporal experience. Any effort to consider or plan for the future is systematically thwarted by three features of incarceration. First, throughout their social organization, prisons are predominantly concerned with one's past transgressions. Second, given the unchanging routine of life in prison, inmates experience and adopt a cyclical system of time reckoning. Third, due to indeterminate sentences, most prisoners have no idea when they will be released.

THE IRREVOCABLE PAST

From the standpoint of the Puritans, who pioneered the use of prisons in America, criminal behavior revealed something irrevocable in the character of the perpetrator. "According to the Puritan reading of the Bible," observes Kai Erikson, "there were only two important classes of people on earth—those who had been elected to everlasting life and those who had been consigned forever to hell."[6] As a result, they did not take the offender's prospects for rehabilitation into account:

> Puritan theories of human development began with the assumption that men do not change a great deal as they mature or are exposed to different life experiences, and in this sense the settlers of the Bay had little faith in the promise that men might "reform" or overcome any pronounced deviant leanings.[7]

A vast body of social science research falsifies the Puritan notion of predestination. It has long been known, for example, that criminal involvement declines rapidly with age, which is not what we would expect to see if human beings were incapable of rehabilitation. Nonetheless, the Puritan theory of justice became "the model for almost every maximum security prison built in America."[8]

Puritans assumed that the criminal precedes the crime. In other words, the source of crime lies within the individual and not the environment. From religious tenets, they inferred that criminal behavior simply reveals what was there all along: an essential flaw of character. In contemporary America, this theology has been largely supplanted by a medical and psychological ideology, but it has parallel implications for institutions that are "correctional" in name only.[9] Now, as then, those who run prisons resist the idea that prisoners can change for the better. The people in their charge are "convicts"; they have been convicted of criminal behavior and must pay their debt to society with intervals of time. Prison administrators fatalistically presume that, no matter what transpires during incarceration, the convict's future will not differ from his or her past. In keeping with this ideology, the structure and procedures in prison focus on the past (i.e., what the inmate did to get here and what has happened since). Prisons impose a new conjugation on human experience. There is only the present (as a result of the past); the future will be more of the same. By allocating little or nothing to rehabilitation, administrators ensure recidivism will occur, which they mistake as evidence in support of this ideology.

The future begins to lose its meaning as soon as the inmate is separated from the nonprison world. With incarceration, the world outside of prison becomes a dream state—a figment of memory and imagination with little or no tangible basis in reality. A prisoner's thoughts concerning the future are grounded in the past of a world that no longer exists. Already, subsequent to sentencing, the prisoner has not been present to witness its ongoing changes. Repeatedly, observes Carceral, fellow inmates rue the fact that the nonprison world they knew is gone, and they have been left behind. In Washington Irving's famous short story, Rip Van Winkle awakens from his slumber to find that he has been absent from the life of his village for at least twenty years. Incarceration brings about something akin to a Rip Van Winkle effect, except that prisoners are frustratingly aware that life is passing them by even as it moves into a future they cannot share. The impact varies with the length of one's sentence. While Carceral was locked up, people in the world outside started using personal computers, the Internet, and telephones with touch screens. For long-term inmates, consequently, adjustment to life outside of prison is quite problematic.

Educational institutions are oriented toward the future. This is why one's education ends at the beginning—a commencement. Contrastingly, social institutions that concern criminal justice are oriented toward the past: the crime one has committed and the temporal retribution one receives as punishment. An emphasis on the past actually begins prior to conviction, during plea bargaining or one's trial. Either way, these proceedings focus on one's past transgressions, not future prospects. In notorious cases, a prisoner's past is fodder for newspapers, TV, and social media. It follows that fellow inmates and members of the staff will be familiar with (or curious about) the particulars of a new inmate's past prior to his or her arrival at the prison. Regardless of whether one is notorious or unknown, however, the court sends an individual to prison with a "judgment of conviction" that specifies one's crime and years to be served as one's sentence.

An emphasis on the past only intensifies after incarceration, where policy and procedures engender a sense of futility. The prison administration will focus on an inmate's past by classifying convicts in terms of crime, sentence, and behavior subsequent to imprisonment. This information is scrupulously recorded and reviewed periodically, forming a permanent file (or "jacket") that follows an inmate if he or she transfers to another facility. It encapsulates an utterly retrospective orientation that ignores an inmate's future potential (which, of course, is not lost on convicts themselves). The length of one's sentence is of primary importance, but no one is quite sure what it will be, which is a powerful contributing factor for the pervasive sense of futurelessness among inmates. In common parlance, we are apt to discuss "the length" of one's sentence as if it were a precise figure, but indeterminate sentences make one's time in prison unknowable.

Futurelessness has experiential and behavioral consequences: all an inmate cares about is here and now. This extreme focus on the present decreases a prisoner's temporal projection. "Convicts have a saying," observes Carceral. "Burn it up! If you want it, and it's available, get all you can." At a minimum-security prison, one kitchen worker called Archie expressed the prevailing attitude: "It's state shit! When it's gone, get more out of the stockroom. The truck comes in every week with supplies. They can order more!" Acknowledging that many inmates steal as much as possible, Carceral suggests that this philosophy of *now* stems from the absence of a knowable future. Janitors steal cleaning supplies to supplement the low pay they receive from the state instead of cleaning their own housing unit. Among kitchen workers, declares Jimmy Lerner, "stealing food is practically a built-in job perk."[10] Here, again, the temporal regime sets the stage for prison dysfunction.

With no future on the horizon, it can be difficult to stay optimistic and stave off desperation. The prison letters of George Jackson are paradigmatic. They track his trajectory toward angry fatalism. His time in prison begins with an indeterminate sentence: "When he was eighteen [i.e., in 1959], Jackson was sentenced from one year to life for stealing $70 from a gas station. He spent the next eleven years in prison, eight and a half of them in solitary confinement."[11] In a letter to his mother on February 25, 1965, he assures her that "I should be out of here this year. I have complied with all of their demands: group counseling, school, clean conduct record. I go to [the parole] board next time they meet."[12] On May 2, 1965, he tells his parents, "I am still in isolation. Nothing has changed since I wrote you last."[13] Poignantly, in a letter written to his mother in June 1965, he is troubled by the temporal uncertainty of his sentence: "I would be happy though to just know how long I will be held, even if it was ten years. I'd feel better knowing."[14] However, in a letter to his father dated September 6, 1965, he relays disappointing news: "They informed me that I 'can forget about the board transfer or the main population facilities here in the prison.' These were their words."[15] Remaining, therefore, in isolation, he is "locked in a cell twenty-four hours a day."[16]

In a letter to his mother on December 23, 1965, Jackson does not believe that he will be kept in such conditions much longer: "A couple of months more of this and I think they will let up on me."[17] In another letter to his mother, dated February 23, 1966, he still assumes some temporal efficacy: "I'll be with you as soon as I can. I've got some clean time in now already and plan to do as well for the rest of this year so that in December they will let me go. They have promised me this anyway."[18] Seven months later, he expresses even greater confidence in the future: "I go to the [parole] board in December and as I have stated before I have met all of their terms. My release is almost assured."[19] Yet he has bad news for his mother in a short letter dated January 3, 1967, where he comes to grips with the fact that his future is unknowable: "I have at least another fourteen or eighteen months to do. Of course I could do the rest of my life here. . . . They gave me no consideration at the [parole] board, the same people that gave me their promise last year."[20] The indeterminate length of his sentence is on his mind when he writes to his sister on January 31, 1967: "My minimum is one year, so I've got seven times more than necessary."[21] Temporal uncertainty is tinged with despair in a letter to a friend on July 15, 1967: "I am in [the] adjustment center here for an undefined amount of time."[22] In his letter to Angela Davis on May 28, 1970, he describes himself as a man with "no tomorrows."[23] One month later, he sends an unequivocal declaration to his editor, Gregory Armstrong: "Desperate men do desperate things."[24] Bereft of hope for a different future, on August 21, 1971, he was shot to death by correctional officers inside of San Quentin prison while trying to escape.

With incarceration, the prisoner is no longer the architect of what will happen. Thomas Meisenhelder argues that a convict's own intentions are eclipsed by an institutionalized future: "The physical and social isolation of the prison removes the prisoner from any subjectively real connection to or control over a future that will take place *outside the institution.* And the future 'inside' the prison is imposed, artificial, and meaningless to the spontaneous life of the inmate."[25] Members of the staff ensure that a prisoner's temporal reality is predominantly retrospective. In part, they do so by deflecting any talk about the inmate's future with responses that invoke his or her past. Prisoners who talk about the future beyond incarceration are viewed as having an "adjustment problem" and will be reprimanded accordingly, as is evident in the following instance witnessed by Carceral:

OFFICER: "You're an inmate!"
PRISONER: "Yeah, but when I get out . . ."
OFFICER: "You're a criminal; you didn't get to prison by going to church."

The prisoner *is* something, something that must be atoned for, yet retribution will not change the past or the future.

In his influential article, "On Being Sane in Insane Places," David Rosenhan describes how he and seven other pseudopatients "gained secret admission to twelve different [psychiatric] hospitals."[26] They discovered that "once labeled schizophrenic, the pseudopatient was stuck with that label."[27] Everything they did was interpreted symptomatically. When, for example, Rosenhan and his confederates recorded field notes, this "was seen as an aspect of their pathological behavior."[28] He concludes that psychiatry "locates the sources of aberration within the individual and only rarely within the complex of stimuli that surrounds him."[29] Prison inmates confront similar circumstances. Members of the staff presume that, based on past behavior, the prisoners in their charge deserve incarceration as well as disrespectful treatment and cannot be changed for the better. From the staff's perspective, writes Sylvester Long, "every word out of an inmate's mouth was a lie and . . . they are con men."[30] The absence of corroborating evidence from a prisoner's past does not dissuade them. "Don't tell me your record isn't bad," a counselor says to Jimmy Baca. "Because you don't have a long rap sheet only means you've gotten away with a lot of things."[31] Obviously, there is no way to refute this argument.

The prison staff seize every opportunity to focus on the shameful details of an inmate's past. When, for instance, Robert Berger's counselor reviews his record, only discrediting information is cited, which indicates the need for reclassification:

"My God," the counselor exclaimed, "you have been in seven prisons, in the Hole three times, have two incident reports, served two sentences back to back, and have even been re-indicted during the first bid. Also, I see that a 'management variable' has been added to your file, resulting in your security level being raised. Additionally, you are a five-time felon. Berger, what is up with you? You're supposed to be a white-collar criminal, but your record here reads like an incorrigible inmate's file."[32]

In diverse situations, a convict's past (prior to and during incarceration) is repeatedly summarized by various members of the staff in order to label the inmate's identity. Bombarded by reminders of past transgressions, inmates are expected to embrace this identity and resign themselves to an institutionalized future. Wherever they interact with staff, prisoners face a recurrent and demeaning question: "You think it's time you took responsibility for your actions?"[33]

Veronica Compton-Wallace, a long-term inmate at Washington Corrections Center for Women, asserts that a prison's "two major objectives" are "retribution and control."[34] Respectively, these aims concern the past and present, not the future. A prisoner's annual hearing offers the staff a formal setting in which to emphasize the past. At this recurrent degradation ceremony, officials review one's crime, sentence, and disciplinary reports. These hearings are consequential. They determine one's classification, with broad ramifications for a prisoner's security level, job, and access to programs that must be completed prior to release. At one of his hearings, Baca's request for schooling is denied, and he objects to this decision: "But the fights; I had to do what I did. You know what's going on. I was defending myself! . . . I know what I was! But I'm trying to change! I'm just asking for a fucking chance!"[35] Mad Dog Madril, a correctional officer, is unmoved by Baca's anguished plea as he gives voice to the chief temporal rubric of retribution: "It's a fucking prison and don't you forget it. You're here to be punished."[36] For Baca and other inmates, these hearings instill a new perspective on the future: "I truly thought they were going to keep me in prison forever."[37]

Carceral endured dozens of such hearings. Over and over again, the staff would recapitulate his past. In the course of these proceedings, a prisoner is required to acknowledge his or her transgressions:

"You were convicted of first-degree murder in 1982 and given a sentence of life?"
"Yes."
"You got into a fight and killed a man?"
"Yes."

"You were twenty years old at the time?"

"Yes." [Actually, he was nineteen.]

"You are appearing before us for your regularly scheduled annual review. It notes here your conduct is good with your last major ticket [i.e., disciplinary report] in 1988."

"Yes."

"This ticket was for the possession of intoxicant with THC. . . ."

"Yes, but I would like to remind the committee that this incident was in 1988, twenty years ago, and I have not been in trouble since."

Twenty years after the incident in question, the hearing committee is still asking Carceral about a disciplinary report for possession of marijuana. Carefully orchestrated, these proceedings concentrate on ritualized recitations of the inescapable past. As Long puts it, "something that happened thirty years ago haunts you in prison, [and] there's no opportunity to change."[38]

A hearing is not about what an inmate hopes for the future; it is about what he or she has done wrong—in the distant and recent past. The prisoner's past earned this present, and the future is irrelevant. Efforts to alter the temporal framework of this script are routinely deflected. At another hearing, for instance, Carceral tells the committee that he is trying to continue his education: "I would like to finish my PhD, go to the community custody system, maybe obtain a job in my area, and parole." But the committee chair rejects Carceral's attempt to envision a very different future for himself: "I think we're getting ahead of ourselves. We have to decide what to do with you today." Only Carceral's classification is at issue, and it is simply a function of his crime and institutional adjustment. Carceral's conversation with Nolen, a fellow prisoner, confirms comparable treatment:

"They only talked about what I did. . . ."

"Program Review Committee?"

"Yeah, they only want to talk about what I did to get here."

"So what else did they say?"

"I'm not being transferred because I have too much time left and need to do a program—a program I can't get unless they transfer me!"

Nolen is trapped in the present by something akin to a catch-22. Another prisoner, Grayson, describes feeling enmeshed at his hearing in a television program that keeps rehashing the past: "There is no way I can change the channel. And, even though I'm the main character, I'm sitting in the chair watching." Like Carceral, neither of them can get the hearing committee to consider the future.

Aside from incarceration, the prison staff is primarily engaged in the recording and classification of misconduct. These processes establish a prisoner's record of institutional adjustment. They contribute to a prisoner's record in disparate ways, but that record is the principal reference for discussions at every hearing, and it is centrally concerned with insubordination. Long complains that "prison administrators are taught to only look at the wrong in an inmate, no matter how much good he does."[39] Long points out that, given the system's sensitivity to misconduct, good deeds go unnoticed:

> They have a random urine test and [there are] two ways to fail. One way is, if you do not give any urine within one hour, then you have fail[ed] the test with no substance. The other way is, if you have had any drugs and they take the test, then you will of course fail and that's a major ticket. The ticket goes into your inmate file to prove that you failed! When you pas[s] that same test, nothing is put into your file. "Why?" It is just as important to know that I passed as it is to know that I failed.[40]

The bureaucratization of an inmate's record makes it difficult to modify one's future (or even think about it) in deliberate fashion.

Progress toward parole is contingent on one's classification, so release is subject to the same institutional disregard for the future. Outside of prison, education represents a fundamental way to alter one's future in purposive fashion. A proper education in prison could be even more valuable, given the clientele in question, but, behind bars, nothing of that sort is available. And, in any case, the Parole Commission will be unimpressed by credentials earned in prison. They will be noted, if at all, on the summary page of the prisoner's hearing record, where there is a single line reserved for the completion of various programs (such as drug treatment) lumped together as evidence of institutional adjustment. As Michael Santos tells us, far more attention will be paid to infractions of any kind, no matter how trivial they may be: "Regardless of what contributions a prisoner makes to the system, or what the offender accomplishes in efforts to prepare himself for a more successful future, only negative adjustments have an impact on records kept by the so-called correctional system."[41]

If release is granted, the decision will be based upon one's irrevocable past: criminal conviction, time served, and record during imprisonment. As we have seen, staying out of trouble is easier said than done, and minor transgressions outweigh major steps forward (such as the completion of one's degree). None of what matters is influenced by a prisoner's efforts at self-improvement. There is, consequently, no sense of personal efficacy for modifying one's future. Instead, there is only learned helplessness. A prisoner often views the decision for or against parole as a mystery or luck of the draw. "I stepped into a hearing one day," says Carceral, "where the commissioner recommended a release date . . . [yet] eventually went from a six-month deferral [his previous status] to an eleven-month deferral of parole. I was lucky my security status didn't change. Others were not as lucky." Having stayed out of trouble, a prisoner named Hawkins earned work release into the community where he was employed for over a year at an automobile repair shop. A previous hearing had given him a six-month deferral. So, Carceral was shocked to learn (from another prisoner) that Hawkins was in segregation awaiting transfer to a maximum-security prison because, at his most recent hearing, the Commission decided "he must do his discharge date" (i.e., an eighteen-month deferral) and upgraded his security classification. The future Hawkins had envisioned was gone. There is an old joke from the workplace, that doing a good job here is like wetting your pants in a dark suit; it gives you a warm feeling, but nobody notices. In prison, a fortiori, good behavior does not affect the future in a dependable way, but bad behavior of any kind (especially crime committed in the unchangeable past) brings about long deferrals that push the future out of sight.[42] Given the certainty of uncertainty, prisoners lack self-confidence in their ability to secure a reliable future. Under such conditions, it is impossible to steer one's actions toward a particular goal.

"All we have is your file; what else is there to examine?" A commissioner says that to Carceral during one of his parole hearings. Strictly speaking, he is correct. The commission has no other direct contact with the prisoner. They meet with an inmate for ten to twenty minutes, perhaps once a year, and, as Long points out, their decision will be based upon the contents of one's file: "The parole board didn't know me, and had never saw my face and just read my file to judge me."[43] As with classification, therefore, the focus of parole deliberations is on past transgressions. Evidence of personal growth and future potential is disregarded. In Carceral's state, life-sentenced prisoners meet with the parole commission. One of them, an acquaintance named Nick, laments his inability to modify the future:

> [The commissioner] wasn't impressed with anything I tried to do after being locked up. The guy told me the board is well aware of the changes which occur with life-sentence inmates. They change the most, since they are incarcerated the longest. Then he reminded me why I was in prison! He wanted to know why I did what I did.

Another prisoner, Hoops, was sentenced to twenty years. He was eligible for parole, but, as he told Carceral in the following exchange, his efforts to gain an early release through evidence of personal reform counted for nothing in the eyes of the commission:

> "It was about six years before my discharge date. I started to realize I wasn't moving. I had been enrolled in self-help, A.A., cognitive intervention, and a religious program. When I reached eleven on twenty, the parole board gave me maximum discharge."
> "Why? Did they say?"
> "The parole board told me my crime was too heinous. No early parole for me. None of the programs mattered, so three more years, I'll be out. Once I learned all that, I dropped out of mostly everything."

Like so many others, this man learned that good deeds do not augur a shorter sentence. We see in this extract the realization of temporal futility. There is nothing he or his colleagues can do to improve their future prospects.

Classification and parole hearings are not the only aspects of life in prison that undermine one's attention to the future. There is no vocational connection between education and subsequent employment. School and work do not offer related trajectories toward a desired future. What incentive is there to earn one's GED? A job, trade school, or college is not the next step. The administration provides no encouragement and very little in the way of resources. When Carceral asks about educational opportunities at a minimum-security prison, the Captain responds, "This is a work center, not a program." As Santos puts it, "Whereas the counselor may be working toward the advancement of his or her career, most prisoners interest themselves only in passing their time as easily as possible."[44]

Incarceration does not foster a future orientation. There is no long-term work ethic. Many prisoners have jobs, but no prisoner has a career. Hard work is not rewarded. "Pay scales in the federal prison system are low," writes Santos, "with average monthly earnings among inmates hovering at less than twenty dollars . . . there is no incentive system for inmates to work hard."[45] Job-related tasks are simple, repetitive, and boring. If a prisoner arrives with any lingering ambition, the temporal regime soon ensures that it is supplanted by the indolent attitude endemic to incarceration. Inmates express contempt for a hard worker with terms like "working fool" or "suck-up." Reflecting on his first days behind bars, Carceral remembers that "I hadn't caught on yet to the prison work ethic: do your job minimally without getting fired."[46] A more experienced prisoner tells Carceral that he walks too fast on the way to their clerical jobs. His coworker would ask, "What's the purpose? Why hurry to have to sit in boredom? Eventually, you'll get it." Carceral would come to understand what his coworker already knew: there is little for them to do; no one cares how well or fast they do it; and that will never change.

Prisoners adopt a new temporal pace to work and life. Their jobs entail unskilled and often demeaning labor. In the case of Robert Berger, a former corporate executive, his food-service job was folding plastic utensils inside paper napkins.[47] Long notes that inmates will accept jobs in prison they would never consent to on the outside.[48] Some jobs have no responsibilities whatsoever; others are just treated as a lark. At one point, Carceral and a coworker inventory dead people for the historical society. They had a recurrent joke: "What's the rush? They're not going anywhere." Eventually, they are given a quota, but nobody enforces it. No one even checks their work, so they just start making things up: "I gave this guy two wives, fourteen children, and three sheep. Think they'll notice?" Like others, he must engage in the pretense of make-work, not to stay out of trouble, but to fend off boredom. Still, minimally at least, a job is something to do, a way to kill time. The only thing worse than having a job is not having one. Unassigned prisoners have only recreation with which to fill the long empty days of incarceration.

There *is* work in prison that rewards effort handsomely, but it happens to be criminal enterprise. With such activities, an inmate makes more money in less time, but that is not the half of it. This prisoner can also abandon the boredom and subservience of menial labor for the seductions of crime and the glamour of evil.[49] With this sort of work, moreover, an inmate can at least imagine and bargain for a different future—one that is chosen instead of imposed, a future that is perhaps ignoble, but one that he or she has a hand in fashioning. It is a future that holds the promise of drama and excitement, one in which the prisoner can be a protagonist rather than a slave. None of this is possible with a job assigned by the prison administration. Ironically, then, the temporal regime tacitly encourages prisoners to participate in an underground economy not unlike that which led to their conviction in the first place.

Most prisoners want no part of criminal enterprise, but that means they have nothing to fill their days, save a futureless cycle of repetitive and mundane activities. Their time is only punctuated by the routine interruptions of an unchanging schedule (counts, meals, etc.). For these prisoners, the pace of life slows to a crawl in a seemingly endless present. Yet, retrospectively, days devoid of memorable activity are forgotten more quickly and more thoroughly than eventful days. It follows that, with so little to remember, prisoners like George Jackson experience the paradox of retrospective temporal compression more intensely than do people in everyday life: "Whatever it was that I lost these last ten years, I lost it suddenly. I can hardly imagine time passing any faster."[50] In an attempt to express the temporal distortion he perceives, Jackson resorts to translating from the standard temporal units of objective time to the standard temporal units of subjective time: "It seems like ten days rather than ten years."[51]

Futurelessness breeds a sense of futility. In turn, futility affects the way prisoners think about their current behavioral options. Why enroll in a parenting class if you have no idea when you will get to see your children? Why sign up for a drug treatment program if you do not anticipate parole in the near future? Nothing here and now is connected to the future beyond release. "I had a social worker tell me that I could take a few years to decide about going to school," recalls Carceral. From the social worker's perspective, "I had plenty of time to take it easy. It was an automatic assumption that I should be lazy." In every setting, inmates are indoctrinated to the unhurried pace of life behind bars.

Inmates do not realize the extent of their indoctrination until they are assigned to work release or granted parole. This tendency is illustrated by two men interviewed by Carceral, both of whom expressed reentry shock in response to the unfamiliar tempo of life outside of prison. One of them, Maxwell, was released after twenty years of incarceration. In his telephone conversation with Carceral, he was astonished by the pace of social inter-action: "People live out here. Time goes by so fast. Especially work! They expect a man to do something!" Similarly, the aforementioned Hawkins, on work release after eighteen years of incarceration, was amazed by the pace of work in an automobile repair shop:

After so long with the state, I got to learn to work again! There is none of that "wait just a moment" then get back to them tomorrow! I was working on a car where I exchanged the battery. The battery sat on the shelf for a while, so I put a thirty-minute quick charge on it. My boss asked me two times, "How's that car doing? Why are we waiting again?" and "Can you speed it up?" I laughed to myself, it's a thirty-minute charge! How can I speed that up? Well, after fifteen minutes, the car was gone and out the door! It was charging on the highway!

For these ex-convicts, as well as their confederates, a significant aspect of the Rip Van Winkle effect is unconscious accommodation to the slow pace of life in prison.

In everyday life, we think about what we hope to do in the future and take steps to realize these goals. Our imagination serves as the vehicle for a kind of time travel. We are, in effect, moving through time toward desired places, events, and identities. Convicts, however, resort to the word "fro-zen" to depict the fact that they are going nowhere. Eighteen when she is imprisoned, Amy Fisher broods about what she is missing:

Many friends did support me at first. When I left for prison, they would promise, "I'll write you. I'll keep in touch." But as one year changed into the next—and I was there seven years—we lost contact. The late teens and early twenties are a very transitional point in people's lives: they go to college, they graduate, they land their first job, they find their first real boyfriend. Later they were even getting married, and I was still sitting in prison, *frozen* in time as a teenager.[52]

In parallel fashion, Berger complains that friends and family have moved on toward their future lives, leaving him behind:

> It's amazing how many letters I received when I first started my bid [i.e., sentence] compared to the amount of mail I receive now. As time goes by people on the outside continue with their lives and issues get pushed into the past. With us it's different. We have no immediate future, and the way things were the day we entered prison is our present. [Our] future will start to happen again upon our release, [but] right now it's *frozen*.[53]

Systematically, a prisoner's environment suppresses the imagination of a future that diverges from current circumstances. According to Ken Lamberton, prisoners "live in a kind of endless present."[54]

Prisoners also counsel each other to be unconcerned with the future. On the face of it, this may appear to be further evidence of having fallen in with bad companions, but it is actually good advice in a predatory environment. For example, Baca's mentor, Macaron, gives him the following instructions on the irrelevance of the future:

> No one will help you here; you're on your own. Fuck family, dreams, hopes, plans; when it comes down to it, you do what you got to do. If you got a parole board hearing in the afternoon and someone jumps your case, you fuck them up, and if you get more time, you get more time.[55]

From this standpoint, one's disregard for the future is a necessary feature of incarceration. Many prisoners cannot afford to worry about the future; they are too busy trying to survive the present.

Convicts adapt to this setting and, in so doing, become complicit with the institutional focus on past transgressions. They contribute to the futurelessness of life in prison by classifying and judging each other in light of their past crimes. "What're you in for?" Lamberton has just entered his new dorm at Florence when he is confronted by that question from a fellow inmate.[56] "It's a long story," he says, not wishing to declare his crime, but the other prisoner persists, "What are you in for?"[57] When Lamberton admits to a sexual relationship with his fourteen-year-old student, he is told, "You can't stay here."[58] Not long after that, he has two fractured ribs and a hole in his head. ("I can see all the way into your skull," says the doctor who stiches his wounds.)[59]

Having developed a hierarchy based on their criminal biographies, prisoners exhibit elective affinity with the temporal regime. Another part of this hierarchy involves bragging about one's criminal exploits and prison experience. Using his cellmate, Kansas, as a prime example, Lerner observes that prisoners embellish their pasts in a game of one-upmanship:

> I have added up all the time Kansas claims to have done and the total is 547 years. He's been down, done time in Sing Sing, Arizona State Prison, Rahway, Marianna, and in Louisiana. He rattles off these credentials the same way a new candidate for our Corporate Fast Track program used to underwhelm me with his Fulbright, Harvard M.B.A., and Yale Law background.[60]

There is, then, an undeniable sense that prisoners collaborate with the temporal regime in the unremitting scrutiny of each other's past.

Prisoners ratify the temporal regime by living in the present. "You spend a lot of time thinking about how awful prison is rather than envisioning your future," writes Piper Kerman.[61] Or they talk about their past rather than their future. This is especially true of long-term inmates, even when they are not elderly. For these prisoners, any attention to the future is tinged with the painful realization that they will not be released for many years, if ever. Weirdly, there is a kind of nostalgia for the way things used to be:

> The Old Heads like to talk about the good old days in the joint—the late sixties and the seventies—when the guards ("the pigs!") were the true enemy instead of fellow convicts. When a Convict Code of Honor prevailed because back then, a Real Convict was a "Straight-up, Stand-up Con!"[62]

Prisoners stake competing claims to having been held in better or tougher conditions, and they relish every opportunity to regale fellow inmates with stories about their previous years of incarceration. Kansas is not an old man, but he wistfully shares memories of a grandiose past with Lerner:

> "Small-time shit, O. G." Kansas shakes his huge skinhead, eyes now filling with the familiar nostalgia that always augurs a long riff back to "the Kansas pen, O. G., where I was running a fucking *meth* lab right out of the bakery— none of this pussy pruno shit these punks got going here, y'unnerstan' what I'm sayin'? Fuck, dawg, I remember one time I was doing a little deuce in Marianna—that's *fed* time, bro, down in Florida, a real stand-up joint."[63]

There is no wondrously imagined future in his reveries; instead, he recounts the places he has been, the suffering he has endured, the small triumphs he has achieved.

Many years ago, Erving Goffman observed that inmates at mental hospitals devise an explanation or justification for their undeniable presence in that stigmatizing setting:

> The low position of inmates relative to their station on the outside, established initially through the stripping processes, creates a milieu of personal failure in which one's fall from grace is continuously pressed home. In response, the inmate tends to develop a story, a line, a sad tale—a kind of lamentation and apologia—which he constantly tells to his fellows as a means of accounting for his present low estate.[64]

Carceral notes that kindred accounts of one's past are equally prevalent in prison. These "crime stories," as he calls them, are autobiographical narratives concerning one's criminal history. As such, they represent significant aspects of discourse in correctional facilities. On the one hand, the prisoner is motivated to assemble and share this story. On the other hand, as Goffman argues, the convict will be "pressed" for this story by everyone else in the prison—including inmates, correctional officers, and members of the staff (especially those who sit on hearing committees or parole boards). The prisoner tells this story again and again, so it becomes well-rehearsed, evolves over time, and varies with the audience. This story is far more than the simple enunciation of one's crime. It is, on the contrary, a chance to highlight the mitigating circumstances that brought about that fateful moment, the ancillary issues that had a pronounced effect on one's punishment, and one's own sense of responsibility or remorse. Be that as it may, by wallowing in the past, prisoners play into the hands of those who would deny them a future of their own contrivance.

THE ENDLESS CYCLE

An all-embracing focus on the past is not the only factor that minimizes attention to the future. There is, as well, the seemingly endless repetition of routine activity. Sunny Jacobs decries "a repetitive cycle of preplanned menus year after year."[65] Prison is a subuniverse of social reality with unique temporal properties, among which is the predominance of a cyclical framework.

During the early days of his imprisonment, when Carceral would hurry to his assigned job, he was operating under the goal-oriented assumptions of a linear framework. "If I hurry, if I do good work, if I am productive now," he reasoned, "I will be rewarded in the future." Having adapted to life in prison, his coworker knows that a future markedly different than the present does not await them, no matter how much (or little) effort they put into their assigned tasks. This more experienced prisoner recognizes that they have an abundance of time and is only interested in killing some of it.

Fundamentally, the pace of life differs for prisoners and correctional officers. Convicts have no place to go and nothing to do, so there is no reason for them to hurry. In contrast, a small number of officers must manage a large number of prisoners, and this problem is exacerbated by overcrowding. Consequently, officers bully convicts to complete every task as quickly as possible. Albert Woodfox was familiar with this drill: "Even on the walk from our cell to the shower we'd be harassed. Guards would call out to us, 'Hurry up. Get in the shower, keep moving.' "[66] Of course, this effort to induce a sense of urgency offers prisoners an opportunity for temporal resistance. And by the same token, officers typically respond slowly, if at all, to requests from prisoners. Axiomatically, prisoners are slow when officers want them to hurry, and officers are slow when prisoners want them to hurry. These indignities demand reprisals, sooner or later. The outcome is an endless cycle of microaggressions on each other's temporal experience.

In the world outside of prison, we are synchronized to the overarching linear time of education, science, government, and the economy. These social institutions have subordinate cyclical patterns, but their hegemonic orientation is linear. Like the rest of us, prisoners have internalized this temporal outlook, but, subsequent to incarceration, it is radically inapplicable. Behind bars, the things that happened today will reoccur tomorrow. There are no reliable benchmarks or milestones. For Baca, "each day was as indistinguishable as the previous one."[67] Tomorrow offers nothing more than an opportunity to repeat your previous activities. With a surfeit of time, why should you try to do things quickly? Anything that is left unfinished will be waiting for you when the sun comes up. Repetition, not progress, is the ruling motif. From a temporal standpoint, incarceration is comparable to being stranded in a totally unfamiliar country.

Convicts experience cyclical time in a threefold sense. First, each day confronts the prisoner with ceaselessly repeating activities. These days are unrelated intervals of time in that they do not represent measurable parts of a journey toward a definite finish line. Outside of prison, one can enumerate a linear series of days leading to a wedding scheduled for the twelfth of December. With indeterminate sentences, the naive convict counting the days until his or her release is courting disappointment. Second, prisoners who cannot abide the futureless circularity of daily routine act up in various ways, which, in cyclical fashion, only lengthens their sentences. Andreas Schroeder summarizes this segment of the pattern:

> All around you you see men letting go and closing the vicious circle, men escaping for a single night with their wives, men plotting revenge that will only double their prison terms, men swaggering in defiance of a machine that isn't paying the slightest attention, its meter simply adding the years, implacably.[68]

Yet, eventually, most prisoners are released, whereupon they typically return to the same circumstances that spawned their criminal conduct in the first place. Repeatedly arrested and returned to prison, this biographical circularity represents the third way in which they experience cyclical time. "Life on the installment plan," that is how Jackson puts it: "three years of prison, three months on parole; then back to start all over again, sometimes in the same cell."[69]

Prisons are punitive and bureaucratic organizations. As such, those in authority seek to standardize the conduct of a captive population—the subordinate and stigmatized people in their custody. Despite notoriously recalcitrant clients, they manage this standardization by means of the calendar and the clock. With the calendar, we have a fixed system by which the year is subdivided. With the clock, we have a mechanical device for the invariant calculation of temporal uniformity. Together, these quantitative devices make for constancy and continuity in the regimentation of time. In everyday life, we employ these devices more or less voluntarily in an effort to coordinate our behavior with that of others. In prison, contrastingly, these devices are used by the temporal regime to impose a uniform schedule on an unwilling population, thereby creating an unchanging and alienating pattern of repetition.

For the prisoner, each day is subdivided into a specified (and unfailingly recurrent) time for sleeping, eating, working, playing, schooling, cleaning, counting, and so on. Every form of activity has a precisely assigned interval of time. Even "unscheduled" time is scheduled. Members of the staff insist on punctuality and attendance and mete out punishment for temporal deviance. One's entire existence is scheduled without courtesy of consultation. The temporal slot for any given activity is established, it seems, mechanistically—not by virtue of one's subjective experience and personal preference. Yet, as elements of a cyclical process, these intervals of time do not accumulate into something more significant. In Woodfox's words, a convict lives "the same day over and over," a relentless and meaningless routine.[70] Thus, life in prison is the temporal equivalent of running on a treadmill; one is engaged in activity but does not perceive oneself to be getting anywhere.

The organization of time conditions temporal experience. With mind-numbing repetition, writes Baca, "days blurred into boring weeks."[71] As a POW, Christopher Burney is similarly deprived of any diversions: "I had already established the routine by which I was to live, with little variation, for five hundred and twenty-six days."[72] The repetition of cyclical time is a reliable recipe for slowing the perceived passage of time, as noted by Ingrid Betancourt: "The days were all alike and seemed to last forever."[73] Cyclical time forces prisoners to inhabit a seemingly eternal now, where they are mired in a glut of time and protracted duration. She admits that "the future no longer interested me, nor did the outside world. They were simply inaccessible to me. I was living the present moment as in an eternity of relentless pain, without the hope it would ever end."[74]

Concentration on the present moment (with genuine disregard for the past or future) dilates one's perception of the passage of time. Each moment may be said to last "forever" in the parlance of those who enter this altered state of consciousness. It is a form of temporal agency (or "time work") that Michael Flaherty terms the "savoring complex."[75] Betancourt's futurelessness is prompted by an unexpected variation on this process. Involuntarily, she is transfixed by circumstances she cannot ignore. The level of concentration and its impact on perceived duration are comparable to what we see in the savoring complex, but the object of her heightened attention is the endless repetition of meaningless experience during her captivity. Ordinarily, one savors what is pleasurable. But what do we call it when that same level of attention is motivated by unsavory yet inextricable conditions? In large part, the futurelessness of prison is occasioned by one's extraordinary focus on the cyclical and inescapable reiteration of goings-on scheduled for the convenience of others.

An institutional obsession with the past and the endless reiteration of cyclical time are related facets of one's temporal experience in prison. A feeling of being ensnared in nonstop repetition is reinforced by the staff's persistent focus on the past. From their standpoint, the future is immaterial. "A man can be in prison for ten years," says Carceral, "but all they want to talk about is his presentence report." Confronted with this attitude, Carceral would think to himself, "Here we go again." The prisoner's past is the central topic of every conversation. No transformation of the prisoner's disposition is anticipated. One is warehoused with only the prospects of a fixed past and recurrent but pointless chores in the future. There is, then, no sense of growth or purpose. Ingrid Betancourt's mournful conclusion helps us see that, in large measure, prisoners' adaptation to cyclical time is forced upon them: "Long years of captivity lay ahead of us. We had to fill the day and not think about the future."[76]

In one way or another, the present recycles the past, and the future recedes from relevance. There is no forward momentum from the past, through the present, into the future. Research by Kathy Calkins examines the temporal experience of patients confined to a rehabilitation center because they suffer from chronic illnesses.[77] She finds that as they adopt a cyclical view of time (an orientation fostered by the clinic), they might retain increasingly uncertain goals but lack any means to obtain them. Carceral witnesses a comparable outlook among his fellow prisoners. Some of them articulate goals they learned in the course of various programs endorsed by the correctional system, but, in all other respects, that same system cultivates a cyclical view of time within which such goals are impertinent.

A linear perspective cannot exist without concern for the future, but the future only recapitulates the past in a cyclical framework. Certain staff members would preface their remarks to Carceral with "After release. . . ." Through these representatives, the correctional institution pays lip service to the value of treatment programs and education, but the overwhelmingly cyclical rhythm and routine of life in prison erodes attention to the future. During incarceration, writes Robert Berger, the time one serves is directionless: "Here, we are not really living, we are not in an environment that allows us to grow and learn. . . . We are not trying to improve our lot in life or trying to make things better. We are stuck."[78] This lack of perceived progress makes for the feeling that time has stopped. Waiting for another gate to be rolled, waiting to be released from another count, waiting for another scheduled shower, prisoners experience an abiding sense of déjà vu.

The timing of an activity, which is utterly inflexible, has been determined by the staff before an inmate even arrives at that correctional facility. "Prisoners are only required to obey like dogs," says Carceral. His evident rancor arises from temporal alienation. The pointlessness of cyclical time is an imposition to which he conforms only at the staff's behest. As a convenience, most events in the world outside of prison begin and end on the hour or the half hour. In prison, however, the schedule is set to five-minute intervals. A count may occur at 5:15 A.M., and recreation may start at 10:20 A.M. The granularity of this schedule is indicative of centralized control over time. This peculiar form of authoritarianism has profound ramifications for temporal experience. It creates a problematic form of lived duration, which, borrowing from Henri Bergson, "gnaws" on a prisoner's psyche, leaving "the mark of its tooth."[79]

One marks the passage of time by noting changes in oneself or the environment. A cyclical system inhibits this process because so little new or noteworthy ever happens. Periods of time are not structured by memorable events; hours blur together, and it is increasingly difficult to notice the passage of time. The cycle repeats itself so quickly that it seems as though nothing is happening and time is abundant. Convicts' complaints are no less repetitive: "Ain't shit to do here!" "Nothing ever changes here." "We do the same shit every day." As variation decreases, dullness increases; a lack of discernible changes exacerbates the feeling that time is passing slowly. Yet, given the routinization of behavior, one's schedule is quickly memorized, and thereafter a prisoner's conduct is more or less automated. As prisoners act without thinking, each standard unit of time is nearly empty of memorable experience. In hindsight, these intervals collapse to the vanishing point due to temporal compression.

A cyclical context alters inmates' time reckoning in two related ways. First, prisoners rid themselves of clocks and calendars. As we have seen, those in positions of authority use these devices to regulate the cyclical activity of life in prison. For inmates, consequently, these devices are worse than superfluous. They magnify the sensation of waiting. By disposing of these devices, prisoners attempt to become oblivious to the linear passage of time. Second, having done so, they become more process oriented in their time reckoning. No one is concerned with finishing anything quickly and moving on to the next task. Rather than setting goals for the future, and measuring progress toward them, they go through the repetitive motions dictated by the day's schedule. In prison, as in everyday life, linear and cyclical systems of time reckoning coexist. Prisoners maintain a residual (and increasingly tenuous) awareness of linear time, but it becomes the subordinate orientation. Once they accept a cyclical orientation, time is primarily manifested as the enactment of standard procedures.

Long-term prisoners are habituated to a cyclical orientation. Action becomes an end in itself, not necessarily because it is fascinating, but as an adaptation to a dearth of novelty and stimulation. One prisoner tells Carceral that he has mopped the same hallway for years: "This is what I do for three hours a day. I take my time and get it done. It's probably the shiniest floor in the prison." He stretches his work to fill the time allotted for it, but he also takes a certain pride in a repetitive task for want of anything else that deserves such devotion. Another prisoner says, "I go to the library every Monday." When the future is identical to the past, that which can be expected has already occurred. Still other prisoners dedicate themselves to exercise or bird-watching. Carceral took up jogging and painting before turning to research and writing. "As I painted," he remembers, "the day would pass by without care." These pursuits offer some consolation but leave the reign of the cyclical system unchallenged.

THE UNKNOWABLE SENTENCE

Technically, of course, there is always a future, but, as with other cyclical systems of time reckoning, prisoners have little or no reason to believe that their future will differ from the status quo. Why not look forward to one's parole? Public perception is that convicts sit in their cells counting down a finite number of days until their release. In fact, most prisoners learn that such calculations are futile. "I was sentenced to six to twenty-three months in prison," states Reginald Hall. "They gave me thirteen to twenty-six years," says his friend, Mike-Mike.[80] "This is a two-to-twelve sentence," Lerner hears from his lawyer.[81] A judge sentences T. J. Parsell to "not less than four and a half years and no more than fifteen years."[82] "It was an indeterminate sentence of six months to ten years," adds Edward Bunker.[83] Like so many others, these prisoners will be released when the state chooses to release them. Given the prevalence of indeterminate sentences and the vagaries of rules and their enforcement, there is no way to calculate that date with any precision. With an indefinite period of captivity, prisoners confront temporal circumstances not unlike those of hostages and POWs.

The widespread fatalism among convicts reflects that of prison administrators—albeit corroborated by repeated failures to extricate themselves from incarceration. Toward the end of his sentence, Carceral was pessimistic and irritated by the formalities: "For me, hope is a thing of the past. It's sanity I need. If they're never going to let me go, I understand. Just don't keep a carrot dangled in front of me." He was first considered for parole in 1993, only eleven years after having been convicted of murder and sentenced to life in prison. Rejected, to be sure, he would be turned down fifteen more times over the following two decades. Prisoners cannot assume that what they do now will mitigate the sentence served for what they did then. Why was Carceral released in 2013 (the seventeenth time he came up for parole) rather than a year or two earlier? The seemingly arbitrary timing suggests that this decision was more attributable to things over which he had no control (i.e., the pressures of mass imprisonment and pervasive overcrowding) than any demonstrated reform of his character. The parole board offered only this cryptic conclusion in its final decision: "You have served sufficient time for punishment."

Programmatically, prison makes inroads on one's attention to the future. Subsequent to incarceration, prisoners find that the future is no longer as important as it once was. This truncated outlook is generated by sentencing procedures as well as members of the prison staff, and it has caustic effects on temporal experience. "Without a definite sense of an attainable future," writes Meisenhelder, "time is likely to be experienced as meaningless, empty, and boring."[84] This mindset brings about toxic levels of protracted duration with no end in sight. For POWs and hostages, the duration of captivity is even more indeterminate, with predictable implications for the perceived passage of time.

Carceral believes that anxiety about parole contributes to futurelessness. The prisoner desires release, of course, but hates being reminded of how long it will take to get there. Yet, by avoiding this subject, prisoners deprive themselves of the preeminent goal. In the resulting vacuum, recurrent events like meals and counts mark the passage of time, but they do not measure progress toward a specific future. It is easy to overlook what does occur because it is so terribly familiar, and there is little or no change in one's physical environment. A cyclical framework engenders passivity. Prisoners know that correctional officers will tell them when one interval ends and another begins. In short, time is perceived to be directionless because it does not move toward the future.

Absent fear of punishment, life behind bars is cheapened because violence is perceived by the perpetrator to engender only that which was already expected: further time to be served in the future. This fatalistic perspective is endemic in prison. It represents the worldview of people who come to presume that the future will be, unavoidably, a continuation of present circumstances. Members of the staff induce this worldview through their control over the rhythm and routine of life in prison. They create a temporal regime that is ruled by the past.

Thus, futurelessness helps us understand the undeniable allure of violence in prison. "I felt as if I had nothing to lose or to live for," recalls Arnold Huskey, "and I acted accordingly."[85] With no future in sight, there is little at stake for the perpetrator except the monotonous repetition of yesterday. And for the audience of fellow convicts, fights are fascinating precisely because they represent improvisational disruptions of cyclical routine.

Chapter Six

MARKING TIME

ǀ

For Oswald Spengler, "it is by the meaning that it intuitively attaches to Time that one Culture is differentiated from another."[1] Just so, incarceration changes temporal reality and alters the way prisoners mark time. The life-style of incarceration demands that they attend to time in new and distinct ways. Simultaneously, their previous methods of marking time become ineffective or injurious to their well-being. The physical setting is small and immutable. One's activities are invariant and repetitious. Temporal inter-vals are short and cyclical. In concert, these environmental factors change the meanings that prisoners attach to time.

But before examining how prisoners mark time, it is worth considering the opposite: their failure to mark time. In common parlance, we may "lose track of time," and, outside of prison, this is often an indicator of enjoyment and liberation from temporal regimentation. Someone on a long holiday, for example, may not know (or care) what day it is.[2] More broadly, people engaged in any challenging but enjoyable activity (such as a game of chess) frequently report losing track of time.[3] On rare occasions, this can even occur in captivity, as when Ingrid Betancourt is reunited with Clara, a member of her political campaign team and fellow hostage: "We spent the rest of the day chatting, unaware of the passage of time."[4]

In prison, however, losing track of time is not typically associated with the enjoyment of one's circumstances. On the contrary, one's inability to mark time is an indicator of mental degeneration. Consider, for instance, the mixture of pity and contempt in Jimmy Baca's description of prisoners on "Nut Run," a cellblock reserved for severely medicated inmates: "Those guys didn't know what day it was or how much time they had served."[5] From a prisoner's standpoint, losing track of time represents a troubling slide toward incompetence. For Tama-Lisa Johnson, it causes considerable embarrassment: "I suck. I really do. I can't believe I just totally forgot it was Thursday and didn't even go to Mass."[6] "The time slips away from me," admits George Jackson ruefully.[7] He does not welcome this perception despite its apparent usefulness for the modification of his own temporal experience during an indeterminate sentence. "I lost track of time and days," writes Baca.[8] His temporal uncertainty makes for alternating bouts of panic or despair.

Losing track of time is brought about by the circumstances of incarceration. With characteristic eloquence, Jacobo Timerman helps us understand the effects of the prison sensorium on temporal experience:

> The cell has a steel door with an opening that allows part of a face, a minimal part, to be visible. The guard has orders to keep the opening shut. Light enters from the outside through a small crack, which acts also as an air vent. This is the only ventilation and light. A faint glow, night and day, eliminating time.[9]

Prisoners in the United States testify to a comparable lack of temporal resources for marking time. There may be no lights in the cell, or the lights may be left on twenty-four hours a day. There may be no windows or bars to see through, as when Billy Sinclair is put into solitary confinement: "The food slot in the solid steel door was the cell's only opening."[10] Consequently, he cannot keep track of time: "I was often disoriented, unable to distinguish night from day because I had forgotten which meal I had eaten last."[11] Likewise, when Piper Kerman is transferred to maximum lockdown, she finds it difficult to mark the passage of time:

> It was easy to lose track of what day it was—there were no newspapers, no magazines, no mail, and since I avoided the TV rooms, no significant way to tell one day from the next. . . . There were no clear windows, so I couldn't even watch the progression of the sun.[12]

Here again, prisoners are caught in a temporal quandary. On the one hand, they do not want to lose track of time, as this bespeaks a stigmatizing incompetence. On the other hand, they also seek to avoid counting standard temporal units (hours, days, etc.) because doing so slows the perceived passage of time. In this chapter, we examine how prisoners develop distinct ways of marking time as a response to the circumstances of their captivity.

ENVIRONMENTAL FACTORS

A particular setting provides only certain ways to mark the passage of time. Other possibilities are simply unavailable. The anthropologist A. R. Radcliffe-Brown confirms this principle with suitably exotic testimony:

> In the jungles of the Andamans it is possible to recognize a distinct succession of odors during a considerable part of the year as one after another the commoner trees and lianas come into flower. . . . The Andamanese have therefore adopted an original method of marking the different periods of the year by means of the different odoriferous flowers that are in bloom at different times. Their calendar is a calendar of scents.[13]

Convicts do not have a succession of trees and flowers coming into bloom. They must make do with what a prison has to offer. By the same token, the Andamanese are not required to stand inside of their cells several times a day to be counted. In large measure, then, the marking of time is determined by a set of impositions that emanate from the physical and cultural environment.

Incarceration limits the individual's sensory experience to a small and unchanging physical setting. In our lives outside of prison, we mark time by virtue of our willful movement across various settings: one's home, one's car or the subway station, one's office, perhaps a bar, any one of several grocery stores or restaurants, and so forth. Prisoners do not have access to anything comparable. "The institution may have no recreational yard or gym, factories, or programs," observe Jeffery Ross and Stephen Richards.[14] Alcatraz Island is only twenty-two acres, about the same size as a private prison where Carceral was held. And, of course, most of that territory is off-limits for the free movement of prisoners. "Because of drastic overpopulation," recalls Baca, "few cons in the prison had their own cells, and hundreds were sleeping on the floor in dormitories."[15] The density of prisoners per square foot is high and typically increasing. Theoretically, this makes for intensified and more diverse social interaction (e.g., urban versus rural communities). However, the prison population is highly homogeneous, so the actual effect is more people quite like yourself telling stories you have heard before.

The upshot is that prisoners have few, if any, opportunities to experience the passage of time in terms of a varied and changing landscape. Robert Berger's comments are apropos:

> The scenery in prison never changes. I wake up in the same room every day, put on the same color clothes, eat at the same table in the mess hall with the same people, walk in the same compound and look at the same scenery day in and day out, year after year.[16]

A small and immutable setting offers little in the way of external stimulation. Very quickly, one's surroundings are overly familiar and uninteresting. Lockdown exacerbates this stimulus deprivation. "I am still confined to this cell," writes Jackson. "It is nine by four. I have left it only twice in the month I've been here for ten minutes each time, in which I was allowed to shower."[17] Yet being released from one's cell is no solution. "The biggest problem with the MCC was that there was nothing to do," states Kerman. She was given recreation "only once a week . . . in what resembled a 1970s elementary school gym."[18]

We see, hear, smell, taste, and touch the physical world. We interact with the setting, as well as other people. Perhaps with this in mind, a punishing uniformity is an essential part of a prison's design. Convicts find themselves waiting for something—anything—to happen. At a minimum-security facility where Carceral was held, he heard a young convict exclaim plaintively, "This is a boring-ass place!" By and large, what might have been used to alleviate his boredom was now unavailable. With waiting and boredom, the mind is frustrated by a dearth of external stimulation, and it is easy to become obsessed with time itself—a recipe for protracted duration. Time is perceived as overabundant and burdensome. In interview after interview, Carceral's fellow prisoners would declare, "Nothing ever changes here!" If no alterations in the setting are registered by one's senses, then the environment offers very little basis for marking the passage of time.

Convicts enter prison fearfully anticipating the threat of constant violence.[19] In time, however, they learn that violence is prevalent but not incessant. At that point, boredom emerges as the more pressing challenge. Rapidly, the novelty of life in prison succumbs to the monotony of an invariant and repetitious schedule, which compounds the lack of sensory stimulation. Outside of prison, people complain about being in a rut, but, not having lived behind bars, they underestimate their temporal latitude. "Month after month," recalls Carceral, "my days consisted of exercising in the morning, working part-time in the kitchen during the afternoon, and watching television at night. That was it. I began to question my own existence: 'Is this all there is?' " His fellow prisoners struggled with similar issues. Maxwell once asked Carceral, "Don't you ever get tired of the same old shit?" During a conversation with Wilkins, Carceral learned a new way to express this frustration:

WILKINS: "I'm beyond being bored."
CARCERAL: "I didn't know there was such a thing."
WILKINS: "Neither did I until I got here."

When "there's nothing to do," as a fourth prisoner put it, one's activities are of negligible help for noting the passage of time.

Segregation reduces a prisoner's world to a single cell where there is almost no schedule whatsoever. In a letter to his mother, Jackson writes, "I am forced to remain in my cell, no fresh air, no sun, twenty-four hours a day in here."[20] Under such conditions, time passes in a slow, unstructured fashion, and it leaves no memorable traces behind: "Each day that comes and goes is exactly like the one that went before."[21] Jackson's temporal experience is not marked by transitions from one place to another. The same is true of prisoners, such as T. J. Parsell, who are held in protective custody: "Inmates on Two-Special were not allowed out of their cells. . . . At chow times, the others went down to base [i.e., the ground floor] while our meals were delivered, usually cold, on Styrofoam plates."[22] In addition, unlike other prisoners, they were not "allowed out of their cells for yard."[23] Diversity in one's activities was an expected (albeit taken for granted) part of every prisoner's former life, so this is a wrenching transition.

Prisoners in the general population enjoy greater mobility, but their activities are repetitive and facile, which blunts the impact of these transitions on temporal experience. In form and content, these brief excursions are nearly as boring as being restricted to one's cell. Jimmy Dunn disparages the deadening circularity of his time in prison: "I'll go to work in that goddamned welding shop, as I do every day, and go through the routine, eat dinner, and get locked up at 4:30. Then I'll get up tomorrow and begin the whole process over again."[24] Berger discovers that the educational programs are no more stimulating: "The drug classes are extremely boring for me, and now I dread going to classes every day."[25] Why not vary your routine? Why not visit different parts of the prison for the sake of novelty and temporal agency? Because you are not allowed to do so, or the necessary options do not exist. Like other prisoners, Dunn and Berger are limited to assigned activities. If they have yard privileges, then they can walk or jog, lift weights, or play basketball. But at best they are left with a narrow and tiresome set of choices.

Penitentiaries manage large populations of prisoners with minimal staffing by means of temporal regimentation. Generally speaking, an inmate's options are few in number, poorly equipped, and staffed by disinterested employees. The tolerated breadth of action is abbreviated to a degree outsiders would find unfathomable. At each of the twelve prisons where Carceral was held, recreation had a regular time slot and a familiar handful of available activities. Prisons schedule time for counts, meals, showers, work, yard, telephone calls, visits, and so on. There is no flexibility; there are no alternatives. As the days and weeks repeat themselves, a new prisoner swiftly commits this routine to memory. The inmate's behavior becomes habitual, which modifies temporal experience. For Baca, "time went by in a continuous ream of uneventful days that fell away in dreary routine."[26] Very little differentiated one moment from the next.

New convicts have a great deal to learn. At first, the sheer volume of novelty is overwhelming. They make mistakes until they realize that their personal preferences are irrelevant. The schedule must be followed to the letter; otherwise, access will be revoked. Long-term prisoners know that if the designated time slot is missed or ignored, then the activity in question is over, gone, no longer an option. They eat their meals fast, says Carceral, having learned that those who do not risk being kicked out of the chow hall before they are finished. At Gladiator School, prisoners were only given ten minutes to eat. Yet doing something for the thousandth time is very different from doing it for the first time, with attendant implications for temporal experience. What was new and challenging is simplified through regimentation and repetition. The sameness of the activity is now the dominant motif. They cannot help but notice that assigned conduct consists of recurrent events. The things they do take (or are permitted to take) a consistent amount of time. Increasingly, then, they mark the passage of time in terms of the sequential steps intrinsic to their activities. Disciplined behavior is converted into the standardization of time.

Subsequent to incarceration, years, months, and weeks become irrelevant. Their primary purpose, to mark the linear passage of time, has little meaning behind bars. Instead, a prisoner's awareness of time shifts to focus on what really matters: short and cyclical segments of the daily schedule. One's temporal orientation is now microscopic and fixated on a timetable devised by those in authority. From this perspective, each day represents a revolving circle of time slots for one's assigned activities. For instance, the prisoner may go to recreation every Wednesday at 9:40 A.M. and return to his or her cell at 10:55 A.M. Most of these time slots range in duration from a few minutes to an hour and a half. They are brief, strictly enforced, and repetitive.

This adaptation to short cycles affects the ways prisoners mark the passage of time. In thought and speech, they refer to time by adopting a new set of standard temporal units.[27] Rather than make arrangements with others using hours and minutes, they are more apt to do so via the sequence of meals, counts, and other scheduled events: "I'll get with you after rec" or "Let's talk before the last count." Carceral is held at the Receiving Center while awaiting transportation to another prison: "I was put into a cell with two other men. We sat for four days waiting on our bus. We received a tray of food three times a day and had to stand for three counts." Their days were structured by a series of shared occurrences instead of abstract units of time. This sequence of events provided a basis for time reckoning as well as interpersonal coordination.

A blinkered focus on the here and now reduces a prisoner's experience of temporal diversity, slowing the perceived passage of time. They pay less attention to next week, next month, and the long-term future. Ordinarily, intervals of time are distinguished from each other by conventional brackets that signal the beginning and ending of the activity in question. Examples include "hello" and "goodbye" in a conversation, the bells that start and stop a class in school, or the opening music and closing credits of a film. It would seem that the prevalence of short temporal cycles in prison implies more, not fewer, brackets. Yet Carceral observes that, in practice, the boundaries between these intervals lose their interest and meaning. By definition, they come and go rapidly. Moreover, the people, places, and activities they "separate" are relentlessly similar. It is increasingly difficult for prisoners to recognize discrete intervals of time as conspicuous entities.

On paper, one's schedule may seem quite busy, but the ironclad routine quickly becomes so familiar, so predictable, that prisoners hardly notice it, much less use it to mark the passage of time. Carceral resorts to a simile when he tries to account for this phenomenon:

> Think of it as making a motion picture. Each frame represents a small change in a series of events. Once they're run through a projector, we perceive them as moving pictures connected together without boundaries. For the prisoner, these intervals merge into one long homogeneous experience. The individual frames aren't seen as discrete events. As the film moves through the projector, this eliminates their distinctiveness.

With his concept of "temporal segregation," Eviatar Zerubavel refers to our efforts to distinguish segments of time.[28] In prison, however, temporal segregation erodes because ostensibly separate intervals reoccur so quickly and with such sameness. Among prisoners, this produces a blur of monotonous and nearly indistinguishable activity, much of which is devoted to killing time. Despite shuffling from one site to another, they do not experience memorably different episodes, and they are left with the impression that "nothing ever happens here."

EXPERIENTIAL FACTORS

The environment fosters experiences that further influence how prisoners mark the passage of time. This analysis distinguishes between the outer and inner sides of imprisonment. Carceral views environmental factors as objective features of the setting, whereas experiential factors are aspects of a convict's subjectivity. In combination, they establish the context within which prisoners note the passage of time. While subjective, the experiential factors are shared by those in captivity. Moreover, these collective sensations favor certain forms of temporality, but not others. Three experiential factors stand out: powerlessness, waiting, and the burden of time.

Life in prison is diametrically opposed to the core value of American culture: autonomy. The temporal version of personal liberty is the ability to do what you want with your time. Yet Carceral often hears prisoners refer to themselves as "state property" because, figuratively speaking, the time they serve is not their own to do with as they please. With incarceration, prisoners lose nearly all control over their temporal experience. Having relinquished personal autonomy, they feel desynchronized with the normal flow of time because they do not move through or modify temporal experience on their own initiative. This enforced inertia brings the circumstances of imprisonment and time itself to the forefront of one's self-consciousness.

A prisoner's schedule has been prearranged by the staff. The daily routine is a given, not something that can be revised according to personal preference. Carceral uses another simile when depicting how it feels to be caught in this system:

> It's like a gear with notches; each notch is a different time slot. As days progress, time slots shift to the next intervals. Time slots mean little or nothing, so a prisoner can't make sharp distinctions between events within his own life. A gear is round, so it cycles back to the beginning notch. And a gear only has so many teeth; these are the limited activities. Subjectively, prisoners see the total pattern as one long continuous duration. Once the gear is running, there's no beginning or end.

What Carceral describes is the mechanical imposition of habitual sensations. One's stream of experience is uniform and crushingly familiar, leaving no sense of progress. Prisoners lack mental forms of memorabilia with which to mark the passage of time.

Correctional officers and other members of the staff decide what prisoners will do, when, and for how long, thereby condemning the convicts in their charge to a reciprocal powerlessness. Loss of control frames the prisoner's experience of time. The staff maintains relentless control of a prisoner's time by means of the daily schedule and intermittent control of a prisoner's time by means of occasional appointments. Members of the staff make these appointments without consulting prisoners beforehand about the timing. Carceral calls our attention to the presumptuousness behind this practice:

> When I was at a minimum-security facility, it amazed me how the staff would simply page a prisoner. They ignored that he may work second or third shift in the community, or that he may be scheduled to do something else. Some of these men would take an afternoon nap when they had nothing else to do only to be awakened by an unscheduled page.

A prisoner can be paged over the public address system at any moment. When summoned, one may be in the shower, on the toilet, or in bed. The presumed availability of prisoners signals their temporal subordination. Though fitful, these incidents clearly symbolize the powerlessness of prisoners vis-à-vis the staff.

George Jackson writes a letter to Joan, a member of the Soledad Defense Committee, immediately after her visit. In this letter he notes, "I've been back in the cell for ten minutes, after waiting forty-five for an escort."[29] Powerless people experience a great deal of waiting. Among prisoners, consequently, it is one of the most prevalent sensations. They stand in line for food, showers, and telephones. They stare at a gate while waiting for a guard to roll it out of the way. Having been called to a meeting with a member of the staff (and expected to arrive without delay), they find themselves waiting for admittance at a security desk. They wait to be counted, and they wait for recreation. They wait for the resumption of regular activities following a weekend or holiday. While people on the outside sometimes have to wait, in prison one waits longer, more often, and without the right to complain or do anything about it. Prisoners who object to the waiting do so with the fatalistic attitude of people commenting on the weather. All concerned view it as a fact of life.

And, of course, prisoners wait for their release. The experienced inmate tries to disregard this issue, thereby moving it into the background of his or her consciousness. Difficulty marking the passage of time is the price one pays for this relief. Still, attending to this possibility, and the stress associated with doing so, intensify toward the end of one's sentence. In this regard, Carceral's comments are instructive:

> The anxiety is progressive. At the beginning of a sentence, most men are angry for getting themselves locked up. Yet, as the prisoner's release date

approaches, he may start counting the days: triple digits, double digits, single digits. Toward the end, anxiety increases exponentially. As one nears release, most are placed with others in the same status. Their conversations focus on release and heighten everyone's anxiety even more.

Waiting, anxiety, and self-conscious attention to time itself make each day seem endless. Convicts know this, but, like Dennis Coleman, they can neither disregard their circumstances nor avoid the consequences: "With only fifty-three more days to go, I'm beginning to notice time passing much more slowly. I don't like it at all. I am aware of the fact that once a prisoner starts noticing time going by, he begins to shake it rough."[30] What they wait for, meanwhile, is inherently uncertain. Their release will be decided by others. Under these circumstances, prisoners become preoccupied with self, situation, and the imagined machinations of those in authority.

A newcomer is not prepared for the amount of waiting that occurs in prison. The inmate must learn to wait, not unlike a child. Convicts sitting or standing around is a common sight, especially at maximum- and medium-security facilities. Prisoners do their own waiting, but they also partake vicariously in the waiting of friends and loved ones. A prisoner tells Carceral, "My mom and dad get their hopes up each time I go to the parole commission. They live hearing to hearing right along with me." For the members of this family, a hearing becomes a new unit of measurement for marking the passage of time. Powerlessness makes for waiting, and waiting shapes temporal experience. "The days were going by so slowly," writes Reginald Hall. "I couldn't stand waiting."[31]

Mass imprisonment coupled with inadequate funding produces overcrowded conditions. With overcrowding, temporal resources become scarce, and waiting is endemic. Each inmate has access to a thinner and thinner slice of time with the various people and opportunities of the prison. "Weekends and holidays were the busiest time" for visits, remembers Parsell, "and if it got crowded, we would be limited to just one hour."[32] The repetition of short intervals erodes the temporal boundaries between events, making it more and more difficult to mark the passage of time. Thus, prisoners and members of the staff view time in radically divergent ways. For members of the staff, time is a limited resource that must be strictly managed. For prisoners, time is overabundant, and they must find ways to kill it.

In every language, vocabulary reflects a people's pragmatic interests. If, as Spengler argues, the meanings we attach to time vary across different cultures, it is because societies use language to think and talk about time in dissimilar ways. Not surprisingly, then, prisoners have developed a unique jargon with which to discuss the nuances of their temporal experience. "I would do two and a half to three years"; that is what other convicts tell Edward Bunker as he awaits sentencing.[33] Later, as a teenager in San Quentin, Bunker insults convicts in nearby cells who were condemned to die for the murder of several people, including children. One of them rebukes Bunker with a customary question: "Why don't you do your own time?"[34] That familiar phrase, "doing time," is an eloquent expression of the fact that there is little else for prisoners to do. Carceral's friend, Maxwell, stops the griping of another prisoner with this curt instruction: "Pull some time, then complain to me." In convict parlance, time is a burden that must be "pulled," and one's temporal experience "drags." "I'm stuck in Folsom Prison," sings Johnny Cash, "and time keeps draggin' on."

Prisoners reveal their inner concerns with the questions they constantly ask each other: "How much time do you have?" or "How many years do you have?" Understandably, they contemplate time, so the length of one's sentence is a marker within their distinctive community. Convicts talk about having been "given" time, but it was not a gift. "The judge gave me ninety days in the county jail," says Bunker.[35] Frequently, the source of one's sentence is represented by an anonymously plural "they," as in these common questions: "How much time do they want you to do?" and "How much time did they give you?" For example, Bunker invokes the anonymous "they" when he describes the fate of an acquaintance: "He was eighteen or nineteen, and they had given him six months."[36] Regardless of its origins, however, the sentence in question must be "served," for it is not the prisoner's time to dispose of as he or she pleases. Bunker provides the following instance: "I had served four years in San Quentin."[37] A prisoner speaks about "serving" time because the sentence is viewed as an imposition.

Prisoners also distinguish between "hard" and "easy" time. When told of a fellow convict's many trips to "seg," one is apt to reply, "You're doing hard time." The longer the sentence, the harder the time. In jail, Rik Scarce would often overhear one prisoner say to another, "You ain't got but three months? Shit, I could do that standin' on my head."[38] Yet this seemingly simple distinction wavers and becomes unclear when examined closely. We should be cautious about putting too much store in it. Serving time becomes harder, not easier, once a prisoner has a date for his or her release. This is evident in the following exchange between Carceral and another convict:

RYERSON: "This is the slowest time ever. I try to go to bed early to push myself into the next day, and then get up and do it again."

CARCERAL: "Are you sleeping?"

RYERSON: "Barely. I'll fall asleep early and wake up in the middle of the night. Then I'll just lay there."

Ryerson's problem with temporal experience intensifies after he receives a date. Prisoners invent illnesses to account for the complaints from those with little of their sentences left to serve. They are said to have "short-timer's disease" or "short-time-itis." They suffer from "going-home-fever" or "gate-fever." This elaborate terminology suggests that, in prison, "easy time" is the El Dorado of temporal experience: desired, sought after, but never really found. There is, rather, hard time and harder time.

"All I have is time." This common expression among prisoners is equally true for those with a little or a lot of their sentence left to serve. It confirms the utter vacancy in their lives. Earlier, we noted prisoners' exasperation at the offhand manner in which members of the staff summon them to an appointment at a moment's notice. They do not appreciate being paged whenever it is convenient for the staff to do so, and they know that they will probably have to wait once they get to their destinations. They may complain, pointedly engage in delaying tactics, and arrive late. Yet, paradoxically, they keep most of these appointments, not out of respect for the staff, but merely to break the cycle of daily tedium. Their rancor at the staff's high-handedness must be tempered by a countervailing interest in altering the emptiness of their temporal experience. They typically obey the summons merely to enliven the present in some small and subservient way. For Carceral, the words associated with time are boredom, meaninglessness, and torture. In prison, time does not heal all wounds. It is, instead, the weapon with which the state wounds prisoners.

ADAPTATIONS

To summarize, then, incarceration imposes certain conditions on prisoners. They contend with three environmental factors: a small and unchanging physical setting, an invariant and repetitious schedule, and short and cyclical segments of time. In addition, they encounter three experiential factors: powerlessness, waiting, and the burden of time. Attending to time as they once did, prior to imprisonment, would take them down a path strewn with impediments and slow their lives to a snail's pace. But there is no need for self-mortification because, like the Andamanese in Radcliffe-Brown's classic ethnography, convicts discover that their unparalleled circumstances afford them new ways to mark the passage of time. In the balance of this chapter, we examine seven of these strategies. Our analysis moves along a continuum between collective and subjective tactics.

Rhythms of the Temporal Regime

Prisoners use the rhythms of the temporal regime to mark the passage of time. Scarce offers the following definition:

> Administrative time constituted the jail's formal, bureaucratic, structural time: the lockdowns (when we were locked in our cells; during a regular day, there was a ninety-minute lockdown following each of the three meals and an overnight lockdown from 11:00 P.M. until 6:00 A.M.), food service times, weekly and three-month changes in the guards' assignments.[39]

This strategy may smack of capitulation, even collaboration, but, in response to his own rhetorical question, Carceral asserts that convicts have no choice in the matter: "Why would one want to mark time by recreation and meals? Yes, there's little meaning in it, but what else is there?"

The marking of time is built into a convict's identification number. These numbers are assigned to inmates in sequential order. As Baca shows us, this enables prisoners to take the measure of each other's temporal experience: "'What's your number?' another asked, to determine when I had come into the joint."[40] A convict's identification number also signals how many times he or she has been sent to prison. Sunny Jacobs recounts how prisons inscribe these numbers with the circularity of recidivism: "Each person is given a number upon arrival. . . . If you already have a number, meaning you are a returnee, then you get a letter in front of your number: A being a two-time loser, B being a three-time loser, and so on."[41] Prisoners use this code to assess two dimensions of time—sequence and frequency—in each other's identity. Thus, Jacobs is "horrified" when she realizes that a fellow convict has returned to prison for "her seventh time."[42]

As a major part of the prison sensorium, a temporal regime rhythmically shapes the sights and sounds of life behind bars. The regularity of one's sensory experience serves as the basis for time reckoning, as noted by Victor Serge: "You soon learn to tell time by the sounds of the prison."[43] Similarly, Timerman recalls "the typical Sunday sounds" during his incarceration."[44] At most correctional facilities, you do not need a clock to know what time it is. Your standard temporal units become screeching announcements over the intercom or the metallic clanging of gates opening and closing. The dictatorial pulse of a prison is also apparent in the staff's control over the lights in one's cell. This temporal regimentation is characteristic of Kerman's experience: "At ten P.M. the lights were turned off abruptly."[45] As Jackson recounts, this forcible marking of time makes it difficult for prisoners to keep idiosyncratic hours: "I get involved in some aspect of the subjects that interest me and before I can extract myself the lights are going off and it is twelve o'clock."[46]

The temporal regime is a chronometric system for the purpose of punitive discipline. Incarceration is centrally concerned with the authoritarian control of one's time. Simultaneously, it is a fountainhead of alienation and a framework for time reckoning. This dualism is the subtext when a fellow inmate, Annette, explains counts to the newly imprisoned Kerman: "They count us five times a day, and you have to be here, or wherever you're supposed to be, and the four o'clock count is a standing count [during which no talking is allowed], the other ones are at midnight, two A.M., five A.M., and nine P.M."[47] Each standing count brings all other activity to a stop:

> The five of us stood silent by our bunks, waiting. The entire building was suddenly quiet; all I could hear was the jangling of keys and the thud of heavy boots. Eventually a man stuck his head into the room and . . . counted us. Then, several seconds later, another man came in and counted us."[48]

When the count is wrong, the whole process is repeated until they get it right. Prisoners use the rhythms of the temporal regime to tell the approximate time of day as well as the day of the week. In the case of personal hygiene, for example, Baca regularly hears a correctional officer shout, "Tier 3, out for showers!"[49] "It's Thursday and Catholic Mass is tonight," notes Christina Dress.[50] For Kerman, "shopping was twice a week in the evening, half the Camp on Monday, the other half on Tuesday."[51]

If, as Radcliffe-Brown puts it, flowers in the jungles of the Andamans embody a kind of calendar, then, by analogy, the temporal regime in prison doubles as a clock and a calendar. This tacit chronometric function is epitomized by Bunker's avowal that convicts find themselves "with nothing to do and meals the mark of passing time."[52] Jimmy Lerner is held in isolation, but he can tell what time it is from the contents of his food trays:

If it's a handful of Rice Krispies and a dented orange (invariably encrusted with a thick white mold), then it must be breakfast time. . . . Peanut butter and jelly means it's about noon, and macaroni and cheese must signify Happy Hour here on the nut wing of the Las Vegas county jail.[53]

In these excerpts, Bunker, Lerner, and other convicts resemble natives on the Andaman Islands. They are not counting minutes, hours, days, or years; they are noting recurrent changes in their environment. It is a cyclical form of time reckoning, not linear or durational.

Christopher Burney comments on the temporal significance of meager lunches during eighteen months of solitary confinement as a POW: "There was also a daily event of great importance, at midday, when the soup was served. . . . There were thus two halves of the day, and I was never sure which was the harder to endure."[54] For Burney, it is the timing of a meal that matters, but this makes him vulnerable to a temporal form of punishment. In retaliation for looking out his window at Allied planes, which was forbidden, his captors do not bring his ration of soup at midday:

I must confess that it was a bleak moment. But the hardest blow was the thought that if I had no soup, I would not only have to fill in the twenty minutes or so which, with delicate spooning, I could spend eating it, but I would also have to be patient for twice as long: the days would be doubled.[55]

What the temporal regime offers can always be withheld, leaving prisoners bereft of any markers for the passage of time.

Churn in Personnel

Prisoners constantly flow into and out of a correctional facility. Moreover, as a total institution that operates twenty-four hours a day, members of the staff, especially correctional officers, must work multiple shifts. In addition, unscheduled turnover among the staff occurs due to promotions, resignations, retirements, and so forth. All of this churn in personnel provides another temporal framework by which prisoners mark the passage of time. Although there is some overlap with the rhythms of the temporal regime, this strategy merits separate discussion.

"I kept time of day and night with meals and shift changes," writes Baca.[56] Prisoners monitor correctional officers as much as officers monitor prisoners. Each officer brings a particular attitude to his or her shift. Depending on the officer in question, there will be specific risks and opportunities, so these shifts represent qualitatively different intervals of time. One officer may be a "hack" while another is "laid-back."[57] As shifts change, the tempo of the day also changes. Prisoners recognize and remember these shift changes, and these transitions become recurrent points of temporal reference in a cyclical world.

Long-term prisoners watch correctional officers start at entry-level positions and progress upward through the ranks. Witness, for instance, this exchange between Desmond and Carceral:

DESMOND: "Do you remember the new guard, Barber?"
CARCERAL: "Yeah."
DESMOND: "He's now a sergeant at Ridgewood."

In a different conversation, Carceral told other prisoners how the current sergeant at Cherryhill's intake unit started at Gladiator School while he was there. Another prisoner complained about one of the officers becoming a social worker. He could not believe that a former officer would be much of an advocate for prisoners. Usually, there are many relatives working for the Department of Corrections, and long-term prisoners can trace these lines of kinship across generations. The comings and goings of the staff mark the passage of time. Prisoners share this knowledge among themselves, much like tribal people without a calendar discuss an unquantifiable past. Across four decades, Albert Woodfox saw that officers, "who often started working at the prison after high school, learned from their uncles, fathers, and grandfathers who were already working at Angola."[58]

There is, as well, "the flow of inmates in and out of the institution," which serves as a further basis for marking the passage of time.[59] Lerner observes that arrivals are conspicuous: "A new fish schlepping his yellow tub through the yard is always an event of great interest."[60] New prisoners meet convicts who have been held at that prison for many years. As a reliable topic of conversation, they will discuss particular places outside of prison, jointly listing the names of those who have served time from these areas. They establish quasi-kinship ties through this process, but they also co-construct a timeline of biographical events. Baca helps us understand that departures are equally remarkable: "It was an event whenever we heard tier gates racking in the distance, because it meant maybe one of us was getting out."[61]

These transitions have temporal significance within the prison community. Terrence was an inmate at Cherryflats for a long time. Carceral recalls the day he learned that Terrence would be transferred to another prison: "You know those people up front have sent my paperwork downtown for approval to go to one of the community centers." Other prisoners monitored his daily status during the period between this announcement and his eventual departure. Once he was gone, they would tell newly arriving prisoners who he was and when he got out. Terrence became part of history in an otherwise ahistorical setting. It is noteworthy, however, that this history is marked by the comings and goings of prisoners and not by standard temporal units.

Even more so, the arrival of a notorious prisoner is a noteworthy and enduring event in the timeline of a particular penitentiary. Mary Kay Letourneau was a middle-school teacher until convicted of a sexual relationship with one of her students. Her trial and subsequent incarceration at the Washington Corrections Center for Women (WCCW) garnered frenzied attention in the media. "Inmates and staff alike are constantly talking about the newest resident of WCCW," reports Dress, another prisoner at that facility.[62] Letourneau's arrival separates time into segments before and after a public event. Later, we examine further variations on this theme as a distinct form of adaptation.

Personal Routine

A fellow prisoner tells Scarce, "You gotta get yourself a routine, man. It's the only way to survive in here!"[63] This is helpful advice from an experienced convict. Held in solitary confinement, however, Jacobs must figure this out for herself, and the resulting schedule is revealing:

> I created a routine for myself. It helped to overcome the feeling of being detached, of free-floating in the absence of a time structure. I would sleep until the smell and sounds of breakfast alerted my senses. Bursting awake, I would quickly wash my face and smooth my hair and wait by the door with my face pressed sideways to the 5" × 5" square of safety glass criss-crossed with wire, waiting for the first sighting of the breakfast cart and the guard. . . .
>
> After exercise, I would eat and then go back to sleep. Yoga filled the next part of my day. Before and after yoga I would pray and meditate. Lunch was another marker in the passage of timelessness. Then I would write or draw or do maths [sic] problems in my head or think about my children, Jesse, my family and cry. . . .
>
> Dinner came cold like breakfast. The removal of the dinner tray marked the beginning of the sensory fasting period during which I made every effort to fill the void with activity until I fell asleep again.[64]

Despite meager resources, she assembles a personal schedule by combining the rhythm of meals with her own daily practices. Through self-discipline, she creates temporal structure within what would otherwise be a featureless stream of experience. Her interjections comprise most of what transpires.

A third strategy for marking time entails focusing on one's own personal routine. The two principal categories are a prisoner's work and leisure activities. Here again, there is some overlap with the temporal regime. Work is assigned and leisure activities are available, but only by dint of those in positions of authority. Nonetheless, both types of activity offer a ready-made framework for one's temporal experience within a setting where there are few such options.

According to Kerman, "prison work gave me a greater sense of normalcy, another way of marking time, and people with whom I had something in common."[65] She works with high-voltage electricity and other "totally inexperienced women," yielding "moments of broad comedy and only occasional bodily injury." The resulting stories structure their temporal experience. Richard Jones and Thomas Schmid echo Kerman's positive assessment:

> In addition to extending his range of contacts with other inmates, a job assignment serves to integrate a new inmate into the daily tempo of prison life. He is required to report for work at a designated time, take coffee and lunch breaks at specified times, and complete his work at a designated time. Any job, no matter how menial, thus serves to mark the passage of time and to introduce the inmate to the daily work schedule."[66]

This generalization, while valid, presents only one side of the argument. The counterpoint, as stated by Thomas Meisenhelder, is that prison jobs have little to offer in this respect because one's temporal experience at work is not marked by a series of memorable events: "One way of marking time is to use one's prison work assignment and its schedule of leisure, work, break, eat, work, break, leisure, as a device for distinguishing one moment from another. . . . Yet, in prison, this is seldom a very satisfactory practice since most prison work is meaningless."[67] Convicts are carrying rocks, not building cathedrals. Using one's work assignment for the purpose of marking time is contraindicated by the "monotonous, unskilled nature of most jobs in the prison."[68]

Carceral's experience bears on this issue. When he worked in the upholstery shop at Cherryflats, he and fellow prisoners would share personalized cakes with each other during short breaks. Before going to work, they would purchase the desired ingredients at the canteen (cupcakes, peanut butter, vanilla cookies, and so on), mix them together, and then heat them in microwave ovens at their living units. Each man created a recipe he felt tasted best. The men would bring these confections to the shop, where they would try each other's cakes and comment on them. "These were," recalls Carceral, "ways to fill moments with memorable events and mark the passage of time." It turned out to be a temporary practice, however, as Gus explained to Carceral in an interview conducted after both men had been transferred out of Cherryflats: "Man, I liked that. When the main ones who were doing it left, it stopped. A couple of the new guys tried it, but it wasn't like you, Benny, Logan, and me. Logan had the best tasting cake to me." On the face of it, this ritual might appear to support the idea that one's job assignment can be an effective way to mark time, but it is worth noting that this welcome distraction was temporary and not an outcome of the work itself, which was always uneventful.

In a similar way, there is a two-edged quality to counts. They interrupt one's current activity because anything the prisoner is doing at that moment must stop. Yet prisoners adapt to this regimentation by developing personal routines that are initiated once they return to their cells. They may use this increment of time during a count to take a brief nap, play cards, or watch television. As with their jobs, however, the repetitiveness of activity during a count blunts its effectiveness in marking time. Consequently, it is more satisfying to create personal routines that operate alongside the rhythms of the temporal regime. "It was the daily routine that kept me focus[ed]," states Sylvester Long. "At 7 [A.M.], I would go to the gym and jump rope or play ping-pong until 8 [A.M.], which was yard time. Then I would go out and run five miles."[69] At one point, Carceral organized his Thursdays around lifting weights: "The guards have a count at 5:00 A.M. Once I see them pass my cell . . . I then make my way to the weight machine. I wave off for breakfast at 6:15. I generally finish at 7:30."

As is evident in the foregoing excerpts, two different temporal systems run alongside each other. Prisoners are aware of clock and calendar time as the backdrop for their activities only to the extent that this knowledge is imposed on them by administrative policies. The objective time of standard temporal units is not otherwise relevant, and maintaining attention to it is counterproductive to the overarching goal, which is killing time. Within their own world, therefore, prisoners are more apt to mark temporal experience in terms of events or activities rather than time, per se. Put differently, prisoners are vaguely aware of day and time in much the same way that someone who is bilingual knows how to speak a second language. This temporal bilingualism is most apparent with adaptations (like those discussed thus far) that are based on the rhythms of the prison regime or when convicts engage in temporal code-switching to describe their schedules to outsiders. Prisoners who rely on purely personal or subjective markers have little or no need for such code-switching, as this statement from Baca demonstrates: "Days, weeks, and months went by, but I hardly recognized them. Only my writing marked the passage of time."[70]

In a related vein, many female convicts use their menstrual cycle to mark time. Members of the staff treat this as another opportunity to impose a sequential structure on inmates' temporal experience. Jacobs illustrates this version of the temporal regime when she recounts the following exchange at the Broward County Jail:

> "I need sanitary pads please."
> "You get one at a time." She handed me a single sanitary pad and an elastic belt.
> "But I have my period. I'll need more than this."
> "You can only have one at a time. Those are the rules. No exceptions."[71]

The more prisoners focus on personal routines, however, the more their days lose resolution and merge together into a timeless blur. These indistinguishable days pass slowly in the present but seem to have passed quickly in retrospect.

Developing Skills

The fourth strategy is an extension of the third: prisoners mark the passage of time by developing skills relevant to their personal routines. "Mondays and Wednesdays were my exercise days," writes Baca. "Every Saturday morning Bonafide and I played chess."[72] Cheyenne Yakima would lift weights each day during recreation.[73] Kenneth Lamberton would walk laps outside on the track.[74] Bunker would meet with other convicts on the yard to swap stories and gossip.[75] There are organized sports, such as basketball and baseball. Kerman adds that "crocheting [was] an obsession among [female] prisoners throughout the system."[76] In short, these skills may be mental, social, or physical, but, given the clientele and the exigencies of life behind bars, physical pursuits are most popular among male prisoners. Certain skills are pertinent to each of these activities. For the purposes of marking time, the key is not simply maintaining a personal routine but rather striving for noticeable improvement. In bodybuilding, for example, the number of repetitions will gradually increase from twenty to thirty per set.

Other prisoners seek to advance their proficiency at educational or intellectual endeavors, marking time along the way. In a letter to his brother, Jackson tells him, "I add five words to my vocabulary each day, five new ones, right after breakfast each morning when I have forty-five minutes to kill."[77] Other convicts may work toward a coveted GED or simply try to improve their skills at reading and writing. This study of time and temporal experience in prison would not have been possible were it not for the fact that Carceral was one of the latter:

> When I was a child, I hated reading and writing. I was always barely getting by in school. I liked writing short stories but could never do it without thousands of mistakes. I still write like this, just ask my coauthor. To help expire time [in prison], I began to fill my days with school. I entered college and found that I enjoy psychology and sociology. I learned to read more and more. It was hard for me to sit and read without being distracted. I began to write after I mostly stopped painting and drawing. The rules allow for prisoners to seek publication for their writings. I found enjoyment in writing about my world. I began to realize that, with all our knowledge in the States, few really know about prison life. To this date, my mind wanders while I read. Yet I can sit down and read longer with fewer distractions. I had to develop my reading and writing skills. Oddly, I disliked these two disciplines, but forced myself to like them.

Carceral's increasing skills at reading and writing cut a series of marks into his temporal experience, which was otherwise severely lacking in content. Later, he would note the passage of time with the acquisition of educational credentials and the publication of his books.

Robert Berger comments on reading his way through prison.[78] "Studying helps me forget that so much of my life is being wasted," adds Andrew Frison.[79] Long includes a list of programs he completed during his fifteen-year sentence.[80] Each of them contributed to his growing self-awareness, but they also represented substantial steps through his temporal experience. Other convicts mark the passage of time by developing their artistic or musical skills. Carceral painted until he turned to reading, writing, and research. At a private prison in the South, he would watch and listen as a fellow convict played his keyboard. Years later, as they corresponded through the mail, he told Carceral that he had switched to a different instrument: "I also have ready access to my guitar, which I love playing, and while playing time just flies by. When not playing, many hours are filled with writing out songs for my picking partner. Many times, I feel there just are not enough hours in the day!" Without music, his temporal experience would revert to its default setting behind bars: an undifferentiated expanse.

Prisoners who mark the passage of time by improving their skills are not using the standard temporal units of clocks and calendars. Developing one's skills is not piecework, where one's output is measured to make rate. Instead, temporal experience is marked by milestones on the path to self-growth. There is no set schedule or mechanical pace to maintain. The temporal regime does not demand their involvement with this activity. As Meisenhelder puts it, there is "a subjective sense of accomplishment" that is "intrinsically engrossing enough" to hasten the perceived passage of time.[81] No one else may care, but, at his or her own pace, the prisoner gains a feeling of change, progress, and achievement. The prisoner's potential is severely limited by programmatic restrictions and lack of resources, but there is all the more reason to derive a sense of satisfaction with something that is an end in itself. In a letter to Carceral, one of his friends doing time in the Walls facility wrote that he was reading books about computers to keep up with recent changes even though he could not use a computer at that prison. He may never lay hands on a computer again, but reading these books creates a structure for his temporal experience.

Watching Television

In correctional facilities, access to television broadcasting is quite variable. At Angola, Billy Sinclair had a television set in his cell, but that is only possible if a convict has the money to purchase one and if the administration permits it.[82] Most prisoners must share "a TV room in the rear of the dorm" or congregate around the television(s) in a dayroom.[83] "We don't have televisions in our cells," reports Jorge Renaud from Texas ("except on the Walls and Ramsey I" wings).[84] Under these more typical circumstances, control of the television is not in the hands of any one inmate: "Depending on the warden's preferences, programs offered on television will range from the basic four networks to ESPN, USA, and various movie channels."[85] Any prisoner who wishes to watch a particular program will need the assent of other prisoners as well as the cooperation of a correctional officer:

> According to policy, every program is to be voted on. All televisions are controlled remotely, by the rover, the officer on the floor who controls the remote. There have been innumerable fights and quite a few riots started by one group of inmates refusing to allow another group to watch what they want.[86]

Female prisoners encounter similar discord: "There is only one TV per fifty women and, predictably, it is a regular point of contention."[87] In short, it is no simple matter to watch a particular television show, although convicts are much more likely to have a radio (or boom box) of their own.

Marking time in prison in terms of television programs is problematic for other reasons, as well. Even if a television is available, the room in question may be otherwise unfurnished. "There were three TV rooms without chairs," for example, when Kerman was transferred to a correctional facility in Oklahoma City.[88] And, even if the room is furnished with chairs, those in authority can arrange things so that two or more television sets compete with each other: "Dueling televisions blared at opposite sides of the small room," observes Kerman when she serves time in Danbury, Connecticut.[89] Moreover, since correctional officers control its temporal availability, they can use the television for petty or vindictive treatment of prisoners, such as "rigidly enforcing the TV hours, much to the displeasure of the insomniacs."[90] As James Paluch points out, watching television inside one's own cell is also difficult given the cacophony that is characteristic of every cellblock: "In the evenings, when the television sets are on and prisoners congregate during 'block-out,' the noise reaches its peak. Even those who decide to stay in their own cells must turn up the volume of their sets to drown out the constant racket."[91]

With a dearth of functional alternatives, however, these problems do not prevent many prisoners from marking time by watching television. The episodic structure of most broadcasting lends itself to this endeavor. Some prisoners will have spent years watching every episode of their favorite program. This can be a solitary experience, but the television is always a special gathering point, so it typically provides a shared encounter with some version of the outside world. In fact, a particular group of prisoners can turn these episodes into regular events. "Wrestling was on Friday nights," recalls Carceral, with "football or basketball over the weekend." The plot twists in daily soap operas become topics of conversation and even a basis for arguments on death row.[92] Other prisoners are equally devoted to the tawdry parade of stories on talk shows: "They spend their free time watching Jerry, Ricki, Montel, and WWF."[93] According to Renaud, the programming is neither random nor uplifting:

There is a running joke in Texas prisons that most television fans can recite every line of every Clint Eastwood movie ever made, because invariably they will be voted in. Rarely are Discovery, PBS, History Channel or any similar shows voted in. The main fare is movies, sports, and, during the daytime, soap operas.[94]

Carceral calls them "professional TV watchers." They serve much of their sentences while sitting in front of a television, living vicariously through its programs in an attempt to escape the monotony of imprisonment.

In a modest way, watching television helps prisoners stay connected to the outside world. The programs are often informative, albeit in tacit and unintended fashion. By watching these programs, a prisoner stays abreast of changes in society. Coincidentally, the local news may take a prisoner back to the community he or she left behind: "Hey, someone stuck up the 7-Eleven where I used to buy cigarettes!" For the most part, however, television programs serve dual and paradoxical functions. On the one hand, they mark the passage of time within a setting where the inhabitants strive to disattend temporal experience. On the other hand, they distract prisoners from cyclical and repetitive routines by means of stories and spectacles that display these same qualities.

Public Events

The foregoing tactics have chronometric advantages. They serve as a basis for marking time because the activity in question is regular, accretionary, or predictable. It is possible, however, to mark temporal experience in terms of public events that are erratic, spasmodic, or unpredictable. These significant occurrences may be fearful or desirable, and they touch everyone's life in the prison—at least vicariously as gossip or folklore. Examples include violence, attempted escapes, new construction, and sex scandals. They constitute temporal milestones in an otherwise barren terrain. For prisoners, they mark a period of time relative to a particular event. They resemble nomadic people in this regard, remembering an unspecified time before or after the flood.

At a mental asylum, Erving Goffman was struck by the contrast between ubiquitous boredom and exceptional events: "Every total institution can be seen as a kind of dead sea in which little islands of vivid, encapturing activity appear. Such activity can help the individual withstand the psychological stress usually engendered by assaults upon the self."[95] He notes that these events offer relief from stressful circumstances, but he does not grasp the temporal significance of this contrast for marking the passage of time. Violence is the "encapturing activity" par excellence. "In my years," says Carceral, "the events I recall most vividly are violent ones. My first fight was within two years of lockup, and I was stabbed." Such events are traumatic for the victim as well as the perpetrator (especially in light of the punishment that commonly follows). For those who witness and gossip about the incident, however, there is relief from sameness, boredom, and an overabundance of empty time. Subsequent gossip is also a kind of temporal agency in that it prolongs their experience of these events. This is another variation on the savoring complex.

Fearful events have the most impact on the prison's collective memory. For all concerned, other events or a period of time can now be remembered as having occurred before or after the fight in question. The perpetrator of violence alters his or her temporal experience, as well as that of the victim. There is massive concentration on the present moment, which slows the perceived passage of time. In addition, the perpetrator usurps time from the rhythm and routine of the temporal regime. Both perpetrator and victim may be reassigned to segregation, which further changes their temporal experience in rather more long-lasting fashion. Those who watch the fight are spellbound by an outbreak of drama in an otherwise drab world. The story is streamlined in the gossip that follows this incident. Precipitating aggression or disrespect is typically unknown or left out of the narrative. Consequently, other prisoners can experience the event very differently. For them, the story may have fearful implications. Given that the violence is misperceived as random, the implication is clear: "I could be next." This gossip makes the environment seem more dangerous (and exciting) than it really is—especially in the eyes of new prisoners. Only later will they realize that such violence is unlikely in the absence of provocation.

The public events prisoners use to mark time need not be violent or fearful. Attempted and successful escapes are milestones in the timeline of a prison. They become chronometric parts of the folklore at that correctional facility. Anthony Manocchio tries to visit Jimmy Dunn on a foggy day, but he is treated with unusual caution by the correctional officers:

The prisoners are kept locked up in their cellblocks until the fog lifts. There have been a number of escapes during foggy weather, so prison officials and guards remain rather tense until the fog lifts. Then the final "fog count" is taken once again, and the "count-is-clear" whistle is sounded.[96]

A memorable event of this sort functions as a temporal landmark in a setting where little else differentiates one period of time from another. Now other events can be dated relative to "that time we were locked down on account of the fog." Two prisoners escaped from Gladiator School while Carceral was there. They used a vacuum cleaner cord to climb down from a second-story window. Once they hit the ground, one man ran but the other climbed a tree right next to the prison. Guards searched the area beneath that tree, but they never looked up to see him. Eventually, both of these men were recaptured, but, for years afterward, prisoners laughed about how much longer it took for the guards to find the man in the tree. As an ongoing part of that prison's folklore, this incident serves as a temporal point of reference.

Major changes to a prison's infrastructure or dramatic revisions of policy offer another way to mark the passage of time. The construction of a new building or the decision to add a bed in each cell becomes another point of reference. Old-timers identify a particular event as something that occurred before or after major renovations. In so doing, they create a sequential structure for their temporal experience. Paluch titles one chapter in his autobiography "The Old Dining Hall" and a second "The New Dining Hall."[97] A new Health Services Unit (HSU) and a new kitchen were built while Carceral was at Cherryflats. Each of these buildings was constructed over a portion of the prisoner recreation area. Thus, with the addition of each building, the recreation yard was reduced in size. Both of these buildings could have been placed in different locations. Once these projects were completed, prisoners could identify a period of time as coming "after the new HSU but before the new kitchen."

As public events, sex scandals serve the same chronometric function—they provide a mutual basis for temporal orientation. At Cherryflats, two prisoners established sexual relationships with two correctional officers. The four of them would spend hours together in one of the offices. Inevitably, these prisoners told others, and someone informed members of the staff. Everyone in the prison was talking about it, and the incident was reported in the local newspaper. Later, another prisoner at Cherryflats had a sexual relationship with a kitchen worker. He disliked the prison so much that he confessed in order to get himself transferred. In a setting where men are deprived of women, such stories are the stuff of legend and daydreams. They constitute the noteworthy elements of a prison's collective memory, shared events that structure temporal experience. Carceral remembers nothing of clocks and calendars at Cherryflats. Instead, his time there was marked by two new buildings, two sex scandals, and one stabbing.

Private Encounters

Prisoners also mark the passage of time by means of personal events and subjective observations. With these tactics, temporal experience is structured by occurrences that affect only a single convict, not the prison population as a whole. These occasions include letters, visits, weddings, the birth of a child, one's graduation or divorce, and the deaths of friends and loved ones. Of course, much the same could be said of people in everyday life, but the unique circumstances of incarceration intensify these events to a degree that is largely unknown outside of prison.

When, for example, Carceral meets with a supportive and cherished confidant, he is engulfed by emotions that flood into the present moment:

> I had a visit from an academic friend. I believe it was the second time I saw her. I was speaking so much and faster than usual that I eventually stopped, noting I should listen for a while. It was truly euphoric to actually have a person want to listen to me about my education, my thoughts. I was aware of time passing, yet much of it disappeared in gulps. Once the visit was over, it took forever to get processed out of the visiting area and walk back to my cell.

Beforehand, he had anticipated this meeting with growing excitement. He savored the memory for months afterward. Yet, not wanting to share the experience with prison gossips, he kept it to himself. The significance of this event partitioned time for him alone.

Some of these personal events and subjective observations are imposed on prisoners by nature or society. Involuntarily, and with an air of regret, Jackson is forced to consider the passage of time during his incarceration. In a letter to his mother, he writes, "You may not know me when you next see me. I find a few new gray hairs every time I look in the mirror. If I live to be thirty, I guess it will be all white."[98] As a POW held in solitary confinement, Christopher Burney attempts to quicken the passage of time by disattending to temporal experience. Yet the local church inadvertently thwarts his efforts:

> I felt less sane after these weeks than ever before, and my condition was not improved when a bell suddenly started to toll the hours. It was a disaster of truly great proportions. The bell was cracked and made a dreadful sound of pain and ugliness. . . . It also multiplied the days, for instead of two periods of waiting, from dawn to soup and from soup to nightfall, there were now twenty-four, each one as long as ever.
>
> The bell never told of progress, never gave a sudden surprise by announcing that the day was further gone than I had thought. Indeed, it seemed to preface every stroke by a sarcastic "it's only . . ."[99]

The unwelcome bell forced Burney to mark the passage of time when he was trying to avoid doing precisely that. By making him time-conscious, it brought about a torturous magnification of his temporal experience.

While some ways of marking time are unwanted intrusions, just as frequently, if not more so, prisoners exhibit behavior or attend to their environment for the express purpose of calibrating temporal experience. We can conceive of these tactics as adaptations, although the degree to which they are voluntary is ambiguous within the context of incarceration. Perhaps it is best to think of them as constrained choices. Having quickly run out of things to do, the captive Burney has recourse to a tried and true method for marking time: "I reached the end of my repertoire and was reduced to the chief stock-in-trade of all those in solitary confinement: pacing up and down the cell."[100] Cigarettes provide another way to gauge the passing hours, as Jackson explains to Joan, one of his supporters: "I just lit my seventy-fifth cigarette of this day. It will be my last—until after breakfast."[101] In segregation, and deprived of his possessions, Carceral contemplates the only thing that setting has to offer: "I did mathematics to occupy my mind. 'Okay,' I'd think to myself, '643 bricks make up this cell. No, no, 648.' " With a resource unavailable to Carceral, Baca and his colleagues resort to an ancient technique for time reckoning: "In the afternoon we'd stand at the bars staring at the windows ten feet beyond, tracking the day's hours through the movements of shadows and light."[102] Lacking even the contrast between shadows and light, Timerman rejoices when a rare visitor arrives to help him fathom his temporal experience: "Once a fly entered the cell, and it was a real holiday watching it flit around for hours, till it disappeared through the small crack by which the jailers communicated with me."[103] In diverse ways, then, we find prisoners subjectively attending to themselves or the environment to mark the passage of time.

THIS FOR THAT

"If nature adores cycles," argues Michael Young, "the conscious mind abhors them. The mind adores difference, especially the kind of small variations from moment to moment that keep people alert."[104] With diabolical diligence, prisons deprive inmates of exactly these "small variations." Correctional facilities occupy very little territory, and the physical setting rarely changes. The range of permissible conduct is quite narrow, leaving prisoners with few behavioral options. On top of that, correctional officers herd inmates through a cyclical schedule of repetitious intervals.

"When events become recurrent and thus habitual," writes Ton Otto, "they become less noticed and remembered by human actors."[105] Shorn of any intervention, this is the mental outcome of incarceration. If prisoners accede to it, they will seem to have hurried through a sentence they can barely remember. Yet the price one pays for this retrospective oblivion is unacceptably steep. The same conditions that make for temporal compression at some uncertain point in the future also bring about a seemingly endless present of sameness and tedium. Rather than submit to temporal emptiness, prisoners devise their own ways of marking time, but there is a self-defeating quality to these tactics.

Prisoners inhabit a setting that is nearly devoid of the temporal markers we take for granted in the outside world. There is almost nothing to do, and boredom is an ineffaceable foe. Burney describes the period of his captivity as "a life where there is little else but time."[106] According to Stephen Stanko, a prisoner's court-imposed sentence "becomes an existence without the events and actions that compose living."[107] This is the temporal experience prisoners would be left with if, in some fashion, they did not mark the passage of time.

In Ken Lamberton's experience, prison is "a place where clocks and calendars are meaningless, where hours and days and months percolate into one homogenous, stagnant pond."[108] Convicts discover that they cannot use the standard temporal units of linear time without incurring the surplus penalty of protracted duration. Attending to hours and days slows the perceived passage of time. Dispensing with our mechanical framework for time reckoning, prisoners instead attend to the sequential occurrences, cumulative processes, or unique events that are available in their immediate environment.

Their tactics parallel those of the people observed so acutely by Karen Blixen when she moved from Denmark to Kenya in 1914 to assume the management of a coffee plantation:

> A clock was entirely an object of luxury in the African highlands. All the year round you could tell, from the position of the sun, what the time was, and as you had no dealings with railways, and could arrange your life on the farm according to your own wishes, it became a matter of no importance.[109]

Temporal experience can be structured by flowers on the Andaman Islands or the position of the sun over East Africa. But it is also possible to gauge temporal experience in other ways: the number of times per day one is counted by correctional officers, the contents of a food tray unceremoniously shoved through a slot in the door to one's cell, or the number of cigarettes one smokes before breakfast. Regardless of whether our circumstances are idyllic or horrific, human beings appear to abhor a temporal vacuum. We mark the passage of time even when it is counterproductive to do so.

It is equally true that convicts confront a singular world. Subsequent to incarceration, they feel compelled to abandon previous temporal benchmarks in favor of those that characterize life in prison. These maneuvers help them to do away with an overabundance of unmarked time. With pathetic and ingenious measures, they structure temporal experience using what they find at hand. More often than not, however, prisoners are troubled by what they embrace and haunted by what they relinquish.

Chapter Seven

RESISTANCE AND TEMPORAL AGENCY

"To prescribe activity is to prescribe a world," declared Erving Goffman; "to dodge a prescription can be to dodge an identity."[1] In the mental asylum that served as the setting for his ethnography, inmates resisted the prescriptions of that total institution by making unauthorized use of what Goffman called "free places," where "ordinary levels of surveillance and restriction were markedly reduced."[2] A divergent view of place is evident in Michel Foucault's treatise on the establishment of penitentiaries.[3] With Jeremy Bentham's panopticon as an architectural model, Foucault argues that those who design prisons aspire to unobstructed surveillance. In his analysis, the physical setting offers no resources for resistance. Goffman and Foucault differ in their assessment of place, but neither of them recognizes time and temporal experience as contested terrain.

During the last two decades, a sizable body of research has been devoted to the study of resistance, but no consensus has emerged on the issue of its efficaciousness, and, almost without exception, temporal dimensions of opposition have been overlooked. Despite Foucault's pessimism, there are intermittent riots, such as the famous uprising at Attica in 1971, and two waves of prison strikes swept across the United States in 2016 and 2018.[4] Yet the megafauna of resistance are comparatively rare events, which, in the absence of closer scrutiny, can be misread as an indicator of widespread quiescence. Recent scholarship corrects this misconception with research on "backstage resistance" and "micro-resistance."[5] In addition, there are efforts to reconceptualize resistance in ways that sensitize us to its real prevalence.[6] Nevertheless, aside from brief attention to "slow playing" in the writings of Jeffrey Ross (i.e., "complying with the direct orders of a CO, but doing so very slowly"), this extensive literature fails to acknowledge that time is the crux of the matter.[7]

The coercive power of the penitentiary is undeniable, but not limitless. Convicts are taken prisoner, but they never fully embrace the temporal regime. Thus, Gresham Sykes compares the prison to an imperial colony: "Like a province which has been conquered by force of arms, the community of prisoners has come to accept the validity of the regime constructed by their rulers but the subjugation is not complete."[8] It follows that the prisoner's view of time is restive and inventive. "Time in prison passes no matter what a prisoner does," writes John Irwin, "but only the most passive or mentally deficient prisoners let time just pass. They *do* time. Most set goals, make plans, lay out strategies."[9] To one degree or another, these strategies entail temporal resistance.

Every prison fails in its effort to control all aspects of the convict's temporal experience. Time changes prisoners, but prisoners also change time. Especially in prison, time offers a chance to assert oneself, an opportunity for gamesmanship, and a resource for insurrection. "I have nothing but time," writes George Jackson.[10] Within the walls of the penitentiary, time becomes the essential field of struggle. This struggle is manifest as "time work" or temporal agency: convicts attempt to control, manipulate, or customize their own temporal experience.[11] With this effort to reestablish temporal autonomy, convicts shoulder some responsibility for their perception of time. Each moment presents a matrix of possibilities. Through the choices they make, convicts exert some influence over their incarceration.

Without intervention of some kind, prisoners confront a "shoreless ocean of time."[12] Victor Serge gives us an inkling of what it is like to anticipate a prison sentence unmitigated by temporal agency:

> The unreality of time is palpable. Each second falls slowly. What a measureless gap from one hour to the next. When you tell yourself in advance that six months—or six years—are to pass like this, you feel the terror of facing an abyss.[13]

His time-induced anguish is echoed in a more recent memoir by T. J. Parsell: "My days dragged by, each one much like the other, until days had become weeks and weeks became months, turning finally into years."[14] The perceived passage of time is excruciating unless the convict intervenes. Rik Scarce is unequivocal: "Inmates *must* mold time for psychic and self-preservation. Otherwise, the time inside the cramped, monotonous jail crawls like molasses in January."[15] In short, time work is necessary. The less effectively prisoners engage in temporal agency, the more torturous serving their sentence becomes.

Nevertheless, declares Cheyenne Yakima, "there's nothing easy about doing time."[16] By way of explanation, Scarce cites the "minimal resources" available for temporal enterprise.[17] Mumia Abu-Jamal elaborates on this point by noting that many convicts have almost no time free from caged circumstances:

> As against any regime imposed on human personality, there is resistance, but far less than one might expect. . . .
>
> It also is true, however, that we have little opportunity to be otherwise, given . . . twenty-two hours locked in cell, followed by two hours of recreation out of cell. Outdoor recreation takes place in a cage, ringed with double-edged razor wire—the "dog pen."[18]

The certainty of reprisals for temporal resistance is another factor. "As one prisoner reminded me during a conversation about taking a stand for our rights to proper and timely medical care," recalls Clare Hanrahan, " 'You're going home soon. We have to stay.' "[19] In prison, furthermore, it is difficult to find any temporal refuge for one's time work. One's past, present, and future are equally repellent, as Richard Jones and Thomas Schmid tell us:

> Doing time is not as easy as it may sound; actually, it is a rather complicated business. For one thing, you must try to keep yourself busy even though there is very little for you to do. . . . You would like to plan for the future, but it seems so far away that it doesn't really seem like it is worth thinking about. Also, thinking about the future tends to make the time drag. You also don't want to think about the past, because eventually you get around to the dumb mistake that got you in here. So, I guess it must be best to think about the present but that is so boring.[20]

Against all odds, then, prisoners must try to exert some control over their own perception of time. Yet they do so within the context of incarceration, which, to say the least, is inhospitable to temporal innovation.

Outside prison, we modify our own temporal experience by pursuing interesting and rewarding careers, socializing with friends and loved ones, traveling to exotic locations, or purchasing various forms of entertainment. Inside prison, where these strategies are unavailable or ineffective, convicts must improvise distinctive tactics to accelerate the pace of life and achieve some relief from monotony. They aspire to do "easy time," not "hard time." According to Carceral, however, easy time is something of a misnomer; it is still troublesome even if less stressful.

"More than anything else," says Scarce, "doing time was about creating completely new meanings for time and developing strategies for fulfilling those new meanings."[21] These strategies for the management of one's own temporal experience help prisoners cope with incarceration. In this chapter, with Carceral as our guide, we consider some of these strategies. The distribution ranges from relatively passive and largely mental techniques to those that are more active and disruptive.

WAITING FOR TIME TO EXPIRE

Timothy Leary condenses life in prison to a single word: "Waiting."[22] Alexander Berkman complains about "the long days of waiting."[23] As Amanda Lindhout puts it, "my own days felt increasingly like a long wait for nothing."[24] "I found out when my new court day was," recalls Reginald Hall, "so I was just waiting."[25] Abu-Jamal outlines the setting: "Imagine living, eating, sleeping, relieving oneself, daydreaming, weeping—*but mostly waiting*, in a room about the size of your bathroom."[26] Jimmy Baca reports "staring at cell walls for hours, days, and months at a stretch."[27] Even Drew Leder, a visiting philosopher, is awestruck by the emptiness: "Everything was unfolding with glacial slowness. . . . I was not just in a waiting room, but in a whole temple of waiting where time was all anybody did and there was plenty of it to kill."[28]

On the face of it, waiting for time to expire is not a form of self-determination. It would be easy to dismiss it as merely the by-product of institutionalization. Yet Harold Garfinkel's research demonstrates that a person's "motivated compliance" with social norms is based on tacit choices.[29] From this standpoint, *choosing* to wait is a species of temporal agency, albeit a relatively passive one. In an unexpected way, moreover, it can be a subtle expression of resistance. Waiting for time to expire, all the while refusing to be changed by the correctional assumptions of the penitentiary, redefines the meaning of one's sentence. Subjectively, there is an understanding that one is enduring the sentence without being altered by it. Thinking about things in this way constitutes "important evidence that he is still his own man."[30] Others may see compliance with the temporal regime, but the prisoner perceives stubborn resistance.

With this covert scheme, prisoners cultivate cognitive immunity to temporal anguish. Peter Pringle gives voice to this defiant stance when, finally, he arrives at an understanding of his own subjective autonomy:

> I had the realisation that all they could do to me was kill me. . . .
>
> This realisation gave me a curious sense of freedom within myself. I knew that while they could keep me physically imprisoned and could put me to death, they could not control my mind or my spirit. Within myself I was free as a bird. In that spirit and realisation I determined to make the best of whatever time might be left to me in his life, regardless of the circumstances.[31]

Pringle concludes that his soul and innermost thoughts are impervious to the rigors of incarceration, which redefines his future temporal experience. He perceives himself to be unchangeable, but, the success of this strategy will prove to be short-lived.

There are exceptions, of course, but a prisoner rarely has any talent at waiting. Most of them are not very good at it, especially at first. This inadequacy has both collective and individualistic facets, but they are two sides of the same coin. American culture does not valorize waiting, so it comes as no surprise that members of our society are typically unprepared for this challenge. Still, this is truer for some than others. In the eyes of one convict, John, this inability to delay gratification is what brings many to prison in the first place: "I know this was definitely my personal downfall. I wanted everything right then. I couldn't wait. And because I couldn't wait I came in here. This is where you have all the guys who didn't want to wait."[32] With incarceration, however, they must learn and choose to wait because it is part of their punishment.

Carceral observes that waiting is what convicts do during the early days of their sentences, when they are still unfamiliar with the alternatives. Yet, inevitably, waiting makes for the experience of protracted duration, so it is rarely the principal strategy throughout one's sentence. Gradually, prisoners become acquainted with other strategies and switch to them during the bulk of their time behind bars. Counting hours and days is an outsider's way to mark the passage of time. Newcomers cling to these customary markers, but experienced prisoners learn to disregard them. Toward the end of their sentences, however, convicts typically revert to waiting as the primary strategy, which creates a frustrating finish for their incarceration. The chasm of time between now and one's release date becomes the sole object of consciousness. The expiration of time is slowed by waiting. Regardless of whether it is at the beginning or at the end of one's sentence, the resulting days are long and monotonous.

To be sure, all prisoners wait—day in, day out—for something or somebody. It is useful, therefore, to distinguish between the waiting inflicted on convicts by the temporal regime and the ways prisoners choose to wait as strategies for the expiration of time. In a general sense, they are all waiting for their freedom. But before that day arrives, if it ever does, there will be plenty of particularized waiting to do. They will wait to be searched and wait for the gates to be rolled. They will wait for the count to clear. They will wait for meals, showers, and access to the yard, canteen, or library. They will wait for work, medical attention, laundry, and toilet paper. They must wait for cellies to get out of bed, stop making noise, or go to sleep. They must wait for telephone calls and visits. Hanrahan notes that correctional officers on certain shifts routinely refused to distribute mail, thereby forcing prisoners to wait for it.[33]

The waiting is occasioned by a lack of resources in combination with a lack of temporal autonomy, but the temporal regime cannot determine *how* convicts do this waiting. The content of this waiting reflects their own choices and decisions; it represents a measure of self-determination. As is always the case, however, it is a severely qualified form of temporal agency—one that is limited by the intrinsic constraints of their circumstances. Indeed, this effort at self-determination is prompted by restrictions imposed upon convicts by the temporal regime. Put differently, they learn strategies for waiting because the setting forces them to do so. Waiting per se does not abbreviate the perceived passage of time. If temporal compression occurs, it is an artifact of the way one waits.

Most prisoners realize that their time is communal as well as personal. They also recognize that paying attention to the passage of time is counterproductive. Attending to time itself slices each interval thinner and thinner, making it seem as if the hour will never end. It follows that they learn to wait without talking about time. Rare instances of deviance are shadows of this norm. A convict named Truck made the norm visible by doing his time in jail poorly, as witnessed by his fellow prisoner, Scarce: "Truck never made the switch from street time to inmate or individual time. . . . Every morning he made a point of announcing to everyone his personal countdown: how many days left until his hearing on a parole violation."[34] Comparable evidence emerges from Carceral's interview with a prisoner named Gus:

> I had a cellie that was a mess. He always talked about the amount of time he *had* to do. But he didn't have any time to do! I think he had like three or four years. He was always worrying about release. It was killing him. Frankly, I got real tired of hearing it since I had so much time to do. Man, he was a whiner.

Truck and Gus's cellie earn the ire of fellow prisoners by violating temporal norms. Waiting poorly, they impose hard time on themselves as well as fellow prisoners.

Waiting is never really avoided during the middle of one's sentence. Rather, a prisoner becomes accustomed to it and learns to divert his or her attention from it. Diversionary behavior will concern us later in the chapter; here, we focus on mental diversions. The prisoner's mind is typically free to wander, so diversionary tactics often include subjective involvement with one's own past or future. In one of his short stories, "Scheherazade," Haruki Murakami's characters hint that time travel is at the heart of storytelling:

> Scheherazade fell silent. From the look of it, she had gone back in time and was picturing the various things that had happened in order, one by one. . . .
> How wonderful it would be, Habara thought, if he, too, could inhabit another time or space.[35]

We should recognize mental time travel as a type of temporal agency, wherein one chooses to inhabit (subjectively at least) a more desirable present.

Likewise, in prison, remembering the past and imagining the future become covert excursions. With the usual bravado, convicts tout their ability to modify temporal experience using mental time travel. A prisoner named Mark commends this stratagem for its capacity to transport him from the here and now of incarceration to other times and places:

> When you're virtually under twenty-four-hour surveillance—like the new prison in Jessup—there's also a way you can *resist* or *escape*. Autistic thinking. Total absorption in fantasy. "I'm building an island and this is what my water source will be, and the kind of plants I'll have. . . ." You can absorb yourself in this for hours and hours and resist being conditioned by the discipline.[36]

In a similar vein, Baca succeeds at escaping the present circumstances of incarceration via mental time travel, but he engages in reminiscence rather than fantasy:

> Occasionally I'd be distracted by the sound of a guard's footsteps or thoughts about the Mexican mafia gunning for me in the prison yard outside. But with nothing else to do but lie there and sweat, I trained my mind to shut out everything around me and travel back in time.[37]

Mark envisions a delightful future, while Baca revisits a cheerful past, but both of them make use of mental time travel to do so.

Baca's memories provide some consolation, but that is not usually the case. Behind bars, every tactic for temporal agency is frequently ineffective or even backfires. Instead of visiting a more desirable time, writes Yakima, "you sit in your cell, accompanied only by memories and regrets."[38] "You think about the years you've wasted that you can never get back," he adds, "years that might have been the best ones of your life."[39] Parsell's efforts are defeated by the prison sensorium: "I tried to take my mind off the situation by reflecting on different times. . . . But none of that worked, because all the sounds and smells of jail kept bringing me back."[40] James Paluch attempts to control the temporal locus of his thoughts, but later admits to failure:

> I try not to think about how I will be forced to repeat this same dreary routine day in and day out for many years to come.[41]
>
>   . . .

Hauntingly, inescapably, I confront myself with the same terrible questions every day: What have I done to myself, and when will this all come to an end?[42]

Daydreaming about future release is equally problematic. Such thinking lengthens the perceived time spent waiting.

Mental time travel is not a simple matter of remembering or imagining better days. In fact, it requires a great deal of subjective discipline to focus on and inhabit a comforting (if fictive) version of one's past or future rather than the ignoble past and cruel present. Without such discipline, which is rarely achieved, the prisoner risks magnifying his or her punishment. Failure has the further consequence of chronic and widespread depression because one merely longs for or misses the past instead of treating it as a temporal refuge. "Just to exist at all in the cage calls for some heavy psychic readjustments," acknowledges Jackson.[43] He reproaches himself for "this morbid depression that owns a little more of my mind each day that passes."[44] Yet he cannot bring himself to refrain from a cognitive process that is the wellspring for his despair: "I think of my personal past quite often."[45]

MANAGING ONE'S TEMPORAL EXPECTATIONS

Temporal experience is subject to our expectations. Moreover, they are collective expectations because of our shared commitment to clocks, calendars, schedules, and the culturally specific rhythms of social interaction. As a result, we can become angry if a web page takes only seconds longer to open than it normally does.

Concerning delay, however, convicts have far more to worry about than a slow internet connection. They must manage their temporal expectations in order to exercise some control over their perception of time. In particular, observes Carceral, long-term prisoners learn to expect the worst but hope for the best. Doing so is a form of temporal agency or time work. This method is motivated by their lengthy experience with the arbitrariness and uncertainty of life in prison.

Managing one's temporal expectations is a cognitive tactic. It proves functional for anyone serving a long sentence to adopt it as a general outlook on incarceration. "We live only for the moment," declares Billy Sinclair, "expecting nothing but the worst."[46] This attitude reflects one's adjustment to an environment that specializes in disappointment: "Kansas stands up, expecting the worst, which is his general worldview."[47] Ingrid Betancourt and other hostages find it equally useful: "Don't ask for anything, don't desire anything."[48]

More specifically, argues Carceral, prisoners must manage their expectations concerning the possibility of being released. Inmates are fixated on release. They discuss the length of their respective sentences and the amount of time they expect to serve. They contemplate their potential release years before they are even eligible to see the parole board. They are undeterred by the likelihood of running afoul of the rules sooner or later, which is commonly expressed in the fatalism of long-term prisoners: "The way most of us old-timers handle the situation is just to assume that everything we do or say is in violation of some rule or other."[49] Coupled with the uncertainty of indeterminate sentences, these prisoners really have no idea when they will be released. Prisoners cope with the resulting stress by managing their temporal expectations. The closer one gets to a parole hearing, the more relevant this strategy becomes.

A seasoned convict named Rashaad explained this tactic to Carceral soon after he entered prison:

RASHAAD: "Look, when you first see the parole board, they will not let you go. You got to expect the worst."
CARCERAL: "Expect the worst?"
RASHAAD: "You got to expect the worst or you will be disappointed."

Carceral never forgot this lesson. When, almost ten years later, he finally met with the parole board, he expected nothing more than a long deferral, which is exactly what he got. He would have to wait twenty-four months before meeting with them again. Ahead of the meeting, he had hoped for a shorter deferral but had not expected it, which took much of the sting out of that decision. Over the ensuing years, Carceral would pass this wisdom on to younger convicts.

Yet one's socialization to life in prison is haphazard. Prisoners often mistrust and disregard each other, so ignorance and misconceptions are widespread. Serving time in this self-imposed isolation, it is easy for them to develop false expectations. A regularly scheduled meeting with the parole board leads them to think that early release is a possibility. They do not realize that many convicts are never granted parole; they remain in prison until their mandatory release date. Their good behavior is unrecognized; the reform of their character is unrewarded. They witness the release of prisoners who committed more serious crimes. They become convinced that the system is arbitrary or rigged against them. If they fail to manage their temporal expectations, regularly scheduled meetings with the parole board become akin to a rollercoaster ride of rising expectations followed by disappointment and dashed hopes.

Even prisoners who know the strategy may be incapable of employing it. Many pay lip service to the tactic of managing one's temporal expectations but are unable to sustain any commitment. It is arduous to expect the worst and hope for the best. In Carceral's experience, more prisoners fail at this strategy than succeed. As a cautionary tale, Carceral recounts a conversation he had with Neville concerning another prisoner named DeShawn:

CARCERAL: "I cannot believe DeShawn's reaction to his hearing yesterday. I was in the bathroom while he was in there talking. One thing he said is that the lady was racist like a motherfucker because another dude with murder got a grant and he didn't. He must not know that dude really did not get a grant. He's only recommended for a grant. Then he said he's going to appeal it because of all the other dudes that got out with less time than him were white. Of course, he said he was going to talk about the guy he thinks has a grant. Dude is a mess."

NEVILLE: "Ever since I known DeShawn, he always thinks he's going home. He was telling another man, like a month ago, he would be out before him. This other guy's date is two months from now. You know you can't go around telling people that. DeShawn's mandatory date is 2016. My mandatory release is 2012. That's when they *have* to let me go. I know you know Zander, DeShawn's cellie. He is down there talking about how DeShawn is getting some weapons, wearing a sheet on his head. You know DeShawn is Muslim. Now he is going terrorist!"

CARCERAL: "I take it you know him well."

NEVILLE: "Yes, I was with him at his last place. He went around for a *whole year*, before a previous hearing, telling other men he was going home. A *whole year*! This time he assumed, because he went through a pre-release investigation, he was getting a grant to leave. So, he did the same thing. A man cannot do that. He did that to himself by telling everyone he was going home. He told *me* that shit. Man, I can't tell him to slow down. He doesn't listen. Now, he is hiding in his room, depressed because they denied him. Pissed off at the world! But he did it to himself."

DeShawn exhibits a recurring pattern of incompetence. He repeatedly fails to manage his temporal expectations, doing hard time as a result. His inability to learn from past mistakes makes him an object of contempt.

To manage temporal expectations, the prisoner must engage in an ongoing process of mind control. This is not a default setting in human consciousness; sustained and purposeful intervention in one's own thoughts will be necessary. An example can be found in Carceral's interview with Gus, a fellow prisoner who reveals his exemplary use of self-talk:

> Every time the thought of release popped into my mind, I said to myself, "They may not release you, Gus, you still have years before mandatory release." I would say this out loud sometimes over and over. These dudes around us are so eager to go home, they will convince anyone else that they're going just because they have an upcoming release hearing.

Time work is laborious; it takes effort to manage one's temporal expectations. The parole board can defer a decision for eighteen months (and do so repeatedly). It can impose a specific condition for release, such as one's completion of a program with a two-year waiting list. A prisoner who assumes the worst is rarely disappointed.

Yet we must not exaggerate the efficacy of these practices. A prisoner's efforts to check temporal expectations do not transpire in a vacuum. The effectiveness of one's temporal agency is limited by the social context over which prisoners have little or no control. Carceral prides himself on being attuned to the temporal reality of life behind bars. Better than most, he understands that "reality is denial after denial without any clear sign of when release will occur." However, his efforts to manage temporal expectations are overturned by irresponsible behavior on the part of a parole agent:

> The first time I was put in for release, the parole agent, who came to inspect the residence where I would be living, told my family that I would be out by December. I reassured my family this person didn't know what he was talking about, but they did not believe that the D.O.C. [Department of Corrections]

would have such an employee. "How could he not know? He's your parole agent." I'm still here. The parole board keeps promising release "next time." Next time and tomorrow have a great deal in common. They never come. Expecting the worst helps. Later, I learned that telling my family I would be released was a "no-no." When the agent visited and told them I'd be out soon, they started living hearing to hearing, date to date, and so did I.

Mind control is necessary but not sufficient. Managing one's temporal expectations is a cognitive stratagem, but it does not operate independently of one's circumstances. Prisoners use this tactic in an attempt to gain the upper hand vis-á-vis the always uncertain time they have left to serve. By and large, however, the intended and unintended workings of the system undermine their efforts.

Simultaneously, hope is part of this strategy and part of the problem. Hope is uplifting, but it impedes one's ability to expect the worst. "In a ferment of anxiety and hope," observes Alexander Berkman, "I count the days and hours, irritable with impatience and apprehension as I near the fateful moment."[50] He enacts the wrong kind of time work, and his hopes are unfulfilled; the parole board refuses to grant him a hearing.[51] Prisoners undermine their own efforts by hoping for the best, but it is often their only recourse. "I know how to do time," boasts Sinclair.[52] In actuality, he is resigned to hoping time away with wishful thinking:

> I had served nearly eight years at Angola. Favrot had predicted that I would spend at least fifteen years in prison. I could not fathom another seven years in Angola. My mind focused on serving ten, perhaps twelve years. Something would happen, had to happen, after ten years.[53]

It is difficult to stifle hope when it is your last resort.

Like the other convicts, Erin George knows that "hope is a dangerous commodity."[54] She tries to protect herself in the customary way: "I keep expectations low."[55] But the systematic dampening of hope is repeatedly overthrown by her own wishful thinking:

> They say that when someone drops a set of keys, it means a prisoner is going home. Now, I'm not a superstitious woman. Intellectually I realize how foolish it is to believe in such a thing. I know that it's ridiculous, but each time

a bunch of keys clatters against the dirty tile floor, always that damn, unreasonable, unquenchable hope insists that maybe it might be true. In the few seconds it takes for rationality to regain control, my mind spins elaborate fantasies of pardons, newfound evidence, and life-restoring lawyers. And despite myself, each time it happens I hope desperately that this time the keys are for me.[56]

In this light, managing one's temporal expectations seems less like a strategy and more like the grim and pitiful struggles of people drowning in time.

DOING YOUR OWN TIME

As noted by Rik Scarce, this principle is part of the folklore at any jail or penitentiary: "One of the first warnings that I had from a fellow inmate was, 'Do your own time, and don't let the time do you.' "[57] Piper Kerman discovers the same tactic at a women's prison.[58] Newly arrived fish may hear it from Old Heads, albeit in this more menacing variation: "Do your own time . . . or someone will make you do theirs."[59] Still, this is not an uncomplicated tactic, as Scarce admits, and failure is consequential: "I was not doing my time very well. As a first timer in the criminal justice system, every day seemed to drag on painfully slowly."[60]

The essence of this strategy is minding your own business. A convict is supposed to avoid trouble, ignore gossip, refrain from hassling the staff, and leave other prisoners alone. There is a negative quality with the focus on what a convict should *not* do. In particular, as we have seen, the individual must not complain about the perceived passage of time because temporal experience is communal: "By shutting up about our time, we helped others do theirs," recalls Scarce.[61] Everyone has a sentence to complete, and it is one's responsibility to do so without intruding on the sentences served by fellow inmates. Benjamin "Pup" Collier "respected other people, did not pay attention to what they were doing."[62] This is not necessarily a morally righteous stance, but it is certainly less stressful and eases the perceived passage of time. Nor is this a purely subjective strategy. If others begin to talk about the nonprison world, a convict may ridicule that topic of conversation or quickly change the subject.

"In here," declares Kansas, "we all got to do our own time"—a hypocritical statement from someone who spends much of his time exploiting others, but, like so many principles, this one is honored more in the breach.[63] It is noteworthy that this principle reflects a common attitude toward other prisoners, as expressed by Jimmy Dunn: "I want nothing to do with them."[64] When prisoners learn about this principle, asserts Stephen Stanko, it brings them to a fork in the road:

> There are two choices: doing your own time or getting caught up in the prison culture. Inmates may keep to themselves inside prison and follow their own morals and beliefs. We call this doing your "own time." However, others choose a life that follows the dictates of the majority of the general population. This choice involves nothing more than doing those things that the majority of other inmates desire, such as taking advantage of the administration when opportunities present themselves, reacting without thought to the emotions of others, and generally going with the flow.[65]

Convicts must *choose* to do their own time, which marks it as a purposeful modification of temporal experience. This path is not forced upon them. It is a form of temporal agency, and the goal is quick expiration of as much time as possible.

"How you do your time is a very personal decision," writes Clare Hanrahan.[66] For that very reason, however, the prisoner's decision to do time in a particular manner also earns admiration or condemnation from his or her colleagues. Gresham Sykes reports a great deal of respect for "a prisoner who 'pulls his own time.'"[67] Contrastingly, two seasoned prisoners who served as mentors for Scarce, Revvs and Zippo, "got upset when other inmates failed to do their own time."[68] The choices in question cannot be reduced to the causal impact of the temporal regime. If that were true, there would be no basis for recriminations. Instead, like George, convicts understand that this strategy arises from some degree of self-determination:

> It all comes down to how I want to do my time. Time is easier if you stay under the radar and keep it together, and as the women who have been doing a long time often say, I'd much rather do my time than have my time do me.[69]

Prisoners are typically depicted as mere victims of architecture and context, but they see themselves as far more than that. "I've crafted my own life in prison," avows George.[70] Convicts believe that, by doing time in one way or another, they can alter the flow of their own temporal experience.

This belief, however, is quite misleading in its implications. As an oft-repeated article of faith, it implies that the strategy is both generally effective and within the reach of every convict, which is unrealistic. There is little supporting evidence, and, in Carceral's experience, this strategy was seldom followed:

> I've found most men cannot do their own time. As a simple example, I once turned a faucet on to let the water get hot. No one was there but me. I left my empty coffee cup next to the running water and stepped away quickly to use the bathroom. When I came back, the water was off because another man could not mind his own business.

It is nearly impossible to do one's own time, given the lack of privacy and other temporal resources. Moreover, "success" can be counterproductive in the long run because, aside from exceptional individuals, this approach to prison life is a recipe for isolation, loneliness, boredom, and the perception that time is passing slowly.

Most prisoners cannot do their own time precisely because meddling in the affairs of others is a seductive distraction. They welcome the way it diverts their own attention from time itself. Carceral notes that convicts "are always interrupting each other and interjecting their comments." They are preoccupied with each other's lives, which is the opposite of doing your own time. Sylvester Long sums it up: "Everybody is in each other's business and gossiping about any and everything."[71] In the crowded conditions typical at most prisons, the convicts are constantly bothering each other, and the state ensures that there is little else for them to do. It is not an environment conducive to doing your own time, as Jackson explains:

> I'm surrounded here by fools, degenerates, and phonies. I suffer a constant bombardment of nonsense from all sides. There is no rest from it even at night. Twenty-four hours a day all my senses must endure the shock of this attack from the lunatic fringe.[72]

Boredom, curiosity, lust, envy, and greed combine to prevent most convicts from doing their own time. Thus, rampant temporal trespassing is characteristic of the prison sensorium. It provokes anger and violence, but, by the same token, it also distracts inmates from time itself and hastens temporal experience.

"Some women never got visits," reports Kerman, "because they had effectively said goodbye to the outside world."[73] A crucial aspect of doing your own time is the subsidiary tactic of ignoring changes in the nonprison world. An inmate once told Carceral, "You can't do time in both worlds." The goal, as articulated by Andreas Schroeder, is temporal compression of one's sentence: "The sooner you give up trying to live your life in two places at once, the sooner your time eases into that long, mindless lope which makes a year only marginally longer than six months, a fin only slightly more drawn out than a deuce."[74] Once again, temporal agency is manifest in the advice prisoners give each other as well as cautionary tales of failure.

Paying attention to life outside of prison slows temporal experience with intense feelings of helplessness and anxiety. Rather than serving as a refuge, one's own consciousness becomes part of the punishment. Stanko's comments are apropos:

> I spent each day wondering what I had lost on the outside while my life dragged along inside. . . . Outside, I was losing my family, my friends, my job, my position in life, future memories, and anything else that might ever provide a smile.[75]
>
> . . . During incarceration, there is little, if anything, that a prisoner can do to help on the outside. A man of the house has now become a man of the cage. . . . The fear of adultery is one that plays most heavily on prisoners.[76]

Convicts who concern themselves with what is going on in the outside world become excruciatingly aware of the passage of time. Jimmy Lerner's description of a fellow inmate elaborates on the harmful effects of one's failure at temporal agency:

> Spoony, all of eighteen, is doing four to ten behind a drug trafficking conviction, measuring out his life with collect calls to Mandy's (mom's) trailer, wondering if Mandy will answer, wondering if she's high, worrying if she's *been* with someone, if she *is* with someone at this very moment—and who is it? Jody? Sancho? And wondering just where Mandy is on the long waiting list for the Salvation Army's drug rehab program.[77]

Lerner's conclusion is no less applicable to other inmates who obsess about life beyond the perimeter of their prisons: "Spoony's doing 'hard time.' "[78]

It becomes dysfunctional for a prisoner to think much about loved ones in the outside world. For Lamberton and other inmates, the "solution" involves severing one's ties with the nonprison world: "Many men prefer to cut themselves off from their previous life and develop a tough layer of indifference to it."[79] Like doing your own time, of which it is a subset, ignoring changes in the outside world is a strategy that demands a level of mental discipline few prisoners possess. As Richard Jones and Thomas Schmid put it, inmates "engage in the practice of 'thought control' to avoid thinking about their loss of control over future events in the outside world."[80] A key part of this process entails substituting a present-time orientation for the future-time orientation with which they entered prison. Yet they are quick to acknowledge that, for most prisoners, this goal is unreachable: "He has never been able to eliminate such thoughts entirely, of course, but he attempts to suppress them when they occur."[81]

Whenever a convict "attempts to suppress them," these efforts are largely blunted by oppositional factors. It is hard for convicts to sustain a genuine disregard for loved ones and their former lives, so ambivalence prevents many prisoners from pursuing this tactic wholeheartedly. Regardless of an inmate's strategic desire for seclusion, ongoing relationships with various people on the outside repeatedly interrupt one's time in prison. There is, as well, a countervailing concern. "Since I've been in prison," says Mike, "the outside world got microwaves, computers, and all that."[82] Its usefulness for managing temporal experience may be dubious, but ignoring changes in the outside world certainly worsens the Rip Van Winkle effect. For this reason, then, as "an inmate approaches the final months of his sentence, his thought control becomes less effective."[83]

There is no shortage of advice in prison. Ironically, advice concerning how to do your own time is one of many ways inmates intrude on each other's temporal experience. Some of it represents a mentor's self-interest; some of it is well-meaning, even altruistic. In any case, most of it falls on deaf ears. Berkman hears good advice from one of his fellow prisoners: " 'Don' think of your time. Forget it. Oh, yes, you can; you jest take my word for't.' "[84] Later, however, he carefully calculates that he will spend "almost 700,000,000 seconds in solitary confinement, and he goes on to compute the probable length of his remaining sentence: "14 years and 2 months."[85]

Of course, Berkman really has no idea how much time he will serve, but these futile calculations have predictable outcomes: "Appalled by the figures, I pace the cell in agitation."[86]

Like Berkman, other prisoners find it impossible to disregard the tract of time that lies ahead of them. Yet thinking about one's sentence can lead to despair. This temporal quandary is vividly illustrated by a passage from Peter Pringle's memoir:

> The enormity of the forty-year sentence now hit me. How on earth could I face forty years in this hellhole? I could not get my mind around that reality. The prospect was simply beyond reason to me. I could think of nothing else. Finally I decided to kill myself; I could see no other solution.[87]

The fact that he "could think of nothing else" does not endorse the efficacy of doing one's own time to modify temporal experience. It is not so simple to banish the future from one's thoughts.

Questionable practicality does not stop seasoned prisoners, such as Dannie Martin, from instructing newcomers to ignore changes in the outside world: "Old convicts tell the young that the best way to do a long sentence is to free the mind of debris left over from the free world. The idea is to acclimatize oneself to the world within the fence or wall and to erase all that lies beyond."[88] Yet new prisoners are cynical and, like Dunn, suspect that this advice comes from someone who inhabits a vastly different realm of temporal experience:

> Any of the old-time cons in the joint will tell you that visits are the worst thing you can have in the penitentiary, because they say all they do is put you on a bum kick. But I'm suspicious that the only reason they say that is because they aren't getting any visits. Generally, there isn't anybody left to visit them. But I haven't gotten that far yet, to the point I think visits are bad. I may someday, but in the meantime, I'll just keep my visits.[89]

This is not to say that the advice is false in some ultimate sense, but its credibility is counterbalanced by the persistent strength of one's social ties during the early years of incarceration.

From a certain distance, these social ties seem to be the essence of humanity, something positive and comforting. Reginald Hall brings us closer to the facts of life in prison, however, where maintaining these social ties can have a toxic impact on one's temporal experience: "I thought about being at home with my mom and my brothers, and my room at home. By then my eyes were like a swimming pool."[90] His effort to do time both inside and outside of the prison leads to chronic depression as well as an unsuccessful suicide attempt.[91]

DISREGARDING DATES AND STANDARD TIME

Here, we begin to address strategies that are more reliably manifest as forms of action. To be sure, there are further dimensions of avoidance, but now we start to see individual and collective interference with the flow of temporal experience. This is most apparent when we examine how prisoners refer to or talk about time.[92] All of their vocabulary is meant to minimize the perceived time that must be served as one's sentence.

Consider, for instance, the well-worn phrase "doing a stretch." Its persistent use can be traced back to at least the nineteenth century. With these words, a prisoner displays a carefree attitude toward what is typically a daunting sentence. Metaphorically, a convict reduces his or her time in prison to something trivial and much less frightening: extending one's limbs in a more or less pleasant effort to relieve muscular tension. The use of this phrase is a kind of temporal alchemy that transforms a lot of hard time into an insignificant event.

Vocabulary always reflects the practical interests of the people in question. In accord with this principle, there is rich variation in prison slang for one's sentence. The use of "spot" and "bit" as temporal euphemisms can be found in Berkman's memoir from the early years of the twentieth century. Note, for example, the temporal compression in this complaint from one of his fellow prisoners: "'Old offender,' they says to the jedge, and he soaks me for a seven spot."[93] Another colleague offers alternative jargon: "'Now he's doin' a five-bit down in Kansas.'"[94]

Words such as "spot" and "bit" diminish the size of a convict's sentence. Years of punishment shrink to something small, manageable, and unworthy of one's concern. This verbal tradition of temporal agency continues in recent autobiographies. Victor Hassine provides the following instance: "'You have to spend more time out of that cell, Victor,' insisted my chess mate and only friend at that time. 'It's not healthy to do a "bit" like that.'"[95]

The same terminology appears in a memoir written by T. J. Parsell: "He and Slide Step also served their first bit together."[96] In a third memoir, Joel Blaeser's friend, Paul, refers to "my state bit."[97]

Multiple types of this terminology coexist in contemporary prisons. "They talked about time in terms of nickels and dimes," recalls Parsell.[98] With this version, convicts equate five- or ten-year sentences with small, nearly worthless coins. Several years in prison can be dismissed with a mixture of contempt and amusement:

> "You back again, Murray?" someone called out to the old con. He was
> elated by the recognition. It conferred status on him.
> "Yeah, I got a nickel this time," he laughed.[99]

Lerner cites "Tooshay, who's doing a dime behind a crack sale gone bad."[100] His cellmate, Kansas, begins one of his stories with "I was doing a little deuce in Marianna."[101]

The linguistic minimizing of one's sentence is a functional attempt at temporal self-delusion. The words bear little resemblance to the actual time one will serve. In extreme variations on this strategy, we witness truly heroic efforts at temporal agency. The scope of this ambition is nicely illustrated when a fellow prisoner explains the meaning of "a stump" to Berkman:

> "Why, you still have two years, Ed," I remind him.
> "Not on your tintype, Aleck. Only one and a stump."
> "How big is the stump?"
> "Wa-a-ll," he chuckles, looking somewhat diffident, "it's one year, elev'n
> months, an twenty-sev'n days. It ain't no two years, though, see?"[102]

Blaeser's assessment of his friend's status betrays a similar level of ambition in regard to temporal fraudulence: "Paul was more than likely going to do all day, meaning life without parole, and would probably never see the streets again."[103] In this rendition, a life sentence is reduced to a single day. Nevertheless, there is little evidence to suggest that this tactic has a profound impact on temporal experience. The ineffectiveness is most apparent in Kareem's lament: " 'The time is getting to me. I've been doing this bit for a long time.' "[104]

The only prisoners who cross days off a calendar are those with little time to serve and a definite release date. Very few convicts are in that category. Even allowing for these criteria, this practice is terribly dysfunctional. Attention to linear time painfully magnifies the remaining temporal experience despite there not being much of it, objectively speaking. Instead, most prisoners strive to disregard dates and standard time as a form of temporal agency. Mike notes the need as well as the poor prospects for this aspiration:

> You sure can't count the amount of time you got to do. Not when the majority of people here have life plus sixty-five, life plus twenty. You don't actually put the sentence out of your mind, because it is always there, impossible to forget. But it's a war you fight battle by battle. You got to go with an innate belief that some way you're going to elude that length of time.[105]

With its reliance on wishful thinking, this effort may be doomed from the start, but the temporal regime provokes improvisational techniques of resistance from his comrades.

Refusing to admit the passage of time is the most extreme of these measures. The idea seems preposterous on the face of it, but outright refusal to acknowledge the ceaseless flow of time is voiced by fictional and nonfictional convicts alike. The Wire, an HBO television series, depicts the lives of drug dealers on the west side of Baltimore. During the twelfth episode of the third season (2004), Barksdale, the kingpin, and several members of his crew are arrested. The police taunt him with the fact that he will do a long stretch in prison, but, in unison, Barksdale and one of his underlings dismiss the impending sentence:

BARKSDALE: "Shit, you only do two days no-how."
UNDERLING: "That's the day you go in and the day you come out."

In this case, at least, art imitates life. George Jackson was imprisoned more than three decades before The Wire was telecast. Yet in a letter to his father, dated October 17, 1967, he makes a comparable effort to disavow the passage of time: "No new problems here. Just waiting it out. Time is on my side. I'm twenty-six now, and I'll be twenty-six when I leave here. Be it forty years from today."[106]

There are, however, more practical methods for disregarding dates and standard time. The fundamental process involves one's cultivation of a genuine obliviousness to clocks and calendars. "My experience is what I agree to attend to," argues William James, one of the founding fathers of psychology.[107] Christina Dress, a convict at the Washington Corrections Center for Women, concurs with his position and makes pragmatic use of it when attempting to manipulate her own temporal experience: "I don't really pay attention to actual days. It's easier that way."[108] Still, time work is necessary; such obliviousness must be accomplished—no easy task given the ubiquity of time-reckoning technology. In order to achieve a genuine level of temporal obliviousness, recalls Jimmy Baca, a prisoner must engage in avoidance rituals:

> When I first arrived, I vowed that I would not think about time because I knew keeping my mind inside the walls, in the present, was going to keep me alive. I didn't have a wristwatch or calendar to mark off days. I never thought about how much time I had done or how much I had left.[109]

Timothy Leary describes another avoidance ritual at a prison in Chino, California. Unlike ordinary convicts, the trustees had to coordinate their work in terms of a calendar. Large red numbers representing each day of the month were pinned to the wall in their office. Each day, they would remove a number for tomorrow, but Leary notices that there "*is no number for today.*"[110] When he asks why, a trustee laughs and says, "'In con terminology, when you wake up in the morning. That day is over.'"

Exceptions to the rule occur when convicts pay attention to time in order to prevent correctional officers from returning them to their cells prematurely. Sunny Jacobs provides this testimony: "I have a watch now . . . but I only use it to time my walks to make sure I get every minute. Other than that it is simply an instrument of torture—self-flagellation with those tiny hands."[111] The two-edged quality of this tactic is evident in her lament, which confirms the reason for disregarding standard time. It is hard to ignore a watch if you have one, but consulting it repeatedly makes for protracted duration. Among prisoners, strategies for temporal resistance often become quandaries in the perceived passage of time. Any success at temporal agency is apt to be meager, fleeting, and counteracted by the side effects of their own tactics.

Time work is defined as an intended effort to alter one's own temporal experience by means of planning and intervention. The desired type of temporal experience will not occur in response to wishful thinking. The prisoner's behavior must be revised to bring about intended change in the perceived passage of time. There is, consequently, the construction of an avoidance ritual, as exemplified by this excerpt from Carceral's interview with Wilkins:

WILKINS: "Yes, I always watch the evening news to see the general events taking place."

CARCERAL: "I know many men who couldn't care less about watching anything when it comes to news."

WILKINS: "There are parts of it that I don't watch!"

CARCERAL: "Like what?"

WILKINS: "Well, when it comes on every night, 5:30. In the beginning, have you noticed how the date is always shown on the front of the guy's desk? Then the camera rolls in on him."

CARCERAL: "Yeah."

WILKINS: "That, and he usually says it's like May 3rd, 2011."

CARCERAL: "Yeah."

WILKINS: "Well, I know this sounds like I'm a nut, but I leave the volume down or have my headset laying on my bed. As soon as I notice they are into the first or second story, then I pick up my headset or turn up the volume. I got tired of every day hearing and seeing the date."

As much as circumstances allow, convicts edit their temporal experience in order to delete any awareness of dates from their consciousness. When effective, this time work brings about an honest unawareness of the calendar, as evident in the following exchange between Carceral and Tyrone in a classroom:

CARCERAL: "Tyrone, what's the date, so I can put it on this paper?"

TYRONE: "Hell, I don't know. If I said, I'd be lying!"

CARCERAL: "You should keep up on that for me!"

TYRONE: "Yeah right. I ain't got a release date; why should I follow what these other players do?"

CARCERAL: "Good question."

TYRONE: "It will only remind me of how much time I got to do to see these people, who *may* let me go."

Tyrone's belligerence reflects the fact that he had been sentenced to life with the possibility of parole in thirteen years. To put it mildly, the date is not a subject he wishes to discuss. Nonetheless, whether they are watching the news, attending class, or engaged in any number of other activities, convicts repeatedly confront challenges to the effectiveness of their temporal agency.

It should come as no surprise that prisoners inhabiting similar situations tend to invent similar tactics for temporal agency. These improvisational forms of time work are diffused across incarcerated populations by rampant recidivism as well as the socialization of newcomers by old-timers. The upshot is that comparable practices can be found in every jail or prison. This is apparent in the way Carceral's observations echo those of Rik Scarce, who records the teachings of a fellow prisoner named Crib:

> So I had this calendar, see, and I was in about a year and the days were just draggin'. And I says, "I gotta do somethin' about this!" The calendar was the first thing to go. Tore it right off the wall. Then I quit readin' th' papers or watchin' th' news. See, that's what'll get you. You see stuff change. . . .
>
> And the news. I never watch the first few minutes of the news 'cause that's when they put the date on there.[112]

The universality of these procedures is a collective response to the obdurate linkage between the circumstances of incarceration and the perceived passage of time. At diverse correctional institutions, prisoners who have never met one another learn the same lessons because they grapple with the same temporal problems.

To summarize, then, prisoners endeavor to diminish their sentences by talking about them with particular terminology, by refusing to admit the passage of time, and by means of various avoidance rituals. A fourth set of tactics for disregarding dates and standard time entails marking or counting only certain intervals of temporal experience. We take up this topic here (instead of the previous chapter) because the behavior at issue is not simply a form of time reckoning. It is, on the contrary, an intended or agentive effort to alter one's own perception of time. As with the aforementioned strategies, the goal is to bring into effect the temporal compression of one's sentence. Only perception can be modified, but that is precisely what matters in these straits.

Carceral becomes acquainted with marking only certain intervals of time in his conversation with Hector, a more experienced colleague:

HECTOR: "When I first got to Gladiator School, one of the other lifers I met told me that the only important thing to remember was the year."
CARCERAL: "So you ignored the months and days?"
HECTOR: "Yeah, I kept saying it's 2001, 2001. I forgot about July this year, which is good!"

From Hector's subjective standpoint, "this year" was at least one month shorter than its objective length. The time he has served seems to have passed a bit more quickly. Another convict named Reno would tattoo a mark on his arm for every year of his incarceration. "Each year I add one," he told Carceral as the latter watched an instance of this time work. Reno had amassed a crosshatch tally on his skin: a repeating pattern of four vertical lines with a fifth diagonal line running through them. Like Hector, he was only counting years. In this fashion, he compressed twelve years of his sentence to a series of small tattoos.

There are fascinating, if quixotic, variations on this theme. Some of them combine refusing to admit the passage of time with counting only certain intervals. Carceral and other long-term prisoners tried to compress temporal experience by marking only presidential elections. He would think to himself, "Four presidents have been elected since I've been down." Sixteen years of incarceration would not sound like that much time when reduced to four barely remembered events. "It's funny how in prison," writes Dress, "you live your life from one eventful date to the next to pass your time."[113] Elaborating on this strategy, Crib teaches Scarce that one can mark and discard time simultaneously:

"I figure it's so long until Christmas, ya know? Then I take off a couple of months. So, like, now—it's really six months until Christmas but for me it's only four."

"I don't follow you."

"I take the next two months and I forget about 'em. Just toss 'em out. Don't even think about 'em. So all of a sudden I look up one day and it's Christmas."[114]

In practice, some counting of standard temporal units takes place in the course of this process, but, in theory, it is supposed to make for temporal compression in the long run. This procedure can be haphazard or surprisingly systematic. The latter possibility is evident when Scarce receives advanced training in the craftsmanship of temporal compression from a convict aptly named Rolls:

> I peered around the partition separating our bunks to ask him why he was still up. It was all about time, he told me. He slept when he wanted to, played endless games of cribbage against himself, ate when he wished (he had his own food stash). Most important, only one day of the week actually counted, Saturday. Saturday? I asked him. "Yeah," he said in a raspy, nicotine-stained tone somewhere between a whisper and normal conversation. "That means another day has passed. See, I only count Saturdays. They're like the last hours of a regular day." Rolls rolled up days of the week like they were one of his Job cigarettes. Sunday through Friday was a blur of sleeping, card playing, and eating. Only Saturday counted. The effect was to make seven weeks feel like seven days.[115]

This strategy is common knowledge among the inhabitants of jails and prisons.[116] There are further permutations, as well, and the sheer variety of this temporal agency bespeaks the terrible urgency that is its motivation.[117]

Despite their prevalence, these tactics are neither natural nor inevitable. For any number of reasons, convicts who know better count the days until their scheduled parole hearing or release, thereby incurring a self-inflicted form of temporal distress. With nothing else to do during a lockdown, Jimmy Lerner resorts to creating "a monthly calendar, drawing little squares and pasting it to the cell wall with state toothpaste."[118] This familiar and seemingly innocuous technology for standard time reckoning is, in fact, an alien and harmful presence within the context of his imprisonment. Staring at it, he realizes that there is nothing to write in any of these "little squares." At home in his kitchen, he remembers, the calendar was always full of his family's activities. He is capsized by this contrast: "I turn my face to the cell wall and, not for the first time, sob quietly against the cinder blocks." For inmates, the perception of time is not random or idiosyncratic. Principles are operative and prisoners ignore them at their peril.

In brief, the details may vary, but most convicts doing a long stretch learn to disregard dates and standard time. Typically, however, these tactics are abandoned near the end of one's sentence, to the detriment of temporal experience. This difficult portion of a prisoner's incarceration becomes all the more so because he or she feels compelled to count the remaining days, as in this passage from Piper Kerman's memoir: "Joyce, from the electric shop, was going home soon. She had drawn the calendar on the blackboard in the shop and would cross off every day that passed with chalk."[119] With a lot of her time left to serve, Kerman is savvy enough to know that mimicking Joyce would be a mistake: "The next seven months stretched out in front of me. I now knew I could do them, but it was still way too early to count the days."[120] Yet, toward the end of her sentence, Kerman relents and suffers the consequences: "My last week in prison was the hardest."[121] The common plight of short-timers, it is owing to the socially structured character of temporal experience.

COMPULSIONS AND PASTIMES

Time work entails the modification of one's own temporal experience, and nearly everything prisoners do is devoted to killing time in an effort to reduce the perceived length of their sentence. For convicts, success is defined as temporal compression. They pursue this elusive prize with a complicated mixture of compulsions and pastimes. These activities are meant to divert their attention away from the passage of time. More or less consciously, they exhibit interventions in the trajectory of temporal experience. Thematically, all of these compulsions and pastimes are proxies for escape from the circumstances of incarceration. The spectrum of these interventions extends from solitary to social practices. Impressively diverse at a glance, this spectrum proves to be more extensive than effective.

Sleeping is at the solitary end of this spectrum. A sleeping convict has shut down his or her attention to the passage of time in prison. "Never wake a sleeping convict," writes Joel Blaeser, "for that is when you're temporarily pardoned."[122] And, when you wake up, there is a little less time to serve. Some sleeping is biologically necessary, of course, but convicts augment the minimum with a great deal more than that, and they interpret all of their sleeping as small victories in the struggle for temporal autonomy. "Many prisoners sleep as much as possible," notes Carceral, and this sleeping has temporal agency as its raison d'être. "You know, you cheat the government ven [*sic*] you sleep," Zippo tells Scarce.[123] "Far too many women attempt to sleep away the hours," asserts Clare Hanrahan.[124] Segregation intensifies the use of this tactic: "Most of the lockdowns sleep sixteen to twenty hours a day and rarely stir off their trays."[125] The same tactic is prevalent among POWs and hostages, such as Ingrid Betancourt: "We passed the time taking siestas, because it was a good way to make the hours go faster."[126]

Sleeping one's sentence away, what could be easier? In fact, it is nothing of the sort. Once again, we confront the problematic ineffectiveness of time work in this setting. As T. J. Parsell points out, the prison sensorium makes for widespread insomnia, not restful slumber: "I tried to sleep away my days, but the noise was maddening. There was a constant drone of inmates yelling, sliding cell doors banging closed, and the shuffling back and forth of convicts."[127] Cheyenne Yakima offers corroborating testimony:

> In jail, sleep is out of the question. All night, every night, all I could hear was the sound of iron doors being opened and slammed shut, keys jingling from the belts of the deputies, toilets flushing, heavy footsteps going back and forth out on the metal catwalk, and, of course, prisoners arguing and discussing their misfortunes.[128]

What is more, Victor Hassine reminds us that sleeping in prison is a perilous activity: "As the number of robberies and assaults surged, the new jailhouse wisdom was that you should always be awake and ready to fight when cells were opened."[129] One's fellow captives are not the only hazard. In *The Gulag Archipelago*, Aleksandr Solzhenitsyn recalls that prisoners were punished for trying "to steal extra sleep."[130] Carceral adds that there is also a thorny issue of mutual courtesy pertaining to temporal discretion. A prisoner attempting to maximize the time he or she spends asleep imposes this tactic on his or her cellmate. This cellmate must wait to perform basic tasks out of respect for the sleeping prisoner, thereby incurring the burden of harder time.

The reverse agency is *not* sleeping as a form of time work. More precisely, a prisoner chooses to be awake when others are asleep. Albert Woodfox provides a detailed rationale for customizing temporal experience in this fashion:

My favorite time of day was two or three in the morning. Everybody was usually asleep. There was no one on the tier out on his hour. The TV volume was low. It was relatively peaceful and quiet. I could concentrate and focus. I liked to read during this time, or think. It was my time to deal with the pressure of being confined in a six-by-nine cell for twenty-three hours a day.[131]

In social interaction, the agency of timing concerns deciding precisely when to do something. One elects to pursue certain activity at an advantageous moment. By staying awake while other convicts slept, Woodfox reserved a bit of time for himself, creating precious intervals he refers to as "my time." This strategy would be problematic for many prisoners, but he was in solitary confinement for most of four decades, so, in his case, it did not conflict with other responsibilities.

Ken Lamberton sketches a scene in which he and fellow convicts fill an otherwise empty interval with physical activity: "We paced inside the cages for hours waiting for housing assignments."[132] Pacing is one of the compulsions through which prisoners attempt to modify their own temporal experience. Among captives of every kind, it is typically thoughtful, intentional, and quite complex. There is a conceptual side to pacing, invisible to the eye, yet crucial to an individual's subjective effort to achieve a measure of temporal compression. In this passage from Alexander Berkman's memoir, we glimpse the self-conscious deliberations that lie beneath the surface of a prisoner's pacing:

But some means must be devised to while away the time. I pace the floor, counting the seconds required to make ten turns. I recollect having heard that five miles constitutes a healthy day's walk. At that rate I should make 3,771 turns, the cell measuring seven feet in length. I divide the exercise into three parts, adding a few extra laps to make sure of five miles. Carefully I count, and am overcome by a sense of calamity when the peal of the gong confuses my numbers. I must begin over again.[133]

Berkman's initial statement marks this activity as a genre of temporal agency, but, in this excerpt, he describes himself working on only a single task. Victor Serge provides instructive contrast by showing us how pacing can be a component of multiple pastimes:

A man in jail . . . paces around his cell, his steps mechanical or self-conscious, depending upon his feeling at the moment. He counts his steps. Eleven! Bad! He gets his pace into rhythm and smiles at having eluded the trap set by an ill-omened number: he gets around the cell in twelve steps. There are many other things to do: you can figure out the necessary time in seconds, note the number of times around, then undertake a complicated calculation of miles traveled. You can make bets with yourself, improvising fascinating games of chance. How many steps, how many times around before the next check by the man on duty, revealed by the faint click of the spyhole?[134]

The hostage Amanda Lindhout combines pacing with mental time travel to escape her current captivity: "On my walks around my room, I blotted out my surroundings and imagined myself pacing the pathways of Stanley Park, moving through groves of tall cedar and along the curving seawall next to the bay."[135] Clearly, pacing involves far more than the restless release of nervous energy. Improvising with one of the few available resources, a prisoner fashions an engrossing line of thought and behavior, thereby shifting attention away from the perceived passage of time.

Exercise is another perennial way to kill time. It is a standard trope of all prison genres, but, behind bars, exercise is not as easy to come by as one might imagine. The necessary equipment is sure to be dilapidated and in short supply. Like Arnold Huskey, convicts often rely on their own ingenuity: "I would ace-bandage peanut butter jars filled with water to each hand and shadow box for a half hour, then go immediately into step-ups on the bed platform, for about two hours or until breakfast trays were delivered to the tray slot."[136] Jimmy Dunn goes to the trouble of getting a particular job, not as an end in itself, but as a kind of meta-work that gives him early access to his favored form of temporal agency:

I always get to the gym first. That's one of the reasons I hassled so much to get the porter's job, so I can get to the gym before the rest of the weight-lifters. This way I'm sure to get the weights and equipment I need.[137]

Dunn declares that "the workout is the high point of my day," but, in this zero-sum game, his success comes at the expense of others.[138]

Many prisoners can only dream of such activity. When Dannie Martin is put into segregation, he discovers that "exercise" is barely distinguishable from pacing:

> Directly in front of my cell is a cage made from wire like that which you see on a hurricane fence. Daily, one or two convicts are allowed in there to walk back and forth like caged wolves. It's called recreation, but I'll probably pass when my turn comes.[139]

Prisoners in the general population do not fare much better, but, as Martin notes, they exhibit a peculiar pattern that is indicative of an abiding concern for temporal agency:

> Convicts always walk around a track counterclockwise, as if to deny time itself, as represented by the clock. It's a losing battle—time always wins. As the years go by, the exercise walks around the track at the prison's perimeter only get more boring.[140]

Carceral confirms that this Sisyphean pattern was the norm at every prison he encountered.

Ernest Dichter calls cigarettes "a modern hourglass."[141] He observes that, in everyday life, "the burning down of a cigarette functions psychologically as a time indicator. A smoker waiting for someone who is late says to himself, 'Now I'll smoke one more cigarette, and then I am off.'"[142] What is more, smoking can be used as a strategy for altering one's own temporal experience. "A cigarette not only measures time," asserts Dichter, "but also seems to make time pass more rapidly."[143] As usual, imprisonment magnifies this relationship. Adam Reed contends that cigarettes are "a quintessential feature" of incarceration: "Something about the ordeal of this modern form of punishment . . . seems to invite inmates, from a range of societies, to smoke and to treat that material with a special kind of reverence."[144]

In prison, cigarettes are one of the principal currencies. You can buy anything with enough of them. T. J. Parsell is traded from one convict to another as a sexual slave for the price of one carton of cigarettes.[145] Here, however, we are interested in the way prisoners use cigarettes as implements of time work. Billy Sinclair's best friend hands him a suicide note and asks him what he thinks of it: "I lit a cigarette," recalls Sinclair, "not really wanting one but needing distraction from the moment. I inhaled deeply."[146] He stalls the forward momentum of that situation and shows us that smoking can be a kind of temporal agency. As the anthropologist Adam Reed puts it, smoking "can even allow [convicts] to open a gap in the time of ordinary experience."[147] His ethnographic research was conducted at the Bomana prison in Port Moresby, the largest urban area of Papua New Guinea. Like convicts in the United States, "the majority of prisoners at Bomana have nothing to do," and smoking "provides them with a much-needed form of occupation."[148] It is noteworthy that the prisoners in his study self-consciously use cigarettes to modify their own temporal experience: "In fact, inmates talk of smoking 'shortening time' (*sotim taim*) or making the prison day pass more quickly."[149] His findings offer further evidence in support of a theory that proposes cross-cultural similarities in the substance of temporal agency.[150]

Like smoking, but with far greater intensity, sexuality can "open a gap in the time of ordinary experience." The effect is paradoxical because ecstatic moments of sexuality narrow the focus of one's attention on the here and now of physical sensations: "Those who leave everyday reality to enter erotic reality . . . become less attentive to both spatial (distant) and temporal (past and future) extremities but more attentive to their centers (local and present)."[151] Yet, for the same reason, sexual ecstasy is characterized by protracted duration, not temporal compression. People commonly report that they perceived time to pass slowly during sex, and no one lacks for protracted duration in prison. A clue to the resolution of this paradox can be found in the preceding quotation from Murray Davis. People in the throes of sexual ecstasy "leave everyday reality," implying that this is another avenue of escape from one's ordinary circumstances. Via sexual time travel, convicts leave the protracted duration of monotony for elongated intervals of ecstasy. Fleetingly, they are transported to a different realm of being.

A fellow prisoner shocks Berkman with the following observation: " 'I have known some men to masturbate four and five times a day. Kept it up for months, too.' "[152] Masturbation is, by far, the most prevalent form of sex in prison. Sylvester Long had a cellmate who could not let his "swipe" (penis) go.[153] "I spent a lot of time masturbating," admits Edward Bunker.[154] Among prisoners, it is something pleasurable to do in a setting where there is very little else to do. As such, it is simply a way to pass the time, a type of temporal agency. "I masturbated, sometimes six times a day," says Jimmy Baca, "I tried anything to pass the time."[155] When Carceral talks with fellow prisoners at Gladiator School, many of the men confide that, while in single cells, they "jagged" (masturbated) six to eight times a day. But consensual and forced sex with others is more transformational of one's temporal experience. For instance, we witness significant distortion in the perceived passage of time when Parsell has obligatory sex with Slide Step: "Each thrust seemed to have an edge of desperation to it. It was as if he held on, for as long as he could, to make each small movement last forever."[156] Parsell also notes that forced sex and consensual sex affect temporal experience in divergent ways: "[During forced sex] I'd slip free of my body, allowing my consciousness to drift someplace else. Anyplace but in the present moment. But [during consensual sex] Paul made me want to stay present. Unlike all the others, he doted on me."[157] In this case, modifying temporal experience may not be the primary motivation, but it is certainly an ancillary effect.

Reading and writing are further methods for mental time travel. Similar to sexuality in this respect, these pastimes can be viewed as types of temporal agency. Charles, one of Drew Leder's informants, refers to reading as a way of withdrawing attention from the passage of time during incarceration: "I was in Supermax and a lot of the brothers in there, they escape by a lot of reading and studying—African history, the Bible, the Koran."[158] For Berkman and countless other prisoners, reading helps to manage their temporal expectations by means of distraction: "By violent efforts of will I strangle the recurring thought of my long sentence, and seek forgetfulness in reading."[159] In the hands of Baca's friend, Marcos, writing offers kindred opportunities for escapism with which to modify one's own temporal experience:

It was tense, and Marcos and I stayed on guard in case the other guys tried to jump us. Marcos didn't mellow out until he started writing another inmate's sister in Los Angeles. He taped her picture on his bunk and was always responding to her perfumed letters full of romantic dreams of their living happily ever after when he got out. He was playing along with her just to fill the time.[160]

His cynical presentation of self adds piquancy to otherwise drab and dangerous days. Whether genuine or cynical, writing is a variant of time work, as Berkman was well aware: "The evening hours have ceased to drag: there is pleasure and diversion in the correspondence."[161]

Reading and writing are comfortingly familiar and seemingly inexpensive. Here and there, they suffice as weapons with which to kill some time. On the whole, however, reading and writing are no more effective than other forms of temporal agency. This type of time work is completely irrelevant for the numberless prisoners who are illiterate. Yet even college-educated prisoners like Kerman find these tactics ineffectual: "I wrote letters and read books. But time was a beast, a big, indolent immovable beast that wasn't interested in my efforts at hastening it in any direction."[162] Moreover, the availability of necessary materials is usually quite limited. Kerman reports that, at her prison, there is "one little rolling bookshelf filled with a bizarre assortment of volumes."[163] Parsell confronts the same problem: "I tried to escape into reading, but the library cart only came twice and by the time it reached us on Two Special, there were only a few books left. They were usually titles that no one there would ever read."[164] In these common circumstances, we witness the institutional suppression of time work through the deprivation of resources. It is more surprising to learn that reading and writing may well be considered illegal activity. "Books, magazines, newspapers were contraband," states Ken Lamberton, and "cards and dominoes were confiscated."[165] It is also the case that any writing is heavily censored, as noted by George Jackson: "I tried to write several times these last couple of weeks but my letters all came back with a note attached explaining what I can and cannot say."[166] A prisoner's collection of reading or writing material typically disappears or is destroyed during frequent shakedowns of the cellblocks.[167]

Previously, we have discussed television as a way for prisoners to mark the passage of time, but it is more than that. Television can be another method whereby one escapes captivity by taking a temporary and cognitive excursion from one's circumstances. In this case, television becomes an agentive strategy for achieving the temporal compression of one's sentence, albeit fleetingly so. Stephen Stanko offers a succinct description of the implications for temporal experience: "Soap operas can turn a long, boring day into what seems minutes, while also placing the prisoner in a state of constant daydreaming."[168] However, it is precisely because of this welcome capacity for escapism and temporal compression that television has complicated, even incongruous, consequences for the ability of prisoners to modify their own temporal experience. These incongruities are laid bare in the evenhanded assessment of Mumia Abu-Jamal:

> After months or years of noncontact visits, few phone calls, and ever decreasing communication with one's family and others, many inmates use TV as an umbilical cord, a psychological connection to the world they have lost. They depend on it, in the way that lonely people turn to TV for the illusion of companionship, and they dread separation from it. For many, loss of TV is too high a price to pay for any show of resistance.[169]

A self-serving type of temporal intervention, watching television, frequently makes for studied passivity and intentional forbearance in all of one's other encounters, rather than insurrectionary opportunism. It is with good reason, then, that those in authority permit televisions, this corrupting form of temporal agency that dampens enthusiasm for more dangerous variants.

"Well, then," says a fellow convict to Berkman, "let's talk about something. It will help while away the time, you know."[170] According to John Irwin, it "is the major way to pass time" during incarceration.[171] We can conceive of it as another variation on escapism, and one rarely lacks the necessary resources, which is to say other convicts. The importance of these conversations is suggested by the effort prisoners put into overcoming all obstacles, even in solitary confinement. At Marion, observes Stephen Richards, "prisoners empty the water out of their toilets and talk from cell to cell through the vacant sewer pipes."[172] Friends may be on different schedules, but prisoners will work around temporal segregation: "When one of us was on the yard the other would call down from the window if he was out on his hour."[173] And, of course, male and female convicts alike talk about each other. As Kerman puts it, "true or not, gossip helped to pass the time."[174] Erin George adds that socializing with other convicts would "make the time go faster."[175]

As previously noted, visits from outsiders are among the atypical intervals during which time seems to pass quickly, but these episodes intensify one's longing for freedom and subsequently slow the perceived passage of time. Generally speaking, the frequency of visits declines over the course of one's sentence, in part because many long-term prisoners eschew them, and the vast majority of prisoners rarely, if ever, receive visitors. The ability to self-induce temporal compression via conversation with one's fellow convicts is no less limited. Political prisoners, hostages, and, in recent decades, POWs, are often kept in isolation. In contemporary American prisons, talking is usually difficult if not impossible while one is held in segregation. Even when there is access to conversation with fellow convicts, one finds that, given nothing to do, there is little to report. Ordinarily, no one has any news, and many inmates were not gifted conversationalists to begin with. Reginald Hall testifies to these limitations: "My cellmates started talking, passing the afternoon. I was bored as hell."[176] Lacking other conversational resources, they recount past exploits over and over again: "All Nard talked about was how he used to be a credit card pickpocket. That's it. That's all he would talk about, day in and day out."[177]

Prisoners also attempt to modify their own temporal experience through play and games. Joel Blaeser recalls "killing time by playing lots of ping-pong" at the Metropolitan Correctional Center in Chicago.[178] At most prisons, but very few jails, convicts can participate in various team sports, such as basketball or baseball. In addition, there may be board games and card games, although their availability is nearly always in question. "Scrabble was even more popular in the unit than cards," writes George. "People would reserve the single battered Scrabble board days in advance."[179] The desirability of these pastimes is suggested by the urgent creativity prisoners display in their absence. Consider, for example, the inventiveness of Jimmy Lerner and his cellmate:

> When two new rolls of toilet paper are finally delivered (three weeks late), Kansas makes us a chess set. An old prison origami hand, he shapes wet toilet paper into pawns, bishops, and even the difficult knights, using state toothpaste . . . as mortar.
>
> We save our lunchtime Kool-Aid to dye half the pieces purple. We let the toothpaste and dye dry overnight. With the pencil stub and the edge of the *Aryan Sentinel* I map out sixty-four squares on the concrete floor.
>
> We play chess all day long.[180]

While absorbed with this game, they become oblivious to the passage of time, yet they are not finished with their temporal agency:

> Our next project is a deck of cards. The lunch and dinner trays often include those little restaurant-style pats of butter with the square cardboard backing.

We save fifty-two of these and Kansas teaches me spades. I teach Kansas
Hollywood rummy.
Before we can construct a backgammon set the lockdown ends.[181]

It is noteworthy that Lindhout and a fellow hostage do fashion a backgammon set from what little they have at hand:

Nigel had crafted playing pieces from our Q-tips—one of us using the cotton
nubs, the other using pieces of the plastic handles, which he's clipped with
his beard-trimming scissors. On a sheet from his notebook, he's drawn two
rows of razoring triangles and then, using a couple of the acetaminophen
tablets and the scissors, carved a set of working dice, itty-bitty white cubes
with tiny numbers written on the sides in pen.
    We played for hours. And then we played for days.[182]

As usual, their temporal experience and time work run parallel to that of
convicts in American prisons.
    Now, however, this line of analysis begins to fold back on itself. With
these data, it is tempting to valorize the human ingenuity of temporal
agency, but playing the same games over and over again can be nearly as
monotonous as the rest of one's time in captivity. Moreover, the availability
of these games is always contingent and clandestine. Lindhout tells us that
she and Nigel must hide the game whenever they "heard footsteps in the
hallway" because it was considered "*haram*" (forbidden) by their captors.[183]
Likewise, at any moment, the games so carefully devised by Lerner and
Kansas could be discovered, seized, and destroyed by correctional officers
as contraband. When all is said and done, this ingenuity is no more effective than other tactics at bringing about the temporal compression of one's
sentence.
    Other compulsions and pastimes are equally contingent and clandes-
tine. Availability is fraught with all manner of arbitrary restrictions, limiting their effectiveness at modifying one's own temporal experience. For
example, when Flaherty asks Carceral if he had access to cigarettes, the
response is not a simple yes or no:

It depended on the date one came into the system. When I first entered the
system, yes, one could smoke inside and outside. Then most prisons banned

smoking inside, but max lockups usually did not. The ones that allowed a person to smoke outside had regulations on where and what time. Then one day they stopped selling all tobacco products, and cigarettes became the most commonly smuggled drug in the system. When they shipped us out of state, the new prison allowed smoking. Many guys, who had been forced to quit, started up again. Over the whole time, one could never smoke in segregation.

In theory, smoking helps prisoners pass the time, but, in practice, a welter of regulations blunts its efficacy.

This lengthy list of compulsions and pastimes is by no means exhaustive. There are, as well, institutionalized activities, such as one's job, schooling, programs, and religious services. Ostensibly, these activities are driven by diverse motivations, but, for most prisoners, they are further tactics for modifying temporal experience. Theodore Davidson observes widespread cynicism at church services and meetings of prisoner organizations: "Often prisoners attend merely to . . . break the routine of prison life."[184] "It was an extra half an hour a week outside my cell"—that is what Sunny Jacobs has to say about her sessions with the guidance counselor.[185] Similarly, Jacobs used her job in the kitchen as a basis for temporal agency: "I would have a bowl of cereal and milk, some fruit, cottage cheese—major delicacies in prison—and to have them *whenever I wanted* was the tastiest part."[186] In jail, adds Rik Scarce, the responsibilities of serving as a trustee "made for a change of pace and helped the hours pass more quickly."[187]

Institutionalized activities are officially sanctioned by those in authority, so there is no need for clandestine arrangements, but availability and effectiveness are no less uncertain. James Paluch identifies the fundamental problem: "A majority of prisoners do not have jobs."[188] At the county jail, Parsell listens to a fellow prisoner complain about the lack of work:

"It's so tight up in this motherfucker," a Black inmate said, "that the only thing you have to do is to get on each other's nerves. You can't even get a job assignment. You got no yard. You got no nothin'. It's enough to drive a motherfucker insane."[189]

Yet, given the monotonous work in prison, convicts with a job assignment are not appreciably more successful at managing their own temporal experience. In this regard, Berkman's comments are illuminating:

Practice lends me great dexterity in the work, but the hours of drudgery drag with heavy heel. *I seek to hasten time* by forcing myself to take an interest in the task. I count the stockings I turn, the motions required by each operation, and the amount accomplished within a given time. But in spite of these efforts, my mind persistently reverts to unprofitable subjects.[190]

He attempts to bring about temporal compression by concentrating on his work, but the stultifying nature of his job foils this endeavor. In accord with Berkman, Clare Hanrahan tells us that, far from serving as a solution, prison jobs are typically part of the temporal problem: "Some work can be completed in just a few hours . . . leaving a lot of idle time to while away at one's workplace."[191] "Since I only worked two hours a day," remembers Hall, "I had a lot of time to kill."[192]

The foregoing survey of compulsions and pastimes is, then, misleading by virtue of its very thoroughness. Its sheer length implies a wealth of effective options for temporal agency, but this is most assuredly not the case. Whenever Carceral considered his own efforts at temporal agency, he was struck by the futility of it all:

The one thing I learned over the years, no matter how busy I would stay, no matter how much I tried to occupy my time in prison, I would always take a breath at the most busiest time and ask myself, "What is the purpose of all this activity?" I'm still in prison. Once I was "activitied-out" for the day, I would realize again how slow and unchanging life was.

Like Carceral, prisoners keep tampering with temporal experience, but typically have little or nothing to show for it. Analytically speaking, some prisoners, in some places, use the aforementioned tactics to alter the perceived passage of time, but, from an empirical standpoint, it is not valid to suggest, even tacitly, that any of them represent sustainable solutions to the problem of temporal experience.

ILLEGAL AND DISRUPTIVE ACTIVITY

In every way imaginable, convicts are attempting to achieve some degree of temporal compression in the perceived passage of time. Yet the undeniable inadequacies of the aforementioned tactics can make for a pervasive sense of despair. "Every day seemed the same," says Blaeser.[193] This monotony sets the stage for obstinate types of temporal agency that issue from a dysfunctional social context. "To deal with the familiar concern of boredom," write Richard Jones and Thomas Schmid, "the familiar tactic of diversionary activities, including involvement in illegal activities, is used."[194] Some of them are less confrontational (such as horseplay, gambling, and drugs), while others are more confrontational (such as insubordination, getting transferred, and instigating trouble). Taken together, they represent potent ways to modify temporal experience, but prisoners who have recourse to these methods will certainly receive more time to serve if caught by those in authority. Will the prisoner get away with it? This question adds an edgy note of piquancy to the endeavor. With illegal and disruptive activities, then, we arrive at frantic efforts and pyrrhic victories.

Donald Roy conducted masterful ethnographic studies of industrial manufacturing in twentieth-century America. His observations revealed extensive shop-floor horseplay among factory machine operatives "in a situation of monotonous work activity."[195] One purpose of this horseplay was temporal compression: "The group interactions thus not only marked off the time; they gave it content and hurried it along."[196] Like panhandling in public places, we should conceive of horseplay as a kind of interpersonal aggression.[197] With horseplay in penitentiaries, the aggression is reactionary in nature and aimed at recouping a measure of temporal autonomy. Relative to industrial workers, prison inmates must contend with boredom that is more encompassing, more severe, and, if left unchecked, more corrosive to one's spirit, but sometimes they employ parallel tactics for altering their temporal experience.

As usual, both male and female convicts make use of this tactic. For instance, Kerman observes fellow inmates "cutting up to make the time pass."[198] And Art Pepper provides a first-person account of his own horseplay:

We had a saying: "To loosen your wig." When you got uptight and really nervous, then you'd "unscrew your cap," and that was the only way I could stand doing the time. I'd get silly and nutty and make weird noises. I'd walk like a spastic. Everybody would be lined up to go to work, and I'd walk right by them shaking and kind of slobbering. And that's when I started getting a reputation as a nut.[199]

His use of "we" and the plural idiomatic ways of referring to this tactic mark it as a collective practice. Pepper and other convicts willfully react to their otherwise highly regulated circumstances with this form of temporal agency, but one's reputation is a steep price to pay for momentary release from the monotony of incarceration.

"On my first day out of isolation," recalls George, "a tattooed, unkempt woman approached me. 'Do you want to play spades?' she asked."[200] Trying to be "as inoffensive as possible," George admits that she does not know how to play spades "or any other card game," but her fellow prisoner does not take no for an answer:

> "You're my partner," said Melinda, my new friend. Melinda introduced the two other players, and we began to play. She was patient, a natural teacher, as she explained the scoring and strategy. Soon I was proficient, and began to play every day, all day. . . .
>
> That's how most people would spend their time. Card games like spades, tonk, five thousand, hearts, and killer—there were hundreds of games I had never heard of. The jail rules didn't allow gambling, but of course it was always part of the game. The usual currency was M&Ms.[201]

Inside and outside of prison, games of chance are forms of time work. By systematically placing the outcome in doubt, they are designed to seize the player's attention and serve as a mental excursion from mundane circumstances. Likewise, gambling on the outcome is a tried-and-true method for intensifying these effects.[202] The upshot is that, customarily, a player experiences some degree of temporal compression.

Analytically, there are four levels of uncertainty and risk in these contests. First, there is the procedural framework of the game, which brings about winners and losers. Second, there is the routine gamesmanship of talking "smack" about one's partner or opponents. George notes that "we garnished every sentence with profanity when the game was in full smack mode."[203] This layer of uncertainty pertains to the risky business of insulting other players. "Talking smack is an oratorical art form," according to George, "a delicate balance of bravado and insult that just skirts the edge of unforgivable offense."[204] The verbal style peculiar to these games is characterized by a great deal of aggression, with the potential for someone taking serious affront and seeking retribution: "More than one card game had been abruptly stopped because of an ill-received insult."[205] Third, there is the fact that gambling is prohibited, as is any altercation that emerges from the mutual insults. There is, then, the very real possibility that one will earn more time in prison with this activity. Fourth, the gambling is dangerous because one cannot rely on the authorities to enforce the resulting debts. Pepper reports that "many people were killed because of debts incurred at the domino tables."[206] Remarkably, all of this risk is undertaken in an effort to accelerate the pace of one's temporal experience.

As of 2019, the Federal Bureau of Prisons reports that 46 percent of inmates are serving time for drug offenses, by far the largest category. In contrast, the second largest category—weapons, explosives, and arson— is only 18 percent. The category devoted to homicide, aggravated assault, and kidnapping is 3.3 percent. It is more than a little ironic that every penitentiary, male or female, is flooded with illegal drugs. "Drugs were all over the jail," observes George.[207] A fellow inmate tells Parsell, "'You can get just about any drug you want in prison: heroin, cocaine, reefer, or speed. Whatever it is you need.'"[208] These drugs reside on a spectrum of consciousness-altering substances, along with prohibited pruno consumption (i.e., home-brewed alcohol) and the equally rampant psychotropic "medicines" dispensed by prison pharmacies. Some of them are legal, some illegal, but, to one extent or another, all of them are used to modify the perceived passage of time.

Despite being held at FCI Englewood, Blaeser meets with no trouble when "smoking lots of weed."[209] "Everyone was getting high," he adds, "so I didn't have to fear being snitched on."[210] Risk is further mitigated by the fact that correctional officers are complicit in this drug trade: "The guards . . . helped sneak in all the tar heroin on the yard."[211] Nonetheless, officers invoke the rules whenever it suits their purpose, with large and lasting consequences for the convict in question. Across twenty years, as we have seen, the parole board would cite Carceral's disciplinary report for a single possession of marijuana. Getting caught with illegal drugs will extend a convict's time in prison, yet these same drugs are highly sought after to alleviate the temporal stress associated with serving one's sentence. It is a treacherous environment, but, by virtue of an irrational calculus, the temporary respite of drug-induced escapism is worth the risk. The circularity of this "solution" is only apparent to those who do not inhabit a prison cell day after day.

In prison, the relationship between drugs and time is multifaceted. There are, to be sure, pharmacological effects, but emotional and temporal experience are really at issue. With drugs, according to Billy Sinclair, convicts find "an escape from the bitter reality of their failed lives."[212] Prisoners can alter temporal experience indirectly by modifying their emotional reactions to incarceration: "I had returned to pills," recalls Sinclair, "taking handfuls of amphetamines. Speed at least kept the demon of despair at bay."[213] For other inmates, notes George, drugs simply render one oblivious to the perceived passage of time: "The hottest items were the drugs that let you sleep until your time was up."[214] As Dannie Martin tells us, many prisoners with no prior history of drug use avail themselves of this tactic, "becoming serious drug addicts" along the way.[215] He learns the motivation for this secondary drug use from a fellow convict: " 'It makes my time a lot easier,' a bank embezzler turned heroin user told me one day."[216]

With horseplay, gambling, and drugs, prisoners attempt to modify temporal experience by minding their own business, in a manner of speaking. Those in positions of authority do not see it this way, of course, so there are intermittent bouts of disregard and enforcement. Still, in essence, the foregoing types of activity are illegal but not terribly disruptive. Understandably, however, the crushing monotony of incarceration motivates more than a few convicts to interrupt the perceived passage of time with reckless forms of insubordination.

Within this category are fine gradations of temporal agency—from opportunism and passive resistance at one end of the continuum to overtly confrontational tactics at the other end. On those rare occasions when there is a lapse in otherwise unrelenting surveillance, convicts can be counted on to take advantage of this opportunity. Jacobo Timerman recounts one such instance, during which his experience of time is altered in a profound, if ephemeral, way:

Tonight, a guard, not following the rules, leaves the peephole ajar. I wait a while to see what will happen but it remains open. Standing on tiptoe, I peer out. There's a narrow corridor, and across from my cell I can see at least two other doors. Indeed, I have a full view of two doors. What a sensation of freedom! An entire universe added to my Time, that elongated time which hovers over me oppressively in the cell.[217]

No confrontation is necessary. All that is required is his willingness to look at what is ordinarily prohibited.

One step further along this continuum, we find various forms of passive resistance that are temporal in nature. They are noteworthy for the clever ways in which convicts take advantage of opportunities that arise within the workings of the temporal regime. Constant administrative efforts to dictate the pace at which prisoners do everything (itself a kind of time work) unintendedly provide an endless stream of occasions for temporal resistance. When, for instance, a correctional officer orders Jimmy Lerner to act quickly, this command presents a temporal basis for a small measure of confrontational leverage: " 'This convict is *slow-playing* me, won't sign for his property.' "[218] In his complaint, this officer invokes an emic term, "slow-playing," which refers to any intentional delay in a prisoner's response. Convicts are just as likely to use the term, as when Lerner describes how his cellmate tries the patience of another correctional officer: "Kansas leisurely gets back in line, slow-playing Bubblecop."[219] It follows that officers will not tolerate procrastination, viewing it quite correctly as a variant of temporal rebellion. Thus, there are repeated threats of retaliation for any perceived delay: " 'You slow-play me and I will personally fuck you.' "[220]

These threats, and the angry vigilance from which they emerge, are by no means delusional. The correctional officers recognize that slow-playing is a willful act of temporal gamesmanship and, as such, a very real threat to their authority. By slow-playing officers, prisoners reassert control over the experience of time (their own as well as that of the guards). These moments are localized, fleeting, and costly, but we fail to grasp the significance of this behavior from the standpoint of a rational calculus. Facing a long and uncertain stay in prison, a moment of temporal autonomy is tantamount to an oasis in a desert of time. From another standpoint, however, this simile is misleading. One finds an oasis; one creates an instance of slow-playing. The latter represents purposeful intervention. Prisoners have no a priori preferences for delay, nor are they inclined to slow the perceived passage of time. It is an encompassing temporal regime that provokes the initiation of slow-playing as an intentional form of resistance.

With a little more effort (and risk), prisoners can transition from passive resistance to outright insubordination. For example, slow-playing is sometimes expanded into explicit noncooperation accompanied by insults for the correctional officers. Andreas Schroeder provides a fine description of such disobedience:

> The guards . . . never entered our rabbit warren in groups of less than three, and if an inmate was wanted by Administration for any reason, one of them simply cupped his hands and hollered through the entrance bars down the tier: "Sinclair! Four-Right-Nine!" I was quite startled the first time I heard that call, because after a brief silence a voice far down the tier distinctly hollered back: "You'll never take me alive copper!" I quickly slid off my bunk to watch the ensuing hassle, but nothing happened and after a while Sinclair was summoned again: "Sinclair! Four-Right-Nine!" Later I found out that this was actually an old ritual, the inmate being summoned automatically hollering his defiance (which varied from the above to responses like "C'mon try and get me, asshole!" and "Try an' make somethin of it, bullmoose!") and settling back for the obligatory second call. That call having been made, and after a decent delay to indicate the appropriate lack of cooperation, the inmate would shuffle down the tier to be administrated unto.[221]

In this case, resistance has become ritualized as inmates strive to balance conflicting temporal desires. They are pulled in two directions, not because of preexisting dispositions, but because their social circumstances engender desires for divergent types of temporal experience: the temporal compression of novelty (i.e., leaving their cells) and the temporal autonomy of insubordination (i.e., delay and insulting the correctional officers).

Yet insubordination is rarely sanitized and ritualized in this fashion. Rose Giallombardo's summary gives us a more accurate picture: "The frustration experienced by these inmates sometimes erupts in a violation of prison rules."[222] Indeed, the lion's share of insubordination is chaotic, confrontational, and dangerous. By the same token, it disrupts the business-as-usual monotony of time behind bars for perpetrator and witnesses alike. This potential for temporal disruption is apparent in the foregoing excerpt, where Schroeder "quickly" slides off his bunk "to watch the ensuing hassle." Ordinarily, his eager anticipation would have been confirmed; insubordination reliably brings about exciting confrontations. Knowingly, then, prisoners devote considerable energy and inventiveness to this endeavor. In one week, at one penitentiary, the convicts are charged with insolence, being out of place, refusal to work, loitering on tier, refusing medication, attempted escape, threatening another inmate, swearing at an officer, threatening an officer's life, and creating a disturbance on the wing.[223]

What does this behavior accomplish? Prisoners know these uprisings are doomed from the start. What is worse, as Jimmy Dunn tells us, they know that insubordination may well prolong their sentences: "Some guys regularly call the bulls a sack of whatever it is they think they are. But that's not really the smart way. All they do is throw you in the hole, and as if that's not bad enough, it adds time to your stay."[224] None of this makes any sense, given their vulnerability to reprisals and the imbalance of power vis-à-vis the temporal regime. Yet none of that makes any difference because this is not about being "smart," to use Dunn's word. If you are thirsty enough for novelty and temporal autonomy, then you drink from those waters even when you know that doing so may be toxic in the long run. One attempts to enliven the passage of time via drama or a burlesque version of confrontation. These encounters have no real function aside from reappropriating a measure of control over one's own temporal experience and, briefly at least, fabricating a different texture in the perceived passage of time.

With still another step along this continuum, efforts to disrupt boredom become dangerous, even deadly. The most serious forms of insubordination morph into efforts at instigating trouble through violence of one kind or another. This time work contributes to the ubiquitous conditions of life inside American prisons, as summarized by Sykes: "Far from being omnipotent rulers who have crushed all signs of rebellion against their regime, the custodians are engaged in a continuous struggle to maintain order—and it is a struggle in which the custodians frequently fail."[225] Jimmy Baca provides the following illustration of such failure: "Because [Texas Red] didn't think he'd had enough visiting time with his wife, he once took the visiting-room guards hostage and initiated his own visiting hours."[226] Needless to say, Texas Red paid a severe penalty for this temporal improvisation. On that day, however, he also spent a bit more time with his wife. It is difficult to quantify but reasonable to ask: How much of the violence that seems so senseless to outsiders is a sensible response from those who seek to reappropriate temporal autonomy?

We can only begin to understand this ceaseless struggle if we see that it is continuous with other kinds of temporal agency. Sometimes, as in the case of Texas Red, it is a struggle for temporal autonomy. Just as often, if not more so, it is a struggle for temporal compression. In accord with this interpretation, Thomas Meisenhelder observes that temporal agency supplies the underlying connectedness of seemingly disparate pursuits: "Prisoners perform some activities simply because they . . . *speed the passage of time*. Insult games, smoke breaks, trips to the canteen, 'rapping,' and *even the more violent acts of fighting or rioting* can all be varieties of the prisoner's creation of time."[227] Without such intervention, the temporal experience of incarceration is dominated by unremitting boredom. Comparable, if less intemperate, motivation can be found among industrial workers, such as one quoted by Clark Molstad in his ethnographic study of a brewery: " 'It's so dull out there *I'd just like to make something happen*, to have something interesting to do or see.' "[228] It is worth emphasizing that this individual was at work, not in prison. Adapting to far more challenging conditions, prisoners have recourse to more extreme types of temporal agency.

It follows that, in large measure, one's fellow convicts are dangerous due to their efforts at temporal agency. "Sometimes," recalls Pepper, "they'd just beat people up because there was nothing else to do."[229] Much of the violence in prison occurs in response to temporal anguish. Moreover, if the state gives prisoners "nothing else to do" with their time, then it is culpable for the resulting violence. Within this context, fighting becomes something akin to a collective pastime—and of a piece with other avocations behind bars. Victor Hassine's assessment of his own circumstances is widely applicable to other penitentiaries: "Violence in Graterford had also become a form of escape for many inmates. In creating and maintaining a predatory environment, these men were able to avoid the reality of imprisonment by focusing all their attention on fighting one another."[230] Some of these combatants are more or less unwitting; many are dimly aware of their role in a larger enterprise; still others are keenly self-conscious as they strive to modify temporal experience. At the latter extreme, as Blaeser explains, temporal envy can even culminate in murderous intent: "Having [an] outdate was good and a curse, as most of the people in Marion have a life sentence and sometimes they will kill you just so you don't go home; this is only out of jealousy because they are leaving in a pine box."[231] These convicts steal time from others, making this the most malevolent form of temporal agency.

Insubordination is dramatic; violence is exciting. Drama and excitement alter the perceived passage of time. Fleetingly, these outbursts alleviate the temporal anguish of boredom for perpetrators and witnesses alike.

"All clashes between prisoners were sporting events," recalls Kerman.[232] Dunn notes the contrast with normal monotony: "A fight in prison— whether you're involved or not—puts an immediate squirt of adrenalin into the system."[233] For Sinclair and fellow convicts, witnessing an assassination is a welcome break from routine: "A large crowd of inmates watched with mixed fascination and excitement."[234] Within this context, violence is knowingly employed and consumed as a strategy for the modification of emotional and temporal experience. Participation opens a door onto another realm of being, as when Schroeder fights another inmate for the use of a card table: "It was terrific. It was absolutely marvelous. It was downright ecstatic, is what it was."[235] Even riots provide opportunities to regain control of the manner in which time transpires. In the midst of a prison uprising, "I am wonderfully, wondrously, *electrically* alive," remembers Lerner.[236] A fellow convict achieves a coveted state of ecstasy: "Kansas, literally bouncing off the walls, Kung-fuing his door, screaming, barking, howling, having the time of his life."[237] Using various types of violence, prisoners attempt "to produce *an increased temporal flow* by usurping, at least transiently, control over what happens now from the institution."[238] These events never last very long (despite perception to the contrary), but their temporal reverberations are extensive, with prisoners "delightedly reenacting and redescribing the scene again and again."[239] In these spectacles and their retelling, they reclaim the ability to dictate the perceived passage of time.

Yet, paraphrasing Michel de Certeau, whatever they win, they cannot keep.[240] An eruption of violence is an astonishing but momentary reprieve. Invariably, order is quickly restored. Moreover, violence is dangerous and costly. Simply being in possession of a weapon is a serious offense. Blaeser tells us, "If I were to get caught with this piece of steel, we were talking at least three years added to my sentence."[241] Even spectators can be swept up in the ensuing punishment. Like Lerner, experienced convicts often retreat from the scene of a violent confrontation, however magnetic it may seem: "When the Shit Jumps Off, unless you want to be up in the mix, it's best to find a hole and pull it over you."[242] The fact that they elect to stay out of trouble rather than participate in or witness an exciting event is indicative of the limited and unsustainable effectiveness of violence as a strategy for modifying temporal experience. Nevertheless, these disincentives are much diminished by long, indeterminate sentences or life without parole. It follows that many prisoners find violence irresistible because, when all is said and done, it remains one line of activity they themselves can initiate, thereby having something to say about the pace of life behind bars.

A further function of insubordination and violence is to provoke a change of scenery by getting oneself transferred to another cell or even a different prison. This is a strategy unto itself for the modification of one's own temporal experience. When, for example, guards tried to add a prisoner to Baca's cell, he "leaped out and hit the guy."[243] Baca is put into solitary confinement, which is what he wanted all along. It was not lost on him (or other prisoners) that violence earned this coveted time alone. Almost certainly, violent insubordination lengthens one's sentence, but Baca had no idea when he might be released, if ever, so there was little or nothing to lose with this gambit. Moreover, he was not punished by being reclassified for segregation. On the contrary, as he put it, "the hole was more like a meditation place for me now."[244] A more radical change of pace can be achieved by having oneself shipped to another penitentiary. During an interview, a fellow convict named Emerson told Carceral that he hoped to be transferred to a different facility. He saw it as a way to alter the perceived passage of time by exchanging the monotony of his current circumstances for the novelty of a new situation:

EMERSON: "You know, everything is different. It takes a while to figure everything out. That helps give me something to do."
CARCERAL: "Changes things around?"
EMERSON: "Yeah, ain't shit to do here."

Troublemakers are punished with more time to serve, and the novelty is likely to be both modest and fleeting, but, for those suffering unrelenting boredom, this transaction may seem like a bargain.

In a related way, even a thwarted escape attempt extricates a prisoner from what has become an overly familiar and onerous setting because that inmate is often transferred to another facility. T. J. Parsell observes that prisoners try to trivialize the transgression, but those in authority are seldom amused: "Inmates referred to running off as breaking camp, but it carried up to five years, which was stacked on top of whatever time you were already serving."[245] Rik Scarce recalls the fate of a fellow inmate, Chepe, who had "walked away from" a minimum-security facility and was subsequently punished by being transferred to a prison with a terrible reputation. At first, Scarce is baffled by what he considers a "stupid" thing to do, but Chepe explains his own elation at the outcome:

> The day Chepe was sentenced for escaping, he returned from court more animated than I had ever seen him, and he was a lively guy. I was surprised. Had he somehow beaten an escape conviction? No. Chepe was stoked because he was heading to prison—*the* prison, Walla Walla State Penitentiary, known, as they all seem to be, as "The Walls." The Walls is Washington State's most formidable house of confinement, a place where male-on-male rape, drugs, and gang warfare were rampant. Conditions there were so bad that the authorities sometimes locked down the entire prison for days or weeks at a time; on those occasions they allowed convicts out of their cells for only one hour a day. Why would anyone want to go to that hellhole? Chepe would be there for years. To me, time at The Walls meant time far worse than what I was experiencing in Spokane County Jail: constant fear, corruption, danger, anxiety.
>
> So why was Chepe beaming? His answer, uttered with a smile and a manic look in his eyes, was chilling. " 'Cause it's a *jungle* in there! You never know what's going to happen next."[246]

Typically, the convict who plays this card finds that all of his or her possessions have disappeared during the transition to another cell or prison.[247] One can obtain more books and pencils, of course, but photographs and journals are irreplaceable. Still, the bigger problems are logistical and existential. The novelty of a new location alters the perceived passage of time, but a prisoner cannot count on being transferred, as there are other forms of punishment for troublemakers, especially repeat offenders. This is something one can do only now and then—and only if the authorities cooperate. Moreover, one prison is very much like another, so any resulting novelty evaporates quickly. Chepe's transfer from jail to prison holds the promise of dramatic differences, but moving from one prison to another is not an equivalent transition. Even when this strategy "works," convicts find themselves in circumstances that have more than a passing resemblance to those they left behind.

DROWNING IN TIME

The circularity in having oneself transferred is the culmination of an over-arching pattern. An immutable schedule is imposed on convicts by the temporal regime of the penitentiary. Convicts spend most of their time in small, unchanging spaces characterized by neglect and overcrowding. Lacking temporal autonomy, inmates are not at liberty to do what they want, when they want, for as long as they want. There are inadequate resources for modifying one's own temporal experience. The staff of the penitentiary focus relentlessly on the convict's past, and they are deeply skeptical about any prospects for rehabilitation. Prisoners avoid marking time via clocks and calendars because doing so engenders a feeling of protracted duration. Yet the ensuing string of identically empty days is typified by blurred repetition, not linear progress toward any definite goal. One's sentence seems to stretch into the future like a vast sea. Prisoners strive to modify their own temporal experience by means of time work, but, more often than not, these strategies are blunted by the temporal regime. Unintendedly, these practices recapitulate the circularity of life behind bars.

Is temporal regimentation the ruling motif of life behind bars? Can convicts modify their own temporal experience? Questions concerning resistance are often couched in terms of either/or arguments, but two things can be true. The people who administer correctional facilities impose a harsh temporal regime on their prisoners, and, ineffectually for the most part, prisoners resist this regime by means of temporal agency. It would be wrong to assert that a temporal regime is inflicted on prisoners who simply assent to its strictures and equally inaccurate to contend that prisoners triumphantly alter their temporal experience whenever they wish to. Rarely, if ever, is the temporal regime so dominant that resistance shrinks to the vanishing point. Nonetheless, temporal agency is not a magic wand that can transform a long, wretched sentence into some kind of lark. "Everything here is on prison time," observes Kerman: "slow motion."[248] Convicts describe temporal experience as the fundamental source of their suffering, which does not suggest that, as a general rule, their time work achieves its ends. Inside and outside of prison, temporal agency is ubiquitous, but, as implied by its name, time work is also laborious; it requires effort, insight, determination, and certain resources. The outcome is always uncertain, but, absent these ingredients, temporal agency is unlikely to accomplish its desired result.

Incarceration fascinates us because, quite apart from issues of crime and punishment, there is something essential to the human condition at the heart of it: "a spiritual exercise, that of forcing oneself to find happiness in the midst of the greatest distress."[249] In tandem, however, the authorities and their prisoners see to it that "happiness" is both scarce and fleeting. Thus, the extensive inventory of time work tactics in this chapter is misleadingly long and varied. Its length and diversity imply that convicts have a large and effective array of tools with which to modify temporal experience. Yet the facts of the matter are by turns dreary and desperate, not efficacious, as inmates mostly fail at this endeavor. In the long run, temporal agency does not quell their time-induced torment. Prisons would be far more popular places if convicts could ameliorate their circumstances at will. "Each day I shaved off another sliver of time," says Baca, but this is a mournful admission, not a declaration of victory.[250] More than anyone else, prisoners are obsessed with time. They devote extravagant attention to lifting its burden from their lives, but they are left with little to show for it. Not incidentally, this tells us something about the socially organized limits of individualistic agency.

The fundamental dialectic of temporal experience is laid bare in that diabolical experiment known as a penitentiary. Simultaneously, human beings are the architects and victims of time. Our circumstances constantly impose temporal structure on us. We resist that structure with all available wit and resources. Still, we must not misunderstand temporal structure as one of the merciless forces of nature. Temporal agency on the part of those who design and administer prisons creates the temporal structure confronted by convicts held captive in these conditions. Like inmates and their keepers, those of us outside of prison establish and reject temporal structure in an ongoing and contested effort to achieve our own shifting and uncertain objectives. By the same token, we cannot celebrate temporal agency without recognizing that one group's creativity is often experienced by another group as temporal insurrection or the externality and constraint of temporal structure. Time is manifest as agency and structure. Both manifestations are products of human ingenuity, and they are viewed as desirable or undesirable depending on where one sits.

Would you recognize that someone was drowning if you watched it happen? In the vast majority of cases, there is very little to see. Every year, roughly half of the children who drown do so in close proximity to their oblivious parents. "Drowning doesn't look like drowning."[251] Dramatizations of drowning in movies and television misrepresent it. These scripted drownings always depict a great deal of splashing, waving, and yelling for help, but real drownings typically lack these explicit signals of distress. "Drowning is almost always a deceptively quiet event."[252] There is little or nothing to hear. A drowning person is suffocating in the water, which makes it difficult or impossible to yell. "Drowning people cannot wave for help," nor can they splash to call attention to themselves.[253] Instinctively, they "extend their arms laterally and press down on the water's surface" because they are frantically focused on lifting their bodies in a vertical fashion to raise their mouths above the water.[254] Ordinarily, they are submerged within twenty to sixty seconds. From start to finish, their brief struggle is barely noticeable to the untrained eye.

Prisoners are drowning in time, but, of course, this is not a perfect analogy. Sooner or later, most of them will be released, at least temporarily, and their struggles in the waters of time are prolonged rather than brief. Despite these deficiencies, this analogy helps us understand the essential predicament of prisoners because the suffering in a penitentiary is primarily temporal. Convicts dread the empty expanse of each new day. Weeks feel like they will never end but then evaporate into the void with so little to remember. There is an omnipresent danger that inmates will surrender to their circumstances and succumb to time. They have too much time and too little control of it. These facts constantly threaten to overwhelm them. Prisoners try this, and they try that, with inventiveness born of desperation. They wish for a shorter sentence, and strain to make time hasten past them, yet mourn like the rest of us when it is gone. With enormous effort and considerable creativity, they achieve only momentary distraction from their grim conditions. Sinking beneath the surface of time, they drown in what most of us thirst for.

NOTES

INTRODUCTION

1. Andreas Schroeder, *Shaking It Rough: A Prison Memoir* (Garden City, NY: Double-day, 1976).
2. Schroeder, *Shaking It Rough*, 5.
3. Schroeder, *Shaking It Rough*, 7.
4. Schroeder, *Shaking It Rough*, 48.
5. Schroeder, *Shaking It Rough*, 48.
6. Schroeder, *Shaking It Rough*, 49. Other prisoners describe protracted duration by translating standard temporal units into idiomatic expressions: "Then, after what seemed an eternity but was only about a week, I had a visitor." See Sunny Jacobs, *Stolen Time* (London: Bantam, 2007), 68.
7. Schroeder, *Shaking It Rough*, 184.
8. Schroeder, *Shaking It Rough*, 184.
9. Becky Pettit and Bruce Western, "Mass Imprisonment and the Life-Course: Race and Class Inequality in U.S. Incarceration," *American Sociological Review* 69 (2004): 151–169; David Garland, ed., *Mass Imprisonment: Social Causes and Consequences* (London: Sage, 2001); Michelle Alexander, *The New Jim Crow: Mass Incarceration in the Age of Colorblindness* (New York: New Press, 2012).
10. See page 3 of "One in 100: Behind Bars in America 2008," http:// https://www.pewtrusts .org/en/research-and-analysis/reports/2008/02/28/one-in-100-behind-bars-in -america-2008.
11. E. Ann Carson, "Prisoners in 2019." U. S. Department of Justice, Office of Justice Programs, Bureau of Justice Statistics, 2020, 3, 10.
12. Peter Wagner and Wendy Sawyer, 2018, "States of Incarceration: The Global Context 2018." Prison Policy Initiative: https://www.prisonpolicy.org/global/2018.html.

13. Stephen Stanko, "Surviving in Prison," in *Living in Prison: A History of the Correctional System with an Insider's View*, ed. Stephen Stanko, Wayne Gillespie, and Gordon A. Crews (Westport, CT: Greenwood, 2004), 177.

14. Stephen Stanko, "Surviving in Prison," 178.

15. Erving Goffman, *Asylums: Essays on the Social Situation of Mental Patients and Other Inmates* (Garden City, NY: Anchor, 1961), 181.

16. Hans Toch, "The Convict as Researcher," in *Sociological Realities*, ed. Irving Louis Horowitz and Mary Symons Strong (New York: Harper & Row, 1971), 497.

17. Jeffrey Ian Ross, Richard S. Jones, Michael Lenza, and Stephen C. Richards, "Convict Criminology and Struggle for Inclusion," *Critical Criminology: An International Journal* 24 (2016): 489–501. See also Jeffrey Ian Ross and Greg Newbold, "Convict Criminology at the Crossroads," *The Prison Journal* 93 (2013): 3–10.

18. Anthony J. Manocchio and Jimmy Dunn, *The Time Game: Two Views of a Prison* (New York: Dell, 1970).

19. Manocchio and Dunn, *The Time Game*, 238.

20. Richard S. Jones, Jeffrey Ian Ross, Stephen C. Richards, and Daniel S. Murphy, "The First Dime: A Decade of Convict Criminology," *The Prison Journal* 89 (2009): 154.

21. John Irwin, *The Felon* (Englewood Cliffs, NJ: Prentice-Hall, 1970).

22. John Irwin, *The Jail* (Berkeley: University of California Press, 1985), xii–xiii.

23. Thomas J. Schmid and Richard S. Jones, "Suspended Identity: Identity Transformation in a Maximum Security Prison," *Symbolic Interaction* 14 (1991): 415–432.

24. Jones et al., "The First Dime," 154. See also Stephen C. Richards and Jeffrey Ian Ross, "Introducing the New School of Convict Criminology," *Social Justice* 28 (2001): 177–190; Jeffrey Ian Ross and Stephen C. Richards, ed., *Convict Criminology* (Belmont, CA: Wadsworth, 2003).

25. Victor Hassine, *Life Without Parole: Living in Prison Today* (Los Angeles: Roxbury, 1996).

26. Thomas J. Bernard, *The Cycle of Juvenile Justice* (New York: Oxford University Press, 1992); George B. Vold, Thomas J. Bernard, and Jeffrey B. Snipes, *Theoretical Criminology*, 5th ed. (New York: Oxford University Press, 2001).

27. Michel Foucault, *Discipline and Punish: The Birth of the Prison* (New York: Vintage, 1979), 293.

28. K. C. Carceral, *Behind a Convict's Eyes* (Belmont, CA: Wadsworth, 2004).

29. Carceral, *Behind a Convict's Eyes*, 8.

30. K. C. Carceral, *Prison, Inc.* (New York: New York University Press, 2006).

31. Carceral, *Prison, Inc.*, 59.

32. Norbert Elias, *Time: An Essay* (Oxford: Blackwell, 1992), 37.

33. Martin P. Nilsson, *Primitive Time-Reckoning* (Lund, Sweden: C. W. K. Gleerup, 1920), 42.

34. Pitirim A. Sorokin and Robert K. Merton, "Social Time: A Methodological and Functional Analysis," *American Journal of Sociology* 42 (1937): 620.

35. Eviatar Zerubavel, *The Seven Day Circle: The History and Meaning of the Week* (New York: Free Press, 1985).

36. Eviatar Zerubavel, "The Standardization of Time: A Sociohistorical Perspective," *American Journal of Sociology* 88 (1982): 1–23.

37. Robert Levine, *A Geography of Time* (New York: Basic, 1997).

38. Zerubavel, *The Seven Day Circle*, 28, 35.

39. Peter L. Berger and Thomas Luckmann, *The Social Construction of Reality* (New York: Anchor, 1966), 27.

40. Eugène Minkowski, *Lived Time: Phenomenological and Psychopathological Studies* (Evanston, IL: Northwestern University Press, [1933] 1970).

41. Alfred Schutz and Thomas Luckmann, *The Structures of the Life-World* (Evanston, IL: Northwestern University Press, 1973), 52.

42. Schutz and Luckmann, *The Structures of the Life-World*, 27.

43. Michael G. Flaherty, *A Watched Pot: How We Experience Time* (New York: New York University Press, 1999); Michael G. Flaherty, "The Perception of Time and Situated Engrossment," *Social Psychology Quarterly* 54 (1991): 76–85; Michael G. Flaherty, "Multiple Realities and the Experience of Duration," *The Sociological Quarterly* 28 (1987): 313–326.

44. Michael G. Flaherty, *The Textures of Time: Agency and Temporal Experience* (Philadelphia: Temple University Press, 2011); Michael G. Flaherty, "Time Work: Customizing Temporal Experience," *Social Psychology Quarterly* 66 (2003): 17–33; Michael G. Flaherty, "Making Time: Agency and the Construction of Temporal Experience," *Symbolic Interaction* 25 (2002): 379–388.

45. Jones et al., "The First Dime," 156, 159.

46. Stephen C. Richards, "USP Marion: A Few Prisoners Summon the Courage to Speak," *Laws* 4 (2015): 100. See also Greg Newbold, Jeffrey Ian Ross, Richard S. Jones, Stephen C. Richards, and Michael Lenza, "Prison Research from the Inside: The Role of Convict Autoethnography," *Qualitative Inquiry* 20 (2014): 439–448.

47. Herbert Blumer, *Symbolic Interactionism: Perspective and Method* (Englewood Cliffs, NJ: Prentice-Hall, 1969), 34–35.

48. Clinton R. Sanders, *Customizing the Body: The Art and Culture of Tattooing* (Philadelphia: Temple University Press, 1989), 173.

49. Gustav Ichheiser, *Appearances and Realities* (San Francisco: Jossey-Bass, 1970), 8.

50. Erin George, *A Woman Doing Life: Notes from a Prison for Women* (New York: Oxford University Press, 2010), 150.

51. See also studies of patients who require lengthy hospitalization: Fred Davis, "Definitions of Time and Recovery in Paralytic Polio Convalescence," *American Journal of Sociology* 61 (1956): 582–587; Julius A. Roth, *Timetables: Structuring the Passage of Time in Hospital Treatment and Other Careers* (Indianapolis, IN: Bobbs-Merrill, 1963); Kathy Calkins, "Time: Perspectives, Markings, and Styles of Usage," *Social Problems* 17 (1970): 487–501; Kathy Charmaz, *Good Days, Bad Days: The Self in Chronic Illness and Time* (New Brunswick, NJ: Rutgers University Press, 1991).

52. Maurice Farber concludes that prison behavior is shaped by inmates' "time perspective, particularly the future outlook," whereas Stanley Cohen and Laurie Taylor describe the mental deterioration of inmates within the context of long-term imprisonment. See Maurice Farber, "Suffering and Time Perspective of the Prisoner," in *Authority and Frustration*, ed. Kurt Lewin (Iowa City: University of Iowa Press, 1944), 208; Stanley Cohen and Laurie Taylor, *Psychological Survival: The Experience of Long Term Imprisonment* (New York: Vintage, 1972). Ian O'Donnell restricts his research to solitary confinement, a situation that is uncommon in crowded American prisons. See *Prisoners, Solitude, and Time* (Oxford: Oxford University Press, 2014). For the vast majority of convicts, what happens to time and temporal experience has little to do with solitude and much to do with

social interaction. We investigate temporal experience across the full spectrum of incarceration.

53. Thomas Meisenhelder, "An Essay on Time and the Phenomenology of Imprisonment," *Deviant Behavior* 6 (1985): 43.

54. Rik Scarce, "Doing Time as an Act of Survival," *Symbolic Interaction* 25 (2002): 304.

1. A TEMPORAL REGIME

1. Michel Foucault, *Discipline and Punish: The Birth of the Prison* (New York: Vintage, 1979), 7.

2. Kai T. Erikson, *Wayward Puritans: A Study in the Sociology of Deviance* (Boston: Allyn and Bacon, 1966), 200.

3. Michael G. Flaherty, "Time, Social Theories of," in *Encyclopedia of Philosophy and the Social Sciences*, vol. 2, ed. Byron Kaldis (Thousand Oaks, CA: Sage, 2013), 1005; see also Martin P. Nilsson, *Primitive Time-Reckoning* (Lund, Sweden: C. W. K. Gleerup, 1920).

4. Emile Durkheim, *The Elementary Forms of the Religious Life* (New York: Free Press, [1915] 1965).

5. Peter L. Berger, *The Sacred Canopy: Elements of a Sociological Theory of Religion* (Garden City, NY: Anchor, 1967), 118.

6. Max Weber, *The Protestant Ethic and the Spirit of Capitalism* (New York: Scribner, [1904–1905] 1958), 157.

7. Anselm Strauss, "Transformations of Identity" in *Human Behavior and Social Processes: An Interactionist Approach*, ed. Arnold M. Rose (Boston: Houghton Mifflin, 1962), 71.

8. Robert Levine, *A Geography of Time* (New York: Basic, 1997), 160.

9. David E. Rohall, Melissa A. Milkie, and Jeffry W. Lucas, *Social Psychology: Sociological Perspectives*, 2nd ed. (Boston: Allyn and Bacon, 2011), 251.

10. Alfred Schutz, *Collected Papers*, vol. 1, *The Problem of Social Reality*, ed. Maurice Natanson (The Hague: Martinus Nijhoff, [1945] 1962), 231.

11. Victor Serge, *Men in Prison* (Oakland, CA: PM Press, [1931] 2014), 32.

12. Erin George, *A Woman Doing Life: Notes from a Prison for Women* (New York: Oxford University Press, 2010), 102.

13. Margaret Mead, *Soviet Attitudes Toward Authority: An Interdisciplinary Approach to Problems of Soviet Character* (New York: Schocken, [1951] 1966), 95. Lest one concludes that communist regimes are unique in this respect, consider the equally brutal treatment that formerly agricultural peasants experienced in the transition to industrial capitalism: E. P. Thompson, "Time, Work-Discipline, and Industrial Capitalism," *Past and Present* 38 (1967): 56–97.

14. Jeffrey Ian Ross and Stephen C. Richards, *Behind Bars: Surviving Prison* (Indianapolis, IN: Alpha, 2002), 65.

15. George, *A Woman Doing Life*, 30.

16. James A. Paluch, Jr., *A Life for a Life* (Los Angeles: Roxbury, 2004), 23. As Erin George puts it, "Every day, I learned, was basically the same." See *A Woman Doing Life*, 33.

17. Jimmy Baca, *A Place to Stand* (New York: Grove-Atlantic, 2001), 246.

18. Jimmy Lerner, *You Got Nothing Coming: Notes from a Prison Fish* (New York: Broadway, 2002), 105.

19. Hartmut Rosa, "Social Acceleration: Ethical and Political Consequences of a Desynchronized High-Speed Society," *Constellations* 10 (2003): 3–52; Hartmut Rosa, *Social Acceleration: A New Theory of Modernity* (New York: Columbia University Press, [2005] 2013); Robert Hassan, *Empires of Speed: Time and the Acceleration of Politics and Society* (Leiden, The Netherlands: Brill, 2009).

20. Timothy Leary, *Jail Notes* (New York: Douglas, 1970), 24.

21. Throughout our analysis, unsourced quotations come from field notes, interviews, or personal correspondence.

22. Eviatar Zerubavel, *The Seven Day Circle: The History and Meaning of the Week* (New York: Free Press, 1985), 131. Zerubavel shows us that, outside of prison, this pattern is not intrinsic to particular days of the week, an observation confirmed by Christopher Burney's experience as a POW: "It was a Wednesday, and the Germans were now treating Wednesdays as Saturdays, sending the staff on leave for the afternoon and abandoning us to that deserted silence which made the day seem twice as long." See Christopher Burney, *Solitary Confinement* (New York: Coward-McCann, 1952), 137–138.

23. George, *A Woman Doing Life*, 34.

24. Michael G. Flaherty, *A Watched Pot: How We Experience Time* (New York: New York University Press, 1999), 40.

25. Robert Berger, *From the Inside: A Prison Memoir* (Lincoln, NE: iUniverse, 2003), 9.

26. Michael Santos, *Profiles from Prison: Adjusting to Life Behind Bars* (Westport, CT: Praeger, 2003).

27. George, *A Woman Doing Life*, 34. "For prison inmates, Christmas is the quietest day of the year," adds T. J. Parsell. See *Fish: A Memoir of a Boy in a Man's Prison* (Cambridge, MA: Da Capo, 2006), 267.

28. Lerner, *You Got Nothing Coming*, 201. "There had been no Christmas or New Year for us that year," recalls Sunny Jacobs, "only another day of sadness and frustration, the same as every other day." See *Stolen Time* (London: Bantam, 2007), 152.

29. Megan Comfort, *Doing Time Together: Love and Family in the Shadow of the Prison* (Chicago: University of Chicago Press, 2008), 40, 42.

30. Rose Giallombardo, *Society of Women: A Study of a Women's Prison* (New York: Wiley, 1966), 133.

31. Stanley Cohen and Laurie Taylor, *Psychological Survival: The Experience of Long Term Imprisonment* (New York: Vintage, 1972), 72. Like Andreas Schroeder, convicts learn that visits disrupt their attempts to manage temporal experience: "The trouble with visits is that they won't let you forget. The more alive you keep your memories of the Street, the worse things look and feel to you Inside. The less you know about what you're missing on the Street, the easier it is to imagine you're not missing anything at all. In order to shake easy time Inside you have to rid yourself of all Outside voices, Outside problems (which you can't resolve in any case) and Outside comparisons with Inside life." See Andreas Schroeder, *Shaking It Rough: A Prison Memoir* (Garden City, NY: Doubleday, 1976), 135.

32. Cohen and Taylor, *Psychological Survival*, 73.

33. Warren TenHouten, "Text and Temporality: Patterned-Cyclical and Ordinary-Linear Forms of Time Consciousness, Inferred from a Corpus of Australian

Aboriginal and Euro-Australian Life-Historical Interviews," *Symbolic Interaction* 22 (1999): 121–137.

34. Murray Melbin, "Night as Frontier," *American Sociological Review* 43 (1978): 3–22.

35. Lerner, *You Got Nothing Coming*, 50. Later, Lerner observes (66), the fish are told that, due to overcrowding, they will remain in "the Fish Tank" for "*another* thirty days."

36. Berger, *From the Inside*; Jorge Renaud, *Behind the Walls: A Guide for Families and Friends of Texas Prison Inmates* (Denton: University of North Texas Press, 2002).

37. Amanda Lindhout and Sara Corbett, *A House in the Sky: A Memoir* (New York: Scribner, 2013), 28.

38. Lindhout and Corbett, *A House in the Sky*, 285.

39. Lerner, *You Got Nothing Coming*, 5.

40. Berger, *From the Inside*.

41. Lerner, *You Got Nothing Coming*, 82.

42. Lerner, *You Got Nothing Coming*, 85.

43. Lerner, *You Got Nothing Coming*, 68.

44. Edith Wharton, *Collected Stories 1911–1937* (New York: The Library of America, 2001), 73.

45. Eviatar Zerubavel, *Hidden Rhythms: Schedules and Calendars in Social Life* (Chicago: University of Chicago Press, 1981).

46. Stephen Stanko, "The Prison Environment," in *Living in Prison: A History of the Correctional System with an Insider's View*, ed. Stephen Stanko, Wayne Gillespie, and Gordon A. Crews (Westport, CT: Greenwood, 2004), 153.

47. George, *A Woman Doing Life*, 33.

48. George, *A Woman Doing Life*, 33.

49. Jacobs, *Stolen Time*, 288.

50. R. Theodore Davidson, *Chicano Prisoners: The Key to San Quentin* (Prospect Heights, IL: Waveland, 1974), 23–24.

51. Stanko, "The Prison Environment," 154.

52. John Irwin, *The Jail* (Berkeley: University of California Press, 1985), 92.

53. "Prisons . . . offer diversions that are unavailable in jails, which are comparatively poorly funded and which house inmates for briefer periods." Rik Scarce, "Doing Time as an Act of Survival," *Symbolic Interaction* 25 (2002): 313.

54. Zerubavel, *The Seven Day Circle*, 38.

55. Lerner, *You Got Nothing Coming*, 50.

56. Lerner, *You Got Nothing Coming*, 50–51.

57. Lerner, *You Got Nothing Coming*, 51.

58. Baca, *A Place to Stand*, 112.

59. Lindhout and Corbett, *A House in the Sky*, 2.

60. Lindhout and Corbett, *A House in the Sky*, 165.

61. Lindhout and Corbett, *A House in the Sky*, 2.

62. Ingrid Betancourt, *Even Silence Has an End: My Six Years of Captivity in the Colombian Jungle* (New York: Penguin, 2010), 64.

63. Betancourt, *Even Silence Has an End*, 515.

64. Betancourt, *Even Silence Has an End*, 484.

65. Betancourt, *Even Silence Has an End*, 129.

66. Barry Schwartz, *Queuing and Waiting* (Chicago: University of Chicago Press, 1975), 19. See also Barry Schwartz, "Waiting, Exchange, and Power: The Distribution of Time in Social Systems," *American Journal of Sociology* 79 (1974): 841–870.

67. William James, *The Principles of Psychology*, vol. 1 (New York: Henry Holt, 1890), 624.

68. Tea Torbenfeldt Bengtsson, "Boredom and Action—Experiences from Youth Confinement," *Journal of Contemporary Ethnography* 41 (2012): 526–553.

69. Anne Line Dalsgård, Martin Demant Frederiksen, Susanne Højlund, and Lotte Meinert, eds., *Ethnographies of Youth and Temporality: Time Objectified* (Philadelphia: Temple University Press, 2014).

70. Erving Goffman, *Asylums: Essays on the Social Situation of Mental Patients and Other Inmates* (Garden City, NY: Anchor, 1961), 5–6.

71. Lerner, *You Got Nothing Coming*, 6.

72. Baca, *A Place to Stand*, 109; Clifford R. Shaw, *The Jack-Roller: A Delinquent Boy's Own Story* (Chicago: University of Chicago Press, [1930] 1966), 57.

73. Peter Pringle, *About Time: Surviving Ireland's Death Row* (Dublin: The History Press Ireland, 2012), 140.

74. Jacobs, *Stolen Time*, 314–315.

75. Victor W. Turner, *The Ritual Process: Structure and Anti-structure* (New York: Aldine, 1969).

76. Albert Woodfox, *Solitary: Unbroken by Four Decades in Solitary Confinement. My Story of Transformation and Hope* (New York: Grove, 2019), 177.

77. Woodfox, *Solitary*, 177.

78. Woodfox, *Solitary*, 177. We find a parallel statement in the writings of Sunny Jacobs: "With all that was going on, daily life in prison remained the same. It could be frustrating but there were times when it was comforting to be carried along by the humdrum routine." See *Stolen Time*, 513. "Any break in the routine truly upsets me" adds Erin George. See *A Woman Doing Life*, 34.

79. Goffman, *Asylums*, 320.

2. TIME AND SPACE

1. See Robert Levine, *A Geography of Time* (New York: Basic, 1997), 95–96. See also Michael G. Flaherty, "Afterword," in *Ethnographies of Youth and Temporality: Time Objectified*, ed. Anne Line Dalsgård, Martin Demant Frederiksen, Susanne Højlund, and Lotte Meinert (Philadelphia: Temple University Press, 2014), 184–185.

2. Daphne Demetry, "Regimes of Meaning: The Intersection of Space and Time in Kitchen Cultures," *Journal of Contemporary Ethnography* 42 (2013): 581.

3. Drawing from Flaherty's theory concerning variation in temporal experience, Stephen Buetow asks if steps can be taken to manage how patients experience time in the course of their medical care. To accelerate the perceived passage of time, for example, he suggests that the "physical environment of the waiting room should be familiar and reassuring to the particular patient clientele, though not monotonous." As we will see, this suggestion stands in stark contrast to the design of prison environments. See Stephen Buetow, "Patient Experience of Time Duration: Strategies for

'Slowing Time' and 'Accelerating Time' in General Practices," *Journal of Evaluation in Clinical Practice* 10 (2004): 24.

4. Jimmy Lerner, *You Got Nothing Coming: Notes from a Prison Fish* (New York: Broadway, 2002), 25.

5. Jimmy Baca, *A Place to Stand* (New York: Grove-Atlantic, 2001), 107.

6. Baca, *A Place to Stand*, 108.

7. Baca, *A Place to Stand*, 109.

8. Stephen Stanko, "Surviving in Prison," in *Living in Prison: A History of the Correctional System with an Insider's View*, ed. Stephen Stanko, Wayne Gillespie, and Gordon A. Crews (Westport, CT: Greenwood, 2004), 177.

9. Baca, *A Place to Stand*, 5.

10. James A. Paluch, Jr., *A Life for a Life* (Los Angeles: Roxbury, 2004), 4.

11. Victor Serge, *Men in Prison* (Oakland, CA: PM Press, [1931] 2014), 9–10. Peter Pringle echoes this imagery: "Being locked in a cell for twelve hours is like being entombed." See *About Time: Surviving Ireland's Death Row* (Dublin: The History Press Ireland, 2012), 136.

12. Lerner, *You Got Nothing Coming*, 46.

13. Lerner, *You Got Nothing Coming*, 214, 228.

14. Lerner, *You Got Nothing Coming*, 203.

15. Timothy Leary, *Jail Notes* (New York: Douglas, 1970), 44.

16. Lerner, *You Got Nothing Coming*, 104; Paluch, *A Life for a Life*, 148.

17. Baca, *A Place to Stand*, 247; Stanko, "Surviving in Prison," 171. See also Sunny Jacobs, *Stolen Time* (London: Bantam, 2007), 122.

18. Lerner, *You Got Nothing Coming*, 105, 120. See also Stephen C. Richards, "USP Marion: A Few Prisoners Summon the Courage to Speak," *Laws* 4 (2015): 99.

19. Paluch, *A Life for a Life*, 4; Erin George, *A Woman Doing Life: Notes from a Prison for Women* (New York: Oxford University Press, 2010), 93.

20. Baca, *A Place to Stand*, 178.

21. Jacobo Timerman, *Prisoner Without a Name, Cell Without a Number* (New York: Knopf, 1981), 3. This cell is in a "clandestine" prison (4). When he is transferred to "a legal prison" (81), his "cell measures nearly two meters in width and three in length." A cell of any kind would have been an improvement for Ingrid Betancourt, who is chained by the neck to a tree after she attempts to escape from the FARC. See *Even Silence Has an End: My Six Years of Captivity in the Colombian Jungle* (New Work: Penguin, 2010), 491.

22. Serge, *Men in Prison*, 35.

23. Jorge Renaud, *Behind the Walls: A Guide for Families and Friends of Texas Prison Inmates* (Denton: University of North Texas Press, 2002).

24. Lerner, *You Got Nothing Coming*, 43.

25. Stephen Stanko, "The Prison Environment," in *Living in Prison: A History of the Correctional System with an Insider's View*, ed. Stephen Stanko, Wayne Gillespie, and Gordon A. Crews (Westport, CT: Greenwood, 2004), 152.

26. Gresham M. Sykes, *The Society of Captives: A Study of Maximum Security Prison* (Princeton, NJ: Princeton University Press, 1958), 5.

27. Stephen Stanko, "A Prisoner's Narrative," in *Living in Prison: A History of the Correctional System with an Insider's View*, ed. Stephen Stanko, Wayne Gillespie, and Gordon A. Crews (Westport, CT: Greenwood, 2004), 141; see also Anthony J. Manocchio

and Jimmy Dunn, *The Time Game: Two Views of a Prison* (New York: Dell, 1970), 30–31.

28. Lerner, *You Got Nothing Coming*, 42.

29. Lerner, *You Got Nothing Coming*, 8; Paluch, *A Life for a Life*, 155; Billy Wayne Sinclair and Jodie Sinclair, *A Life in the Balance: The Billy Wayne Sinclair Story* (New York: Arcade, 2000), 21.

30. Stanko, "Surviving in Prison," 171.

31. In segregation, Paluch finds "a sink that does not work." See *A Life for a Life*, 155; see also Robert Berger, *From the Inside: A Prison Memoir* (Lincoln, NE: iUniverse, 2003).

32. Clifford R. Shaw, *The Jack-Roller: A Delinquent Boy's Own Story* (Chicago: University of Chicago Press, [1930] 1966), 150.

33. R. Theodore Davidson, *Chicano Prisoners: The Key to San Quentin* (Prospect Heights, IL: Waveland, 1974), 27. More recently, Baca's latrine in a Mexican jail was "a hole in the floor." See *A Place to Stand*, 81.

34. Paluch, *A Life for a Life*, 135.

35. Sykes, *The Society of Captives*, 4.

36. George, *A Woman Doing Life*, 10.

37. Lerner, *You Got Nothing Coming*, 5; Leary, *Jail Notes*, 22.

38. Harold Garfinkel, "Conditions of Successful Degradation Ceremonies," *American Journal of Sociology* 61 (1956): 420–424.

39. Sinclair and Sinclair, *A Life in the Balance*, 66.

40. Christopher Burney, *Solitary Confinement* (New York: Coward-McCann, 1952), 90.

41. Lerner, *You Got Nothing Coming*, 6.

42. Baca, *A Place to Stand*, 160.

43. Baca, *A Place to Stand*, 55. See also Lerner, *You Got Nothing Coming*, 69.

44. Davidson, *Chicano Prisoners*, 24.

45. Davidson, *Chicano Prisoners*, 24–25.

46. Aleksandr Solzhenitsyn, *The Gulag Archipelago* (New York: Harper & Row, 1973), 502.

47. Davidson, *Chicano Prisoners*, 25. Erin George echoes his observation from the standpoint of a different era and gender: "The inmates [in segregation] are allowed almost nothing inside their cells." See *A Woman Doing Life*, 71.

48. Sinclair and Sinclair, *A Life in the Balance*, 316.

49. Solzhenitsyn, *The Gulag Archipelago*, 481.

50. Baca, *A Place to Stand*, 121.

51. George, *A Woman Doing Life*, 66.

52. Sinclair and Sinclair, *A Life in the Balance*, 158; Lerner, *You Got Nothing Coming*, 97.

53. Berger, *From the Inside*.

54. Sinclair and Sinclair, *A Life in the Balance*, 316; Timerman, *Prisoner Without a Name, Cell Without a Number*, 3.

55. Lerner, *You Got Nothing Coming*, 31.

56. Baca, *A Place to Stand*, 96.

57. Shaw, *The Jack-Roller*, 151.

58. Baca, *A Place to Stand*, 98.

59. Paluch, *A Life for a Life*, 10.

60. Paluch, *A Life for a Life*, 10.

61. Sinclair and Sinclair, *A Life in the Balance*, 40–41, 167.

2. TIME AND SPACE
62. Sinclair and Sinclair, *A Life in the Balance*, 86; see also George, *A Woman Doing Life*, 71.

63. Paluch, *A Life for a Life*, 151.

64. Baca, *A Place to Stand*, 109.

65. Baca, *A Place to Stand*, 159–160. In Canadian punishment cells, "the prisoner sits all day on the freezing tiles." See Andreas Schroeder, *Shaking It Rough: A Prison Memoir* (Garden City, NY: Doubleday, 1976), 147.

66. Lerner, *You Got Nothing Coming*, 201.

67. Paluch, *A Life for a Life*, 19.

68. Baca, *A Place to Stand*, 201.

69. Lerner, *You Got Nothing Coming*, 101.

70. Lerner, *You Got Nothing Coming*, 120.

71. Paluch, *A Life for a Life*, 135.

72. Baca, *A Place to Stand*, 1. See also Pringle, *About Time*, 128.

73. Lerner, *You Got Nothing Coming*, 29.

74. Davidson, *Chicano Prisoners*, 9.

75. Davidson, *Chicano Prisoners*, 24; Lerner, *You Got Nothing Coming*, 203.

76. Albert Woodfox, *Solitary: Unbroken by Four Decades in Solitary Confinement. My Story of Transformation and Hope* (New York: Grove, 2019), 285.

77. John Irwin, *The Jail* (Berkeley: University of California Press, 1985), 91. Andreas Schroeder confirms the same pattern in prison: "Our rooms are fitted with brilliant 200-watt bulbs, and at 6:00 A.M. the guards flick them on and pound on the plywood walls shouting our names." See *Shaking It Rough*, 85.

78. Manocchio and Dunn, *The Time Game*, 29.

79. Lerner, *You Got Nothing Coming*, 44.

80. Baca, *A Place to Stand*, 179. See also Sunny Jacobs, *Stolen Time* (London: Bantam, 2007), 359; Solzhenitsyn, *The Gulag Archipelago*, 228.

81. Manocchio and Dunn, *The Time Game*, 46; see also Baca, *A Place to Stand*, 112. At Pine Ridge Camp in Canada, there were "night counts every two hours." See Schroeder, *Shaking It Rough*, 197.

82. Solzhenitsyn, *The Gulag Archipelago*, 479–480. See also Pringle, *About Time*, 154.

83. Baca, *A Place to Stand*, 123–124. Likewise, in Canadian punishment cells, "it's pitch black in there." See Schroeder, *Shaking It Rough*, 147.

84. Paluch, *A Life for a Life*, 135.

85. Sinclair and Sinclair, *A Life in the Balance*, 14–15; see also Lerner, *You Got Nothing Coming*, 121. Peter Pringle, the Irish POW, encountered the same circumstances at Portlaoise Prison: "The fluorescent overhead lights were on day and night." See *About Time*, 154.

86. Davidson, *Chicano Prisoners*, 25.

87. Paluch, *A Life for a Life*, 4.

88. Lerner, *You Got Nothing Coming*, 43.

89. Baca, *A Place to Stand*, 2.

90. Baca, *A Place to Stand*, 96.

91. Baca, *A Place to Stand*, 201.

92. Lerner, *You Got Nothing Coming*, 6. His perspective is echoed in comments from Billy Sinclair: "A brooding sense of despair was etched in every scar and crack of the dirty green walls that surrounded me." See Sinclair and Sinclair, *A Life in the Balance*, 164.

93. Davidson, *Chicano Prisoners*, 26.

94. Lerner, *You Got Nothing Coming*, 143. See also Baca, *A Place to Stand*, 119: "From the southeast corner of the field where we were sitting, the expanse of parched grass spread with a dirt track around it."

95. Paluch, *A Life for a Life*, 137.

96. Baca, *A Place to Stand*, 114.

97. Sinclair and Sinclair, *A Life in the Balance*, 68; see also Baca, *A Place to Stand*, 119: "Cons were scattered out, separated by race: north of the handball courts was the iron pit filled with tattooed Aryan warriors muscling up; beyond that were boxers sparring and pounding the speed bags and body bags in a dirt ring; more Chicanos and blacks played baseball at the southwest corner; and at the northwest corner teams divided by race ran up and down the cement basketball courts."

98. Erving Goffman, *Relations in Public: Microstudies of the Public Order* (New York: Basic, 1971), 304.

99. Baca, *A Place to Stand*, 81.

100. Sykes, *The Society of Captives*, 4.

101. Lerner, *You Got Nothing Coming*, 29.

102. Michel Foucault, *Discipline and Punish: The Birth of the Prison* (New York: Vintage, 1979), 200.

103. Sinclair and Sinclair, *A Life in the Balance*, 15.

104. Sinclair and Sinclair, *A Life in the Balance*, 102.

105. Lerner, *You Got Nothing Coming*, 30.

106. Baca, *A Place to Stand*, 110.

107. Stanley Cohen and Laurie Taylor, *Psychological Survival: The Experience of Long Term Imprisonment* (New York: Vintage, 1972), 58.

108. Sykes, *The Society of Captives*, 7.

109. Thomas Meisenhelder, "An Essay on Time and the Phenomenology of Imprisonment," *Deviant Behavior* 6 (1985): 44. "Stimulus deprivation," Timothy Leary agrees, is an apt way to understand the prison environment. See *Jail Notes*, 44.

110. Woodfox, *Solitary*, 33. Likewise, Sunny Jacobs refers to "the sameness of days." See *Stolen Time*, 193.

111. Stanko, "Surviving in Prison," 178. Similarly, Erin George mourns her separation from the sight of nature, even during outdoor recreation: "The rec yard was small, about the size of half a basketball court, and surrounded by a two-story cinderblock wall. It was capped by a heavy metal grate and chicken wire, so I couldn't see the trees or grass, and not even a leaf could make its way to me." See *A Woman Doing Life*, 8.

112. Burney, *Solitary Confinement*, 8.

113. Baca, *A Place to Stand*, 149.

114. George, *A Woman Doing Life*, 96.

115. George, *A Woman Doing Life*, 95.

116. Lerner, *You Got Nothing Coming*, 32–33.

117. Sinclair and Sinclair, *A Life in the Balance*, 320.

118. Baca, *A Place to Stand*, 1.

119. Sinclair and Sinclair, *A Life in the Balance*, 59, 172; Paluch, *A Life for a Life*, 9.

120. Woodfox, *Solitary*, 37. Later in his memoir, he recounts the following incident: "Soon after I arrived a prisoner on the tier tried to intimidate me. It started in the

shower. He made comments about my body. I kept on showering. I dried off, put my clothes on, and went into the day room. He was sitting at a table playing cards. I grabbed the mop bucket, walked up to him, and split his head open with it. He was taken to the hospital, where he was treated, and he was returned to the same floor and cellblock where I was. Now he knew not to fuck with me and so did everyone else." (60)

121. Paluch, *A Life for a Life*, 9.
122. Paluch, *A Life for a Life*, 10.
123. Irwin, *The Jail*, 92. "The first thing that hit me was the noise," adds Andreas Schroeder. "Over a steady backdrop of clashing steel doors and shrilling hinges there is incessant shouting, arguing, [and] irritated commands." See *Shaking It Rough*, 62.
124. Paluch, *A Life for a Life*, 17. T. J. Parsell provides parallel testimony: "Noise echoed from everywhere, making it hard to hear anyone. Screaming, yelling, the rumble of rollers, the pulling of release brakes, and the sounds of a hundred sliding cell doors." See *Fish: A Memoir of a Boy in a Man's Prison* (Cambridge, MA: Da Capo, 2006), 49.
125. Baca, *A Place to Stand*, 110.
126. Paluch, *A Life for a Life*, 17; italics in original. In contrast, POWs and political prisoners may be forbidden to speak above a whisper. See Serge, *Men in Prison*, 52; Solzhenitsyn, *The Gulag Archipelago*, 481.
127. Baca, *A Place to Stand*, 110.
128. Sinclair and Sinclair, *A Life in the Balance*, 40. One's sleep also is disrupted by security procedures: "Every two hours during the past two nights a guard has stomped into the room, his boots thudding so loudly on the floor that I woke up every time." See Schroeder, *Shaking It Rough*, 198.
129. Jack Henry Abbott, *In the Belly of the Beast: Letters from Prison* (New York: Random House, 1981), 45.
130. Abbott, *In the Belly of the Beast*, 44–45.
131. Lerner, *You Got Nothing Coming*, 121.
132. Baca, *A Place to Stand*, 210.
133. Lerner, *You Got Nothing Coming*, 5, 104. "While in clandestine prisons," remembers Jacobo Timerman, "I was almost always cloistered in a cell close to the torture chamber." From this vantage point, he hears other prisoners screaming. Later, at a legal prison, he still listens to the grief of fellow inmates: "Often, I hear prisoners weeping." See *Prisoner Without a Name, Cell Without a Number*, 77, 82.
134. Lerner, *You Got Nothing Coming*, 105. Female prisoners hear the same insults: "Someone cursed, 'Shut the fuck up! Stupid bitch!'" See Jacobs, *Stolen Time*, 61.
135. Baca, *A Place to Stand*, 210. Billy Sinclair notes that quiet is a sign of impending violence. See Sinclair and Sinclair, *A Life in the Balance*, 117, 150.
136. Leary, *Jail Notes*, 24.
137. Lerner, *You Got Nothing Coming*, 119.
138. Lerner, *You Got Nothing Coming*, 19, 28.
139. Virginia Woolf, *A Room of One's Own* (New York: Harcourt, Brace, Jovanovich, 1929).
140. Lerner, *You Got Nothing Coming*, 262.
141. Baca, *A Place to Stand*, 192.
142. Stanko, "Surviving in Prison," 171.

143. Davidson, *Chicano Prisoners*, 9. Jimmy Lerner offers corroboration: "The general-population cellblocks were already at double occupancy with two men sharing a cell designed for one." See *You Got Nothing Coming*, 66.

144. George, *A Woman Doing Life*, 23.

145. George, *A Woman Doing Life*, 23.

146. Lerner, *You Got Nothing Coming*, 146–147.

147. Lerner, *You Got Nothing Coming*, 147.

148. Sinclair and Sinclair, *A Life in the Balance*, 104.

149. Sinclair and Sinclair, *A Life in the Balance*, 147.

150. Solzhenitsyn, *The Gulag Archipelago*, 451.

151. Martin Demant Frederiksen, *Young Men, Time, and Boredom in the Republic of Georgia* (Philadelphia: Temple University Press, 2013), 142. Jimmy Baca is confronted by kindred circumstances in a Mexican jail: "The cell could accommodate at most twenty prisoners, but it held about sixty." See *A Place to Stand*, 81.

152. Lerner, *You Got Nothing Coming*, 37.

153. Lerner, *You Got Nothing Coming*, 41.

154. Lerner, *You Got Nothing Coming*, 42.

155. Lerner, *You Got Nothing Coming*, 58.

156. Lerner, *You Got Nothing Coming*, 44.

157. Paluch, *A Life for a Life*, 12.

158. Paluch, *A Life for a Life*, 12.

159. Baca, *A Place to Stand*, 193.

160. George, *A Woman Doing Life*, 39.

161. George, *A Woman Doing Life*, 21.

162. George, *A Woman Doing Life*, 18.

163. George, *A Woman Doing Life*, 9.

164. George, *A Woman Doing Life*, 19.

165. George, *A Woman Doing Life*, 18.

166. George, *A Woman Doing Life*, 20.

167. George, *A Woman Doing Life*, 21.

168. George, *A Woman Doing Life*, 40.

169. George, *A Woman Doing Life*, 40.

170. Leary, *Jail Notes*, 45.

171. Serge, *Men is Prison*, 53.

172. Abbott, *In the Belly of the Beast*, 121.

173. Sykes, *The Society of Captives*, 77; Billy Sinclair concurs with his assessment: "I had two choices on the Big Yard—and there was no middle ground—fight and accept the criminal code or submit and be another's [*sic*] man's pussy." See Sinclair and Sinclair, *A Life in the Balance*, 216.

174. Abbott, *In the Belly of the Beast*, 121, italics in original; Sykes, *The Society of Captives*, 78.

175. Paluch, *A Life for a Life*, 94; Sinclair and Sinclair, *A Life in the Balance*, 122.

176. Lerner, *You Got Nothing Coming*, 99.

177. Lerner, *You Got Nothing Coming*, 153. See also Baca, *A Place to Stand*, 113, 212; Sinclair and Sinclair, *A Life in the Balance*, 18, 100.

178. George, *A Woman Doing Life*, 29.

179. George, *A Woman Doing Life*, 29.

180. Stanko, "Surviving in Prison," 172.
181. Amy Fisher and Robbie Wolliver, *If I Knew Then* . . . (New York: iUniverse, 2004), 179.
182. Stanko, "Surviving in Prison," 171.
183. Leary, *Jail Notes*, 79.
184. Paluch, *A Life for a Life*, 8–9. Similarly, Peter Pringle reports senseless violence: "One of the ordinary prisoners [he considers himself a POW], whom I later learned was a bit off the head, attempted to stab me one day as I was walking back from the handball alley." See *About Time*, 73–74.
185. Sinclair and Sinclair, *A Life in the Balance*, 111, 121.
186. Baca, *A Place to Stand*, 120.
187. Stanko, "Surviving in Prison," 173; "I have seen inmates bludgeoned or stabbed," he adds, "because they took a piece of chicken from another convict."
188. Sinclair and Sinclair, *A Life in the Balance*, 98; see also 121 where, Sinclair asserts, "each day an inmate was stabbed, killed, raped, or brutalized."
189. Paluch, *A Life for a Life*, 10.
190. Jack Katz, *Seductions of Crime: Moral and Sensual Attractions in Doing Evil* (New York: Basic, 1988), 3. Recently, there have been efforts to establish a "sensory history." See John David Smith, "What Did the Civil War Smell Like?" *The Chronicle of Higher Education*, October 17, 2014, B16.
191. Woodfox, *Solitary*, 233.
192. Thomas Meisenhelder supports this observation: "Prison inmates experience a heightened sense of self-consciousness." See "An Essay on Time and the Phenomenology of Imprisonment," 44.
193. Michael G. Flaherty, *A Watched Pot: How We Experience Time* (New York: New York University Press, 1999), 91.
194. Michael G. Flaherty, "The Perception of Time and Situated Engrossment," *Social Psychology Quarterly* 54 (1991): 80.
195. Abbott, *In the Belly of the Beast*, 76.
196. Manocchio and Dunn, *The Time Game*, 12–13.

3. TEMPORAL ALLOWANCES

1. Timothy Leary, *Jail Notes* (New York: Douglas, 1970), 44.
2. Jimmy Baca, *A Place to Stand* (New York: Grove-Atlantic, 2001), 185.
3. Rik Scarce, "Doing Time as an Act of Survival," *Symbolic Interaction* 25 (2002): 305.
4. Scarce, "Doing Time as an Act of Survival," 304.
5. Stephen Stanko, "Surviving in Prison," in *Living in Prison: A History of the Correctional System with an Insider's View*, ed. Stephen Stanko, Wayne Gillespie, and Gordon A. Crews (Westport, CT: Greenwood, 2004), 182; Stephen Stanko, "The Prison Environment," in *Living in Prison: A History of the Correctional System with an Insider's View*, ed. Stephen Stanko, Wayne Gillespie, and Gordon A. Crews (Westport, CT: Greenwood, 2004), 156.
6. Stanko, "Surviving in Prison," 171.
7. John Irwin, *The Jail* (Berkeley: University of California Press, 1985), 93.
8. Jorge Antonio Renaud, *Behind the Walls: A Guide for Families and Friends of Texas Prison Inmates* (Denton: University of North Texas Press, 2002), 53. Eddie Griffin

expresses similar frustration: a prisoner "must await permission to enter or exit at almost every stop. A man becomes peeved." See Stephen C. Richards, "USP Marion: A Few Prisoners Summon the Courage to Speak," *Laws* 4 (2015): 97.

9. James A. Paluch, Jr., *A Life for a Life* (Los Angeles: Roxbury, 2004), 134.
10. Piper Kerman, *Orange Is the New Black: My Year in a Women's Prison* (New York: Spiegel & Grau, 2011), 36.
11. Kerman, *Orange Is the New Black*, 60.
12. Albert Woodfox, *Solitary: Unbroken by Four Decades in Solitary Confinement. My Story of Transformation and Hope* (New York: Grove, 2019), 351.
13. Richard S. Jones and Thomas J. Schmid, *Doing Time: Prison Experience and Identity Among First-Time Inmates* (Stamford, CT: JAI, 2000), 29.
14. Ken Lamberton, *Wilderness and Razor Wire: A Naturalist's Observations from Prison* (San Francisco: Mercury House, 2000), 193–194.
15. Robert Berger, *From the Inside: A Prison Memoir* (Lincoln, NE: iUniverse, 2003), 175.
16. Berger, *From the Inside*, 175.
17. Edward T. Hall, *The Dance of Life: The Other Dimension of Time* (Garden City, NY: Anchor Doubleday, 1983); Robert Levine, *A Geography of Time* (New York: Basic Books, 1997).
18. Javier Auyero, *Patients of the State: The Politics of Waiting in Argentina* (Durham, NC: Duke University Press, 2012).
19. Erin George, *A Woman Doing Life: Notes from a Prison for Women* (New York: Oxford University Press, 2010), 23; see also Stanko, "Surviving in Prison," 178.
20. Jacobo Timerman, *Prisoner Without a Name, Cell Without a Number* (New York: Knopf, 1981), 105.
21. Paluch, *A Life for a Life*, 136. "Segregated prisoners," George adds, "are allowed three hours of rec a week." See *A Woman Doing Life*, 71.
22. Baca, *A Place to Stand*, 181.
23. Paluch, *A Life for a Life*, 137. The same conditions can be found at a prison for women, where segregated inmates are "placed in one of the enclosed miniature rec yards, one inmate per cage. It looks like a series of outdoor dog runs." See George, *A Woman Doing Life*, 71.
24. Jimmy Lerner, *You Got Nothing Coming: Notes from a Prison Fish* (New York: Broadway, 2002), 62.
25. Billy Wayne Sinclair and Jodie Sinclair, *A Life in the Balance: The Billy Wayne Sinclair Story* (New York: Arcade, 2000), 92.
26. Kerman, *Orange Is the New Black*, 285.
27. George, *A Woman Doing Life*, 90.
28. George, *A Woman Doing Life*, 103.
29. Alice Goffman, *On the Run: Fugitive Life in an American City* (Chicago: University of Chicago Press, 2014), 11.
30. Kerman, *Orange Is the New Black*, 216. For convict Richard Jones, the time limit was even shorter: "10 minutes." See Jones and Schmid, *Doing Time*, 58. Likewise, Sunny Jacobs was "allowed one ten-minute call per day." See *Stolen Time* (London: Bantam, 2007), 297.
31. Stanko, "Surviving in Prison," 171.
32. Kerman, *Orange Is the New Black*, 215. That Kerman's wait is typical, not exceptional, is confirmed by Jones and Schmid: "There are usually long lines of inmates waiting

to use the telephones, and time limits, which are enforced by the inmates themselves, are placed on the length of phone calls." See *Doing Time*, 15.

33. George, *A Woman Doing Life*, 8.

34. Lerner, *You Got Nothing Coming*, 106, 121. In jail, Billy Sinclair remembers, an inmate
clique decided when (or if) other inmates could use the telephone, turning this privilege into a basis for extortion. See Sinclair and Sinclair, *A Life in the Balance*, 18.

35. Berger, *From the Inside*, 109. "We were allowed one phone call a month," recalls
Berger, when he is placed in segregation. See 13.

36. Jorge Renaud points out that, in Texas, "access to the general library is considered a
privilege that can be revoked." See *Behind the Walls*, 81. See also Woodfox, *Solitary*, 125.

37. George, *A Woman Doing Life*, 104.

38. George, *A Woman Doing Life*, 104. "Visits were 25–30 minutes long" in Peter Pringle's case. See *About Time: Surviving Ireland's Death Row* (Dublin: The History Press
Ireland, 2012), 157.

39. George, *A Woman Doing Life*, 103.

40. Kerman, *Orange Is the New Black*, 59.

41. Jacobs, *Stolen Time*, 504.

42. Kerman, *Orange Is the New Black*, 60. See also Michael G. Flaherty, "Time and the
Horizon of Poignancy: Notes on Temporally Induced Sorrow," *KronoScope: Journal
for the Study of Time* 12 (2012): 90–103.

43. Kerman, *Orange Is the New Black*, 59.

44. Lerner, *You Got Nothing Coming*, 69.

45. Lerner, *You Got Nothing Coming*, 69.

46. Kerman, *Orange Is the New Black*, 61. Convict Richard Jones provides corroboration:
"The time went by so fast" [during a visit]. See Jones and Schmid, *Doing Time*, 69.
"The visit was over in the blink of an eye as always," adds Sunny Jacobs. See *Stolen
Time*, 549.

47. Jones and Schmid, *Doing Time*, 15–16.

48. Kerman, *Orange Is the New Black*, 215.

49. Megan Comfort, *Doing Time Together: Love and Family in the Shadow of the Prison*
(Chicago: University of Chicago Press, 2008), 43.

50. Baca, *A Place to Stand*, 180.

51. Paluch, *A Life for a Life*, 46.

52. Paluch, *A Life for a Life*, 137. At Mountjoy Prison, Peter Pringle was permitted fewer
opportunities for personal hygiene: "We were allowed a bath once a week when we
paraded in small groups to the bath house." See *About Time*, 32.

53. Sinclair and Sinclair, *A Life in the Balance*, 22.

54. Ingrid Betancourt, *Even Silence Has an End: My Six Years of Captivity in the Colombian Jungle* (New York: Penguin, 2010), 17.

55. Jacobs, *Stolen Time*, 111.

56. Lerner, *You Got Nothing Coming*, 35, 37. There is "no hot water in cells," adds Stephen
Stanko. See "The Prison Environment," 150.

57. George, *A Woman Doing Life*, 10.

58. Renaud, *Behind the Walls*, 11.

59. Renaud, *Behind the Walls*, 8.

60. Paluch, *A Life for a Life*, 27.

61. Stanko, "Surviving in Prison," 178.

62. Paluch, *A Life for a Life*, 29.
63. Clifford R. Shaw, *The Jack-Roller: A Delinquent Boy's Own Story* (Chicago: University of Chicago Press, [1930] 1966), 159. See also Pringle, *About Time*, 70.
64. George, *A Woman Doing Life*, 42.
65. George, *A Woman Doing Life*, 89.
66. Lerner, *You Got Nothing Coming*, 10.
67. Lerner, *You Got Nothing Coming*, 11.
68. Lerner, *You Got Nothing Coming*, 12.
69. Sinclair and Sinclair, *A Life in the Balance*, 322; Paluch, *A Life for a Life*, 9.
70. George, *A Woman Doing Life*, 71–72. See also Shaw, *The Jack-Roller*, 111; Sinclair and Sinclair, *A Life in the Balance*, 22, 198.
71. Christopher Burney, *Solitary Confinement* (New York: Coward-McCann, 1952), 22.
72. Aleksandr Solzhenitsyn, *The Gulag Archipelago* (New York: Harper & Row, 1973), 207. See also Timerman, *Prisoner Without a Name, Cell Without a Number*, 81.
73. Lerner, *You Got Nothing Coming*, 11.
74. Baca, *A Place to Stand*, 114. Albert Woodfox is given the same amount of time for a meal: "Once seated, we had fifteen minutes to eat." See *Solitary*, 33.
75. Berger, *From the Inside*, 105.
76. R. Theodore Davidson, *Chicano Prisoners: The Key to San Quentin* (Prospect Heights, IL: Waveland, 1974), 27.
77. Baca, *A Place to Stand*, 179.
78. Solzhenitsyn, *The Gulag Archipelago*, 205.
79. Paluch, *A Life for a Life*, 155.
80. Timerman, *Prisoner Without a Name, Cell Without a Number*, 4.
81. Lerner, *You Got Nothing Coming*, 205.
82. Timerman, *Prisoner Without a Name, Cell Without a Number*, 105.
83. Clare Hanrahan, *Jailed for Justice* (Asheville, NC: Celtic Wordcraft, 2002), 91.
84. Hanrahan, *Jailed for Justice*, 91.
85. Mary Ellen Klas, "Teen Inmates in Florida Denied Food for Talking," *Tampa Bay Times*, Wednesday, June 29, 2016, 1A, 7A. "Depriving inmates of food is against the law in Florida's prisons," adds Klas, "but when it happens, it rarely gets reported."
86. Berger, *From the Inside*, 3.
87. Richards, "USP Marion," 94.
88. See Auyero, *Patients of the State*.
89. Michael Santos, *Profiles from Prison: Adjusting to Life Behind Bars* (Westport, CT: Praeger, 2003), 92.
90. John Mirowsky and Catherine Ross, "Paranoia and the Structure of Powerlessness," *American Sociological Review* 48(1983): 228–239.
91. Barbara Adam, *Timescapes of Modernity: The Environment and Invisible Hazards* (London: Routledge, 1998).
92. Paluch, *A Life for a Life*, 51. See also Sinclair and Sinclair, *A Life in the Balance*, 67. Some prisoners cannot bring themselves to use this strategy. See Jacobs, *Stolen Time*, 151.
93. Sylvester Long, *I Made It Through the Storm: My Fifteen Year Walk in State Prison* (Bloomington, IN: 1st Books Library, 2002), 412.
94. Lerner, *You Got Nothing Coming*, 101–102. "O. G." is an abbreviation of his nickname, Original Gangsta.

4. SERVING TIME

1. Albert Woodfox, *Solitary: Unbroken by Four Decades in Solitary Confinement. My Story of Transformation and Hope* (New York: Grove, 2019), 171.
2. Eviatar Zerubavel, *Hidden Rhythms: Schedules and Calendars in Social Life* (Chicago: University of Chicago Press, 1981), 142–143.
3. Fyodor Dostoevsky, *The House of the Dead* (New York: Grove, [1862] 1957), 20; italics in original.
4. Robert Berger, *From the Inside: A Prison Memoir* (Lincoln, NE: iUniverse, 2003), 4.
5. Sylvester Long, *I Made It Through the Storm: My Fifteen Year Walk in State Prison* (Bloomington, IN: 1st Books Library, 2002), 584.
6. Fred Davis, "Why All of Us May Be Hippies Someday," *Trans-Action* 5 (1967): 15.
7. Karen Stein, "Time Off: The Social Experience of Time on Vacation," *Qualitative Sociology* 35 (2012): 351.
8. Stanley Cohen and Laurie Taylor, *Psychological Survival: The Experience of Long Term Imprisonment* (New York: Vintage, 1972), 89.
9. Sunny Jacobs, *Stolen Time* (London: Bantam, 2007), 280. She suffers extreme anxiety when she leaves her cell under her own initiative. See 281.
10. Erin George, *A Woman Doing Life: Notes from a Prison for Women* (New York: Oxford University Press, 2010), 34.
11. Long, *I Made It Through the Storm*, 61.
12. Jimmy Baca, *A Place to Stand* (New York: Grove-Atlantic, 2001), 186.
13. Dostoevsky, *The House of the Dead*, 9.
14. Barry Schwartz, "Deprivation of Privacy as a 'Functional Prerequisite': The Case of the Prison," *The Journal of Criminal Law, Criminology, and Police Science* 63 (1972): 229–239.
15. Robert Gifford, *Environmental Psychology: Principles and Practice*, 2nd ed. (Boston: Allyn and Bacon, 1997), 182.
16. Cohen and Taylor, *Psychological Survival*, 79.
17. Cohen and Taylor, *Psychological Survival*, 79.
18. Cohen and Taylor, *Psychological Survival*, 81.
19. Clare Hanrahan, *Jailed for Justice* (Asheville, NC: Celtic Wordcraft, 2002), 44.
20. Hanrahan, *Jailed for Justice*, 71. Hanrahan adds that such surveillance is especially problematic for female inmates: "Both the strip search and the pat-down search are a particularly disturbing fact of prison life, given the very high percentage of imprisoned women who report a past history of physical or sexual abuse." (44)
21. George, *A Woman Doing Life*, 14.
22. Piper Kerman, *Orange Is the New Black: My Year in a Women's Prison* (New York: Spiegel & Grau, 2011), 167.
23. Amy Fisher and Robbie Wolliver, *If I Knew Then . . .* (New York: iUniverse, 2004), 137.
24. Jimmy Lerner, *You Got Nothing Coming: Notes from a Prison Fish* (New York: Broadway, 2002), 35.
25. Stephen Stanko, "A Prisoner's Narrative," in *Living in Prison: A History of the Correctional System with an Insider's View*, ed. Stephen Stanko, Wayne Gillespie, and Gordon A. Crews (Westport, CT: Greenwood, 2004), 141.
26. Victor Serge, *Men in Prison* (Oakland, CA: PM Press, [1931] 2014), 54.

27. Jorge Renaud, *Behind the Walls: A Guide for Families and Friends of Texas Prison Inmates* (Denton: University of North Texas Press, 2002), 7. At intake, Reginald Hall is not fearful, but he is already troubled by the lack of privacy: "Standing there I realized that it wasn't so much that I felt scared, it was more the waiting and being around so many different people that was beginning to wear on me." See Reginald L. Hall, *Memoir: Delaware County Prison* (Mountainside, NJ: Writersandpoets.com, 2004), 2.

28. Long, *I Made It Through the Storm*, 339.

29. Alfred Schutz, *The Phenomenology of the Social World* (Evanston, IL: Northwestern University Press, [1932] 1967), 163.

30. Schutz, *The Phenomenology of the Social World*, 165.

31. Baca, *A Place to Stand*, 204.

32. Berger, *From the Inside*, 49.

33. Fisher, *If I Knew Then*, 175.

34. Hanrahan, *Jailed for Justice*, 92. POWs also endure temporal trespassing: "Guards came into each hut during the night and made a count. If a prisoner had his head under the covers, they would pull the covers back to see the man in the bed. This caused considerable aggravation and disturbance during the night." See Peter Pringle, *About Time: Surviving Ireland's Death Row* (Dublin: The History Press Ireland, 2012), 50. In addition, temporal trespassing helps us understand violations of proper sequence in social interaction, as noted by Sunny Jacobs: "I think that everyone should knock before they peep their head in to see if I'm on the john—not while they knock be looking in already." See *Stolen Time*, 194.

35. Woodfox, *Solitary*, 336–337.

36. Berger, *From the Inside*, 72.

37. Long, *I Made It Through the Storm*.

38. Edward T. Hall, *The Dance of Life: The Other Dimension of Time* (New York: Anchor Doubleday, 1984).

39. Zerubavel, *Hidden Rhythms*.

40. Richard H. Anson and Barry W. Hancock, "Crowding, Proximity, Inmate Violence, and the Eighth Amendment," *Journal of Offender Rehabilitation* 17 (1992): 123–132.

41. "*Hurry up and wait* seems to be the standard operating jailhouse philosophy," writes Jimmy Lerner. See *You Got Nothing Coming*, 17.

42. Rik Scarce, "Doing Time as an Act of Survival," *Symbolic Interaction* 25 (2002):306.

43. "There had been seizures, diabetic emergencies, a heart attack, a throat slashing, and a girl who hanged herself," recalls Sunny Jacobs. "The pregnant girl had her baby on the way to the hospital, in the driveway of the local fire department because we couldn't summon help soon enough." See *Stolen Time*, 260.

44. Sunny Jacobs states that "it took for ever [sic] to get to see the doctor." See *Stolen Time*, 458.

45. Baca, *A Place to Stand*, 110.

46. Billy Wayne Sinclair and Jodie Sinclair, *A Life in the Balance: The Billy Wayne Sinclair Story* (New York: Arcade, 2000).

47. James A. Paluch, Jr., *A Life for a Life* (Los Angeles: Roxbury, 2004), 27.

48. Mark Iutcovich, Charles E. Babbitt, and Joyce Iutcovich, "Time Perception: A Case Study of a Developing Nation," *Sociological Focus* 12 (1979): 71–85; Hall, *The Dance of Life*; Robert Levine, *A Geography of Time* (New York: Basic, 1997); Allen C. Bluedorn,

The Human Organization of Time: Temporal Realities and Experience (Stanford, CA: Stanford University Press, 2002).

49. Peter L. Berger and Thomas Luckmann, *The Social Construction of Reality* (New York: Anchor Doubleday, 1966).

50. Max Weber, *Economy and Society: An Outline of Interpretive Sociology* (Berkeley: University of California Press, [1921] 1978).

51. George, *A Woman Doing Life*, 95.

52. George, *A Woman Doing Life*, 96.

53. Jeffrey Ian Ross and Stephen C. Richards, *Behind Bars: Surviving Prison* (Indianapolis, IN: Alpha, 2002).

54. Megan Comfort, *Doing Time Together: Love and Family in the Shadow of the Prison* (Chicago: University of Chicago Press, 2008), 40.

55. Michael Santos, *Profiles from Prison: Adjusting to Life Behind Bars* (Westport, CT: Praeger, 2003), 93.

56. Santos, *Profiles from Prison*, 93.

57. Santos, *Profiles from Prison*, 111.

58. George Herbert Mead, *Mind, Self, and Society* (Chicago: University of Chicago Press, 1934), 90, 122.

59. Michael G. Flaherty, *A Watched Pot: How We Experience Time* (New York: New York University Press, 1999), 96.

60. In prison, as in Argentina, there is a politics of waiting. See Javier Auyero, *Patients of the State: The Politics of Waiting in Argentina* (Durham, NC: Duke University Press, 2012).

61. George, *A Woman Doing Life*, 42.

62. Berger, *From the Inside*, 30.

63. Renaud, *Behind the Walls*, 104.

64. Renaud, *Behind the Walls*, 108.

65. George Jackson, *Soledad Brother: The Prison Letters of George Jackson* (New York: Bantam, 1970), 19.

66. George, *A Woman Doing Life*, 14.

67. Berger, *From the Inside*, 30.

68. Renaud, *Behind the Walls*, 108.

69. Lerner, *You Got Nothing Coming*, 20.

70. Jacobs, *Stolen Time*, 417.

71. William A. Reese and Michael A. Katovich, "Untimely Acts: Extending the Interactionist Conception of Deviance," *The Sociological Quarterly* 30 (1989): 159–184.

72. Erving Goffman, *Asylums: Essays on the Social Situation of Mental Patients and Other Inmates* (Garden City, NY: Anchor, 1961), 5–6; italics added.

73. Fisher, *If I Knew Then*, 138.

74. Fisher, *If I Knew Then*, 138–139.

75. Baca, *A Place to Stand*, 125–126.

76. Fisher, *If I Knew Then*, 140.

77. Renaud, *Behind the Walls*, 31.

78. Renaud, *Behind the Walls*, 32.

79. Michel Foucault, *Discipline and Punish: The Birth of the Prison* (New York: Vintage, 1979), 3.

80. Emile Durkheim, *The Rules of Sociological Method* (New York: Free Press, [1895] 1964).

81. Associated Press, "Florida to Parole 'Prison Houdini' after 36 Years," *Tampa Bay Times*, July 15, 2016, 9B.
82. Associated Press, "Florida to Parole 'Prison Houdini' after 36 Years," 9B.
83. Associated Press, "Florida to Parole 'Prison Houdini' after 36 Years," 9B.
84. Associated Press, "Florida to Parole 'Prison Houdini' after 36 Years," 9B.
85. Michael A. Hallett, "Race, Crime, and For-profit Imprisonment: Social Disorganization as Market Opportunity," *Punishment & Society* 4 (2002): 369–393.
86. Erving Goffman, *Stigma: Notes on the Management of Spoiled Identity* (Englewood Cliffs, NJ: Prentice-Hall, 1963).

5. NO FUTURE ON THE HORIZON

1. Thomas Meisenhelder, "An Essay on Time and the Phenomenology of Imprisonment," *Deviant Behavior* 6 (1985): 45, italics in original.
2. Peter L. Berger, *The Sacred Canopy: Elements of a Sociological Theory of Religion* (New York: Anchor, 1990) 69.
3. Peter L. Berger and Thomas Luckmann, *The Social Construction of Reality* (New York: Anchor Doubleday, 1966), 103.
4. Berger and Luckmann, *The Social Construction of Reality*, 26.
5. Michael G. Flaherty and Gary Alan Fine, "Present, Past, and Future: Conjugating George Herbert Mead's Perspective on Time," *Time & Society* 10 (2001): 147–161.
6. Kai T. Erikson, *Wayward Puritans: A Study in the Sociology of Deviance* (Boston: Allyn and Bacon, 1966), 189.
7. Erikson, *Wayward Puritans*, 196–197.
8. Erikson, *Wayward Puritans*, 204.
9. Peter Conrad and Joseph W. Schneider, *Deviance and Medicalization: From Badness to Sickness* (St. Louis, MO: C. V. Mosby, 1980).
10. Jimmy Lerner, *You Got Nothing Coming: Notes from a Prison Fish* (New York: Broadway, 2002), 164.
11. George Jackson, *Soledad Brother: The Prison Letters of George Jackson* (New York: Bantam, 1970), front matter.
12. Jackson, *Soledad Brother*, 45.
13. Jackson, *Soledad Brother*, 54.
14. Jackson, *Soledad Brother*, 58.
15. Jackson, *Soledad Brother*, 67.
16. Jackson, *Soledad Brother*, 68.
17. Jackson, *Soledad Brother*, 70.
18. Jackson, *Soledad Brother*, 73.
19. Jackson, *Soledad Brother*, 78.
20. Jackson, *Soledad Brother*, 82.
21. Jackson, *Soledad Brother*, 85.
22. Jackson, *Soledad Brother*, 98.
23. Jackson, *Soledad Brother*, 228.
24. Jackson, *Soledad Brother*, 245.
25. Meisenhelder, "An Essay on Time and the Phenomenology of Imprisonment," 45, italics in original.

26. David L. Rosenhan, "On Being Sane in Insane Places," *Science* 179 (1973): 251.

27. Rosenhan, "On Being Sane in Insane Places," 252.

28. Rosenhan, "On Being Sane in Insane Places," 253.

29. Rosenhan, "On Being Sane in Insane Places," 253.

30. Sylvester Long, *I Made It Through the Storm: My Fifteen Year Walk in State Prison* (Bloomington, IN: 1st Books Library, 2002), 80.

31. Jimmy Baca, *A Place to Stand* (New York: Grove-Atlantic, 2001), 162.

32. Robert Berger, *From the Inside: A Prison Memoir* (Lincoln, NE: iUniverse, 2003), 173.

33. Baca, *A Place to Stand*, 162.

34. Veronica Compton-Wallace, *Eating the Ashes: Seeking Rehabilitation within the US Penal System* (New York: Algora, 2003), 10.

35. Baca, *A Place to Stand*, 163.

36. Baca, *A Place to Stand*, 163.

37. Baca, *A Place to Stand*, 163, 164.

38. Long, *I Made It Through the Storm*, 390. On the outside, contrastingly, insurance companies are known to raise our rates after a single speeding ticket, but they do so only for a few years.

39. Long, *I Made It Through the Storm*, XXX.

40. Long, *I Made It Through the Storm*, 540–541.

41. Michael Santos, *Profiles from Prison: Adjusting to Life Behind Bars* (Westport, CT: Praeger, 2003),57.

42. An extra pair of jeans can lengthen one's sentence: "It would affect your time if you got written up for extra clothing just as much as if you got caught for some serious offence." See Sunny Jacobs, *Stolen Time* (London: Bantam, 2007), 397.

43. Long, *I Made It Through the Storm*, 585.

44. Santos, *Profiles from Prison*, 75.

45. Santos, *Profiles from Prison*, 75.

46. K. C. Carceral, *Behind a Convict's Eyes* (Belmont, CA: Wadsworth, 2004), 30.

47. Berger, *From the Inside*.

48. Long, *I Made It Through the Storm*.

49. Jack Katz, *Seductions of Crime: Moral and Sensual Attractions in Doing Evil* (New York: Basic, 1988).

50. Jackson, *Soledad Brother*, 239. See also Arthur Koestler, *Dialogue with Death: The Journal of a Prisoner of the Fascists in the Spanish Civil War* (Chicago: University of Chicago Press, [1946] 2011), 119–120. Further support can be found in Ingrid Betancourt's memoir: "The days seemed endless, stretching cruelly and slowly between anguish and boredom. In contrast, the weeks, months, and, later on, years seemed to accumulate at breakneck speed." See *Even Silence Has an End: My Six Years of Captivity in the Colombian Jungle* (New York: Penguin, 2010), 109. Despite spending significant time in captivity, admits Betancourt, "I had trouble remembering what I'd done on the previous day." See 131. "Of the following days I remember little in particular," adds Christopher Burney, "because nothing happened." See *Solitary Confinement* (New York: Coward-McCann, 1952), 13. Jimmy Baca provides a similar assessment: "I can't remember much happening except a relentless tedium." See *A Place to Stand*, 190. For analysis of this phenomenon, see Michael G. Flaherty, *A Watched Pot: How We Experience Time* (New York: New York University Press, 1999), 25–27, 110–112.

51. Jackson, *Soledad Brother*, 215. There are other versions of this translation, such as the following excerpt from a memoir by Sunny Jacobs: "So far I have been locked up for one year and two months. It feels like I am living another lifetime, and yet in some ways it feels like just yesterday that I was with Jesse and the kids." See *Stolen Time*, 186. For theoretical discussion, see Michael G. Flaherty, "An S-shaped Pattern in the Perceived Passage of Time: How Social Interaction Governs Temporal Experience," *Language & Cognition* 10 (2018): 1–25.

52. Amy Fisher and Robbie Wolliver, *If I Knew Then . . .* (New York: iUniverse, 2004), 140–141; italics added.

53. Berger, *From the Inside*, 111; italics added.

54. Kenneth Lamberton, *Wilderness and Razor Wire: A Naturalist's Observations from Prison* (San Francisco: Mercury House, 2000), 92.

55. Baca, *A Place to Stand*, 131. "He [Macaron] advised me not to give the future or the past much thought," adds Baca. See 116.

56. Lamberton, *Wilderness and Razor Wire*, 157.

57. Lamberton, *Wilderness and Razor Wire*, 157.

58. Lamberton, *Wilderness and Razor Wire*, 158.

59. Lamberton, *Wilderness and Razor Wire*, 162.

60. Lerner, *You Got Nothing Coming*, 196.

61. Piper Kerman, *Orange Is the New Black: My Year in a Women's Prison* (New York: Spiegel & Grau, 2011), 124.

62. Lerner, *You Got Nothing Coming*, 172. For outsiders, it is tempting to think that prisoners are obsessed with their future freedom. Jimmy Baca corrects this misconception: "Most people might assume that cons spend their time thinking about what they're going to do when their time is up, fantasizing about the women they're going to fuck and scams they're going to run, or planning how they're going to go straight and everything will be different. I did think about the future sometimes, but more and more it was the past my mind began to turn to, especially during those first days and nights in solitary." See *A Place to Stand*, 133. The past is more accessible than the future and, with a proper dose of nostalgia, more comforting. Yet Baca observes that killing time was the initial impetus: "Revisiting the past wasn't about seeking comfort at first, it was just something to do, like push-ups." See 134.

63. Lerner, *You Got Nothing Coming*, 195–196; italics in original.

64. Erving Goffman, *Asylums: Essays on the Social Situation of Mental Patients and Other Inmates* (Garden City, NY: Anchor, 1961), 66–67.

65. Jacobs, *Stolen Time*, 502.

66. Albert Woodfox, *Solitary: Unbroken by Four Decades in Solitary Confinement. My Story of Transformation and Hope* (New York: Grove, 2019), 336.

67. Baca, *A Place to Stand*, 246.

68. Andreas Schroeder, *Shaking It Rough: A Prison Memoir* (Garden City, NY: Doubleday, 1976), 59. See also Woodfox, *Solitary*, 283: "They'd build a case against a prisoner, write him up, take him to disciplinary court, sentence him to more time—and the cycle continues."

69. Jackson, *Soledad Brother*, 31. Erin George provides supporting testimony: "I watch the same people granted parole only to return within six months to a year, over and over again. Many have been in and out five and six times since I began in 1987." See *A Woman Doing Life: Notes from a Prison for Women* (New York: Oxford University

Press, 2010), 147. Albert Woodfox offers corroboration from his personal experience: "Nothing was different my second time at Angola. I was assigned the same dorm on the trustee side, Cypress 1. I had the same job, working in the fields." See *Solitary*, 43. In one study, "two-thirds . . . of released prisoners were arrested for a new crime within three years, and three-quarters . . . were arrested within five years." See Matthew R. Durose, Alexia D. Cooper, and Howard N. Snyder, "Recidivism of Prisoners Released in 30 States in 2005: Patterns from 2005 to 2010—Update," Department of Justice, Office of Justice Programs, Bureau of Justice Statistics: https://www.bjs.gov/index.cfm?ty=pbdetail&iid=4986.

70. Woodfox, *Solitary*, 206.
71. Baca, *A Place to Stand*, 22.
72. Burney, *Solitary Confinement*, 14.
73. Betancourt, *Even Silence Has an End*, 131.
74. Betancourt, *Even Silence Has an End*, 131.
75. Michael G. Flaherty, *The Textures of Time: Agency and Temporal Experience* (Philadelphia: Temple University Press, 2011), 31.
76. Betancourt, *Even Silence Has an End*, 376.
77. Kathy Calkins, "Time: Perspectives, Markings, and Styles of Usage," *Social Problems* 17 (1970).
78. Berger, *From the Inside*, 65–66.
79. Henri Bergson, *Creative Evolution* (New York: Dover, [1907] 1998), 46.
80. Reginald L. Hall, *Memoir: Delaware County Prison* (Mountainside, NJ: Writersandpoets.com, 2004), 94–95.
81. Lerner, *You Got Nothing Coming*, 9.
82. T. J. Parsell, *Fish: A Memoir of a Boy in a Man's Prison* (Cambridge, MA: Da Capo, 2006), 198.
83. Edward Bunker, *Education of a Felon* (New York: St. Martin's, 2000), 94.
84. Meisenhelder, "An Essay on Time and the Phenomenology of Imprisonment," 45.
85. Stephen C. Richards, "USP Marion: A Few Prisoners Summon the Courage to Speak," *Laws* 4 (2015): 101.

6. MARKING TIME

1. Oswald Spengler, *The Decline of the West* (New York: Knopf, [1922] 1932), 130.
2. Karen Stein, "Time Off: The Social Experience of Time on Vacation," *Qualitative Sociology* 35 (2012).
3. Mihaly Csikszentmihalyi, *Beyond Boredom and Anxiety* (San Francisco: Jossey-Bass, 1975).
4. Ingrid Betancourt, *Even Silence Has an End: My Six Years of Captivity in the Colombian Jungle* (New York: Penguin, 2010), 257.
5. Jimmy Baca, *A Place to Stand* (New York: Grove-Atlantic, 2001), 211. Outside of prison, losing track of time is also viewed as evidence of confusion or disorientation. When checking to see if someone has suffered a concussion, it is common practice to ask that person a series of questions concerning time: What year is it? What month is it? What day of the week is it?

6. Christina Dress with Tama-Lisa Johnson and Mary Kay Letourneau, *Mass with Mary: The Prison Years* (Victoria, BC: Trafford, 2004), 102.

7. George Jackson, *Soledad Brother: The Prison Letters of George Jackson* (New York: Bantam, 1970), 110.

8. Baca, *A Place to Stand*, 93. See also 125.

9. Jacobo Timerman, *Prisoner Without a Name, Cell Without a Number* (New York: Knopf, 1981), 3–4.

10. Billy Wayne Sinclair and Jodie Sinclair, *A Life in the Balance: The Billy Wayne Sinclair Story* (New York: Arcade, 2000), 21.

11. Sinclair and Sinclair, *A Life in the Balance*, 23.

12. Piper Kerman, *Orange Is the New Black: My Year in a Women's Prison* (New York: Spiegel & Grau, 2011), 269–270. See also Baca, *A Place to Stand*, 178. These observations are echoed by Sunny Jacobs when she is held in the Broward County Jail, Fort Lauderdale, Florida. Like other new prisoners, she is placed in a cell where there is "constant fluorescent lighting." Later, she returns to this issue: "Nothing changes to delineate day from night. There is just the routine." Finally, she itemizes what is missing: "There is no sense of time here. No day; no night. There are no clocks, no calendars, no windows, no sky." See Sunny Jacobs, *Stolen Time* (London: Bantam, 2007), 72, 113, 116.

13. A. R. Radcliffe-Brown, *The Andaman Islanders* (New York: Free Press, [1922] 1964), 311–312.

14. Jeffrey Ian Ross and Stephen C. Richards, *Behind Bars: Surviving Prison* (Indianapolis, IN: Alpha, 2002), 36.

15. Baca, *A Place to Stand*, 192.

16. Robert Berger, *From the Inside: A Prison Memoir* (Lincoln, NE: iUniverse, 2003), 175.

17. Jackson, *Soledad Brother*, 41.

18. Kerman, *Orange Is the New Black*, 283, 285.

19. Richard S. Jones and Thomas J. Schmid, *Doing Time: Prison Experience and Identity Among First-Time Inmates* (Bingly, UK: Emerald Group, 2000).

20. Jackson, *Soledad Brother*, 86.

21. Jackson, *Soledad Brother*, 110. Similarly, Amanda Lindhout recalls that "every minute was basically the same as the last, every hour like the one just past." See *A House in the Sky: A Memoir* (New York: Scribner, 2013), 210.

22. T. J. Parsell, *Fish: A Memoir of a Boy in a Man's Prison* (Cambridge, MA: Da Capo, 2006), 53.

23. Parsell, *Fish*, 53.

24. Anthony J. Manocchio and Jimmy Dunn, *The Time Game: Two Views of a Prison* (New York: Dell, 1970), 41.

25. Berger, *From the Inside*, 139.

26. Baca, *A Place to Stand*, 204.

27. Outside of prison, people use "time reference" for various purposes during conversation. See Chase Wesley Raymond and Anne Elizabeth Clark White, "Time Reference in the Service of Social Action," *Social Psychology Quarterly* 80 (2017): 109–131.

28. Eviatar Zerubavel, *Hidden Rhythms: Schedules and Calendars in Social Life* (Chicago: University of Chicago Press, 1981), 103.

29. Jackson, *Soledad Brother*, 248. With comparable wording, Peter Pringle describes "a long wait for the escort to arrive." See *About Time: Surviving Ireland's Death Row*

(Dublin: The History Press Ireland, 2012), 143. In the same vein, Sunny Jacobs shows us that inmates wait for all manner of permissions: "I had submitted the usual request for a visit but it was taking an interminable time to get an answer." See *Stolen Time*, 175. Likewise, it takes a year for Peter Pringle to get a typewriter and ream of paper. See *About Time*, 178.

30. Andreas Schroeder, *Shaking It Rough: A Prison Memoir* (Garden City, NY: Doubleday, 1976), 126.

31. Reginald L. Hall, *Memoir: Delaware County Prison* (Mountainside, NJ: Writersandpoets.com, 2004), 113.

32. Parsell, *Fish*, 269.

33. Edward Bunker, *Education of a Felon* (New York: St. Martin's, 2000), 94.

34. Bunker, *Education of a Felon*, 118.

35. Bunker, *Education of a Felon*, 208.

36. Bunker, *Education of a Felon*, 36.

37. Bunker, *Education of a Felon*, 128.

38. Rik Scarce, "Doing Time as an Act of Survival," *Symbolic Interaction* 25 (2002): 307.

39. Scarce, "Doing Time as an Act of Survival," 304.

40. Baca, *A Place to Stand*, 179.

41. Jacobs, *Stolen Time*, 314.

42. Jacobs, *Stolen Time*, 431.

43. Victor Serge, *Men in Prison* (Oakland, CA: PM Press, [1931] 2014), 39.

44. Timerman, *Prisoner Without a Name, Cell Without a Number*, 84.

45. Kerman, *Orange Is the New Black*, 51.

46. Jackson, *Soledad Brother*, 57. See also Baca, *A Place to Stand*, 97.

47. Kerman, *Orange Is the New Black*, 43.

48. Kerman, *Orange Is the New Black*, 45. For descriptions of standing counts at male prisons, see Jimmy Lerner, *You Got Nothing Coming: Notes from a Prison Fish* (New York: Broadway, 2002), 46 and James A. Paluch Jr., *A Life for a Life* (Los Angeles: Roxbury, 2004), 59, 164.

49. Baca, *A Place to Stand*, 110.

50. Dress et al., *Mass with Mary*, 52.

51. Kerman, *Orange Is the New Black*, 68.

52. Bunker, *Education of a Felon*, 119. Like other prisoners, Sunny Jacobs marks time by means of her own hunger: "My stomach is my clock. It tells me that it is lunchtime." See *Stolen Time*, 125.

53. Lerner, *You Got Nothing Coming*, 5.

54. Christopher Burney, *Solitary Confinement* (New York: Coward-McCann, 1952), 16–17.

55. Burney, *Solitary Confinement*, 145.

56. Baca, *A Place to Stand*, 142.

57. Ross and Richards, *Behind Bars*.

58. Albert Woodfox, *Solitary: Unbroken by Four Decades in Solitary Confinement. My Story of Transformation and Hope* (New York: Grove, 2019), 25. The same is true among female prisoners: "We went through a number of superintendents and I had many different guards assigned to me through my years on death row." See Jacobs, *Stolen Time*, 263. See also Dannie M. Martin and Peter Y. Sussman, *Committing Journalism: The Prison Writings of Red Hog* (New York: Norton, 1993).

59. Meisenhelder, "An Essay on Time and the Phenomenology of Imprisonment," 49.
60. Lerner, *You Got Nothing Coming*, 144.
61. Baca, *A Place to Stand*, 181.
62. Dress et al., *Mass with Mary*, 35–36.
63. Scarce, "Doing Time as an Act of Survival," 312. Stephen Richards offers the same prognosis: "Convicts at Marion either went crazy or devised strict daily disciplines to pass the time alone in their cells." See "USP Marion," 101. See also Sylvester Long, *I Made It Through the Storm: My Fifteen Year Walk in State Prison* (Bloomington, IN: 1st Books Library, 2002), 535.
64. Jacobs, *Stolen Time*, 136–137. Peter Pringle resorts to the same strategy: "I developed a routine," he recalls, "by structuring and varying my days, albeit within the prison confines." See *About Time*, 171 and 176.
65. Kerman, *Orange Is the New Black*, 93.
66. Jones and Schmid, *Doing Time*, 77.
67. Thomas Meisenhelder, "An Essay on Time and the Phenomenology of Imprisonment," *Deviant Behavior* 6 (1985): 49.
68. Gresham M. Sykes, *The Society of Captives: A Study of Maximum Security Prison* (Princeton, NJ: Princeton University Press, 1958), 29.
69. Long, *I Made It Through the Storm*, 533.
70. Baca, *A Place to Stand*, 197.
71. Jacobs, *Stolen Time*, 65–66.
72. Baca, *A Place to Stand*, 182, 194.
73. Cheyenne Valentino Yakima, *If I Could Paint Tomorrow: A Prisoner's Story* (Bloomington, IN: 1st Books Library, 2001).
74. Kenneth Lamberton, *Wilderness and Razor Wire: A Naturalist's Observations from Prison* (San Francisco: Mercury House, 2000).
75. Bunker, *Education of a Felon*.
76. Kerman, *Orange Is the New Black*, 116.
77. Jackson, *Soledad Brother*, 142.
78. Berger, *From the Inside*.
79. Michael Santos, *Profiles from Prison: Adjusting to Life Behind Bars* (Westport, CT: Praeger, 2003), 173.
80. Long, *I Made It Through the Storm*.
81. Meisenhelder, "An Essay on Time and the Phenomenology of Imprisonment," 50.
82. Sinclair and Sinclair, *A Life in the Balance*, 66.
83. Sinclair and Sinclair, *A Life in the Balance*, 104.
84. Jorge Renaud, *Behind the Walls: A Guide for Families and Friends of Texas Prison Inmates* (Denton: University of North Texas Press, 2002), 11.
85. Renaud, *Behind the Walls*, 51.
86. Renaud, *Behind the Walls*, 52.
87. Jacobs, *Stolen Time*, 312.
88. Kerman, *Orange Is the New Black*, 265.
89. Kerman, *Orange Is the New Black*, 273.
90. Kerman, *Orange Is the New Black*, 252.
91. Paluch, *A Life for a Life*, 18.
92. Sinclair and Sinclair, *A Life in the Balance*.
93. Lerner, *You Got Nothing Coming*, 175.

94. Renaud, *Behind the Walls*, 53.
95. Erving Goffman, *Asylums: Essays on the Social Situation of Mental Patients and Other Inmates* (Garden City, NY: Anchor, 1961), 69–70.
96. Manocchio and Dunn, *The Time Game*, 44.
97. Paluch, *A Life for a Life*.
98. Jackson, *Soledad Brother*, 70. Jackson was a month shy of thirty when he died.
99. Burney, *Solitary Confinement*, 116–117.
100. Burney, *Solitary Confinement*, 20. See also Pringle, *About Time*, 170.
101. Jackson, *Soledad Brother*, 232.
102. Baca, *A Place to Stand*, 181.
103. Timerman, *Prisoner Without a Name, Cell Without a Number*, 35.
104. Michael Young, *The Metronomic Society: Natural Rhythms and Human Timetables* (Cambridge, MA: Harvard University Press, 1988), 87.
105. Ton Otto, "Times of the Other: The Temporalities of Ethnographic Fieldwork," *Social Analysis* 57 (2013): 68.
106. Burney, *Solitary Confinement*, 15.
107. Stephen Stanko, "Surviving in Prison," in *Living in Prison: A History of the Correctional System with an Insider's View*, ed. Stephen Stanko, Wayne Gillespie, and Gordon A. Crews (Westport, CT: Greenwood, 2004) 177.
108. Lamberton, *Wilderness and Razor Wire*, 31.
109. Karen Blixen, *Out of Africa* (London: Penguin, [1937] 2011), 49.

7. RESISTANCE AND TEMPORAL AGENCY

1. Erving Goffman, *Asylums: Essays on the Social Situation of Mental Patients and Other Inmates* (Garden City, NY: Anchor, 1961), 187.
2. Goffman, *Asylums*, 230. See also Jill A. McCorkel, "Going to the Crackhouse: Critical Space as a Form of Resistance in Total Institutions and Everyday Life," *Symbolic Interaction* 21 (1998): 227–252.
3. Michel Foucault, *Discipline and Punish: The Birth of the Prison* (New York: Vintage, 1979).
4. Alejo Stark, "Containing the Surplus Rebellion: Prison Strike/Prison Riot," *New Global Studies* 14 (2020): 193–203.
5. Ben Crewe, "Power, Adaptation, and Resistance in a Late-Modern Men's Prison," *British Journal of Criminology* 47 (2007): 256; Ashley T. Rubin, "The Consequences of Prisoners' Micro-Resistance," *Law & Society Inquiry* 42 (2017): 138. See also Michael Gibson-Light, "Ramen Politics: Informal Money and Logics of Resistance in the Contemporary American Prison," *Qualitative Sociology* 41 (2018): 199–220.
6. Melissa Munn and Chris Bruckert, "Beyond Conceptual Ambiguity: Exemplifying the 'Resistance Pyramid' through the Reflections of (Ex-)Prisoners' Agency," *Qualitative Sociology Review* 6 (2010): 137–149; Ashley T. Rubin, "Resistance as Agency? Incorporating the Structural Determinants of Prisoner Behaviour," *British Journal of Criminology* 57 (2017): 644–663.
7. Jeffrey Ian Ross, "Resisting the Carceral State: Prisoner Resistance from the Bottom Up," *Social Justice* 36 (2009–2010): 33.

8. Gresham M. Sykes, *The Society of Captives: A Study of Maximum Security Prison* (Princeton, NJ: Princeton University Press, 1958), 48. As Andreas Schroeder puts it, "everything in a human being revolts against being stuffed into a cage." See *Shaking It Rough* (Garden City, NY: Doubleday, 1976), 152.

9. John Irwin, *The Warehouse Prison: Disposal of the New Dangerous Class* (Los Angeles: Roxbury, 2005), 100; italics in original.

10. George Jackson, *Soledad Brother: The Prison Letters of George Jackson* (New York: Bantam, 1970), 80.

11. Michael G. Flaherty, "Time Work: Customizing Temporal Experience," *Social Psychology Quarterly* 66 (2003): 17.

12. Alexander Berkman, *Prison Memoirs of an Anarchist* (New York: New York Review of Books, [1912] 1999), 167.

13. Victor Serge, *Men in Prison* (Oakland, CA: PM Press, [1931] 2014), 56.

14. T. J. Parsell, *Fish: A Memoir of a Boy in a Man's Prison* (Cambridge, MA: Da Capo, 2006), 298. Peter Pringle invokes the same imagery when he reports that "the time dragged." See *About Time: Surviving Ireland's Death Row* (Dublin: The History Press Ireland, 2012), 35.

15. Rik Scarce, "Doing Time as an Act of Survival," *Symbolic Interaction* 25 (2002): 315; italics in original. Sunny Jacobs expresses the same sense of urgency: "But a few months was like for ever [sic]—even the hours could become for ever [sic] if you didn't do something to stave off the tedium that could steal your will." See *Stolen Time* (London: Bantam, 2007), 193.

16. Cheyenne Valentino Yakima, *If I Could Paint Tomorrow: A Prisoner's Story* (Bloomington, IN: 1st Books Library, 2001), 21. See also Victor Hassine, *Life Without Parole: Living in Prison Today* (Los Angeles: Roxbury, 1996), 142.

17. Scarce, "Doing Time as an Act of Survival," 317.

18. Mumia Abu-Jamal, *All Things Censored* (New York: Seven Stories, 2000), 42–43. See also Parsell, *Fish*, 38.

19. Clare Hanrahan, *Jailed for Justice* (Asheville, NC: Celtic Wordcraft, 2002), 79.

20. Richard S. Jones and Thomas J. Schmid, *Doing Time: Prison Experience and Identity Among First-Time Inmates* (Bingly, UK: Emerald Group, 2000), 141–142.

21. Scarce, "Doing Time as an Act of Survival," 305.

22. Timothy Leary, *Jail Notes* (New York: Douglas, 1970), 94. Peter Pringle resorts to repetition: "waiting and waiting." See *About Time*, 206.

23. Berkman, *Prison Memoirs of an Anarchist*, 85.

24. Amanda Lindhout and Sara Corbett, *A House in the Sky: A Memoir* (New York: Scribner, 2013), 165.

25. Reginald L. Hall, *Memoir: Delaware County Prison* (Mountainside, NJ: Writersandpoets.com, 2004), 76.

26. Abu-Jamal, *All Things Censored*, 55; italics added.

27. Jimmy Baca, *A Place to Stand* (New York: Grove-Atlantic, 2001), 4.

28. Drew Leder, *The Soul Knows No Bars: Inmates Reflect on Life, Death, and Hope* (Lanham, MD: Rowman & Littlefield, 2000), 1.

29. Harold Garfinkel, *Studies in Ethnomethodology* (Englewood Cliffs, NJ: Prentice-Hall, 1967), 53.

30. Goffman, *Asylums*, 55.

31. Pringle, *About Time*, 163.
32. Leder, *The Soul Knows No Bars*, 141.
33. Hanrahan, *Jailed for Justice*.
34. Scarce, "Doing Time as an Act of Survival," 308.
35. Haruki Murakami, *Men Without Women* (New York: Knopf, 2017), 128, 139.
36. Leder, *The Soul Knows No Bars*, 44–45. Further evidence can be found in the memoir by Andreas Schroeder. While in solitary confinement, he imagines that he is rebuilding his house: "Just before being arrested I'd built myself a small house on a mountain in B.C.; now, to keep my mind working busily enough to ignore my body, I started the project all over again, making every cut, digging every hole, driving every nail, painting every board, reconstructing the entire building in my mind." See *Shaking It Rough*, 150. Likewise, Albert Woodfox imagines himself on vacation: "I fantasized about going to Yosemite National Park, which I'd seen in a National Geographic program on TV." See *Solitary: Unbroken by Four Decades in Solitary Confinement. My Story of Transformation and Hope* (New York: Grove, 2019), 183.
37. Baca, *A Place to Stand*, 134. One finds comparable strategies in the memoirs of POWs and hostages. As Amanda Lindhout puts it, "I passed the time by escaping in my mind." See *A House in the Sky*, 348. She "could pass two hours imagining one meal in granular detail"(222). See also Christopher Burney, *Solitary Confinement* (New York: Coward-McCann, 1952), 8–10.
38. Yakima, *If I Could Paint Tomorrow*, 54.
39. Yakima, *If I Could Paint Tomorrow*, 36. See also Berkman, *Prison Memoirs of an Anarchist*, 165.
40. Parsell, *Fish*, 175.
41. James A. Paluch, Jr., *A Life for a Life* (Los Angeles: Roxbury, 2004), 31.
42. Paluch, *A Life for a Life*, 105. See also Amy Fisher and Robbie Wolliver, *If I Knew Then . . .* (New York: iUniverse, 2004), 142.
43. Jackson, *Soledad Brother*, 18.
44. Jackson, *Soledad Brother*, 50.
45. Jackson, *Soledad Brother*, 51.
46. Billy Wayne Sinclair and Jodie Sinclair, *A Life in the Balance: The Billy Wayne Sinclair Story* (New York: Arcade, 2000), 136.
47. Jimmy Lerner, *You Got Nothing Coming: Notes from a Prison Fish* (New York: Broadway, 2002), 216.
48. Ingrid Betancourt, *Even Silence Has an End: My Six Years of Captivity in the Colombian Jungle* (New York: Penguin, 2010), 482.
49. Martin and Sussman, *Committing Journalism*, 283.
50. Berkman, *Prison Memoirs of an Anarchist*, 346.
51. Berkman, *Prison Memoirs of an Anarchist*, 347.
52. Sinclair and Sinclair, *A Life in the Balance*, 319.
53. Sinclair and Sinclair, *A Life in the Balance*, 124.
54. George, *A Woman Doing Life*, 135. See also Jacobs, *Stolen Time*, 442.
55. George, *A Woman Doing Life*, 135.
56. George, *A Woman Doing Life*, 173.
57. Scarce, "Doing Time as an Act of Survival," 303.
58. Piper Kerman, *Orange Is the New Black: My Year in a Women's Prison* (New York: Spiegel & Grau, 2011), 84.

59. Lerner, *You Got Nothing Coming*, 172.

60. Scarce, "Doing Time as an Act of Survival," 303.

61. Scarce, "Doing Time as an Act of Survival," 309.

62. Michael Santos, *Profiles from Prison: Adjusting to Life Behind Bars* (Westport, CT: Praeger, 2003), 17.

63. Lerner, *You Got Nothing Coming*, 83.

64. Anthony J. Manocchio and Jimmy Dunn, *The Time Game: Two Views of a Prison* (New York: Dell, 1970), 37.

65. Stephen Stanko, "Surviving in Prison," in *Living in Prison: A History of the Correctional System with an Insider's View*, ed. Stephen Stanko, Wayne Gillespie, and Gordon A. Crews (Westport, CT: Greenwood, 2004) 179.

66. Hanrahan, *Jailed for Justice*, 79.

67. Sykes, *The Society of Captives*, 102.

68. Scarce, "Doing Time as an Act of Survival," 307.

69. George, *A Woman Doing Life*, 83.

70. George, *A Woman Doing Life*, 37.

71. Sylvester Long, *I Made It Through the Storm: My Fifteen Year Walk in State Prison* (Bloomington, IN: 1st Books Library, 2002), 474.

72. Jackson, *Soledad Brother*, 110.

73. Kerman, *Orange Is the New Black*, 111.

74. Schroeder, *Shaking It Rough*, 135–136.

75. Stanko, "Surviving in Prison," 172.

76. Stanko, "Surviving in Prison," 181.

77. Lerner, *You Got Nothing Coming*, 200; italics in original.

78. Lerner, *You Got Nothing Coming*, 200. See also Berkman, *Prison Memoirs of an Anarchist*, 239: "The memory of the life 'outside' intensifies the misery."

79. Kenneth Lamberton, *Wilderness and Razor Wire: A Naturalist's Observations from Prison* (San Francisco: Mercury House, 2000), 101.

80. Jones and Schmid, *Doing Time*, 97.

81. Jones and Schmid, *Doing Time*, 114. Andreas Schroeder is more pessimistic: "It's hard not to think about what's going on outside. I find I can't really stop myself." See *Shaking It Rough*, 7.

82. Leder, *The Soul Knows No Bars*, 56.

83. Jones and Schmid, *Doing Time*, 114.

84. Berkman, *Prison Memoirs of an Anarchist*, 141.

85. Berkman, *Prison Memoirs of an Anarchist*, 231.

86. Berkman, *Prison Memoirs of an Anarchist*, 231.

87. Pringle, *About Time*, 168.

88. Dannie M. Martin and Peter Y. Sussman, *Committing Journalism: The Prison Writings of Red Hog* (New York: Norton, 1993), 128.

89. Manocchio and Dunn, *The Time Game*, 190. Mumia Abu-Jamal gives us a very different view of visits—one that is in accord with the advice from old-timers: "Over five years have passed since that visit, but I remember it like it was an hour ago; the slams of her tiny fists against the ugly barrier; her instinctual rage against it—the state-made blockade raised under the rubric of security, her hot tears. They haunt me." See *All Things Censored*, 62.

90. Hall, *Memoir*, 85.

91. Hall, *Memoir*, 86.
92. For an analysis of time reference in everyday life, see Chase Wesley Raymond and Anne Elizabeth Clark White, "Time Reference in the Service of Social Action," *Social Psychology Quarterly* 80 (2017): 109–131.
93. Berkman, *Prison Memoirs of an Anarchist*, 430.
94. Berkman, *Prison Memoirs of an Anarchist*, 167.
95. Hassine, *Life Without Parole*, 12.
96. Parsell, *Fish*, 121.
97. Joel Blaeser, *Letters from Marion: A Deadhead's Journey from Peace to a Super Max Prison* (Milwaukee, WI: Big House, 2015), 153.
98. Parsell, *Fish*, 48.
99. Sinclair and Sinclair, *A Life in the Balance*, 102.
100. Lerner, *You Got Nothing Coming*, 161.
101. Lerner, *You Got Nothing Coming*, 196.
102. Berkman, *Prison Memoirs of an Anarchist*, 302.
103. Blaeser, *Letters from Marion*, 154.
104. Hassine, *Life Without Parole*, 141.
105. Leder, *The Soul Knows No Bars*, 88.
106. Jackson, *Soledad Brother*, 110.
107. William James, *The Principles of Psychology*, vol. 1 (New York: Henry Holt, 1890), 402.
108. Christina Dress with Tama-Lisa Johnson and Mary Kay Letourneau, *Mass with Mary: The Prison Years* (Victoria, BC: Trafford), 106. Sunny Jacobs relies on the same tactic: "I didn't count the days and months but I did keep track of the years. I was twenty-seven when this began and I was now thirty-eight years old." See *Stolen Time*, 429.
109. Baca, *A Place to Stand*, 246.
110. Leary, *Jail Notes*, 77; italics in original.
111. Jacobs, *Stolen Time*, 186.
112. Scarce, "Doing Time as an Act of Survival," 311. Crib admits that there is a price to pay: "'That's what fucks you up when you get back on the streets. If you ain't watched no TV for a while, you ain't gonna be ready for all the changes. But it works while you're in.'"
113. Dress et al., *Mass with Mary*, 54.
114. Scarce, "Doing Time as an Act of Survival," 311.
115. Scarce, "Doing Time as an Act of Survival," 310.
116. Scarce, "Doing Time as an Act of Survival," 310: "So many other inmates knew of Roll's strategy that it must have been handed down in jails and prisons from time immemorial."
117. See, for example, Santos, *Profiles from Prison*, 196: "Time now passes differently. I divide the years into two parts rather than twelve months; in winter I feel close to summer, and in the heat of summer I feel the holidays rapidly approaching."
118. Lerner, *You Got Nothing Coming*, 185–186.
119. Kerman, *Orange Is the New Black*, 99.
120. Kerman, *Orange Is the New Black*, 187.
121. Kerman, *Orange Is the New Black*, 293. As Sunny Jacobs puts it, "short time is always harder. The short-timers lived a schizophrenic existence, bodily here but mentally there." See *Stolen Time*, 527.

122. Blaeser, *Letters from Marion*, 23.

123. Scarce, "Doing Time as an Act of Survival," 309.

124. Hanrahan, *Jailed for Justice*, 95.

125. Lerner, *You Got Nothing Coming*, 213. See also Paluch, *A Life for a Life*, 137.

126. Betancourt, *Even Silence Has an End*, 247.

127. Parsell, *Fish*, 54.

128. Yakima, *If I Could Paint Tomorrow*, 50. "It was impossible to sleep or even to rest," adds Peter Pringle. See *About Time*, 152.

129. Hassine, *Life Without Parole*, 24.

130. Aleksandr Solzhenitsyn, *The Gulag Archipelago* (New York: Harper & Row, 1973), 203.

131. Woodfox, *Solitary*, 182.

132. Lamberton, *Wilderness and Razor Wire*, 214.

133. Berkman, *Prison Memoirs of an Anarchist*, 214. See also Lerner, *You Got Nothing Coming*, 85.

134. Serge, *Men in Prison*, 47. From Sunny Jacobs, we get this comparable account: "Taking small steps, placing one foot directly in front of the other, I paced off the length of the concrete floor. Six steps. It was six steps from the door to the toilet, which had no lid and gaped at me, mocking me with its rude presence. I turned back towards the door again. Six steps. I could walk these six steps as much as I liked and there was nothing to stop me. Back and forth—to the door, to the toilet—I began to pace." See *Stolen Time*, 108–109.

135. Lindhout and Corbett, *A House in the Sky*, 220.

136. Stephen C. Richards, "USP Marion: A Few Prisoners Summon the Courage to Speak," *Laws* 4 (2015): 102.

137. Manocchio and Dunn, *The Time Game*, 135.

138. Manocchio and Dunn, *The Time Game*, 141.

139. Martin and Sussman, *Committing Journalism*, 121. There was a similar arrangement at Marion, where Arnold Huskey was "given an opportunity to go outside into an individual rec cage for a single hour's exercise." See Richards, "USP Marion," 102.

140. Martin and Sussman, *Committing Journalism*, 50. See also 215.

141. Ernest Dichter, *The Psychology of Everyday Living* (New York: Barnes & Noble, 1947), 89.

142. Dichter, *The Psychology of Everyday Living*, 89.

143. Dichter, *The Psychology of Everyday Living*, 89.

144. AdamReed, " 'Smuk Is King': The Action of Cigarettes in a Papua New Guinea Prison," in *Thinking Through Things: Theorising Artefacts Ethnographically*, ed. Amiria Henare, Martin Holbraad, and Sari Wastell (London: Routledge, 2007), 32–33.

145. Parsell, *Fish*, 223.

146. Sinclair and Sinclair, *A Life in the Balance*, 162.

147. Reed, " 'Smuk Is King,' " 34.

148. Reed, " 'Smuk Is King,' " 35.

149. Reed, " 'Smuk Is King,' " 35

150. Michael G. Flaherty, "An Erotics of Time: Toward the Cross-Cultural Study of Temporal Experience," *Revista de Antropologia da UFSCar* 9 (2017): 7–27; Michael G. Flaherty, Betina Freidin, and Ruth Sautu, "Variation in the Perceived Passage of Time: A Cross-National Study," *Social Psychology Quarterly* 68 (2005): 400–410;

Michael G. Flaherty, Lotte Meinert, and Anne Line Dalsgård, eds., *Time Work: Studies of Temporal Agency* (Oxford, UK: Berghahn, 2020); Anne Line Dalsgård, Martin Demant Frederiksen, Susanne Højlund, and Lotte Meinert, eds., *Ethnographies of Youth and Temporality: Time Objectified* (Philadelphia: Temple University Press, 2014).

151. Murray S. Davis, *Smut: Erotic Reality/Obscene Ideology* (Chicago: University of Chicago Press, 1983), 20.

152. Berkman, *Prison Memoirs of an Anarchist*, 441.

153. Long, *I Made It Through the Storm*.

154. Edward Bunker, *Education of a Felon* (New York: St. Martin's, 2000), 43.

155. Baca, *A Place to Stand*, 125.

156. Parsell, *Fish*, 160.

157. Parsell, *Fish*, 241.

158. Leder, *The Soul Knows No Bars*, 45.

159. Berkman, *Prison Memoirs of an Anarchist*, 230.

160. Baca, *A Place to Stand*, 54–55.

161. Berkman, *Prison Memoirs of an Anarchist*, 180.

162. Kerman, *Orange Is the New Black*, 67.

163. Kerman, *Orange Is the New Black*, 265.

164. Parsell, *Fish*, 54. See also Irwin, *The Jail*, 93.

165. Lamberton, *Wilderness and Razor Wire*, 155.

166. Jackson, *Soledad Brother*, 84.

167. Berkman, *Prison Memoirs of an Anarchist*, 214; Baca, *A Place to Stand*, 230.

168. Stanko, "Surviving in Prison," 182; see also Fisher, *If I Knew Then . . .*, 194. "After dinner," writes Arnold Huskey, "I would allow myself to turn on the television." See Richards, "USP Marion," 102. That he decides when to watch is evidence of temporal agency in the timing of his activity.

169. Abu-Jamal, *All Things Censored*, 43. At Angola, Albert Woodfox knew "guys who arranged their whole day around what would be on television." See *Solitary*, 335.

170. Berkman, *Prison Memoirs of an Anarchist*, 197.

171. John Irwin, *The Jail* (Berkeley: University of California Press, 1985), 93.

172. Richards, "USP Marion," 94. Popular topics include "a person's roots and origins, women, and music," but prisoners can also be observed "telling jokes to pass the time." See Paluch, *A Life for a Life*, 138; Blaeser, *Letters from Marion*, 62.

173. Woodfox, *Solitary*, 329. See also Jacobs, *Stolen Time*, 301.

174. Kerman, *Orange Is the New Black*, 140.

175. George, *A Woman Doing Life*, 18.

176. Hall, *Memoir*, 8.

177. Hall, *Memoir*, 8, 21. See also Woodfox, *Solitary*, 44.

178. Blaeser, *Letters from Marion*, 21.

179. Erin George, *A Woman Doing Life: Notes from a Prison for Women* (New York: Oxford University Press, 2010), 18.

180. Lerner, *You Got Nothing Coming*, 108. See also Paluch, *A Life for a Life*, 138.

181. Lerner, *You Got Nothing Coming*, 109. In a related vein, the famous jazz musician, Art Pepper, transforms a cup into a musical instrument. See Art Pepper and Laurie Pepper, *Straight Life: The Story of Art Pepper* (New York: Schirmer, 1979), 171.

182. Lindhout and Corbett, *A House in the Sky*, 185.

183. Lindhout and Corbett, *A House in the Sky*, 185.

184. R. Theodore Davidson, *Chicano Prisoners: The Key to San Quentin* (Prospect Heights, IL: Waveland, 1974), 24.

185. Jacobs, *Stolen Time*, 135.

186. Jacobs, *Stolen Time*, 323; italics added.

187. Scarce, "Doing Time as an Act of Survival," 309.

188. Paluch, *A Life for a Life*, 62.

189. Parsell, *Fish*, 38.

190. Berkman, *Prison Memoirs of an Anarchist*, 131; italics added.

191. Hanrahan, *Jailed for Justice*, 83.

192. Hall, *Memoir*, 98. As attested to by Art Pepper, many of the "jobs" in prison are ludicrously fictional: "They gave me a job with a little pan and a little broom and I swept the yard. In the morning, after everybody went to work, I would go out and sweep for a couple of hours, and then after supper I'd sweep for maybe an hour, and it was really funny." See Pepper and Pepper, *Straight Life*, 176.

193. Blaeser, *Letters from Marion*, 181.

194. Jones and Schmid, *Doing Time*, 113.

195. Donald Roy, " 'Banana Time': Job Satisfaction and Informal Interaction," *Human Organization* 18 (1959–1960): 158–168.

196. Roy, " 'Banana Time': Job Satisfaction and Informal Interaction," 162.

197. Mitchell Duneier and Harvey Molotch, "Talking City Trouble: Interactional Vandalism, Social Inequality, and the 'Urban Interaction Problem,' " *American Journal of Sociology* 104 (1999): 1263–1295.

198. Kerman, *Orange Is the New Black*, 183.

199. Pepper and Pepper, *Straight Life*, 177. See also Pringle, *About Time*, 40.

200. George, *A Woman Doing Life*, 16.

201. George, *A Woman Doing Life*, 16.

202. Erving Goffman, "Fun in Games," in *Encounters: Two Studies in the Sociology of Interaction* (Indianapolis: Bobbs-Merrill, 1961); Erving Goffman, "Where the Action Is," in *Interaction Ritual: Essays on Face-to-Face Behavior* (New York: Pantheon, 1967).

203. George, *A Woman Doing Life*, 17.

204. George, *A Woman Doing Life*, 16–17.

205. George, *A Woman Doing Life*, 18.

206. Pepper and Pepper, *Straight Life*, 278.

207. George, *A Woman Doing Life*, 10.

208. Parsell, *Fish*, 121.

209. Blaeser, *Letters from Marion*, 110.

210. Blaeser, *Letters from Marion*, 110.

211. Blaeser, *Letters from Marion*, 110.

212. Sinclair and Sinclair, *A Life in the Balance*, 101.

213. Sinclair and Sinclair, *A Life in the Balance*, 121.

214. George, *A Woman Doing Life*, 11.

215. Martin and Sussman, *Committing Journalism*, 295.

216. Martin and Sussman, *Committing Journalism*, 295.

217. Jacobo Timerman, *Prisoner Without a Name, Cell Without a Number* (New York: Knopf, 1981), 5.

218. Lerner, *You Got Nothing Coming*, 21; italics in original.
219. Lerner, *You Got Nothing Coming*, 32.
220. Lerner, *You Got Nothing Coming*, 30.
221. Schroeder, *Shaking It Rough*, 20.
222. Rose Giallombardo, *Society of Women: A Study of a Women's Prison* (New York: Wiley, 1966), 134.
223. Sykes, *The Society of Captives*, 43–45.
224. Manocchio and Dunn, *The Time Game*, 30.
225. Sykes, *The Society of Captives*, 42.
226. Baca, *A Place to Stand*, 182.
227. Thomas Meisenhelder, "An Essay on Time and the Phenomenology of Imprisonment," *Deviant Behavior* 6 (1985): 48; italics added.
228. Clark Molstad, "Choosing and Coping with Boring Work," *Urban Life* 15 (1986): 231; italics added.
229. Pepper and Pepper, *Straight Life*, 143.
230. Hassine, *Life Without Parole*, 37.
231. Blaeser, *Letters from Marion*, 243.
232. Kerman, *Orange Is the New Black*, 142. See also Jacobs, *Stolen Time*, 315.
233. Manocchio and Dunn, *The Time Game*, 157.
234. Sinclair and Sinclair, *A Life in the Balance*, 128.
235. Schroeder, *Shaking It Rough*, 72.
236. Lerner, *You Got Nothing Coming*, 397; italics in original.
237. Lerner, *You Got Nothing Coming*, 397.
238. Meisenhelder, "An Essay on Time and the Phenomenology of Imprisonment," 47; italics added.
239. Schroeder, *Shaking It Rough*, 109. Convicts alter the perceived passage of time by extending the temporal reach of drama or illicit activity: "For the next several days the camp crackles and pops with breathless descriptions of the wild party held last Friday night in Hut Six" (148).
240. Michel de Certeau, *The Practice of Everyday Life* (Berkeley: University of California Press, 1984), xix.
241. Blaeser, *Letters from Marion*, 244.
242. Lerner, *You Got Nothing Coming*, 248.
243. Baca, *A Place to Stand*, 193.
244. Baca, *A Place to Stand*, 193.
245. Parsell, *Fish*, 37. In addition to serving more time, these convicts are punished with reassignment to more secure prisons. See Schroeder, *Shaking It Rough*, 139.
246. Scarce, "Doing Time as an Act of Survival," 313–314.
247. Baca, *A Place to Stand*, 193. See also Jackson, *Soledad Brother*, 97.
248. Kerman, *Orange Is the New Black*, 60.
249. Betancourt, *Even Silence Has an End*, 139.
250. Baca, *A Place to Stand*, 160.
251. Mario Vittone, "Drowning Doesn't Look Like Drowning," *Slate*, June 4, 2013.
252. Vittone, "Drowning Doesn't Look Like Drowning."
253. Vittone, "Drowning Doesn't Look Like Drowning."
254. Vittone, "Drowning Doesn't Look Like Drowning."

SELECTED BIBLIOGRAPHY

The following books (and two articles) contain autobiographical material describing various forms of captivity. Their vivid stories provide first-person testimony concerning involuntary confinement. We have examined these autobiographical accounts for what they can tell us about time and temporal experience under the peculiar constraints of incarceration.

Abbott, Jack. *In the Belly of the Beast: Letters from Prison*. New York: Random House, 1981.

Abu-Jamal, Mumia. *All Things Censored*. New York: Seven Stories, 2000.

Baca, Jimmy Santiago. *A Place to Stand*. New York: Grove, 2001.

Berger, Robert L. *From the Inside: A Prison Memoir*. Lincoln, NE: iUniverse, 2003.

Berkman, Alexander. *Prison Memoirs of an Anarchist*. New York: New York Review, [1912] 1970.

Betancourt, Ingrid. *Even Silence Has an End: My Six Years of Captivity in the Colombian Jungle*. New York: Penguin, 2010.

Blaeser, Joel. *Letters from Marion: A Deadhead's Journey from Peace to a Super Max Prison*. Milwaukee, WI: Big House, 2015.

Bunker, Edward. *Education of a Felon*. New York: St. Martin's Griffin, 2000.

Burney, Christopher. *Solitary Confinement*. New York: Coward-McCann, 1952.

Carceral, K. C. *Behind a Convict's Eyes*. Belmont, CA: Wadsworth, 2004.

——. *Prison, Inc.* New York: New York University Press, 2006.

Compton-Wallace, Veronica. *Eating the Ashes: Seeking Rehabilitation Within the US Penal System*. New York: Algora, 2003.

Dostoevsky, Fyodor. *The House of the Dead*. New York: Grove, [1862] 1957.

Dress, Christina with Tama-Lisa Johnson and Mary Kay Letourneau. *Mass with Mary: The Prison Years*. Victoria, Canada: Trafford, 2004.

Fisher, Amy and Robbie Woliver. *If I Knew Then.* . . . Lincoln, NE: iUniverse, 2004.

George, Erin. *A Woman Doing Life: Notes from a Prison for Women.* New York: Oxford University Press, 2010.

Hall, Reginald L. *Memoir: Delaware County Prison.* Mountainside, NJ: Writersandpoets .com, 2004.

Hanrahan, Clare. *Jailed for Justice: A Woman's Guide to Federal Prison Camp.* Asheville, NC: Celtic Word Craft, 2002.

Hassine, Victor. *Life Without Parole: Living in Prison Today.* Los Angeles, CA: Roxbury, 1996.

Irwin, John. *The Felon.* Englewood Cliffs, NJ: Prentice-Hall, 1970.

——. *The Jail: Managing the Underclass in American Society.* Berkeley: University of California Press, 1985.

Jackson, George. *Soledad Brother: The Prison Letters of George Jackson.* New York: Bantam, 1970.

Jacobs, Sunny. *Stolen Time: The Inspiring Story of an Innocent Woman Condemned to Death.* London: Bantam, 2007.

Jones, Richard S. and Thomas J. Schmid. *Doing Time: Prison Experience and Identity Among First-Time Inmates.* Stamford, CT: JAI, 2000.

Kerman, Piper. *Orange Is the New Black: My Year in a Women's Prison.* New York: Spiegel & Grau, 2011.

Koestler, Arthur. *Dialogue with Death.* Chicago: University of Chicago Press, [1946] 2011.

Lamberton, Kenneth. *Wilderness and Razor Wire: A Naturalist's Observations from Prison.* San Francisco, CA: Mercury House, 2000.

Leary, Timothy. *Jail Notes.* New York: Douglas, 1970.

Leder, Drew. *The Soul Knows No Bars: Inmates Reflect on Life, Death, and Hope.* Lanham, MD: Rowman & Littlefield, 2000.

Lerner, Jimmy A. *You Got Nothing Coming: Notes from a Prison Fish.* New York: Broadway, 2002.

Lindhout, Amanda. *A House in the Sky: A Memoir.* New York: Scribner, 2013.

Long, Sylvester. *I Made It Through the Storm: My Fifteen Year Walk in State Prison.* Bloomington, IN: 1st Books Library, 2002.

Manocchio, Anthony J. and Jimmy Dunn. *The Time Game: Two Views of a Prison.* New York: Dell, 1970.

Martin, Dannie M. and Peter Y. Sussman. *Committing Journalism: The Prison Writings of Red Hog.* New York: Norton, 1993.

Paluch, James A., Jr. *A Life for a Life.* Los Angeles, CA: Roxbury, 2004.

Parsell, T. J. *Fish: A Memoir of a Boy in a Man's Prison.* Cambridge, MA: Da Capo, 2006.

Pepper, Art and Laurie Pepper. *Straight Life: The Story of Art Pepper.* New York: Schirmer, 1979.

Pringle, Peter. *About Time: Surviving Ireland's Death Row.* Dublin: The History Press Ireland, 2012.

Renaud, Jorge Antonio. *Behind the Walls: A Guide for Families and Friends of Texas Prison Inmates.* Denton: University of North Texas Press, 2002.

Santos, Michael G. *Profiles from Prison: Adjusting to Life Behind Bars.* Westport, CT: Praeger, 2003.

Scarce, Rik. "Doing Time as an Act of Survival." *Symbolic Interaction* 25 (2002): 303–321.

Schmid, Thomas J. and Richard S. Jones. "Suspended Identity: Identity Transformation in a Maximum Security Prison." *Symbolic Interaction* 14: 415–432, 1991.

Schroeder, Andreas. *Shaking It Rough: A Prison Memoir*. Garden City, NY: Doubleday, 1976.

Serge, Victor. *Men in Prison*, trans. Richard Greeman. Oakland, CA: PM Press, [1931] 2014.

Shaw, Clifford R. *The Jack-Roller: A Delinquent Boy's Own Story*. Chicago: University of Chicago Press, [1930] 1966.

Sinclair, Billy Wayne and Jodie Sinclair. *A Life in the Balance: The Billy Wayne Sinclair Story*. New York: Arcade, 2001.

Solzhenitsyn, Aleksandr I. *The Gulag Archipelago*. New York: Harper & Row, 1973.

Stanko, Stephen, Wayne Gillespie, and Gordon A. Crews (eds.). *Living in Prison: A History of the Correctional System with an Insider's View*. Westport, CT: Greenwood, 2004.

Timerman, Jacobo. *Prisoner Without a Name, Cell Without a Number*. New York: Alfred A. Knopf, 1981.

Woodfox, Albert. *Solitary: Unbroken by Four Decades in Solitary Confinement. My Story of Transformation and Hope*. New York: Grove, 2019.

Yakima, Cheyenne Valentino. *If I Could Paint Tomorrow: A Prisoner's Story*. Bloomington, IN: 1st Books Library, 2001.

INDEX

Abbott, Jack Henry, 61, 65, 69
Abu-Jamal, Mumia, 192–193, 225, 275n89
acceleration, 23, 193, 232
access, 28, 36, 38, 72, 220; cultural value
of, 77; lack of, 74, 79–80, 84, 114, 119,
163; to library, 75–76; regulation of,
43, 86, 95, 260n36; requests for, 94;
scheduled, 34, 88, 116; status and,
40; temporal limits on, 73, 78, 91–93,
97–98, 108, 168; unscheduled, 89
action, 154–155, 209; absence of, 188;
breadth of, 163; inhibition of, 47, 72,
74, 97, 120; projection of, 133
activity, 71, 120, 190, 217; allowances for,
85, 97, 117, 128; disruptive, 229–240;
diversity of, 162–163; illegal, 46,
229–240; initiation of, 239;
interruption of, 172, 178; management
of, 21, 91, 154, 163–164; memorable,
145, 183; off-unit, 42; outdoor, 28; rate
of, 19, 30, 114; repetition of, 92, 145,
149–152, 158, 164–165; restriction of,
118, 163; rhythm of, 50, 178; routine,
23; timing of, 30, 41, 72, 111, 154, 219,
278n168; work-related, 176
Adam, Barbara, 95
advice, 105, 147, 207–208

aggression, 61, 184, 230–231
Albion, 103
Alcatraz, 46, 160
Alderson, 27, 102
alienation, 109; temporal, 151, 154, 172
ambiguity, 121–122
amusements, 41–42. *See also* distractions;
temporal agency, resources for
anger, 167, 234; fatalism and, 136;
overcrowding and, 62; retribution
and, 130; security procedures and,
75; temporal trespassing and, 206.
See also rage
Angola, 46; Billy Sinclair and, 51, 53, 63,
67, 78, 114, 181, 202; Albert Woodfox
and, 59, 175, 267n69, 278n169
anguish, 11, 68, 139; time-induced, 152,
192, 194, 237, 242, 266n50
annual hearing, 139–143, 147, 149
anticipation, 9, 42, 133. *See also*
projection, temporal
antistructure, 43–45
anxiety, 202, 206, 240, 262n9;
architecture and, 47; predatory
environment and, 65; release and,
167–168; temporal regime and, 119.
See also fear

290

INDEX
fatalism, 73, 84, 157, 167, 199; prison
administrators and, 134, 156;
progress toward, 136. *See also* futility;
resignation
FCI Englewood, 232
fear, 54, 65, 68, 184, 240
feces, 54, 59, 104
feelings, 51–52, 133, 154
The Felon, 6
field notes, 13–14
fighting, 2, 59; exploitation and, 65, 139,
257n173; fascination with, 157, 184;
punishment for, 122; as temporal
agency, 237; theft and, 8; women and,
63. *See also* violence
file, 125, 136, 141–142. *See also* record
filth, 53, 68
fish, 39; advice for, 203; arrival of, 47, 58,
61; exploitation of, 65; lockdown of,
28, telephone and, 36. *See also* intake
Fisher, Amy, 66, 103, 106, 124–125, 127,
146
Fish Tank, 35, 47, 54, 63–64, 250n35.
See also intake
Flaherty, Michael, 4, 102, 104, 132;
research interests of, 3; research
methods and, 13, 227; study of
temporal agency and, 11, 152; study
of temporal experience and, 11, 24,
251n3, 266n50, 267n51
Florence State Prison, 46–47, 54, 105, 147
Fluvanna Correctional Center for
Women, 15, 21, 65, 115
folklore, 183–185, 203
Folsom, 46, 169
food, 86–87, 113; denial of, 89, 261n85.
See also meals
food trays. *See* meal trays
Fort Dix, 80, 118
Foucault, Michel, 7, 13, 18, 58, 128, 190
Frederiksen, Martin Demant, 63
freedom, 19, 62, 194–195, 233, 267n62;
longing for, 225; loss of, 100
frequency, 72; access and, 97; control
of, 76, 93; identification numbers
and, 171–172; temporal experience
and, 79

friends, 51, 59, 111, 146–147, 221; time
with, 78, 81, 100, 225
frisking. *See* pat-down search
frustration, 21; access and, 89;
boredom and, 162; delay and,
68, 80; indifference and, 73;
micromanagement and, 97, 101;
noise and, 60; in outside world,
79; overcrowding and, 62; policy
revisions and, 94; scarcity and, 72,
84–85; schedules and, 24, 35, 251n78;
with security procedures, 110, 258n8;
stimulus deprivation and, 59, 161;
temperature and, 54; temporally
induced, 41, 99, 120, 135, 235; visits
and, 82
futility, 120, 135; temporal, 143, 155, 229.
See also resignation
future, 9, 188, 192; attention to, 132, 143,
148–149, 153, 156; confidence in,
132, 137; disregard for, 138, 141, 155,
164, 208; dystopian, 41; as frame
of reference, 133, 150; imagination
of 145, 147; inability to modify,
142–143, 157; involvement with,
196–197; irrelevance of, 133, 140, 147,
152, 267n55; meaning of, 135, 139;
meaninglessness of, 137, 153, 156;
progress toward, 51, 146, 156–157;
redefinition of, 194; as temporal
refuge, 198; unknowable, 136–137.
See also temporal orientation,
to future
futurelessness, 136, 145, 147, 151–152,
156–157

gambling, temporal agency as, 230–233
games, 73; temporal agency as, 226–227,
231
gamesmanship, temporal, 52, 191, 231, 234
Garfinkel, Harold, 51, 193
gates, 74; waiting for, 75
gender, 16; autobiographies and, 15;
counts and, 89; churn in personnel
and, 270n58; doing time and, 203;
drugs and, 51, 232; gossip and, 225;
horseplay and, 230; intake and,

skills, 179
slang, 2, 209
sleeping, 37; danger of, 218; deprivation
of, 56, 60, 68, 106, 218, 256n128;
surveillance while, 106; temporal
agency as, 217–219
slow-playing, 122, 191, 234
smoking. *See* cigarettes
snitching, 121
social institutions, 133, 150
social interaction, 21, 57; fitness for,
101–102; impediments to, 114;
organization of, 27, 109, 114; pace of, 79,
146; patterns of, 43, 263n34; regulation
of, 72; rhythms of, 161, 198; temporal
agency in, 230; temporal framework
for, 34–35, 107, 109; timing in, 109, 219
socialization, 9–10, 133, 199, 214–215
social sciences, 12, 16, 67, 134
society, 9, 115, 169; changes in, 183; debt
to, 131, 134; modern 27, 41, 194, 221;
premodern 9, 27, 175
Soledad, 46
solitary confinement, 23, 48; celebration
of, 54; conversations in, 225–226;
desire for, 239; legal limits of, 126;
mental time travel during, 274n36;
odors in, 54 61; overcrowding
versus, 125; personal routine in, 176,
271n63; POW in, 186–187; stimulus
deprivation and, 59-61, 159; temporal
experience and, 69; time in, 124, 136,
173, 207, 219
solitude, 106; loss of, 101, 104–105;
segregation and, 127
Solzhenitsyn, Aleksandr, 52, 56, 63,
87–88, 218
sonic competition, 60
sorrow, temporally induced, 81
sounds, 172. *See also* noise
Special Housing Unit (SHU), 80
Spengler, Oswald, 158, 169
Spokane County jail, 240
staff, 84, 86–87, 90, 101; availability of,
106–107, 109–110; chastisement from,
109, 111; corruption of, 51, 98; days
off, 24, 28; discretion of, 94, 108,

117–118, 120, 126, 178; lights and, 55;
perspective of, 138–139, 153, 156, 241;
primary activity of, 141; schedule and,
30–31, 97, 152, 154, 157, 166; speech of,
153; turnover of, 117–118, 174
standard temporal units, 164, 172,
245n6; counting of, 160, 173, 195,
202, 216–217; emptiness of, 154;
measurement of time and, 129, 178,
181, 189; protracted duration and, 11,
69; rhythm and, 19; translation of, 145,
245n6, 267n51
Stanko, Stephen, 4, 32–33, 49, 66, 74, 80,
103, 188, 204, 206, 260n56
staring, 57–58, 63
status, 109, 125–127, 168, 210; temporal, 91;
transitions in, 20
Stave Lake Camp, 1–2
Stein, Karen, 100
stigma, 12, 151, 160; management of, 131,
149
stimulus complexity, 68–69
stimulus deprivation, 23, 155, 161–162, 176,
255n109
Strauss, Anselm, 20
stress, 58, 62–65, 68, 107, 183–184; coping
with, 199, 232; temporal, 87–88, 109,
167
strikes, 190
strip search, 57, 75–76, 78, 82, 102, 262n20
structure, 43–45, 182. *See also* temporal
experience, structuring of; temporal
structure, ambivalence toward
subordination, 151; temporal, 167
suffering, 65, 120, 128, 133; sonic, 61
suicide, 49, 59, 61, 208–209, 221
Sumter Correctional Institution, 89
sunrise, 29
sunset, 28–29
surveillance, 18, 58, 68, 101–103, 110;
architecture of, 58, 190; intrusive, 55,
107; lapses in, 190, 233
survival, 68
sweat, 54, 64
Sykes, Gresham, 49, 191, 204, 236;
enforced intimacy and, 58; fear and,
65; intake and, 51